Making 21st Century Knowledge Complexes

T0330608

The world has changed profoundly since the publication of the influential book *Technopoles of the World*. As policy-makers and practitioners attempt to harness science, technology and innovation to create dynamic and vibrant cities many wonder how relevant Manuel Castells and Peter Hall's messages are today. Twenty years later, this book returns to their concepts and practices to update their message for the 21st century.

Making 21st Century Knowledge Complexes: Technopoles of the World Revisited argues that the contemporary technopole concept encompasses three new dimensions. First, building synergy between partners is vital for the success of complexes. Second, the correct governance arrangements are critical to balance competing interests inevitable in any science city project. Third, new evaluation mechanisms are indispensable in allowing policy-makers to steer their long-term benefits.

Through twelve case study chapters and two chapters of detailed comparative analysis, this book provides academics, policy-makers and practitioners with critical insights in understanding, managing and promoting today's high-technology urban complexes.

Julie Tian Miao is Lecturer in Urban Planning and Development, University of Glasgow, UK.

Paul Benneworth is a Senior Researcher at the Center for Higher Education Policy Studies (CHEPS) at the University of Twente, the Netherlands.

Nicholas A. Phelps is Professor of Urban and Regional Development, The Bartlett School of Planning, University College London, UK.

Regions and Cities

Series Editor in Chief:
Susan M. Christopherson, *Cornell University, USA*

Editors:
Maryann Feldman, *University of Georgia, USA*
Gernot Grabher, *HafenCity University Hamburg, Germany*
Ron Martin, *University of Cambridge, UK*
Martin Perry, *Massey University, New Zealand*

In today's globalised, knowledge-driven and networked world, regions and cities have assumed heightened significance as the interconnected nodes of economic, social and cultural production, and as sites of new modes of economic and territorial governance and policy experimentation. This book series brings together incisive and critically engaged international and interdisciplinary research on this resurgence of regions and cities, and should be of interest to geographers, economists, sociologists, political scientists and cultural scholars, as well as to policy-makers involved in regional and urban development.

For more information on the Regional Studies Association visit www.regionalstudies.org

There is a **30% discount** available to RSA members on books in the *Regions and Cities* series, and other subject related Taylor and Francis books and e-books including Routledge titles. To order just e-mail alex.robinson@tandf.co.uk, or phone on +44 (0) 20 7017 6924 and declare your RSA membership. You can also visit www.routledge.com and use the discount code: **RSA0901**

Making 21st Century Knowledge Complexes

Technopoles of the world revisited

Edited by
Julie Tian Miao, Paul Benneworth
and Nicholas A. Phelps

LONDON AND NEW YORK

First published 2015
by Routledge
2 Park Square, Milton Park, Abingdon, Oxon OX14 4RN

and by Routledge
711 Third Avenue, New York, NY 10017

First issued in paperback 2018

Routledge is an imprint of the Taylor & Francis Group, an informa business

© 2015 selection and editorial material, Julie Tian Miao, Paul Benneworth and Nicholas A. Phelps; individual chapters, the contributors

The right of the editors to be identified as the authors of the editorial material, and of the authors for their individual chapters, has been asserted in accordance with sections 77 and 78 of the Copyright, Designs and Patents Act 1988.

All rights reserved. No part of this book may be reprinted or reproduced or utilised in any form or by any electronic, mechanical, or other means, now known or hereafter invented, including photocopying and recording, or in any information storage or retrieval system, without permission in writing from the publishers.

Trademark notice: Product or corporate names may be trademarks or registered trademarks, and are used only for identification and explanation without intent to infringe.

British Library Cataloguing in Publication Data
A catalogue record for this book is available from the British Library

Library of Congress Cataloging in Publication Data
Making 21st century knowledge complexes : Technopoles of the world
    revisited / edited by Julie Tian Miao, Paul Benneworth and
    Nicholas A. Phelps.
    pages cm
    Includes bibliographical references and index.
    1. Research parks. 2. Research parks – Case studies. 3. Castells,
    Manuel, 1942– Technopoles of the world. I. Miao, Julie Tian.
    II. Benneworth, Paul. III. Phelps, N. A. (Nicholas A.)
    T175.7.M35 2015
    607.2 – dc23
    2014046916

ISBN 13: 978-1-138-33966-8 (pbk)
ISBN 13: 978-0-415-72779-2 (hbk)

Typeset in Times New Roman
by Florence Production Ltd, Stoodleigh, Devon, UK

In memory of
Sir Peter Hall (1932–2014);
a great scholar, colleague, mentor, supervisor,
partner, thinker, President and inspiration

For
Theodore Hendrick and Leanne Marie
Aili He, Haijun Miao and Wang

Contents

SECTION 5
Conclusions 273

Figures

Tables

Contributors

Alberto Albahari is a post-doc research fellow at the School of Industrial Engineering of the Universidad de Málaga (Malaga, Spain) where he teaches Management. His main research interests deal with innovation management, knowledge-intensive environments and academia–industry relations.

Paul Benneworth is a senior researcher at the Center for Higher Education Studies at the University of Twente in the Netherlands. His research interests are related to the relationships between knowledge production and society, through university–society interaction, technological clusters, innovation and technological development, and their relation to wider societal and governance networks and systems.

Luis Carvalho is senior researcher at the European Institute for Comparative Urban Research (Euricur). His research interests are in the fields of the territorial economy, urban management and the geography of knowledge and innovation.

Antònia Casellas is Assistant Professor at the Geography Department, Universitat Autònoma de Barcelona. Her research is engaged with the theoretical and policy analysis of the triad: economic viability and ecological responsibility, governance and social innovation, and urban/regional restructuring processes.

David R. Charles is Professor of Innovation and Strategic Management and Deputy Head of Lincoln Business School at the University of Lincoln in the UK. His main research interests include innovation management, regional innovation policies and university-business collaboration, and the role of universities in their wider urban and regional contexts.

Sharifah R.S. Dawood is a senior lecturer in the Geography Section, School of Humanities, Universiti Sains Malaysia. Her research interests cover economic geography, knowledge-intensive business services, regional development and innovation, and urban sociology. She has published chapters for the OECD Reviews of Higher Education in Regional and City Development, journal articles for Environment and Planning C, and established research networking with the Asian Development Bank.

Henry Etzkowitz is president of the Triple Helix Association and editor-in-chief of the journal *Triple Helix*. He is also a visiting professor at the University of London, Birkbeck and Special Advisor to the Shandong Academy of Science and Technology. Henry is author of *Athena Unbound: The advancement of women in science and technology (CUP) and Triple Helix*; *University-industry-government innovation in action* (Routledge); and his next book is titled *The entrepreneurial university wave*.

Wei-Ju Huang (Astor) is Assistant Professor at the Department of Urban Planning, College of Planning and Design, National Cheng Kung University, Taiwan. Her research mainly focuses on deepening the understanding of the nature of spatial planning by applying institutional analysis and comparative research to contemporary planning issues, especially at an urban and regional scale.

Milana A. Korotka (m.a.korotka@utwente.nl) is a PhD researcher of HRM at the School of Management and Governance, HRM Department of the University of Twente. She received her MSc degree in European Studies (Regulation track) from the Public Administration Department at the University of Twente.

Tim May is Professor and Co-Director of the Centre for Sustainable Urban and Regional Futures (SURF), University of Salford, Manchester, UK. Professor May's current work investigates the relationship between epistemic communities and communities of practice and explores values and learning in urban environments.

Julie Tian Miao is a lecturer in Urban Planning and Development at the Department of Urban Studies, University of Glasgow. Her research focuses on innovation systems, regional development and urban transformation. She is particularly interested in comparing the different development approaches toward the knowledge economy between the East and West.

Beth Perry is Reader and Co-Director of the Centre for Sustainable Urban and Regional Futures, University of Salford, Manchester, UK. Since 2011 she has been Director of the Greater Manchester Local Interaction Platform for Mistra Urban Futures, a centre for sustainable cities with partners in Sweden, Kenya and South Africa.

Nicholas A. Phelps is Professor of Urban and Regional Development at the Bartlett School of Planning. His interests cover the economic geography of multinational enterprises and foreign direct investment, the theory of urban economic agglomeration and the politics and planning of suburbs.

He recently co-edited a special issue of the journal Environment & Planning C on the subject of 'Science and the city'.

Tiago Ratinho holds a PhD from the University of Twente having defended his thesis on the impact of business incubation in 2011. His research interests are in the fields of Entrepreneurship, Strategy, and Technology Transfer. He currently teaches at the Merrick School of Business at the University of Baltimore.

Roland Scherer is Head of the Research Center for Regional Science at the Institute for Systemic Management and Public Governance at the University of St Gallen (Switzerland). His main activities include basic research, applied research as well as consulting in the field of Regional Development. A particular focus lies on projects on cross-border cooperation and multi-level governance.

Simone Strauf is Senior Researcher at the Institute for Systemic Management and Public Governance at the University of St Gallen (Switzerland). Her main research interest lies in Regional Science with a particular focus on impact monitoring and the contribution of higher education institutions to regional development.

Mário Vale is a Full Professor at the Institute of Geography and Spatial Planning and a researcher at Centre for Geographical Studies at the University of Lisbon. He was a Fulbright Visiting Scholar at the Department of Geography at UCLA (University of California Los Angeles) in 2013. He was President of the Portuguese Association of Geographers (2004–08) and Vice-Chair of the Regional Studies Association (2008–11).

Willem van Winden is Professor of Urban Knowledge Economy and Strategy at Amsterdam University of Applied Sciences. He has published widely on urban knowledge-based development and related topics, and he works as advisor for a number of large cities.

Foreword

We have aspired in this volume to pull together a book that, despite consisting of a set of individual chapters, nevertheless coheres together around a single message with a useful scientific contribution. This makes edited books strongly dependent on the existence of communities of scholars who are working with sufficient overlap and common interests to generate a clear and coherent message. The origins for this book lay in discussions between the editor Nick Phelps and Professor Yong-Sook Lee at the Department of Public Administration, Korea University. Together with the support of Korea's Science and Technology Policy Institute, they organised a symposium and field visit on the theme of science parks and innovation policy in Seoul, Korea in October 2011.

This symposium sought to place on the academic agenda the issue of what kind of new spatial forms were emerging as a consequence of the ubiquity of the idea of innovation as a central driver for almost every policy field. What had previously been a concern restricted to departments of economic affairs was spreading out to affect health, science, housing, transport and environmental fields, seeking to stimulate and promote innovation as central policy goals. This policy ubiquity was clearly having a profound effect on the spatial forms associated with innovation; the suburban campus technopoles identified by Sir Peter Hall and Manuel Castells in 1994 were clearly being overtaken by new kinds of economic space, in city centres, in networked form, outside cities, and even in new kinds of suburbs. Over the course of the day and around ten highly stimulating papers, a group including the editors of this present volume coalesced with a clear interest in continuing to take this debate forward.

A selection of the papers from the conference were selected for publication in a special issue of the Pion journal *Environment & Planning C: Government and Policy*, which at the time of writing has just gone to print (volume 32, issue 5). But at the same time, there was interest in sustaining the momentum among the participants, and the wider scholarly community, in a number of different ways. In 2012, the three editors organised a conference session on Technopoles of the World, seeking to broaden out the discussion beyond the very narrow focus of the STEPI event (new spatial forms of technopoles). The focus of the session that emerged at the Regional Studies Association European Conference 2012 in Delft sought to revisit how the idea of technopoles as drivers of regional development had evolved in the twenty years since the publication of Castells and Hall's seminal text.

In the course of the five sessions in May 2012, it became clear that there was a great deal of scholarly interest in these discussions, and spurred by the wide thematic and geographical scope of the papers presented, the editors of this volume decided to submit a proposal into this *Cities and Regions* book series. We were delighted with the response of the publisher and Routledge for the speed with which they issued a contract. In the last year, the book has settled down around twelve selected contributions that tell a convincing story of how the idea has spread into new parts of the world, into new kinds of spatial configurations, and into new integrated policy frameworks.

We hope this volume does not mark the end of the journey of our community of interest in technopoles and economic development. We were delighted to be involved in a research network funded by the UK's Leverhulme Trust exploring the global dimensions of new science park forms. Led by Professor Dave Valler, Oxford Brookes University, who was involved in the original symposium in Korea, the network has the ambition of exploring how the growing internationalisation and delocalisation of science is affecting the local spaces created as foci for critical mass in science- and innovation-based economic development. Through a mixture of discussions, new publications and research, we envisage that this network will build on the momentum generated by the special issue, and that we hope is sustained by this book, to ensure there is no simple reversion to the idea of science parks as 'high technology fantasy' policy panaceas.

So we acknowledge that this book has been heavily dependent on this community of interest around celebrating and reflecting on two decades of technopoles concepts. First, we would like to thank Yong-Sook, Hjungyoo Kim and STEPI for mobilising this fascinating community, and all those involved at the STEPI event for contributing to a fertile discussion. Second, we would like to thank Sally Hardy and Lesa Reynolds at the Regional Studies Association for providing us with the platform and the network to amplify our message, and to connect with a wider grouping who laid the foundation for this volume. Third, we would like to thank Rob Langham, Natalie Tomlinson and Lisa Thomson for their enthusiasm and support in bringing this volume to fruition. Fourth, we would like to thank our authors for the good humour with which they have endured our efforts to co-ordinate and stimulate them in making the best possible contributions, which we hope they now are fully able to appreciate.

But perhaps the greatest acknowledgement must be made to the man who set this whole train of thinking in motion. It is with deepest sadness that we admit that the entire meaning of this volume changed forever at the end of July 2014. What had been planned as a celebration of two decades of what to us was a seminal text shifted profoundly with the passing of Sir Peter at the age of 82. It is not just that Sir Peter had inspired us twenty years ago, with powerful writing that echoed through the years to give a call to arms for a new generation to discuss, debate, reflect and extend technopoles thinking. We also felt ourselves lucky for him to personally endorse our project with a rousing launch presentation at the Delft conference, which we had hoped would form the introduction to this book.

Although that introduction was not possible, his message in Delft emerges in many of the contributions we have, stories of policy-makers trying to create new kinds of living and working, with new forms of city branding and marketing to advertise this globally, involving complex new organizational forms, public–private hybrids. It is clear that in the field of urban science policy, as with so many other fields, Sir Peter initiated and inspired a group of scholars active in raging debates of contemporary significance. It is our fervent hope that this volume will be able to contribute in some way to sustaining the debate and to encourage others to seek inspiration in his writing to better understand the contemporary world and its challenges. As a team each with our own relationship to Sir Peter, we cannot help but be greatly affected by this loss, but at the same time hope that we are able to use this book to provide a fitting memorial to this important dimension of his intellectual legacy.

The Editors, October 2014

Section 1

Introduction

1 Technopoles of the world

Changes, dynamics and challenges

Julie Tian Miao, Paul Benneworth and Nicholas A. Phelps

1.1 Introduction

Since the publication of Manuel Castells and Peter Hall's (1994) seminal work *Technopoles of the World* (Routledge), there has been increasing interest in these knowledge infrastructures from not only the academic but also the political and policy spheres. Even more so than when their volume was written, these high-technology spaces have evolved and thrived in the context of the emergence of the new knowledge economy and they have attracted a host of imitative followers (cf. Hospers, 2006). To a great extent, the enthusiastic development of technopoles or science parks worldwide can be seen as following an inductive theorising logic in which policy-makers and other stakeholders have been inspired by the success of places such as Silicon Valley and Cambridge (UK). Those that have advocated and developed new technopoles or science parks seek to reap analogous rewards to these places, rooted in the fundamental assumption that developing the appropriate infrastructure is sufficient for innovation activities and high-tech industries to prosper in these carefully cultivated complexes. Nevertheless, Castells and Hall were not backward in warning of the potential economic wastefulness of technopole initiatives, and in particular highlighting the long-term commitment required for the necessary innovation synergies to take shape. Indeed, they placed a figure on the time required, stating that between fifteen and twenty-five years is the norm for the full impacts of a technopole to become evident (Castells and Hall, 1994: 236).

With twenty years having passed since the publication of *Technopoles of the World*, the moment therefore seems ripe to revisit how these promising new knowledge spaces have performed economically, reflecting on both those that had been created by 1994 and those spaces created in the wake of these early ground-breaking initiatives. This provides a means to systematically explore the features of the contemporary technopoles and to reflect on the challenges that have accompanied their growth. The time is also ripe for a reconceptualisation of technopoles, now that so much more is known about the contours of what Rutten *et al.* (2014) have termed the 'social knowledge economy'. The key challenge is that the ubiquity of knowledge exchange and creation empowered by new information and communications technologies (ICTs) infrastructures has placed a critical question mark over the importance of physical places in the ecology of new knowledge creation. In other words, if knowledge can be exchanged globally, mediated through technologies, then what are the conceivable advantages of creating physical platforms, industrial complexes and campuses to facilitate exchange between geographically proximate partners?

But at the same time it is clear that there remains a physical dimension in knowledge exchange, particularly related to the importance of exchanging tacit knowledge (know-how and know-who). Tacit knowledge is created through social learning processes underpinned by intense and regular interactions, and the reality is that physical proximity – if not necessary – is certainly greatly supportive of these intense interactions (Gertner, Roberts and Charles, 2011). Highly innovative firms active in global knowledge networks need to be anchored to territories by having a shared interest in these places, which may emerge in the knowledge communities associated with technopole complexes (Yeung, 2009). Therefore, what is critical is understanding how place-specific knowledges – with the capacity to anchor firms active in global innovation networks – build up around these complexes, and in particular the role they play within multi-scalar knowledge production, circulation and exploitation processes.

Ideas such as the importance of the knowledge base for a territory (Keeble and Wilkinson, 1999), the rescaling of innovation management (Perry and May, 2007) and the re-organising of power structures (Christopherson and Clark, 2010) are gradually emerging within academic debate. To make sense of the knowledge base of the territory, scholars are paying more attention to the social assets of a place, the dynamics and solidification of knowledge stock and the scale and scope of knowledge diffusion (Rutten *et al.*, 2014). In terms of innovation management, while the call for 'strategic regions' (Pierre and Andersen, 2012) is gaining momentum, greater effort has also been devoted to decision-making processes at local and city levels (Glaeser, 2011), with an increasing realisation that, suitably equipped, cities have great potential to take the lead in stimulating entrepreneurship and innovation. Decentralisation and deregulation have been pushed to a new horizon in current administrative structures, a trend not only visible in developed countries but also in developing ones too.

1.2 Technopoles in the 21st century

In this volume we have sought to engage with these emerging debates and new characteristics when revisiting the topic of technopoles in the contemporary context. As well as re-establishing attention on a work that we think is worthy of wider consideration, we also aim to provide a significant update to *Technpoles of the World* in the light of developments during the last two decades. Our ultimate intention with this volume is to provide a comprehensive reflection on the relevance of technopole concepts and practices in the conditions of the new century, as well as to evaluate the changing forms and functions of knowledge facilities and industrial complexes in both developed and developing countries. In order to achieve this goal, contributors to this volume were asked to pay particular attention to three overarching themes that characterise what might be thought of as the 21st century technopole, namely:

- the way technopoles provide synergies between actors that function as wider innovation milieux,
- the role played by governance arrangements in determining the success of technopoles, and
- the practicalities of how the implementation of these conceptual models creates (or indeed does not create) economic success and improved innovative performance.

With respect to the first of these overarching themes, this book explores the scales and scope of contemporary technopoles as real innovation milieu, particularly given the distanciation possible between innovators empowered by new technologies. In the original volume two decades ago, Castells and Hall defined the milieu of innovation as:

> the social, institutional, organizational, economic, and territorial structures that create the conditions for the continuous generation of synergy and its investment in a process of production that results from this very synergistic capacity, both for the units of production that are part of the milieu and for the milieu as a whole.
>
> (ibid., p. 9)

Two dimensions of this definition could prove to be highly relevant in the contemporary context. First is what are the conditions and leadership styles that are necessary for cultivating these 'fertile structures'. What we see increasingly is close partnerships between public and private actors in the inception, development, management and exploitation of technopole projects. This manifests itself in the increasingly blurred planning boundaries around these industrial complexes, and a growing overlap between the scientific, cartographic and social spaces that are articulated around technopoles. The second dimension is whether and how physical proximity still plays a significant role in creating synergy between actors within a system. We already noted in 1.1 that contemporary changes have challenged the traditional wisdom that the key supportive processes in technopoles were stimulated by the physical proximity of the relevant players. Even in 1994, it was evident to Castells and Hall that such an approach was doomed to failure without the creation of dynamic interactions and networks between them in support of technological development and innovation. And we are driven by the advent of the 'information economy' to reflect critically on the role of physical proximity, whether it is doomed to become increasingly irrelevant, or whether leading innovative actors are finding ways to support their innovativeness and competitiveness by creating new kinds of physical interactive knowledge spaces.

Our second overarching theme in the volume lies in foregrounding the importance of governance and policy in current theoretical technopole debates. The starting point for Castells and Hall (1994) was to explore the processes of industrial re-organisation and relocation associated with the increasing emergence of the post-industrial knowledge economy. The relationship between industrial re-organisation on the one hand, and industrial relocation on the other, was addressed through a 'descriptive-analytical' methodology (Church, 1995) with a detailed account of evolutionary and institutional dynamics. But one issue that was not really touched upon in the original volume was the way in which the urban dynamics of these particular places were shaped by these highly localised knowledge facilities. Of course this partly reflects the fact that technopoles were seen as being a sub-urban or ex-urban/rural phenomenon, rather than something to be inserted into the existing contested and scarce fabric of existing urban assemblages. The spatial separation of the majority of the cases they chose led Castells and Hall to add a chapter on 'Metropolis as innovation milieu' in order to at least attempt to provide some comparison of urban and suburban technopoles.

The realisation that many technopoles are now embedded within the sprawling suburbs of metropolitan areas (Phelps, 2012), along with a growing number of studies that have sought to understand the active placing of science in cities (Benneworth *et al.*, 2011), have physically linked or even merged these once isolated knowledge facilities with the established metropolis. There is a realisation that there are new dynamics associated with what Yigitcanlar (2010) refers to as knowledge-based urban development (KBUD). The increasing importance of KBUD processes has in turn raised new questions about technopoles, such as their functions in the formation and dynamics of city regions and their role in the agglomeration economy, as well as more practical issues around their management, governance, financing and land use planning. The governance structure of technopoles and their financing, in particular, is in need of an urgent solution – an urgency that is only increasing given the current financial austerity in most countries. It is clear that a new multi-disciplinary dialogue is necessary to meaningfully create useful connections between concepts of multi-level governance in networks and those of contemporary industrial innovation and restructuring.

In terms of the third overarching theme, this book seeks to make much clearer and more explicit connections between conceptual explorations and the underlying practical inspirations. Our primary concern in this book has therefore not been the economic and social achievements of technopoles per se, but rather the underlining conditions and structural features that have led to such achievements, and indeed the factors that have worked against and undermined their wider economic and societal contributions. We have been concerned to avoid a simplistic reduction of these contributions to nothing more than a cost-benefit spreadsheet calculation. The volume is particularly concerned with accounting for the characteristics of the firms and the technopoles, their regional economic and institutional conditions, and understanding and evaluating how their specialisation and/or diversity has led to their regional economic development contributions. In this regard, a wider geographical range of cases has been necessary in this volume to ensure coverage of the diversified economic-social contexts of contemporary technopoles, particularly as shall become clear the extension of the concept from North America, Europe and Japan into emerging economies. Our geographical coverage here includes both a number 'stars' and 'forefathers' of technopoles studied in the original book, as well as many newcomers and latecomers in the technopole family. The contemporary technopole landscape covers both facilities in advanced economies, embedded in (potentially highly supportive) urban environments, as well as those in less-developed economies, where these knowledge facilities have to be built from scratch. We have sought to provide wide coverage of examples of both of these categories of technpoles.

We of course hope the thematic coverage and geographical scope of the book permits a timely and valuable contribution to the existing literature about science parks, urban science and technopoles. In making this contribution, we have been partly inspired by a desire to build on the findings, claims and concepts emerging in a scientific conversation that has been unfolding now for three decades. Many published works on this subject are based on a single case study and/or a single nation, such as Allen Scott's (1989) *The Technopoles of Southern California*, Hilary Sunman's (1986) *France and her Technopoles*, as well as Massey, Quintas and Wield's (1992) *High-tech Fantasies*. It is clear that the academic literature is only now starting to catch up with the emergence of serious technopole complexes in developing countries, with the notable exceptions of Susan Walcott's (2003) *Chinese Science and Industrial Technology Parks*, and Luciano Ciravegna's (2012) *Promoting Silicon Valleys in Latin America: Lessons from Costa Rica*. At the same time, these contributions are primarily focused on a single case, and we hope to complement the depth of these studies with a broad selection representing the diversity of contemporary technopoles.

There are of course a number of other volumes that have started to develop the international comparative understanding of technopoles and high-technology urban spaces. Studies with an international breadth include Nicos Komninos's (2002) *Intelligent Cities*, which draws lessons from Europe and the USA, although in reality his treatment of technopoles comes as an aside to a thorough analysis on the consequences arising from the digitalisation of the innovation process. Likewise Steve Graham's (2003) *The Cybercities Reader* focuses exclusively on the information society. Francisco Carrillo's

(2006) *Knowledge Cities* explores this phenomenon mainly from the urban planning perspective, paying more attention to social capital and intellectual capital. Conversely, Colin Barrow's (2001) *Incubators: A Realist's Guide to the World's New Business Accelerators* focuses more on practical issues such as running and choosing incubators rather than theoretical exploration. We hope readers find that this volume lives up to these aspirations and helps to sustain what we believe to be a vital debate with practical, policy and scholarly ramifications.

1.3 Conception, contribution and unsolved questions

Given that the inspiration for our edited book came directly from the influential work by Castells and Hall (1994), it is worth perhaps very briefly returning to that book in order to set out clearly the intellectual context within which this volume has emerged. It was Castells and Halls that popularised the term 'technopole' around the world, in academic, policy-maker and practice communities. At their time of writing, this particular industrial complex appeared to be 'so physically similar', and was defined by the authors as 'specific forms of territorial concentration of technological innovation with a potential to generate scientific synergy and economic productivity' (ibid., p. 10). They created a classification of six technopole categories, including:

1 Spontaneous innovative milieu that had formed around highly innovative supply chains and clusters.
2 'Science cities', complexes consisting exclusively of co-located research activities without any direct link to manufacturing.
3 'Technology parks' that seek to deliberately induce technological growth by attracting highly innovative firms.
4 National programmes that sought to create a network of national technopoles, represented by the case of Japan's Technopolis programme.
5 'Quintessential innovative milieux' located within core metropolitan areas, in which innovative milieux were often deeply embedded in an existing urban fabric.
6 Technopoles under construction, where it was possible to intimately study and report on the practices that underpinned attempts to create these archetypal future technology spaces.

In revisiting the technopole phenomenon, and this classification, it is necessary to reflect on socio-economic changes in the intervening period. There have been huge transformations in the nature of the information economy, a process that continues unabated to this date, along with the increasing importance of the creative-cultural economy (Comunian *et al.*, 2010). A new class of labour, the so-called 'creative class', has emerged in recent decades because of their apparent impressive capabilities to drive innovation, not merely the symbolic analysts of technological innovation (Reich, 1991), but those with knowledge useful in creating value in this new cultural creative economy. Florida (2002a) pointed out with his *Rise of the Creative Class* that the desire of this group for a stimulating and pleasant urban environment could have significant consequences for technopoles (see also Florida, 2002b). Certainly, the message was that policy-makers seeking to create, plan and construct innovative spaces should certainly bear in mind the locational preferences of this new group.

Second, the importance of cities, and in particular core urban areas, is gaining weight both in economic and political terms. The old desire for 'garden style', or 'campus style' technopoles is becoming increasingly unattainable given the space constraints faced within metropolitan cores. Third, with the increasing involvement of public agents in entrepreneurial activities, and the predominance of public-private partnership as the foundation of knowledge-based urban development, the issue of governance and power structure involved in constructing such industrial complexes is becoming increasingly challenging. Against the backdrop of these changes, there is decreasing value in defining technopoles in terms of their specific spatial configuration, although space does matter more than simply being a way of stimulating innovative synergy. Indeed, it is not clear whether the idea of a six-fold classification has great relevance these days because technopoles are evolving many parallel functions with multiple and sometimes overlapping organisational principles. Given these changes, and especially the importance of diversification, it is natural that the chapters in this volume are themselves very diverse in reporting technopoles that are so varied in their physical compositions, the key stakeholders involved, and the emerging developmental narratives.

Keeping these changes in mind, we have sought in this volume to contribute in four areas:

- First, we aim to provide a degree of coherence in a muddied set of debates dealing with the perennially wicked issues around science parks, technopoles, the urbanisation process and knowledge-based development. To do this, what we have sought to do is solicit contributions from a range of qualitative and quantitative backgrounds, and different disciplinary perspectives, in order to facilitate building a common knowledge base from the 'stylised facts' we see emerging from each contribution.
- Second, in adopting an explicitly international comparative perspective on technopoles and cognate phenomena, we have also attempted to bring a range of diversity in our contributions, and avoid simply repeating simplistic narratives of 'Silicon Somewheres' (following Hospers, 2006). The case studies in this volume cover both developed and developing economies, successful and less successful cases, and both established and newcomers in the technopole family. This allows a degree of reflection on the comparisons and contrasts between ranges of environmental conditions.

• Third, we have sought to engage with policy and practice debates, by synthesising the findings in the introduction and concluding chapters (Chapters 1 and 14). Although we cannot go as far as Castells and Hall in offering a recipe for technopoles, we do have a reasonably clear set of messages for policy-makers, all relating to the needs to create local coalitions that strengthen places' positions within wider corporate innovation systems. Although the environment is becoming more dynamic, policy-makers need to find a way to offer stability to technopole projects and identify lead actors able to provide continuity, particularly as increasing numbers of incumbent R&D firms reduce their overall R&D efforts.

• Fourth, the contributors to this edited book all adhered to the central themes of reflecting the lessons learnt from Castells and Hall's original book, examining the contemporary features of and challenges facing technopoles, and critically examining their potentials and added values. This ensures a degree of consistency in the approach and reference points adopted in the chapter contributions, as we will see later.

1.4 Updating *Technopoles*: the structure of the present volume

This book presents case studies covering North America, Europe and Asian Pacific regions, and is structured around the three dimensions mentioned in 1.1 as a means of linking the chapters together. The first of these dimensions is the issue of synergy, the means by which technopoles create their competitive advantage. Our key concern here has been in understanding who is leading synergy-building processes, and the roles that geographical scales play in affecting the ways in which localised collective mobilisations can be created between innovative actors. The second dimension is that of the relationships between urban science governance processes and processes of city regional development, in the context of an ever tighter interweaving of innovation spaces into urban fabric necessitating increasingly complicated technopole governance structures. These complexities are closely related to the third of those dimensions, namely the political and policy tensions in seeking to promote technopole development, including tensions between stimulating aggregate and niche growth, creating attractive place images as against effective place synergies, and governmental re-organisation to create scales of governance that reflect technopoles' physical footprints. Each of the chapters deals in their own ways with these concepts, although clearly different elements come in different ways to the fore in each contribution. The structure of the book has been ordered around three main dimensions, which are important in the course of the book. Alongside the introduction and concluding chapters (Chapters 1 and 14 respectively), there are three sections that cover one of these substantive dimensions; synergy management, technopole governance, and evaluating technopoles.

1.4.1 Synergy management: who, how and where

Section 2 is concerned with the issue of how technopoles act as vehicles for the creation of synergies between different actors within a technopole. Our starting point is understanding synergy as a potential for better information flow between actors in different societal spheres as a result of a techno-pole effect (Castells and Hall, 1994, p. 224). The idea of synergy implies that technopoles have a systemic dimension, and that they are places that host specific kinds of knowledge from which participants are able to derive unique competitive advantage, making them the place to be for any companies wishing to access that knowledge (Gertler, 1995). This definition of synergy strongly implies a system level analysis where there is, as Marshall (1920) famously described, an 'industrial atmosphere'. There are certainly concepts that help to explain how these activities function, including neo-Marshallian industrial districts (Amin and Robins, 1991), Porter's (1998) clusters, or Morgan's (1997) learning regions. However, underneath this systemic nature is a critical question about the dynamics of the networks and connections that create these systemic effects. Particularly important here is the issue of who is leading the process, how interactions could be accumulated, and where the most beneficial environment for such interactions to happen can be found.

There is often a tendency in analyses to focus on the role of the private sector in playing leadership roles in knowledge-sharing processes, configuring synergetic networks by mobilising partnerships with universities, governments and other partners. However, in Chapter 2 Henry Etzkowitz draws our attention to the growing entrepreneurial capabilities of universities in North America. He situates this analysis in an evolutionary perspective, tracing what he characterises as three phases of entrepreneurial universities, first gaining autonomy, then commercialising intellectual property, and then proactively improving the efficacy of its regional innovation environment. Underpinning these behavioural changes has been a recognition that such behaviours are necessary to generate knowledge, secure funding, and promote technopole development, given the importance of two-way flow between knowledge institutions in innovation as well as an increasingly knowledge-based society. Drawing on examples from MIT and Stanford, and placing those developments in the context of exemplars in Brazil and Europe, Etzkowitz makes it clear that part of the strength of the technopole concept has been its capacity to react to changing fundamentals; the technpole concept is one that appears inherently elastic.

The traditional way of promoting university-industry linkages, according to the original Castells and Hall (1994) study, was based around setting aside a specific piece of land where these two different groups could physically be brought together, without consideration for the underlying motives and drives of the different partners, which as Etzkotwitz indicates, are critical for delivering behavioural changes. This raises the question of how interactions can be stimulated to produce longer-term synergies given the increasing question marks that are placed next to this model. In Chapter 3, Korotka and

Benneworth explore this issue further in the context of the Netherlands, where universities have adopted important and sometimes decisive roles in knowledge-based urban development. However entrepreneurial they may be, the first obstacle that any university has to overcome in building co-operation is to address the fact that their interests in co-operation are by no means the same as those of business partners; little is known of the reasons why academic researchers choose to engage with businesses, particularly when such research often carries the suspicion of being tainted by its application. Using the technopole of Kennispark Twente as its case study, the authors sought to address this question alongside the issue of what types of proximity influence academics' choice to collaborate. Drawing upon a survey of active academic collaborators, their research found that in Kennispark, academics co-operate with external partners based on organisational and social proximity regardless of their location. This had led the authors to suggest that physical proximity is not intrinsically important to how Kennispark benefits its participants, but instead it is other forms of proximity that matter (cognitive, organisational and social). But at the same time there was a recognition that these proximities were produced by the campus form, and therefore there was a need for more reflection on precisely how technopoles could promote other forms of proximity through physical proximity.

This 'proximity paradox' (Broekel and Boschma, 2012) discussed by Korotka and Benneworth is also taken up by Winden and Carvalho in Chapter 4. Focusing on synergy management from technopoles' shareholders' perspective, the authors studied six self-styled knowledge locations in five European cities (Aachen, Arhus, Coimbra, Dublin and Eindhoven). Again, question marks were placed against the importance of geographical proximity to creating the synergistic benefits, the authors drawing on corroborating statements from technopole practitioners. It is these practitioners who have increasingly come to realise that knowledge exchange and learning are socially-situated practices, operating through different multi-scalar networks and spatial configurations. In seeking to manage and support synergies in that new environment, there were four broad types of synergy management tools that had become widely used to stimulate and cultivate other forms of proximities through co-locating, including 1) design for interaction; 2) managing the tenant mix; 3) shared facilities; and 4) promoting networks and communities. At the same time, and in line with other contributions, they highlighted the potential of physical design to support interpersonal exchanges, and argued that technopoles' authorities certainly benefit from better knowledge about the dynamics of innovation process.

All these cases obtained from North America and Europe, to some extent, signal a paradigm shift in the way technopoles are both theorised and managed, irrespective of whether their origins lie in spontaneous or planned complexes. In Chapter 5, Charles examines in detail the evolution of one particular sub-class of technopoles, namely science cities, which he defines in line with Castells and Hall (ibid., p. 10) as 'strictly scientific research complexes, with no direct territorial linkage to manufacturing'. This 'first generation' of science cities was normally planned separately from the urban fabric in order to physically separate pure science research from the potential disturbances and distractions of urban life. Science cities over time have developed new visions, partnerships, funding and spatial organisations as they have sought to create synergies between these campuses and the wider urban system, to use these campuses' creative engines to drive the wider urban economy. Funding is one of the main challenges facing these planned complexes' capabilities with regard to creating dynamic urban science projects. While in the case of North America, its national and state governments have delegated funding responsibilities to local initiatives (Chapter 2), in the UK and many continental European countries, central and regional governments are still responsible for providing the finance for science cities. This difference might explain why the key entrepreneurial drivers of these place-based activities in the US are the universities, while in Europe, public sector organisations have adopted increasingly entrepreneurial personae.

1.4.2 Space, place and governance

Another notable feature of the 'new wave' of science cities is the absence of major city-building activity, but instead a focus on leveraging existing science resources to meet cities' future developmental needs. As a result, what we could find in contemporary science cities is a closer physical and functional connection between urban knowledge spaces. This emerging feature raises the question of whether the distinction between technopoles and metropolitan areas remains valid in the contemporary context. While addressing this question satisfactorily might require a much longer time span, it is possible to consider the conflicts that emerge when urban and knowledge spaces are merged together, both from interferences between different kinds of governance structures as well as spatial planning structures. It is for this reason that although governance is at most an implicit theme in the original *Technopoles* volume, it has to be placed absolutely centrally in contemporary technopole analysis. In their original book, Castells and Hall (ibid., p. 1) described the prototype information society (emphasis added):

> [it] consists of a series of low, discreet buildings, usually displaying a certain air of quiet good taste, and set amidst impeccable landscaping in that standard real-estate cliché, a campus-like atmosphere . . . which are now legion on the *periphery* of virtually every dynamic urban area in the world.

Moreover, innovation and creation activities were supposed to be separated from manufacturing:

> quite a number of the people in the buildings of these new technopoles do not usually make anything, though somewhere else, often not many

miles away, in rather similar buildings – sometimes of slightly less elegance – other people are making the things they invent here.

(ibid., p. 2)

These stereotypical images of technopoles have been redefined by the growing, or reoccurring, awareness that urban cores and cities are still the leading drivers of economic development, particularly during the times of austerity and economic crisis. Therefore, Beth Perry and Tim May in Chapter 6 rightly point out that the ever-growing importance of knowledge and innovation in the post-industrial or post-Fordist economy:

collide and collude with writings concerning the emergence of new networked and distributed forms of governance and multi-level arrangements which highlight the relevance of the 'city' and more recently 'city-regions' as appropriate units of analysis and action in both political and economic terms.

(p. 107 of this volume)

But the coupling between knowledge and urban spaces is far from a simple task, whose complexity starts from the diverse and sometimes even contradictory expectations of participants in knowledge creation processes as to the kinds of knowledge that can be created. As Perry and May point out, the significance of knowledge can be viewed through a variety of different lenses, including at the very least the economic, political, socio-cultural and scientific, each of which highlights different facets of knowledges that are important for stakeholders in particular knowledge coalition. Successful knowledge-based urban development projects must reflect stakeholders' various interests in these kinds of knowledge, and develop appropriate governance structures to ensure that those different assumptions, expectations and needs can be clearly articulated and resolved within the formal constraints of territorial projects. Perry and May illustrate their argument with a detailed case study of England's Science City Project, where the authors convincingly demonstrate how, in the absence of a meaningful concept of knowledge, loopholes emerged in locally tailored development strategies and also provoked a range of conflicts, both between central and local governments and different local government bodies themselves.

This complicated governance structure of technopoles is not exclusive to England but also occurs in Asia-Pacific regions, in part a consequence of public governance norms that are often more strictly top–down in their development approaches. In Chapter 7, Wei-Ju Huang provides a timely update of Taiwan's Hsinchu project, a typical technology park initiative examined by Castells and Hall. Castells and Hall described Hsinchu as a relatively loose university initiative, with much in common with Sophia-Antipolis, France and Cambridge, UK, a centrally planned initiative with limited connection to its surrounding area. Although three decades have passed since its inception, there has not been a substantive shift in Hsinchu's enclave nature to any significant degree. Huang brings together the concepts of spaces of dependence (following Cox, 1998) and the territorial structure of the state to examine the nature of the governance conflicts in two collaboration initiatives: Hsinchu Science City Development Plan and the Governor Forum. The first failed because of central government restructuring alongside the loss of public funding; the second largely ignored interest divergences between the partners and the longer-term issue of development targets. Echoing Charles's (Chapter 5) findings, the case of Hsinchu suggests that two elements are crucial, namely a clear vision for science parks and a feasible funding plan. Huang also reaches a number of other interesting conclusions, including the need to avoid overstating high-tech sectors' specific preferences at the expense of social and environmental concerns both within the science park areas and their wider regional setting. The most desirable state is a more balanced urban development strategy catering for both economic and social wellbeing in the core, as well as peripheral areas.

The relation between metropolitan core and suburban areas in knowledge-based urban developments is the explicit focus of Mario Vale in Chapter 8, who presents the cases of Madrid and Lisbon. Castells and Hall already highlighted the importance of metropolitan cities as the milieu of innovation two decades ago, although neither of these two cities featured specifically in their analyses. Vale places his case studies in the context of the emerging cognitive-culture economy, in which creativity and culture-related sectors are becoming increasingly important in terms of job and wealth creation. But the spatial impacts of this cognitive-cultural economy are physically shaped by the existing post-Fordist urban structure, something that in old industrial cities (such as Madrid and Lisbon) is characterised by dereliction and vacancy. Most planned science park projects in Madrid and Lisbon, therefore, were constructed in old industrial suburbs where industrial sites became available. Their existence provided foundations for these suburban areas to actively plan for the exploration of new opportunities in the emerging cognitive-cultural economy. As a result, these suburban localities found themselves coming into competition with the metropolitan core for the attraction of investment and job creation. In the absence of governance mechanisms and planning frameworks to co-ordinate between core and suburban areas in tandem with declining public funding, the suburban locations have been losing out rather than adding value to these core areas. One of the remedies proposed by the author, in light of some successful small-scale innovative regeneration practices, is for policies to move away from mega-projects imported from elsewhere and to focus on place-based actions.

The specifications of Spain, especially its effort in using science parks to promote city regeneration, are explored further in Chapter 9 by Antònia Casellas. The author explicitly points out that, at least in Spain, science parks carry the dual functions of economic growth and land development, and that these two functions do not always hang together seamlessly. Governance structure is again a focus in Casellas' chapter, but unlike the case of Hsinchu (Chapter 7), where central government dominates both governance arrangements and operational practicalities, in Spain science parks tend to be embedded within their cities and regions (an issue also emerging in Chapter 8). The stylised case of Barcelona provides an advanced model of building multi-level sector co-operation, and of leveraging private investment through public seed funding. The efficiency of this 'Barcelona model' in promoting innovation activities across the city region was nevertheless somewhat undermined by the overwhelming focus on land development and physical regeneration. Casellas warns of the potential vicious cycle of over-focusing on physical development, and neglecting the soft environment, innovation capability, and R&D activities necessary to create innovative milieu. Spain's historical public policy tradition of using land development as a means of driving economic growth, in Casellas' point of view, has something to do with the large proportion of SMEs in its economic fabric. Their limited capacity to assemble capital for investment, a situation only aggravated by the current economic crisis scenario, makes it difficult to generate sufficient private investment in science parks' development. This finding underscores the importance of considering both the characteristics of individual science parks and the wider context in which any evaluation of their overall economic contribution must necessarily take place – an issue addressed in the following section.

1.4.3 Heterogeneity and technopoles' evaluation

Many of the narratives that have been developed around science parks have been developed on the basis of claims of success that have drawn upon evaluations of those science parks. But as we noted in 1.4.2, any attempt to evaluate science parks must necessarily go beyond a simple accounting cost-benefit approach and explore the range of contributions they make, economically, socially, but also administratively and in policy contexts. The evaluation point was perhaps made most trenchantly by Massey, Quintas and Wield (1992) who noted that the simple lesson of UK science parks in the 1980s was that the single most important thing you could do to make a science park succeed was to locate it in a buoyant economy, in the case of the UK ideally in the 'Golden Triangle' of Oxford–London–Cambridge. But that rather begged the question and led them in their analysis to point to the proliferation of 'high-tech fantasies' propelled by a belief that it was the science park, rather than pre-exsiting economic success, which lay at the root of the creation of these innovative spaces. Likewise, in this section, we have sought to get beyond straightforward stories selling success, but to place that success in the context of what barriers have been overcome, and what tensions and failures have been encountered in the course of creating those science parks.

Although Chapter 10 is, like Chapter 9, about science parks in Spain, it offers a solid complement to Casellas' qualitative exploration. Albahari quantatively tested the influences of heterogeneity on science parks' performances in Spain. Albahari noticed that the significant parks' characteristics in influencing regional added value were their age, size, characteristics of the management teams, level of technological development in their host region, and the level of university involvement. Among the companies' features, their size and R&D intensity were found important for them to benefit from a science park's location. These findings are interesting when compared to the current understanding of technopoles. First, with regard to the influence of a science park's age, Castells and Hall argued that a long-term commitment was one precondition for the emergence of synergy in technopoles. However, in Albahari's study, the age of science parks was found to have a non-linear effect, with both younger and older parks outperforming mid-aged parks. Second, in connection with the question of location, Albahari found statistically significant benefits for science parks locating in less innovative regions, although without further replication this result is not conclusive. Third, it was found that the more companies located on science parks, the better the companies' innovation performance, suggesting that agglomeration still plays a positive role in science parks' functioning. However, the data here were not able to distinguish either different types of agglomeration nor proximity, topics that could clearly benefit from future research.

The influence of the companies' heterogeneity on their performances is likewise the focus of Tian Miao in Chapter 11, which presents the case of a less-known science park in Central China, Optics Valley China, a research context that clearly affected the evaluation indicator selection. In this chapter, Miao illustrated the impact of companies' different ownerships, something that has particular saliency on their internal resources, external networking activities, and overall innovation performances, in a country like China where there has been a very rapid transformation. Data from a survey of companies revealed that public-controlled companies took the lead in all three dimensions. This puzzling finding was explained with three detailed case studies on companies with different ownerships. Her findings hinted that: first, having a focus on a single research sector matters; second, having a focus on a single region matters, and; third, the particular nature of transition was also important. Therefore, this chapter strongly suggests that the environment within which a science park is embedded is an important enabler and/or constrainer of its performance. Evaluations of these 21st century industrial complexes should always put their research in context.

Dawood and Phelps in Chapter 12 demonstrate the importance of regional economic and institutional environment with two Malaysian cases. As with the picture emerging from the previous chapters, it is not automatically safe to assume that technopoles locating similar industries together in less-developed regions will be successful in cultivating Marshallian externalities. Conversely, what Charles (this volume) terms the third wave of science cities, by locating within established urban areas, seeks to take advantage of the latter's diverse economic structure. Dawood and Phelps explicitly explored the extent to which technology parks in Malaysia could leverage externalities related to Marshallian specialisation and externalities related to industry diversity or related variety. Against those expectations, their survey of two representative technology parks yielded disappointing results: they neither built up a strong specialised economy nor leveraged a diverse economy. However, such findings are perhaps unsurprising given their national background. In Malaysia, there is a weak science and technology policy framework, a lack of scale and associated diversity in either the national capital city region and other urban centre economies upon which the two parks might leverage. As things stand, the Malaysian technology parks do seem quite a long way away from a position where they are able to stimulate synergy building processes, and further feed back benefits into their host regions.

Although the above three chapters are all focused on park-level analysis, Strauf and Scherer's contribution in Chapter 13 evaluates technopoles' regional contribution. Assisted with a comparative analysis of six European science parks, they propose a framework for the evaluation of the regional impact of technopoles based on five factors: (a) links between academic and extra-faculty research; (b) promotion of the knowledge transfer; (c) entity co-ordinating the knowledge transfer; (d) promotion of start-ups and; (e) co-operation with regional enterprises. A case study on the University and Research Centre Tulln in Austria illustrated the process of building these factors, which has the potential for developing into a comprehensive regional synergic network. But the importance of a well-organised management team (cf. Chapter 10), and their skills in cultivating synergy among different components (cf. Chapter 4) is also highlighted by the author here. The most substantive contribution made by this chapter is to note that better public accountability is needed to trace the cost and gains of these investments. The chapter suggests that the construction of a clear cause-effects chain was necessary to be able to successfully and meaningfully evaluate regional outcomes and impacts against the relevant objectives in a specific case. As a consequence of this, different technopoles should come up with different evaluation plans that take into account their specific vision and regional conditions. An implication of this chapter is also that strategic policy-makers and technopole practitioners should be aware of the shelf-life of their plans, visions and evaluation frameworks, and be prepared to update them periodically to take into account both what has been achieved internally and the effects of the changing technopole context.

In the final chapter, we try to draw the threads together by first summarising the lessons learned from the cases we covered in this volume, reflecting and comparing them with those highlighted in Castells and Hall's original visit of these industrial complexes. It is clear from the various contributions that there are some common issues emerging across the chapters. The idea of a technopole has in the context of the knowledge economy been fractured, and we see a plurality of new ideal types and best practices examples. Yet, this plurality runs the risk of obscuring the similarity of the kinds of processes that all of these spaces – whether located at the heart or the edge of the city, in capitals or peripheries, and in developed or developing countries – have in common. What remains to be better understood is how these pluriform technopoles are reflections of wider changes in the way that knowledge capital is created, circulated, transmitted, transformed and utilised in this new knowledge economy. Nevertheless, on the basis of the case studies, it is possible to see some intriguing glimpses of the way places, spaces and territories remain important for knowledge creation processes. From that, we are able to then build upon these experiences to make some tentative suggestions for building, structuring, and (re)vitalising technopoles, and in particular to ensure that they do not become a crude spatial fetishism of the high-technology fantasy but instead help to leverage multi-scalar innovation networks to drive territorial economic development. Here we admit that drawing lessons from such diverse projects across the world, which themselves are perhaps still the most important experimental fields of coupling science, technology, economy and space, is not an easy task. But to make technopole initiatives relevant in the 21st century it is necessary to deal with these questions, inconsistencies and tensions. Our aim is partly to replicate Castells and Hall, not just in terms of the content we offer, but also partly to help trigger and sustain a debate of great scientific and practical importance, and which can form the basis of wider attention and further studies.

References

Amin, A. and Robins, K. (1991) 'These are not Marshallian times', in R. Camagni (ed.), *Innovation networks: Spatial perspectives*, London: Belhaven.

Barrow, C. (2001) *Incubators: A realist's guide to the world's new business accelerators*. London: John Wiley & Sons.

Benneworth, P., Hospers, G.J., Jongbloed, B., Leiyste, L. and Zomer, A. (2011) 'The "science city" as a system coupler in fragmented strategic urban environments?'. *Built Environment*, *37*(3): 317–35.

Broekel, T. and Boschma, R. (2012) 'Knowledge networks in the Dutch aviation industry: The proximity paradox'. *Journal of Economic Geography*, *12*(2): 409–33.

Carrillo, F. (2006) *Knowledge cities*. London: Butterworth-Heinemann.

Castells, M. and Hall, P. (1994) *Technopoles of the world: The making of twenty-first-century industrial complexes*. London: Routledge.

Christopherson, S. and Clark, J. (2010) 'Limits to "The Learning Region": What university-centered economic development can (and cannot) do to create knowledge-based regional economies'. *Local Economy*, *25*: 120–30.

Church, A. (1995) 'Book review: Technopoles of the world. The making of 21st century industrial complexes'. *Transactions of the Institute of British Geographers*, *20*: 123–4.

Ciravegna, L. (2012) *Promoting Silicon Valleys in Latin America: Lessons from Costa Rica*. London: Routledge.

Comunian, R., Faggian, A. and Li, Q.C. (2010) 'Unrewarded careers in the creative class: The strange case of bohemian graduates'. *Papers in Regional Science*, *89*(2): 389–410.

Cox, K.R. (1998) 'Spaces of dependence, spaces of engagement and the politics of scale or: Looking for local politics'. *Political Geography*, *17*(1): 1–23.

Florida, R. (2002a) *The rise of the creative class: And how it's transforming work, leisure, community and everyday life.* New York: Perseus Book Group.

Florida, R. (2002b) 'The economic geography of talent'. *Annals of the Association of American Geographers*, *92*(4): 743–55. doi: 10.1111/1467–8306.00314.

Gertler, M. (1995) ' "Being there": Proximity, organisation and culture in the development and adoption of advanced manufacturing technologies'. *Economic Geography*, *71*(1):1–26.

Gertner, D., Roberts, J. and Charles, D.R. (2011) 'University-industry collaboration: A CoPs approach to KTPs'. *Journal of Knowledge Management*, *15*(4): 625–47.

Glaeser, E. (2011) *Triumph of the city: How our greatest invention makes US richer, smarter, greener, healthier and happier.* London, Basingstoke and Oxford: Pan Macmillan.

Graham, S. (2003) *The cybercities reader.* London: Routledge.

Hospers, G.J. (2006) 'Silicon somewhere? Assessing the usefulness of best practices in regional policy'. *Policy Studies*, *27*.

Keeble, D. and Wilkinson, F. (1999) 'Collective learning and knowledge development in the evolution of regional clusters of high technology SMEs in Europe'. *Regional Studies*, *33*(4): 259–303.

Komninos, N. (2002) *Intelligent cities.* London: Routledge.

Marshall, A. (1920) *Principles of economics.* London: Macmillan.

Massey, D., Quintas, P. and Wield, D. (1992) *Hi-technology fantasies.* London: Routledge.

Morgan, K. (1997) 'The learning region: Institutions, innovation and regional renewal'. *Regional Studies*, *31*(5): 491–503.

Perry, B. and May, T. (2007) 'Governance, science policy and regions: An introduction'. *Regional Studies*, *41*(8): 1039–50.

Phelps, N.A. (2012) *An anatomy of sprawl.* London: Routledge.

Pierre, C. and Andersen, B. (2012) 'New strategic dynamics in the Arctic region'. *Institute for Foreign Policy Analysis*, April (6): 4–9.

Porter, M.E. (1998) *On competition.* Boston, MA: Harvard Business School.

Reich, R. (1991) *The work of nations.* London: Simon & Schuster.

Rutten, R., Benneworth, P., Boekema, F. and Irawati, D. (eds) (2014) *The social dynamics of innovation networks.* London: Routledge.

Scott, A. (1989) *The technopoles of Southern California.* Los Angeles: UCLA Press.

Sunman, H. (1986) *France and her technopoles.* Cardiff: CSP Economic Publications.

Walcott, S. (2003) *Chinese science and industrial technology parks.* London: Ashgate.

Yeung, H.W. (2009) 'Situating regional development in the competitive dynamics of global production networks: An East Asian perspective', in H.W. Yeung (ed.) *Globalizing regional development in East Asia: Production networks, clusters, and entrepreneurship.* London: Routledge.

Yigitcanlar, T. (2010). 'Making space and place for the knowledge economy: Knowledge-based development of Australian cities'. *European Planning Studies*, *18*(11): 1769–86.

Section 2

Synergy management

Who, how and where

2 The entrepreneurial university as a technopole platform

A global phenomenon

Henry Etzkowitz

2.1 Introduction

The university is moving from the periphery to the center of the technopole concept as it is transformed from a provider of human capital to a source of new technologies and jobs. The 'capitalization of knowledge' is at the heart of a new mission for the university, linking universities to users of knowledge more tightly and establishing the university as an economic actor in its own right and as an instigator of regional development. Even as the university and other knowledge-producing institutions are viewed as a generator of future economic growth in ever more direct ways, an entrepreneurial university might appear to be a contradiction in terms and an antithesis of the Ivory Tower academic model. However, the entrepreneurial university transcends and incorporates previous academic dichotomies (ivory-tower/polytechnic; research/teaching) in a new synthesis. The entrepreneurial university is an emergent phenomenon that is a result of the working out of an 'inner logic' of academic development that previously expanded the academic enterprise from a conservator to an originator of knowledge.

Originating as a medieval institution for the conservation and transmission of knowledge, the university has evolved over the centuries into an institution in which knowledge is also created and put into use. Research became an inextricable part of the teaching process as teaching extended from dissemination of available knowledge to include methodologies that retrieve lost knowledge. Research was expanded to an increasing number of disciplines as reliable methods were formulated, enabling students to participate in the creation of new knowledge as part of their training. Practical implications were discerned in some of these research results, especially in the sciences, and steps were taken to put them to use.

Academic entrepreneurship is an extension of teaching and research activities, on the one hand, and the internalization of technology transfer and firm-formation capabilities, taking a role traditionally played by business and industry, on the other. Peter Hall (1985) early on noted the need for 'Better links between educational-scientific policy and regional urban policy' (p. 49). This disjuncture is still apparent as the UK reduced, rather than increased funding for universities in the wake of the 2008 economic downturn (Etzkowitz and Ranga, 2011). Rather than pouring resources into existing universities and founding new ones, as it did in the early post-war period, the UK opted for a counterproductive austerity strategy. Although various measures may be cited, such as the local interpretation of the US Small Business Innovation Research Programme, these efforts are small in scale and scope. The UK has failed to fully capitalize on its major comparative international advantage, the under-utilized innovation potential in its academic sphere (Etzkowitz, 2010). Universities and offshoot campuses are one key but very specific and perhaps under-researched element of technopoles. This chapter analyzes the emergence of the university as an entrepreneur, the internal and external impetuses for this development, and its enhanced role in the creation of Technopoles.

2.2 The transition to an entrepreneurial university

We usually think of an entrepreneur as an individual, who takes great risks to initiate a new activity, while organizations typically perform the function of institutionalizing and perpetuating an activity. However, organizations may also play the entrepreneurial role as Schumpeter noted in his analysis of the role of the Department of Agriculture in creating the US agricultural research system (1949). Indeed most individual entrepreneurs are members of groups, whose complementary skills and resources are required to make an entre- preneurial act possible.

Entrepreneurship is thus a quintessentially organizational phenomenon, even when its collective nature is hidden by individualistic ideological precepts. Although the idea of the entrepreneurial university has been widely accepted, there is still considerable skepticism of its validity.

There are three stages and phases to the development of the university as an entrepreneur, with each modality building upon the other, in a usual but by no means necessary order. In an initial phase (*University Entrepreneur One*) the academic institution takes a strategic view of its direction and gains some ability to set its own priorities, either by raising its own resources through donations, tuition fees and grant income or through negotiations with resource providers. This is the sense in which 'entrepreneurial university' is used by Burton Clark in his analysis of European universities extracting themselves from virtually total Ministry control down to the number of students that may be recruited in each discipline (1999). European universities, that formerly received almost their entire income by government subvention, are undergoing the painful process of diversification, forming alumni associations to connect with their graduates and establishing fundraising offices, long a staple of US academia.[1]

In a second phase (*University Entrepreneur Two)* the academic institution takes an active role in commercializing the intellectual property arising from the activities of its faculty, staff and students. In this phase, a university typically establishes its own technology transfer capabilities, in-sourcing them from firms to which they may have been contracted, such as the Research Corporation in the US, or through devolution of system-wide offices as in the State University of New York and the University of California to individual campuses. Universities with significant intellectual property potential, like Stanford, received an immediate boost in income from having their own staff in more direct contact with the faculty. Similarly, research powerhouses, such as Oxford, Cambridge and Imperial, in the UK, very quickly became leaders in technology transfer and firm-formation once they turned their minds to it. Universities with fewer research resources to commercialize, not surprisingly, take a longer time to ramp up. However, some schools with modest resources, such as Arizona State and the University of Utah, that have made tech transfer and firm formation an equal priority with education and research, have achieved higher rates of valorization than many of their resource-rich competitors.

In a third phase (*University Entrepreneur Three*), the academic institution takes a proactive role in improving the efficacy of its regional innovation environment, often in collaboration with industry and government actors. Although these phases were identified as taking place sequentially in the development of the Massachusetts Institute of Technology (MIT), non-linear and even reverse sequences may be identified, for example, in the experience of the Blekinge Institute of Technology in Sweden, which took off from phase three.[2] Regional government and business actors identified establishment of an academic institution as part of a strategy to make the transition from a declining industrial region to knowledge-based industry, in this case software. They successfully lobbied the national government and the Blekinge Institute of Technology was founded. Thus, the transition to the entrepreneurial university can also take off from a teaching as well as a research-oriented school.

2.3 MIT as entrepreneurial academic exemplar[3]

MIT's nature, as an academic anomaly, has been misinterpreted by some observers who expected that it would inevitably conform to the Research University model, i.e., follow Harvard. Instead, MIT has become the exemplar of an entrepreneurial university model that is designed to take the lead in creating a Technopole. Although MIT has developed research to great distinction, including involvement in collaborations with its Cambridge neighbour, Harvard is imitating MIT more than the other way around. Harvard's new science campus in Allston, temporarily halted by the 'great recession' was intended to surpass MIT in technology development and firm-formation.[4] Many other US universities, as well as universities across the world, have taken up this entrepreneurial objective. Indeed, some such as Kanpur in India, Cambridge in the UK, and Skolkovo in Russia, have hired MIT to help them create university-led Technopoles. For MIT, this was not a new mission but was part of the intent of its founders.

MIT was founded during the mid-19th century as a university with a strategic purpose, the renewal of the Boston region, an early US high-tech conurbation. This academic project was based on the strategic vision of its founder William Barton Rogers, a professor of geology at University of Virginia, who moved to Boston in order be located in a region that had a need for such an enterprise. The industrial infrastructure of the Boston region, based upon textiles and machines, had emerged in the early 19th century. Rogers obtained industry donations and political support to gain a share of the Massachusetts land grant, a unique application of the law supporting academic foundations with a practical intent, that at the time, typically focused on agriculture.

MIT, however, was for several decades after its founding only a 'down payment' on the grand scheme of founder, William Barton Rogers. The school's resources were only sufficient to train undergraduates, not to engage in research, technology transfer or industrial consultation. Thus, MIT only performed one of the several tasks for industry that its fellow Land Grant universities were performing for agriculture. It was not until the end of the 19th century that MIT began to engage more directly with industry, other than sending out trained graduates. By then, MIT had gained sufficient resources to inaugurate research and did so by hiring in consulting engineers as professors. At the time, these independent engineers were a main source of research for firms, engaged to perform specific tasks, as needed. An unintentional side effect of bringing consulting engineers into the university as researchers was that they continued their consulting practices and thus established a link between the university and industry that was already commonplace in agriculture.

During the early 20th century, MIT's involvement with industry was structured through a series of organizational innovations that legitimated the interaction between the academic and business spheres. This included the invention of the one-fifth rule regulating consultation and the utilization of contracts to formalize hitherto informal university-industry ties and the patent system to protect intellectual property. What emerged were the traditional academic committee process to review inventions and an external organization, the Research Corporation, to market the patents to industry. The next step was the creation of organization within the university, the technology transfer office, to carry out this task on a more intensive basis. In either format, as a branch of the university or as a freestanding entity, a search mechanism was introduced to identify commercializable knowledge within the university and to market it to potential users.

During the 1930s MIT played a leading role in developing a regional innovation strategy, based upon several instances of high-tech firm-formation that had already occurred by the 1920s. However, to generalize these instances and systematize the capitalization of knowledge, gaps had to be filled, such as providing business advice and seed capital to professors who might have commercializable technologies but lacked these other key elements that had previously been available only to a relatively few academics. This was the context in which a new organizational format, the venture capital firm, was invented by academic, business and governmental leaders, out of elements drawn from these institutional sources, in support of firm formation.

The governors of New England, as early as the 1920s, had called together the region's leadership to address the problem of industrial decline. Since universities were an especially prominent part of the region's infrastructure, it is not surprising that they were included in the call. This had the unexpected consequence of introducing an element of novelty into the typical public–private partnership, cresting a triple helix configuration. First, bringing the representatives of the three institutional spheres together in the New England Council provided an audience for Karl Compton, the president of MIT who, together with fellow MIT administrators, had formulated the concept of firm formation from academic research as an economic development strategy. This approach was based on extending an available focus on 'new products' as a possible basis of economic development, taking it one step further. The very process of including actors from these various backgrounds in the strategy review and formulation process provided access to the resources required to implement the eventual plan. By moving the 'new product' approach from the industrial sphere and tying it to the academic research process, the MIT group, in effect, formulated a 'linear model' of innovation.

Second, in addition to providing a receptive venue for the concept of firm formation from academia, the Council provided a venue for its specification as an organizational strategy that led to the invention of the venture capital firm. Compton had previously, unsuccessfully, tried to introduce the general idea of science-based economic development at the national political level. However, it did not find a receptive audience due to prevailing views that too much new technology was possibly the cause of depression and un-employment. New England, with its history of industrial growth based on technological innovation, from at least the early 19th century provided an exception to the general rule of technological skepticism that was the prevailing ideology at the time. The basic elements (financial resources, human capital, technological innovation) were available in the region. The university-industry-government network created by the New England Council could call upon individuals such as Ralph Flanders who had moved from the industrial sphere, as President of a Vermont tool company to the political sphere as Senator from Vermont, with an intervening stint as member of the board of the Boston branch of the Federal Reserve Bank. Such persons were available to encourage the necessary legislation. MIT's senior faculty could be called upon as advisors to review candidate technologies and recent graduates could be hired as technology scouts.

Third, the New England Council provided a network to put the concept into effect. Several elements had to be brought together in order to invent the venture capital firm. These included changes in law to allow financial institutions to invest part of their capital in more risky ventures than previously allowed. Moreover, persons with technical expertise were needed to seek out and review candidate technologies for commercialization, as well as individuals with business expertise to guide the firm-formation process. Finally, someone with an overview of all the elements of the process was required to knit these elements together into a coherent organization.

The Harvard Business School happened to have on its faculty a professor, Georges Doriot, who had taken an interest in new firm formation in contrast to the vast majority of the faculty who were focused on issues of existing, typically, large firms. Graduates, especially those who had taken his course in 'manufacturing', could be recruited to work in an organization concerned with firm formation. Thus, American Research and Development (ARD) was founded in 1946 to assist academic firm-formation efforts with seed capital, coaching and mentoring. The firm sent out scouts to visit university labs to identify prospects, although widespread publicity about the foundation of ARD also brought in a large number of unsolicited proposals from hopeful entrepreneurs.

A university-industry-government network, instantiated in ARD, to promote regional development was built on a substrate of academic institutions such as MIT that were already producing commercializable technologies and that already had experience in transferring technology to industry through consultation, patenting and licensing. In addition, a business school, with a limited focus on entrepreneurship and entrepreneurial skills, was available at Harvard. President Compton provided the necessary leadership to put these elements together into a coherent organizational format. Operating within the context of the New England Council, MIT took the Innovation Organizer (IO) role in renewing the regional Technopole by anchoring it to an academic substrate, while also playing a key role in inventing the venture capital firm, a hybrid organization providing support as well as investment.[5]

The University's 'third mission' of economic and social development, is transformed from being merely a facilitator for transferring technology to individual firms to being a force for fostering regional economic and social development. Instead of a focus on an individual patent or technology transfer regime, there is a concern with the university playing a broader role in its region. Sometimes, as in Portugal, where regional political entities are weak, the university plays a role of 'regional innovation organizer (RIO)', bringing together local businesses and municipalities to develop an innovation strategy.[6] In this case the university's convening role is primary, bringing relevant actors together to identify local strengths and weaknesses and find a way to fill gaps. Like the New England Council, and similar groups such as the Amsterdam Knowledge Circle or the Pittsburgh High Tech Council, the objective is to leverage existing resources, and attract new ones, to create a regional growth dynamic. The novel element in these efforts is the enhanced expectations for universities to contribute more than their traditional educational and research resources.

2.4 Transcending the linear model

The entrepreneurial university encompasses and extends the Research University, enhancing it by joining a reverse linear dynamic to the classic linear model. The entrepreneurial university takes a pro-active stance in putting knowledge to use and in broadening the input into the creation of academic knowledge. Thus, it operates according to an interactive rather than a linear model of innovation. The linear model, starting from research and moving to utilization, is complemented by a reverse linear model moving from problems in industry and society, seeking solutions in science. Once the two processes operate in tandem, often through the university's technology transfer office, moving relevant knowledge and technology out of the university and its liaison office, bringing problems in, an interactive process is generated in which each linear starting point enhances the other. The university's incubator facility, housing both firms generated from academic research and firms brought into the university's orbit by entrepreneurs seeking a closer connection to the academic scene to enhance their firm, exemplifies the interactive dynamic.

The classic linear model presumed a progression from research to development to innovation and product introduction in which the university was centrally involved only in the first phase, transferring research results with commercial potential. The first step toward an academic entrepreneurial ethos is increased sensitivity to results with practical potential followed by a willingness to participate in the realization of this potential. This change often occurs through the attention that outsiders pay to academic research for this reason. Thus, in the early twentieth century MIT established a faculty committee to consider patenting discoveries made on campus after finding that some visitors to campus were taking the practical implications of faculty research to market as their own. Interactions with venture capitalists and business angels have led other academics to enter into projects to commercialize their research. The founding of biotechnology firms such as Genentech and Synergen during the late 1970s and early '80s exemplify this collaborative process. Finally, academics themselves discern the practical implications of their research as in the classic closing sentence of Watson and Cricks' 1953 note in *Nature* announcing the double helix model that 'It has not escaped our attention [. . .].'

The next step to an entrepreneurial academic ethos is the realization that working on practical problems posed by non-academics can have a dual potential. On the one hand, such work meets the needs of supporters of the academic enterprise and provides support to that enterprise. On the other hand, these research tasks for others may lead to the posing of new research questions with theoretical potential. The Materials Characterization Center at the University of Puerto Rico operates on the basis of this dual focus, training its graduate students to pursue both tasks in tandem. An earlier generation of basic researchers, such as Columbia University physicist Isidor Rabi, focused on disciplinary advance, realized the theoretical potential of their practical work on Second World War weapons problems and, in the post-war period, revised their conception of science accordingly.

The interactive model both brings together the two linear models as well as generating an interaction between them in which basic research questions arise from addressing practical problems and vice versa. The potential of an interactive model became apparent during the Second World War when physicists working on engineering problems in wartime research projects such as radar, who believed that they had put aside their academic interests, started generating theoretical questions that they would address later. Thus, scientists who had previously opposed federal funding of research, fearing that they would lose their academic freedom, enthusiastically embraced it after the war. While holding to an ideology of basic research, many continued their work on practical problems in the post-war period, some continuing with military research while others shifted to civilian problems. Despite this revolution in the role of the basic researcher, conceptual reformulation of the academic role lagged practice until the growth in commercialization of research that began during the 1980s and '90s and has been ongoing since, albeit at different rates in various venues.

A two-way flow of influence is created between the university and an increasingly knowledge-based society as the distance among institutional spheres is reduced. Universities negotiate partnerships with start-up firms, emanating from academic research in which they invest intellectual and financial capital in exchange for equity in these firms. They also make broad arrangements with R&D intensive firms for funds in exchange for preferred access to patent rights and adjunct faculty status for company researchers. Such firms may locate on campus as at the University of Bochum in Germany, the Centennial campus of North Carolina State University and prospectively at the College of Natural Resources at the University of California, Berkeley. The content and formats for teaching, research and linkage itself are also affected. The assumption of an active role in economic development leaves existing academic missions in place, but it also encourages them to be carried out in new ways.

The entrepreneurial university model can be expressed in four inter-related propositions:

- Proposition 1: *Interaction*. The entrepreneurial university interacts closely with the industry and government; it is not an ivory tower university isolated from society.
- Proposition 2: *Independence*. The entrepreneurial university is a relatively independent institution; it is not a dependent creature of another institutional sphere.
- Proposition 3: *Hybridization*. The resolution of the tensions between the principles of interaction and independence are an impetus to the creation of hybrid organizational formats to realize both objectives simultaneously.

- Proposition 4: *Reciprocality.* There is a continuing renovation of the internal structure of the university as its relation to industry and government changes and of industry and government as their relationship to the university is revised.

Propositions One and Two may also be institutional principles of a research and teaching university; it is the confluence of all four elements that make for a full-fledged entrepreneurial university.

2.5 The American entrepreneurial university

To be an entrepreneur, a university has to have a considerable degree of independence from the state and industry but also a high degree of interaction with these institutional spheres. In academic systems following the Humboldtian model of close ties to the state, on the one hand, and professional autonomy guaranteed by civil service status, on the other, the university was an arm of the Ministry of Education with little ability to set its own strategic direction. The achievement of relative autonomy from the state, a process that was initiated in Europe relatively recently, occurred in the early 19th century in the US.

Academic independence from direct state control was secured in the US as an outcome of the Supreme Court decision in the Dartmouth College case of 1819. A schism at Dartmouth College left two groups struggling for control. One group reorganized as Dartmouth University and tried to obtain control by having the state of New Hampshire revise the charter that had established the College. The representatives of the original College argued that the state could not revise a charter, once granted. In supporting this position the Court defined universities as 'private eleemosynary institutions' stating that trustees and professors were not public officers nor were they extensions of 'civil government' (Hofstader and Metzger, 1961). The case had broader implications in the extension of its general principles of institutional autonomy from charitable to business corporations, becoming the legal basis for increasing independence of corporations from state control.

The ability to take independent initiatives is based on the premise that the university is not a subordinate element of a hierarchical administrative structure such as a Ministry of Higher Education. If a university system operates as it formerly did in Sweden where the Ministry of Higher Education decided how many students will be admitted each year to each discipline, there is hardly a possibility to have sufficient autonomy on which to base an entrepreneurial university. It has been argued that universities did not come into independent existence in France until the 1970s in a devolution that occurred as a side effect of reforms made in response to the student movements of the 1960s. Until quite recently, the various faculties were directly linked to the National Ministry and universities were hardly an organizational framework, let alone autonomy (Musselin, 2004).

To this day European Professors are often selected through national compe-titions that make a strategy such as Terman's 'steeple building' at Stanford, creating a critical mass of professors on a special topic difficult if not impossible to realize. Terman's strategy was to identify a nascent field with theoretical and practical potential and hire several professors with research specialties in this area, in effect forming a proto center, while linking them to departments in which they would teach more broadly than their special research area. This strategy allowed the university to fulfill three missions simultaneously that otherwise might have been at odds with each other.

Although the formation of firms by academics is not a new phenomenon, it is only recently that universities have accepted and indeed encouraged their staff to take this step. Moreover, faculty members who participate in the formation of firms are also retaining their faculty positions, after taking a leave to start the firm. MIT was the first academic institution during the early post-war era, followed by Stanford, to have a significant number of faculty members participate in the organization of firms, creating an entrepreneurial culture at these universities that encouraged other faculty and graduate students to emulate their actions. Frederick Terman, Engineering Professor and Dean, provided the prototype in mentoring his masters students Hewlett and Packard to commercialize a device that they had developed on campus under his tutelage during the late 1930s.

An occasional phenomenon prior to the Second World War, firm-formation from academia became a steady stream in the post-war era. The venture capital model, invented to fund the early stages of university research commercial-ization, expanded beyond that purview to ever later stages of firm formation. Nevertheless, ARD and some of its peers continued to seek out investment opportunities in academia. During the 1970s and '80s academic-industry relations developed rapidly in the US in response to increased international competition. The incremental evolution of products within existing industries was inadequate to insure economic growth. Academia was thus brought into new, relatively independent, alignment with industry. There was both a need to introduce new technologies into existing industries and to create industries based on new technology.

There were precursors earlier in the century for accomplishment of this task, but integration of research with application is now the basis of a policy for civilian technology development, a model previously confined to the military sector (Etzkowitz *et al.*, 1999). Federal policy to encourage commercializa-tion research preceded the well-known Bayh Dole Act, but that Act had a significant effect in encouraging a broader range of universities to become involved as a condition of receiving federal research funds. The Small Business Innovation Research (SBIR) programme legitimized government funding of start-ups under the guise of extending basic research projects into the realm of utilization. State governments also became more active, funding centers at universities to produce and transfer useful research as well as supplying seed capital to firms originating from academia. Taken together, the US created an immanent national policy of academic entrepreneurship and public venture capital. This 'hidden industrial policy' functioned in an uncoordinated and decentralized manner, leaving it up to academic entrepreneurs to knit various initiatives together to help support their firm formation efforts along with resources from family, friends and angels.

2.6 The European entrepreneurial university

We have also witnessed the spread of academic-industry relations to countries in Europe and Latin America with different cultural and academic traditions, research and industrial backgrounds. An entrepreneurial university can also be based on the teaching role of the university, by introducing entrepreneurial training into the curriculum. In this model, which has been explicitly developed in Sweden and Brazil, students are expected to play the entrepreneurial role in taking research out of the university and making it into firms, playing the role of technical entrepreneurs. In this model, firm formation is less tied to advanced research, although it may be based upon it but is more connected to what has been taught in entrepreneurship courses.

European universities have established training programmes in entrepreneurship designed to create firms, as well as educate students in the new discipline. Although US universities increasingly have entrepreneurship training programmes in their business schools and 'greenhouses' to encourage student entrepreneurs, there is a greater focus in Europe on student, rather than faculty, entrepreneurs in part because of differences in academic norms and cultures. The European Entrepreneurial University educates and graduates organizations as well as individuals. The focus on educating entrepreneurs and training groups of students as firms may explain some of the rapid rise in firm formation in Sweden, a country previously noted for its complex of large technology firms tied to a comprehensive social welfare system.

Many Swedish academic spin-off firms arise from teaching programmes in Entrepreneurship rather than from faculty research. For example, the Entrepreneurship Center at Linkoping University produces 100 spin-offs per year from its training activities and through extensions of its programme at other Swedish universities. In the Linkoping model students move from courses into pre-incubator facilities where they can try out their ideas and develop their business plans with advice from consultants recruited from industry. The best prospects are then invited into an incubator facility, often with funding arranged. The Entrepreneurship Center at Chalmers University in Gothenburg trains groups of students who first go through a recruitment and application process that encourages the development of a firm formation concept and then evaluates it as the basis for acceptance into the programme.[7]

The role of students in European academic entrepreneurship is not new. It can be especially seen in the foundation of chemical and optical firms, e.g., Zeiss Jena in Germany in the mid to late 19th century, often by the students of leading academic researchers. These firms typically maintained contact with

academia through consulting relationships that persisted through the generations. As some of these firms have downsized in recent years some of the
traditional format for university-industry relationships have declined at academic institutions such as Milan Polytechnic. These have been replaced by
new initiatives that broker student projects in firms and incubator space for
firm formation.[8]

2.7 The Brazilian entrepreneurial university

The Brazilian Entrepreneurial academic model can be seen as a synthesis of
the US and European variants. On the one hand, academic entrepreneurship
emerged in Brazil as a survival strategy when research funding precipitously
declined in the early 1980s. Research as an explicit academic mission had only
recently been introduced into an academic system with largely training
functions, despite the long-time existence of a few specialized research units.
Universities that were determined to persist in this new mission looked to
develop new sources of material and ideological support for this goal and the
means to realize it. The incubator was imported from the US as an organizational format to translate academic research into economic activity (Etzkowitz,
Mello and Almeida, 2005).

Academic entrepreneurship also took a broader format to address broader
social problems as well as economic issues. Thus, the incubator concept was
translated from a high-tech business-firm development format into a low-tech
service cooperative initiative, translating the organizational expertise developed in the initial project to address the deep inequalities endemic to Brazilian
society. Entrepreneurial education was also introduced as part of general
education, rather than being confined to engineering and business students,
the traditional human resource of entrepreneurial activities. Just as students
learn to write an essay expressing their personal thoughts or a scientific report,
utilizing evidence to support a thesis, so they are also being taught to write a
business plan, setting forth an objective and the means to realize it, along with
a 'market test'.[9]

Academic entrepreneurship thus becomes part of the teaching mission of
the university, intruding an entrepreneurial ethos to a broader population
on the grounds that it is equally relevant to the arts and social sciences as
to engineering and the sciences; to low-tech as well as high-tech ventures.
Academic entrepreneurship is being translated to a non-academic population
through the Popular Cooperatives and other university-originated social
programmes (Almeida and Etzkowitz, 2010). More recently, the Innovation
Law of 2004 has inspired the creation of 'the firm in a lab', a joint academic
research group and business firm that produces research results, journal articles
and marketable products at one and the same time in a common unit housed
within the university. This hybrid entity saves resources by lessening the need
to duplicate facilities, since the early stages of spin-off can legitimately take
place within the academic lab. Addressing the Valley of Death created by the

necessity to make an early separation between academic research and the conduct of business remains an issue in the US.

2.8 Experiential education: filling a gap in Stanford's innovation system[10]

Several entrepreneurially minded students and recent graduates, working through Stanford's Student Government, organized the StartX Accelerator, an experiential educational coaching and mentoring project, to assist their fellow students' entrepreneurial ventures. The project was led by a recent graduate who had attempted to organize a firm as an undergraduate but realized that he lacked sufficient knowledge and skills. He found the entrepreneurial courses and assistance available on campus useful but insufficient to help him achieve his objective. The StartX initiative began from this premise and has developed from relatively modest beginnings as a student 'lab' into a complex entrepreneurial support structure that has attracted significant resources, both human and financial.

StartX operates according to a quasi-academic model, applied to groups rather than individuals, and is largely conducted experientially, with mentoring and coaching, although occasional lectures are offered. The moments of StartX includes (1) an application process; (2) co-location with sister firms on the accelerator premises, (3) mentoring and coaching, and (4) a demo day 'graduation'. Founders are undergraduate students, masters, PhDs, post-doctoral fellows and professors, who share a common experience founding a company that creates an atmosphere of trust and information sharing among the programme's participants. The StartX admissions process is analogous to the admissions process for many universities in the US. Each team of entrepreneurs applies to StartX by submitting an application and going through an interview. The first round of the application consists of short essays and a short video pitch and the second round consists of a two-minute pitch in front of a panel – one minute on the team and one minute on the company. Only by succeeding in both rounds does a team get into the StartX programme. In many ways, StartX is a re-invention of ARD, the original venture capital firm, recuperating many of the features of a pro-bono coaching and mentoring organization that also offered seed capital. StartX believes that its location in Silicon Valley makes that service unnecessary due to the proliferation of angel and venture funding in the region. However, if the model were transferred to universities in less start-up funding rich environments, such an additional service might be included.[11]

The StartX home on the first floor of the AoL Building in the Stanford Research Park, adjacent to the academic campus, is amenable to the needs of software and Internet firms that merely require computers as their development tools but lacks wet lab space required by biotech firms. Nevertheless, several nascent biotech firms have gone through the StartX process. Although they have found it useful in assisting honing the firms' presentation and business approach, they are not able to carry forward the technical side of the firm at StartX. To gain the university's support in filling the perceived gap in incubator wet lab space at Stanford, several StartX firm founders in the biological science space requested a meeting with Stanford's President John Hennessey. They met at a café near the university to discuss their strategy in preparation for the meeting with the President. All of the petitioners had successfully formed firms but had faced difficulties in acquiring lab facilities to carry on their experimentation. One founder said that when he had initially mentioned his intention of founding a firm to his PhD supervisor he had been told to leave the lab. Nevertheless, he returned the next day and the two reconciled, with the faculty member eventually supporting the formation of the firm. Others described taking leaves of absence from PhD programmes that lacked a direct method of crediting firm-formation activities as part of the degree programme. One deliberately dropped out after the masters in order to insure retaining control of her intellectual property. Two complained that their leaves of absence were only valid for two years in comparison to UC Berkeley that allowed a three-year leave. The author, a coach for the meeting preparation, suggested that instead of leaves of absence, that firm formation should be included along with publications as part of the outputs of an entrepreneurial university PhD programme.

A 2005 participant observation study of the Stanford Office of Technology Licensing (OTL) conducted by the author identified an 'excluded middle' of inventors with commercializable research that was not being moved forward. OTL, with twenty-five staff members, was primarily focused on serial entrepreneurs, whom they had worked with on successive commercialization projects, and did not have sufficient resources to seek out inventors who did not come to them directly. Occasionally, such an inventor was incentivized to find their own way to OTL but this was the exception rather than the rule. For example, a biology professor who did not believe in commercialization of research but wanted to see his invention built found a PhD student in the engineering school who was interested in founding a firm. He made that the condition of realizing the biology professor's goal of building his device and together they went through the OTL marketing and licensing process. But this idiosyncratic example illustrated the existence of a broader entrepreneurial support gap at Stanford, even though a solution was found in this particular case.

Filling a gap in a support structure for spin-off activity in an already highly productive innovation system produced a significant increase in firm formation at Stanford University (Etzkowitz, 2013b). The StartX phenomenon demonstrates that the world's leading entrepreneurial university located in the world's most productive innovation conurbation has been operating below its potential and is amenable to improvement. The broader significance of this case is that it is a targeted intervention, based on research into strengths and weaknesses of an academic innovation system and its context. As significant and attractive an initiative as StartX is, it should not be misread as a 'one size fits all' cure for what ever ails an aspiring university's efforts to contribute to regional economic and social development. Rather, the case is a prescription to fill gap(s) and connect the dots between existing resources, a bottom-up process in this instance.

2.9 Conclusion: the entrepreneurial university as a technopole platform

The contemporary entrepreneurial university is the latest step in an academic progression in which the new task emanates as a controversial departure from previously accepted academic missions and eventually is integrated with the old and becomes accepted in its own right. These transitions were controversial. Thus, the introduction of economic and social development as an academic mission called into question the purpose of the university as a research institution, for some academics, even as the introduction of research as an academic mission disturbed the taken-for-granted assumption of the university as a single purpose educational institution.

Research is now accepted as a traditional academic mission but this was not always the case. In the late nineteenth century, when a few research-oriented professors at Stanford University argued that research should be an equal mission in the university along with teaching, many traditional professors objected, arguing that the mission of the university is education. However, those faculty members who were conducting research typically responded that by discovering new knowledge, we can raise the training of the students to a higher level. It is more productive for them to do research as a way of learning and participate with us in doing research as opposed to passively sitting and learning through lectures. Thus, there was a debate and a discussion over whether this new mission of research should be accepted within the university. A 'game of legitimation' took place in which the new objective was tied to the old task. Moreover, it was held that the two activities were more productively done together than carried out separately.

To this day there is a tension between research and teaching in the university. It is a question that will never be settled but it is a productive tension because professors have found that they do better research if they are working with students. It also helps in the training of students to be doing research. Nevertheless, overemphasis on one or the other task produces conflicts of obligation. For example, if the professor becomes too involved in research and moves away from education then that creates a problem and tension in the university. This tension is a persisting one but nevertheless it is found to be more productive and cost effective to have these two missions together. That is why research and teaching are integrated into an increasing number of universities worldwide.

Similarly we are experiencing a debate about whether the third mission of economic and social development should be integrated into the university. Again, it is objected that it is a conflict with research for the researcher to be involved in translating the research into a technology and product (Rimer, 2003; see also Bok, 2003). Indeed, conflicts emerge between the financial interest in the company and following the research idea as an end in itself. However, these are conflicts that are managed as rules are established to regulate participation in firm formation, just as the one-fifth rule was established early in the 20th century to regulate consultation. Indeed, the new rules are often extensions of those worked out to regulate previous conflicts.

It can be expected that this new function of economic and social development will be integrated into the university much as research was integrated with teaching in an earlier era, with incubators adjoining classroom and laboratory facilities in the universities of the future. Conducting the activities separately is not as productive of basic research or applied research or technology and new product development. It is more productive to see innovation as non-linear where basic research problems can come out of practical issues as well as problems in a discipline. As each new mission is incorporated within the university, it restructures how the previous one is carried out. Thus, as research is assumed as an academic mission, how to do research is taught to students, thus making it part of the educational mission.

Each new mission is also found to provide a new source of legitimation and support for the previous missions. As students perform research tasks as part of their education, new knowledge is generated. Thus research becomes incorporated in the teaching mission and teaching in the research mission. Similarly, economic development provides a new legitimation for research as it contributes to expanding that activity. The second academic revolution also expands the number of universities. As the thesis of knowledge-based economic development takes hold every region wants its own university. Attracting the best students and professors in some areas becomes an economic development strategy that expands the growth of the academic enterprise. Some of these changes are internal developments within the academy, such as the development of the research group that has firm-like qualities. Thus, the Research University shares homologous qualities with a start-up firm even before it directly engages in entrepreneurial activities.

The entrepreneurial university is an efflorescence of embryonic characteristics that exist 'in potentio' in any academic enterprise. Theories of the university typically fail to account for the metamorphosis of a medieval institution based on charitable and eleemosynary principles into one capable of generating regional economic growth and of playing a primary, rather than a secondary, role in society. Instead, they argue for confinement to whatever has previously been accepted as academic roles and statuses, such as teaching and research, isolation or a close connection to the state. Rather, the entrepreneurial academic transition is the next stage in the development of a unique institution that incorporates and amplifies previous objectives, e.g., research and education even as it assumes new ones for economic, social and regional development in an organizational instantiation of the Hegelian dialectic. In the transition from industrial to knowledge-based society, industrial clusters and technopoles increasingly rely on universities, with their research, education and entrepreneurial capabilities, to secure a 'smart specialization' niche[12] in the global arena.

Notes

1 The lack of experience with academic fundraising has opened up a market for consultants to roleplay asking for money with newly minted university fundraisers who lack experience or are from cultures where such a question is considered to be impolite.
2 Author interview with Per Eriksson, Rector of Blekinge Institute of Technology, Stockholm, 2001.
3 This section draws upon Etzkowitz (2002).
4 Personal communication form John Marlin, Harvard graduate and participant in alumni reunion tour where this claim was made, 2007.
5 See Etzkowitz, 2008.
6 Interview with Industrial Liaison Director, University of Aveiro, 2001.
7 Interview with Matts Lundgren, Chalmers University, 2001. www.entrepreneur. chalmers.se
8 Author interview with Sergio Campo dall'orto, Indubator Director, Polytechnico Milano, 2002.
9 Interviews with Prof Ednalva de Morais and Prof Bermudez, University of Brasilia; Jose Aranya and Jose Pimento-Bueno, Pontifical Catholic University of Rio de Janeiro, 2002.
10 This section draws upon Etzkowitz (2013a).
11 Author interview with Cameron Teitleman, StartX founder and CEO, 2012.
12 See http://ec.europa.eu/invest-in-research/pdf/download_en/kfg_policy_brief_no9. pdf

Bibliography

Almeida, M., Mello, J. and Etzkowitz, H. (2010) 'Social innovation in a developing country: invention and diffusion of the Brazilian cooperative incubator'. *International Journal of Technology and Globalisation*, *1*(2): 258–77.
Bok, D. (2003) *Universities in the marketplace: The commercialization of higher education*. Princeton, NJ: Princeton University Press.
Castells, M. and Hall, P. (1994) *Technopoles of the world: The making of 21st century industrial complexes*. London: Routledge.
Clark, B. (1999) *Creating entrepreneurial universities: Organizational pathways of transformation*. New York: Pergamon.
Etzkowitz, H. (1983) 'Entrepreneurial scientists and entrepreneurial universities in American academic science'. *Minerva*, *21*(2–3): 1573–871.
Etzkowitz, H. (1999) 'Public entrepreneur: The trajectory of United States science, technology and industrial policy'. *Science and Public Policy*, *26*(1): 53–62.
Etzkowitz, H. (2002) *MIT and the rise of entrepreneurial science*. London: Routledge.
Etzkowitz, H. (2008) *The triple helix: University-industry-government innovation in action*. London: Routledge.
Etzkowitz, H. (2010) 'Entrepreneurial universities for the UK: A "Stanford University" at Bamburgh Castle'. *Industry and Higher Education*, August, *24*(4): 251–6.

Etzkowitz, H. (2013a) 'StartX and the paradox of success: Filling the gap in Stanford's entrepreneurial culture'. *Social Science Information*, *52*(4).

Etzkowitz, H. (2013b) 'Silicon Valley at risk? Sustainability of a global innovation icon'. *Social Science Information*, *52*(4).

Etzkowitz, H., Gulbrandsen, M. and Levitt, J. (2001) *Public venture capital: Sources of government funding for technology entrepreneurs* (2nd edn). New York: Aspen/Kluwer.

Etzkowitz, H., Mello, J. and Almeida, M. (2005) 'Towards "meta-innovation" in Brazil: The evolution of the incubator and the emergence of a triple helix'. *Research Policy*, *34*(4): 411–24.

Etzkowitz, H. and Ranga, M. (2009) 'A transKeynesian vision of government's role in innovation: Picking winners revisited'. *Science and Public Policy*, *36*(10): 799–808.

Hall, P. (1985) 'Technology, space and society in contemporary Britain'. In Castells, M. (ed.) *High technology, space and society* (p. 49). Newbury Park: Sage.

Marshall, J. (1819) 'Chief Justice John Marshall's Opinion in the Dartmouth College Case, 1819'. In R. Hofstadter and W. Metzger (eds) (1961) *American higher education: A documentary history*. Chicago, IL: University of Chicago Press, pp. 213–19.

Musselin, C. (2004) *The long march of French universities*. London: Taylor & Francis.

Rimer, S. (2003) 'A warning against mixing commerce and academics'. *The New York Times*, Wed. 16 April D9.

Schumpeter, J. (1949) 'Economic theory and entrepreneurial history'. In *Essays on economic topics*. Port Washington, NY: Kennikat Press.

3 Back to the future of high technology fantasies?

Reframing the role of knowledge parks and science cities in innovation-based economic development

Milana A. Korotka, Paul Benneworth and Tiago Ratinho

3.1 Introduction

Charles and Wray (2010) argued that the rise of science cities since 2000 could only be understood as a reframing of Castells and Hall's (1994) notion of technopoles in ways that made the concept both digestible to and usable by policy-makers (see also Chapter 5, this volume). This formed the basis for a huge expansion of both academic and policy interest in the idea of investing in science facilities as an integral part of urban development policy (Perry and May, 2011; Benneworth *et al.*, 2011). Nowhere is this illustrated better than the OECD (2011) who identified the ingredients that contribute to the recipe for a successful 'science city', highlighting the different national contexts within which science cities are currently being developed (see also Anttiroiko, 2004). But this framing of science cities provides a stark reminder of the limits of these models' policy application. We have already experienced two waves of 'policy bubble' in neo-endogenous models, namely the 1980s enthusiasm for science parks and the 1990s enthusiasm for clusters (Quintas, Wield, and Massey, 1992; Martin and Sunley, 2003).

So are we now standing on the verge of a similar 'science city' bubble? Of course the lessons of these past episodes are not that these original ideas or analyses were in some way flawed. Rather, as academic concepts were absorbed by policy-makers, they transformed subtly and lost their original rigour in this process of translation, evolving into quasi-concepts or policy concepts, becoming coded and over-coded into simplistic policy recipes (cf. Bøås and McNeill, 2004; Böhme and Gløersen, 2011; Lagendijk and Visser, 2014). This chapter seeks to place these emerging ideas of urban science into the context of a potential third wave of potential 'irrational exuberance' around technopoles, which we characterise as being primarily concerned with models of knowledge-based urban development (KBUD), highlighted by Perry and May (2010):

> a dominant consensus [which] has emerged around the need to increase the inter-relationships between universities and their localities for the mutual benefit of all involved ... cities and city-regions are adopting a number of strategies and policies designed to build science cities, knowledge capitals, silicon alleys or technology corridors.
>
> (p. 6)

This chapter contributes to debates around technopoles and science cities by focusing on the KBUD processes potentially created by these new kinds of urban space (neo-technopoles). We focus on one specific KBUD process, namely their hosting of communities of mutually interacting individuals who are undertaking socialised learning and hence building collective and unique knowledge assets that in turn become the basis of that territorial advantage. These communities are solving innovation problems, and in so doing build up unique useful knowledges with external value (Benneworth and Ratinho, 2014a). We draw on Yigitcanlar's (2010) notion of Knowledge Community Precincts (KCPs) to understand how science cities function, highlighting the importance of proximity in developing shared understandings and common knowledge pools. Our starting point in this chapter is that while much of the literature assumes that the private sector is the appropriate focus for stimulating KBUD processes, there are many examples emerging of where universities play important – even decisive – roles in those physical developments. This raises for us an interesting question, given universities' and firms' divergent interests and needs in knowledge production. We therefore question in this chapter whether physical proximity alone is a sufficient reason for academics and businesses to collaborate given these different orientations, while trying at the same time to avoid creating a 'strawman' argument, because clearly where there are no knowledge overlaps, physical proximity alone will rarely lead to collective innovation (cf. Chapter 5 this volume).

In this chapter, we focus on one side of the university–firm collaboration nexus, namely those academics involved in technopole developments. Our overall research question is how can KCPs and their underlying shared knowledge resources contribute to participating academics' needs. We explore two issues – the extent to which one such KCP project functions as a "science park at regional scale" creating an active knowledge community, and also the motivations of academics participating in that KCP towards local collaboration activities. A hallmark of our case study is that Kennispark represents a place where the issue of physical proximity is salient, where a knowledge community of entrepreneurs has emerged from a university and therefore there are prima facie grounds to expect that there may be a level of interaction. From this we place limits upon science city concepts and policies, contributing to a wider debate regarding the role of science and 21st century industrial complexes.

3.2 Literature review

3.2.1 From technopoles to knowledge community precincts

The publication of *Technopoles of the World* (Castells and Halls, 1994) sparked a huge interest in the use of high-technology industrial complexes as a means of driving innovation-based economic development. The book emerged at the same time as a realisation of the increasing importance of knowledge capital as driving productivity growth and economic development (Romer, 1994; Solow, 1994; Temple, 1998). With KBUD becoming increasingly important, cities functioned as critical loci of knowledge-based development, facilitating interaction and knowledge exchange between innovators, and hence driving knowledge accumulation (Knight, 1995). Knowledge provided cities with competitive advantage; any firm seeking to access a relatively distinct ('tacit') piece of knowledge was required to engage with actors in the host territory (Gertler, 1995).

This provided at least an explanation of why those cities already endowed with successful high-technology clusters were successful. But the question still arose of how to turn this into a more generalised concept of economic change, or indeed, to develop meaningful policy recommendations from it. Silicon Valley's success in particular spawned a rash of attempts by policy-makers to duplicate its successes, leading to what Hospers (2006) referred to as the rise of 'Silicon Somewheres', pale imitations of 'the original industrial core of the revolution in information technology'(Castells and Hall, 1994, p. 12). Somewhere between the problematic notion of the ubiquitous Technopole and the knowledge economy was a realisation that the nature of economic production was changing in ways with distinctly urban dimensions (Charles and Wray, 2010; see also Chapter 5).

A key feature of knowledge was that not all forms of knowledge were easily transferred over space, and some kinds of knowledge, referred to variously as tacit knowledge, know-how, knowing-in-action, were best transferred in personal contacts through social learning processes (Nonaka and Takeuchi, 1995; Garud, 1997; Amin and Roberts, 2008). KBUD analyses have therefore sought to explicate the precise processes by which knowledge-based urban agglomerations can facilitate knowledge spillovers and social interactions that encourage knowledge combination and creation supporting urban competitiveness (Yigitcanlar and Velibeyoglu, 2008; Perry and May, 2010). But there is a peculiar nebulousness to the idea of 'urban' in these concepts, and to more precisely specify how the city can facilitate spill-overs, Yigitcanlar (2010) develops the idea of a knowledge community precinct (KCP). A KCP is a physical development (a precinct) that brings together different knowledge actors who interact intensely around specific innovation projects, thereby creating specific kinds of knowledge embedded within these learning communities (Amin and Roberts, 2008; Gertner, Roberts and Charles, 2011). Those local knowledges in turn are attractive to external users, making these KCPs 'places to be' in particular global innovation networks, thereby binding external actors to these precincts and increasing these host cities' relative strength in wider urban networks (Smith, 2003; Perry and May, 2010; Yeung, 2009).

3.2.2 Local KCP connections boosting external network strengths

Benneworth *et al.* (2011) refer to the proliferation of policy interventions seeking to promote KCP benefits in particular city-regional territories as 'urban science' (following Anttioiko, 2004; Perry and May, 2010; 2011), in a sense representing what Lagendijk and Visser (2014) might call the coding-overcoding of the technopole urban development concept. Urban science studies following this definition have focused on physical developments emblematical of projects by which policy-makers have sought to create KBUD benefits locally (Benneworth, Hospers and Timmerman, 2009). To understand the innovation contributions made by KCPs, we argue that they have some commonalities with incubators, providing three dimensions that define a successful business incubator – *viz.* infrastructure, business support and access to networks (Ratinho, 2011), albeit at a larger scale and with broader scope, extending beyond what Lundvall (2007) calls the core of the regional innovation system into the wider policy and educational environment. KCPs may have both passive and active elements, both passively creating opportunities for actors to interact as well as actively undertaking interventions to simulate interaction between participants (Benneworth and Ratinho, 2014a). These active elements have become particularly important in cities lacking strong existing networks and clusters of innovators, within processes of constructing regional advantage or developing smart specialisation strategies (Asheim, Boschma and Cooke, 2011; McCann and Ortega-Argilés, 2013).

If one considers a Knowledge Community Precinct as a science park extended to the urban scale (cf. Anttiroiko, 2004), then KCPs' active elements integrate those individuals active in research and innovation projects within organisations hosted within the precinct. Miller (2014) argues that there are three kinds of mechanisms by which active benefits can be constructed in urban science settings, namely creating linkages and networks, providing complementary services to accelerate innovation and supporting technologies with long lead-times. Likewise, Ratinho and Henriques (2010) argue that urban science parks bring together relevant innovation actors in ways that can stimulate the intense interactions necessary for effective innovation-led growth alongside effective management that provides suitable support services for high-technology entrepreneurs.

We contend that three kinds of intervention might potentially support these interactions, corresponding to the three elements provided by incubators, but qualitatively different in terms of their underlying scope and scale.

1   They offer *infrastructure* for co-location, physically creating a single district where various actors come together and have the opportunity to

undertake shared activities within the district through mechanisms such as joint ventures, shared equipment or Living Labs.

2   They may seek to *mobilise knowledge communities* within these precincts, running activities from informal network meetings to formal cluster groupings that bring people with similar interests and knowledge together in the hope of mobilising interaction between them.

3   They oversee the emergence of an *entrepreneurial ecology* around the site based upon services that are necessary to exploit the opportunities that emerge when co-located interacting actors see opportunities for novel innovative activities. These activities may involve facilitating technology entrepreneurship, providing business development advice, signposting actors to those that may be able to help them, or running various kinds of funding competition for innovative and creative ideas.

3.2.3 Proximity and KBUD in knowledge community precincts

These three KCP dimensions suggest that physical proximity is immediately obvious as a salient variable, in particular with reference to active interventions mobilising networks that may involve partners located outwith the formal campus. This reflects a shift in the nature of the knowledge economy given the increasing importance of virtual interactive technologies that facilitate geographically extended learning communities, what Benneworth and Ratinho (2014b) refer to as the 'social knowledge economy'. With knowledge being created through social interactions, people are increasingly finding it easier to interact with those with whom they share common characteristics, without necessarily being physically co-located with them. Hence, it is not just geographical proximity (co-location) that may be germane for interaction but also other forms of proximity creating preconditions for social interactions and collective knowledge creating, proximities that Boschma (2005) stylises as organisational, institutional, cognitive and social.

All kinds of proximity function by facilitating interactions that actors are already trying to undertake, rather than encouraging otherwise unconnected actors to interact and co-innovate simply because they are 'proximate'. Indeed, Broekel and Boschma (2012) highlight what they call the 'proximity paradox', where innovative actors may choose to interact with physically remote actors because of their social preferences and capital that make those cartographically-distant interactions far more productive than those with local actors. Conversely Caniëls, Kronenberg and Werker (2014) posit the existence of a personal dimension to proximity – the idea of a 'click' between two people – that cannot be explained in terms of the embedding of people (organisations, epistemic communities, cultures) in various contexts but is specific to the people and personalities involved.

On that basis, we seek to question the assumption that academic scientists automatically have interest in the knowledge being generated within the KCPs that exist around their research activities. Although some KCPs have an open innovation ethos bringing together different firms in similar fields with collaboration potential (see Chapter 4, this volume), more typically they attempt to create knowledge concentrations incorporating upstream (academic) and downstream (commercial) knowledge. While the regional development literature might present heuristics of knowledge creators and knowledge exploiters working harmoniously within regional contexts to create globally-valuable knowledge (cf. Cooke, 2005), this ignores these communities' divergent interests in shared knowledge creation. Without a fundamental basis for cooperation, there will not be the social interactive activities that create collective knowledge resources (and hence the KBUD effects).

We therefore argue that more attention needs to be paid to the basis for cooperation between KCPs and whether interactions are sufficient to create shared knowledge resources that are attractive and valuable to those immediately outside the KCP (creating network effects anchoring powerful external partners within local networks, Yeung, 2009). We problematize the notion of academics automatically choosing to work with local innovative actors simply because of geographical proximity effects (cf. *inter alia* Broekel and Boschma, 2012; Caniels *et al.*, 2014; Fromhold-Eisebeth, Werker and Vojnic, 2014). Academic engagement involves balancing potential negative effects on the universality of the research against the positive effects that engagement might bring in terms of access to resources, knowledge and expertise externally (Baldini, Grimaldi and Sobrero, 2007; Lam, 2010; Bozeman *et al.*, 2012). More work remains to be done on understanding academics' precise motivations for engaging with non-academic partners and in particular industry (d'Este and Perkmann, 2011; Gulbrandsen, Mowery and Feldman, 2011).

In this chapter, we focus on how proximity features within academics' motivations for engaging with local actors, asking 'why do academics choose to engage with non-academic research partners within KCPs?' Our starting point is that academics' knowledge exchange activities complement their own research networks (Benneworth and Charles, 2005). In choosing to work with local firms in a KCP, proximity must provide a competitive advantage in these wider academic networks within which research excellence is judged. Effective KCPs are those best able to help participating academics meet their own research needs; thus we ask the following operational research questions:

- What do the KCPs' academics seek to derive from business engagement with external partners?
- What types of proximity influence academics' choice to cooperate with local/distant firms?
- How can KCPs build 'useful proximity' in this context?

To address this question, we focus on one particular KCP, the case of Kennispark in the east of the Netherlands, where regional actors including university, the public sector and firms have tried to create a single knowledge district for the Twente region. We first examine the nature of the KCP on the basis of documentary analysis, mapping the efforts placed into building infrastructures, both physical infrastructures but also the 'softer' community networks supporting new innovative activities within the Kennispark. We then examine, on the basis of an academic survey from the participating university, the University of Twente, their engagement behaviours and their underlying rationales. That in turn provides the basis to reflect on the overarching question posed in the introduction to this chapter, namely how KCPs and their underlying shared knowledge resources can contribute to participating academics' needs to be excellent in wider academic/scholarly networks.

3.3 Introduction to the Kennispark case study

3.3.1 An overview of Kennispark Twente

The knowledge park (Kennispark), situated in Twente region (see Figure 3.1) of the Netherlands, is a business incubator and urban science project underpinned by a strong entrepreneurial vision and beneficial location. The University of Twente (UT) has an integrated entrepreneurial culture, diversified funding base, tight relationships with internal organisations and produces applied research of excellent quality (Lazzaretti and Tavoletti, 2007).

Figure 3.1 The position of the Twente region in Europe
Source: IYC, 2005 (Courtesy of Faculty ITC, Univ. Twente).

UT consistently ranks among the most entrepreneurial universities in the Netherlands and Europe, with more than 700 firms emerging from the university in the last twenty years. In 2013, Elsevier magazine (a Dutch language analogue of *The Economist*) declared UT the 'most entrepreneurial university' in its national valorisation ranking of Dutch universities.

But this situation has not arisen in a vacuum: UT is a relatively young and innovative university in an old industrial region (a lengthier treatment of its history is available in Benneworth and Hospers, 2007). Founded in 1961, UT's main regional mission was to support the textiles industry with diversification by increasing the number of highly trained engineers (Schutte, 1999). However, in the 1970s, UT suffered as the textiles industry declined, leading to calls to close the university, and UT reinvented itself as a source of new industries, developing strong leadership and support structures to promote entrepreneurship (Clark, 1998). Today, the university has 10,000 students and 3,300 staff in social and technical sciences, with a research focus in five areas (each with a corresponding research centre, listed in brackets): nanotechnology (MESA+); telematics and information technology (CTIT); biomedical technology and technical medicine (MIRA); innovation and governance studies (IGS); and geo-information science and earth observation (ITC).

The university is actively engaged with regional industry, regional policymakers and business-support organisations, including the municipality, the Chamber of Commerce, the regional development agency, the province, the region and national actors. The university has actively engaged with regional intermediaries since the 1970s (with the creation of the Provincial Regional Development Agency), participating in the creation of a Business and Technology Centre (BTC) to the south of its campus, the development of land adjacent to the BTC and university into a Business and Science Park (BSP), and more latterly, the integration of the BSP and university campus into a single knowledge space, 'Kennispark' (Knowledge Park). Kennispark unites existing university and BSP facilities and new facilities stimulating firm location on the former university campus, including the nanotech fabrication centre (the High Technology Factory) and former university laboratories converted into a business centre (the Gallery project).

3.3.2 Methodology

This chapter reports fieldwork research undertaken within (and elsewhere reported as) Korotka (2012), extended in the course of 2013–14 with additional desk research. The exploratory study considered mechanisms underpinning the development of localised knowledge pools within KCP formation. The UT was chosen because of its history in developing Kennispark; the first fieldwork element involved a review of documents exploring the creation of the KCP in terms of the infrastructure, the networks and the business support developed in Kennispark. This was complemented with a survey exploring how and why academics choose to collaborate with business partners, and the circumstances under which local/regional partners might be chosen over national/regional partners. A survey was undertaken of academic researchers from the UT's five research institutes (MESA+, MIRA, CTIT, ITC, and IGS), researchers being asked whether proximity benefited research, or whether its benefits were restricted to separate valorisation activities.

The survey questionnaire aimed to foreground the role of proximity in scientific/commercial interactions, exploring the circumstances under which local/regional partners might be chosen over national/regional partners. The questionnaire consisted of seven screens, including an invitation message introducing the study and fourteen questions, as well as demographic questions regarding age, gender, research position and research experience, thereby providing the opportunity to cross-tabulate the answers in analysis as well as comparing how opinions vary between sub-groups. As the questionnaire was focused on the researchers' attitudes towards partnership with external partners, it also included questions regarding the primary location of those external partners, their primary form of contact, frequency of co-operation, rationales and barriers for effective partnership, and facilitators for the co-operation. Closed-ended questions were chosen as the questions format with multiple-choice options for the answers, with a five-point Likert scale for the ranking type answers. To ensure that the researcher was actively involved in university co-operation (i.e., had knowledge of the field), this factor was a screening choice in the first question, and those who had not collaborated with industry were thanked for their interest and the survey closed to them. In total 1144 academics from five research institutes of Kennispark were approached to participate with a total of 199 academics replying, 62 reporting contacts with external partners.

3.4 Kennispark as a knowledge community precinct

Kennispark has been hailed by the Kerngroep Innovatie as the most important engine of the Dutch knowledge economy (Kerngroep Innovatie, 2012), perhaps slightly hyperbolic when one considers the strengths of the Eindhoven Brainport complex (see Chapter 4, this volume). Nevertheless, a series of important Dutch policy and analytic reports (including a national economic development strategy, the national spatial strategy, a cluster analysis, and a cluster observatory) highlighted something distinctive about Kennispark's environment for the transformation of technology into new businesses. Kennispark represents a distinctive model for a high-technology business incubator unit, operating not at the level of a single building, but at the level of the Knowledge Precinct, an integrated technology campus covering around 6,000 employees. In this section we explore the extent to which Kennispark provides each of the three dimensions identified in 3.2.2, the extent to which the urban science project as a KCP is able to create district-level infrastructure, mobilise knowledge communities and a supportive entrepreneurial ecology.

First, in infrastructure terms Kennispark acts as a central focus and meeting point for regional high technology industry, with around two thirds of firms active in R&D in the region located partly or wholly in the Kennispark area. Kennispark has been created as a single integrated space bringing together the formerly adjacent but separate university campus and Business and Science Park to create a single integrated space of around 150ha. The university facilities have been physically replanned (the entire campus has been rebuilt since 1998) to open it up to business around a central 'Education and Research Square', the south side of which is the new Gallery building. Former university lecture theatres have been redeveloped as an innovation centre for knowledge-intensive companies actively engaged in open innovation with connections to the university. The site is overseen by the Kennispark Twente Foundation, a joint initiative of the Province of Overijssel, the City of Enschede, the University of Twente and the Saxion University of Applied Sciences, and managed by the BTC on behalf of the site investors.

Second, in terms of business support Kennispark has developed a complex set of support for new and growing business, targeting the different elements and stages of business growth, explicitly to mobilise knowledge communities. A key element is support for starting entrepreneurs, continuing the work begun by the Temporary Entrepreneur Position (the TOP programme, which has produced around 400 companies in 25 years), providing business advice, a temporary loan, a physical location and contact with a university research group for potential high-technology starters. Another key element of the business support are the various financial support streams that are co-ordinated through Kennispark, including the Twente Technology Fund, the Innovation Fund Enschede and financing from the regional venture capital (VC) firm, PPM Oost. A range of supports and subsidies are available for growing technology businesses to accelerate their innovative activities and support the development of innovative clusters (Kerngroep Innovatie, 2012).

Finally, Kennispark represents a relatively dense innovation ecosystem built up from a wide degree of overlapping networks. The TOP model is based on firms created by embedding entrepreneurs in networks to access the various different kinds of capital embedded within those networks, whether that is business advice, scientific knowledge, business mentoring or help in building businesses. Over time, a number of these firms have grown and become highly successful, and have placed their own resources at the disposal of new companies, whether creating new spin-offs themselves, providing business advice for new start-ups, or indeed creating markets for start-ups by buying their services. A number of regional high-technology companies including spin-offs formed the Twente Technology Circle (TKT) that helped starting and growing companies to access the resources – particularly advice and contacts – required to stimulate high technology innovation-based growth. Kennispark sought to function as a 'network of networks' connecting various existing regional networks, by making them more transparent and therefore making it easier for starting and growing entrepreneurs to maximise the benefits they were able to access through the networks.

Despite the relatively rosy picture presented by the narrative, as well as the awards and plaudits that Kennispark has received for its work in knowledge exchange, there remain some barriers to effective collaboration between universities and external partners. Freitas and Verspagen (2009) argued that despite the physical co-location of all these activities, there are in fact only relatively sporadic interventions and weak engagement of channels between universities and their users. Benneworth and Hospers (2007) problematize a lack of analytical literature related to UT's entrepreneurial activity, with a clear empirical gap in tracing how particular activities within a KCP have regional-level consequences (cf. Benneworth and Ratinho, 2014a).

3.5 Interaction behaviours of Kennispark academics

The following two sections provide the empirical evidence to explore Kennispark's regional consequences as a KCP by exploring how important physical proximity was to academic participants. This reports on the basis of the sixty-two academics reporting active involvement in various kinds of external co-operation, from collaborative research, problem-solving activities, student placement activities, creating spin-off companies, working with start-ups and informal networking activities. The most popular kind of association with external parties came through collaborative research (32 per cent), with 25 per cent taking part in problem-solving activities. Over 20 per cent were involved with informal networking activities, and 19 per cent in student placement activities. A very small portion of the sample was concerned with working with start-ups and creating spin-off companies – 11 per cent and 3 per cent respectively (see Figure 3.2 below). For those academics involved

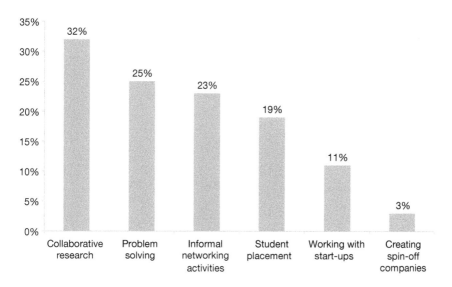

Figure 3.2 Types of activities (per cent of respondents)

in external engagement, collaborative research and problem-solving (i.e., intensive knowledge-exchange activities) were the most frequent kinds of interaction.

Second, despite the knowledge-intensity of the main kinds of interaction, the primary location of external partners of the academics was national (53 per cent) and with the least active collaboration happening on the local KCP level (Figure 3.3).

However, despite the relatively limited importance of local co-operation, modes of communications between academics and their partners suggested that social modes of interaction were important. Around 60 per cent of the

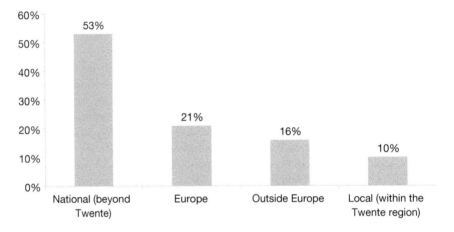

Figure 3.3 The location of external partners (per cent of respondents)

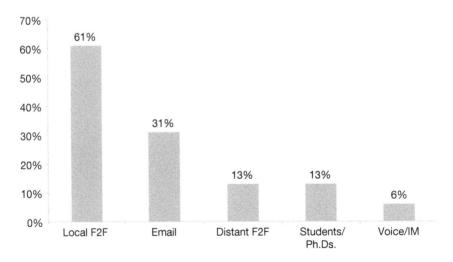

Figure 3.4 Primary form of contact (per cent of respondents)

academics surveyed reported a preference for face-to-face meetings with their external partners, while the lowest number of researchers used telephone/skype/Instant messaging (6 per cent) as a primary form of contact with their external partners (Figure 3.4).

3.6 Motivation, constraints and facilitation for UI co-operation

At first reading, there is a slightly contradictory element to these findings: namely, that despite not favouring working with local partners, academics working with external partners are involved in knowledge-intensive activities (joint research and problem solving) using 'social knowledge exchange' approaches as the basis for those interactions (face-to-face meetings). To understand the dynamics of this contradiction in more detail, we now turn our attention to *why* they interact with external partners, and why despite their partners being remote, they are choosing for intensive, personal forms of interaction that involve physical proximity. Respondents were given a choice of seven reasons for why they interacted with external partners (shown in Figure 3.5) with the pattern of answering suggesting three kinds of reasons for working with external partners.

- The most common set of responses related to *the practicalities of carrying out research*, namely developing future research opportunities (73 per cent agree, 15 per cent strongly agree) and maintaining useful contacts (60 per cent agree; 27 per cent strongly agree).
- The next set of motivations were to *increase their research's impacts*, whether seeing their research outcomes implemented in innovative technologies (56 per cent agree, 19 per cent strongly agree) or out of a sense of responsibility to contribute to social and economic development (55 per cent agree, 19 per cent strongly agree).
- The least common set of reasons related to *undertaking excellent research*, whether supporting world-class research (52 per cent agree, 13 per cent strongly agree), developing an international research career (39 per cent agree, 5 per cent strongly agree), or accessing public research grants (37 per cent agree, 15 per cent strongly agree).

In terms of the types of proximity that mattered to co-operating academics, they were asked to rank what was important to them in external collaboration for each of Boschma's five dimensions. We operationalised each of Boschma's five dimensions into a simple descriptive of a kind of interaction indicative of each kind of proximity. Cognitive proximity emerges through frequent interaction; organisational proximity by being in similar informal networks; social proximity is a form of trust; institutional proximity is shared values; and geographical proximity is being locally proximate. For each of these descriptives, we asked whether that characteristic was useful for supporting

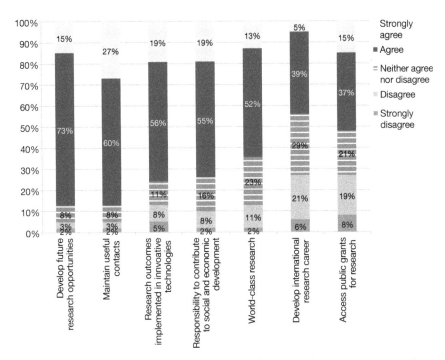

Figure 3.5 Motivation for activities with external partners (mean score, per cent)

something of core interest to the academic (i.e., research) or was useful for the valorisation elements of the activity. For the first variable, cognitive proximity via frequent interaction, we therefore asked whether they interacted frequently with partners, first because it helped their research, or second because it helped the valorisation activities. Each of these questions was formulated to elicit a response using a five-point Likert-scale variable from 'strongly disagree' to 'strongly agree'. Table 3.1 below shows the results. For each of the ten questions, the table below first gives absolute scores and percentages of respondents giving the respective answer (the column) to the question (the row). The operational prompts used in this question are provided below (see also Korotka, 2012).

The pattern of location of external partner influenced by five dimensions of proximity demonstrates that academics agree to co-operate with an external partner located in any area if the co-operation is supported by a high level of proximity. Furthermore, it is worth mentioning which dimension of proximity is the most important for different location of external partners. First, for external parties, academics consider social proximity as the most important dimension of proximity. Second, academics chose institutional proximity as the most significant in co-operation with national external partners. Third, cognitive and social proximity is equally important in co-operation with European

Table 3.1 Role of proximity in UI co-operation (crosstab)

Type of proximity	Question Considering your most important activities with industrial partners . . .	Answer									
		Strongly disagree		Disagree		Neither agree nor disagree		Agree		Strongly agree	
		Count	%	Count	%	Count	%	Count	%	Count	%
Cognitive (frequent communication)	. . . frequent communication with industrial partners helps to conduct innovative projects more effectively.	1	2%	6	10%	17	27%	35	56%	3	5%
	. . . more frequent interaction with companies allows us to conduct research independently.	2	3%	20	32%	27	44%	10	16%	3	5%
Organisational (informal networks)	. . . informal networks with firms help to control innovative projects more effectively.	2	3%	9	15%	22	35%	27	44%	2	3%
	. . . communication with firms through informal networks gives more flexibility in research.	3	5%	10	16%	19	31%	26	42%	4	6%
Social (trust)	. . . working with industrial partners I trust helps me to raise the effectiveness of innovative projects.	1	2%	4	6%	11	18%	36	58%	10	16%
	. . . I prefer to work with different partners on each project to maintain my independence.	2	3%	15	24%	20	32%	20	32%	5	8%
Institutional (shared values)	. . . I find it easier to work with firms that share my ways of working, research culture and values.	0	–	6	10%	10	16%	36	58%	10	16%
	. . . I will work with any industrial partner if it leads to quality publications or patents.	4	6%	18	29%	8	13%	26	42%	6	10%
Geographical (local)	. . . working with local firms helps me to organise and co-ordinate my innovative projects more effectively.	2	3%	9	15%	31	50%	19	31%	1	2%
	. . . I will work with local firms only to acquire high-quality research grants.	17	27%	22	35%	16	26%	7	11%	0	–

Table 3.2 Location of external partner vs proximity ratings (average)

Location	Proximity				
	Cognitive	*Organization*	*Social*	*Institutional*	*Geographical*
Local	3.8	3.3	4.3	3.7	3.5
National	3.5	3.3	3.8	3.9	3.1
Europe	3.7	3.1	3.7	3.5	3.4
Global	3.3	3.4	3.5	3.9	2.7
Average	3.6	3.3	3.8	3.8	3.2

partners. Finally, institutional proximity was primarily important for inter-action with global partners, perhaps reflecting researchers' need for a common approach (the shared values) to projects that guide work towards mutually usefully conclusions at a distance, i.e., without continuous contact and interaction (Table 3.2).

3.7 Knowledge Park Twente – 'seedbed' of regional innovation?

In this chapter, we have sought to contribute to understanding how 'techno-poles' can function as knowledge community precincts where there is social learning between innovative partners active in research and valorisation networks by hosting. This provides a means of updating the Castells and Hall's technopoles concept given the changes over the last two decades that have seen knowledge creation become a much more distributed process where geography nevertheless still matters (Rutten *et al.*, 2014). In our study we found that academics are co-operating with external partners rather actively: local knowledge communities appear to be more engaged with partners at the national and international levels than the regional. We interpret this as being a consequence of the relatively limited involvement of local businesses in the local knowledge community, with a number of honourable and high profile exceptions. To create a more nuanced understanding of how technopoles can function in the age of a social knowledge community, we now return to our original research questions.

Our first question related to what academics nationally located within KCPs sought to achieve through their engagement with external partners. Our findings were unambiguous in this area – external engagement was primarily related to the practicalities of undertaking research, secondarily to making their research useful in applications and for society in general, and finally, as part of carrying out excellent research. Our second question related to what types of proximity could influence KCP academic's choices to co-operate with local and distant external partners. In Kennispark, academics co-operate with external partners based on organisational and social proximity regardless of their location. Yet, results show that regardless of the researchers' background, research experience, type of activity, frequency of co-operation or form of contact they will work with distant external partners as long as that supports high quality research. Our third question was how KCPs could build useful proximity. From our results that KCP actors use forms of interaction more suited for social learning processes, we infer that proximity of some kind is important (cf. 3.2.3). But the results – in terms of the lack of prevalence of local interactions – corroborate our findings that physical – geographical – proximity is not important to how Kennispark benefits its participants, but instead it is other forms of proximity that matter (cognitive, organisational and social).

The results achieved in this study contribute to the extensive theoretical discussion on knowledge transfer and the role played by specific knowledge transfer spaces – technopoles – in knowledge-based urban development. As the literature review shows an empirical gap in quantitative analysis of academics' choices in co-operation with industry, this study contributes to the quantitative analysis research on UI partnership. What was examined in this study represented the attitude of academics towards partnership with business. It confirmed the notion that social, organisational, strategic and institutional proximity can contribute to the development of an effective network between local and external actors. While geographical proximity in the sense of being permanently located next to similar partners is not a first-order prerequisite for building effective relationships between university and industry (Ratinho and Henriques, 2010) there does appear to be a second-order relationship here. The KCP as a physical space is important for building particular kinds of proximity between actors, and to further reflect on this we highlight three key stylised facts that we infer on the basis of our study findings:

- Academics are engaged in knowledge exchange with users (collaborative research and problem solving)
- Research is carried out underpinned by social learning processes (face-to-face meetings even with those firms not located on Kennispark).
- Academics feel cognitive, organisational and social proximity with those agents.

We therefore feel that it is reasonable on this basis to argue that *something about Kennispark* seems to be contributing to creating the locational benefits, even if those locational benefits are not entirely reducible to physical proximity emerging from co-location. Critically, to our mind, this is something that neither analyses of Kennispark in particular or studies of KCPs in general have yet addressed, namely how place-specific activities contribute to building cognitive, organisational and social proximity. Clearly, if academics and external users are working together on a piece of research or via a student placement, then this interaction generates shared languages, routines, expectations and understandings that provide cognitive and social proximity. We further contend that this issue – how place-specific knowledge sites develop non-place specific proximities – requires further analysis, in particular its relationship with the wider research and valorisation networks within which actors are situated.

This is a piece of exploratory research seeking to understand how physical knowledge production locations (which we conceptualise as knowledge community precincts) are changing given the emergence of the social knowledge economy. Therefore, we must necessarily be modest in the wider claims that we make but at the same time we acknowledge that there is increasing realisation that knowledge production is not a purely localised process. We argue that KCPs contribute to forming proximity between academics and users, but that other kinds of proximity may be more important than the purely geographical. We can make an educated guess as to how the interactions between academics and external users build proximities (cf. Gertner *et al.*, 2011), but it is much harder to discern precisely what the role of the KCPs is in building these shared knowledge bases, repertoires, norms and collective understandings as the basis for effective collaboration. This would represent the obverse of Boekel and Boschma's (2012) 'proximity paradox' – that despite knowledge exchange being able to take place anywhere, locality remains important in building proximities between academics and external users. We conclude in contending that if technopoles are to retain their salience as a 21st century spatial form (as this volume seems to suggest) then it will be as much because of their promotion of non-spatial as spatial forms of proximity, a situation that would demand much further reflection and consideration from the field.

Acknowledgements

The authors would like to thank the respondents to the survey for their time and candour, without which this research would not have been possible. The authors would also like to acknowledge the support of the Dutch Organisation for Scientific Research (NWO) DATALAB project at the University of Twente for technical support in administering the survey. We would also like to thank Julie Tian Miao for her invaluable comments on a series of earlier drafts of this chapter. Any errors or omissions remain the authors' responsibility.

Bibliography

Amin, A. and Roberts, J. (2008) 'Knowing in action: Beyond communities of practice'. *Research Policy. 37*(2): 353–69.

Anttiroiko, A.V. (2004) 'Science cities: Their characteristics and future challenges'. *International Journal of Technology Management, 28*(3): 395–418.

Asheim, B.T., Boschma, R. and Cooke, P. (2011) 'Constructing regional advantage: Platform policies based on related variety and differentiated knowledge bases'. *Regional Studies, 45*(7): 893–904.

Baldini, N., Grimaldi, R. and Sobrero, M. (2007) 'To patent or not to patent? A survey of Italian inventors on motivations, incentives, and obstacles to university patenting'. *Scientometrics, 70*: 333–54.

Benneworth, P.S. and Charles, D.R. (2005) 'University spin off companies and the territorial knowledge pool: Building regional innovation competencies?'. *European Planning Studies*, *13*(4): 537–57.

Benneworth, P.S. and Hospers, G.J. (2007) 'Urban competitiveness in the knowledge economy: Universities as new planning animateurs'. *Progress in Planning*, *23*(1): 3–102.

Benneworth, P.S. and Ratinho, T. (2014a) 'Reframing the role of knowledge parks and science cities in knowledge based urban development'. *Environment & Planning C*, *32*(5): 784–808.

Benneworth, P.S. and Ratinho, T. (2014b) 'Regional innovation culture in the social knowledge economy', in R. Rutten, P. Benneworth, D. Irawati and F. Boekema (eds) *The social dynamics of innovation networks*. London: Routledge.

Benneworth, P.S., Hospers, G.J., Jongbloed, B., Leiyste, L. and Zomer, A. (2011) 'The "science city" as a system coupler in fragmented strategic urban environments?'. *Built Environment*, *37*(3): 317–35.

Benneworth, P.S., Hospers, G.J. and Timmerman, P. (2009) 'Who builds "science cities" and "knowledge parks"? High technology firms mobilising heterogeneous commercialisation networks', in R. Oakey, S. Kauser, A. Groen and P. v.d. Sijde (eds) *New technology based firms in the new millennium Vol 7*. London: Elsevier.

Bøås, M. and McNeill, D. (2004) 'Ideas and institutions: Who is framing what?' (pp. 1–12), in M. Bøås and D. McNeill (eds) *Global institutions and development: Framing the world?* London: Routledge.

Böhme, K. and Gløersen, E. (2011) 'Territorial cohesion storylines: Understanding a policy concept'. Spatial Foresight Briefing 2011: 1. Luxembourg. Available at: www.spatialforesight.eu/tl_files/files/editors/dokumente/Brief-2011-1-111025.pdf (accessed on 27 January 2015).

Boschma, R.A. (2005) 'Proximity and innovation: A critical assessment'. *Regional Studies*, *39*(1): 61–74.

Bozeman, B., Youtie, J., Slade, C.P. and Gaughan, M. (2012). 'The "dark side" of academic research collaborations: Case studies in exploitation, bullying and unethical behavior'. In annual meeting of the Society for Social Studies of Science (4S) October (pp. 17–20).

Broekel, T. and Boschma, R. (2012) 'Knowledge networks in the Dutch aviation industry: The proximity paradox'. *Journal of Economic Geography*, *12*(2): 409–33.

Caniëls M.C.J., Kronenberg, K. and Werker, C. (2014) 'Conceptualizing proximity in research collaborations' (pp. 221–38), in R. Rutten, P. Benneworth, D. Irawati and F. Boekema (eds) *The social dynamics of innovation networks*. London: Routledge.

Castells, M. and Hall, P. (1994) *Technopoles of the world: The making of 21st century industrial complexes*. London: Routledge.

Charles, D.R. and Wray, F. (2010) 'Science cities in the UK', Melbourne 2010 Knowledge Cities World Summit, Melbourne, 16–19 November.

Clark, B. (1998) 'The entrepreneurial university: Demand and response'. *Tertiary Education and Management*, *4*(1): 5–16.

Cooke, P. (2005) 'Regionally asymmetric knowledge capabilities and open innovation: Exploring "Globalisation 2" – a new model of industry organisation'. *Research Policy*, *34*: 1128–49.

d'Este, P. and Perkmann, M. (2011) 'Why do academics engage with industry? The entrepreneurial university and individual motivations'. *Journal of Technology Transfer*, *36*: 316–39.

Fromhold-Eisebith, M., Werker, C. and Vojnic, M. (2014) 'Tracing the social dimension in innovation networks – from conceptualization to empirical testing' (pp. 121–40), in R. Rutten, P. Benneworth, D. Irawati and F. Boekema (eds) *The social dynamics of innovation networks*. London: Routledge.

Freitas, I.M.B., Verspagen, B. (2009) 'The motivations, organization and outcomes of university-industry'. Available at: www.socialsciences.leiden.edu/cwts/news/scoreboard.html (accessed on 28 October 2014).

Fromhold-Eisebith, M. Werker, C. and Vojnic, M. (2014) 'Tracing the social dimension in innovation networks – from conceptualization to empirical testing' (pp. 121–39), in R. Rutten, P. Benneworth, D. Irawati and F. Boekema (eds) (2014) *The social dynamics of innovation networks*. London: Routledge.

Garud, R. (1997) 'On the distinction between know-how, know-why and know-what', *Advances in Strategic Management, 14*: 81–101.

Gertler, M. (1995) '"Being there": Proximity, organisation and culture in the development and adoption of advanced manufacturing technologies'. *Economic Geography, 71*(1): 1–26.

Gertner, D., Roberts, J. and Charles, D. (2011) 'University-industry collaboration: A CoPs approach to KTPs'. *Journal of Knowledge Management, 15*(4): 625–47.

Gulbrandsen, M., Mowery, D. and Feldman, M. (2011) 'Introduction to the special section: Heterogeneity and university–industry relations'. *Research Policy, 40*(1): 1–5.

Hospers, G.-J. (2006) 'Silicon somewhere? Assessing the usefulness of best practices in regional policy'. *Policy Studies, 27*(1): 1–15.

Kerngroep Innovatie (2012) 'Innovatiesprong Twente: Naar meer inhoudelijke focus en vernieuwing van de aanpak. Hoofdlijn van de strategie voor het innovatiebeleid en de governance voor de periode 2012–2015'. Available at: http://ris.enschede.nl/stukken/09638/download.html_ (accessed on 28 October 2014).

Korotka, M.A. (2012) 'Proximity factors influencing academics' decisions to co-operate with industry – a case study of the University of Twente's research institutes'. Unpublished MSc thesis. Available at: http://purl.utwente.nl/essays/62013/ (accessed 8 April 2012).

Knight, R.V. (1995) 'Knowledge-based development: Policy and planning implications for cities'. *Urban Studies, 32*(2): 225–60.

Lam, A. (2010) 'What motivates academic scientists to engage in research commercialization: "Gold", "ribbon" or "puzzle"?'. *Research Policy, 40*: 1354–68.

Lagendijk, A. and Visser, G. (2014) 'The travels of the Creative City. Boosting creativity and innovation in Amsterdam and Leiden' (pp. 201–20), in R. Rutten, P. Benneworth, D. Irawati and F. Boekema (eds) *The social dynamics of innovation networks*. London: Routledge.

Lazzaretti, L. and Tavoletti, E. (2007) 'Higher education excellence and local economic development: The case of the entrepreneurial University of Twente'. *European Planning Studies, 13*(3): 475–93.

Lundvall, B.-Å. (2007). 'National Innovation Systems – Analytical Concept and Development Tool'. *Industry & Innovation, 14*(1): 95–119.

McCann, P. and Ortega-Argilés, R. (2013) 'Modern regional innovation policy'. *Cambridge Journal of Regions, Economy and Society, 6*(2): 187–216.

Martin, R. and Sunley, P. (2003) 'Deconstructing clusters: Chaotic concept or policy panacea?'. *Journal of Economic Geography, 3*(1): 5–35.

May, T. and Perry, B. (2011) 'Urban research in the knowledge economy: Context, content and outlook'. *Built Environment*, *37*(3): 352–67.

Miller, S. (2014) 'The Strathclyde Technology and Innovation Centre in Scotland's innovation system'. *Regional Studies, Regional Science*, *1*(1): 145–51. Available at: www.tandfonline.com/doi/full/10.1080/21681376.2014.944208 (accessed on 28 October 2014).

Nonaka, I. and Takeuchi, H. (1995) *The knowledge creating company: How Japanese companies create the dynamics of innovation.* New York: Oxford University Press.

OECD (2011) 'Regions and Innovation Policy', *OECD Reviews of Regional Innovation*, OECD Publishing, pp. 25–84. Available at: www.oecd.org/document/2/0,3746,en_2649_37429_47721730_1_1_1_37429,00.html (accessed on 28 October 2014).

Perry, B. and May, T. (2010) 'Urban knowledge exchange: Devilish dichotomoies and active intermediation'. *International Journal of Knowledge-based Development*, *1*(1/2): 6–24.

Perry, B. and May, T. (2011) 'Urban research in the knowledge economy: Content, context and outlook'. *Built Environment*, *37*(3): 352–67.

Quintas, P., Wield, D. and Massey, D. (1992) 'Academic-industry links and innovation: Questioning the science park model'. *Technovation*, *12*(3): 161–75.

Ratinho, T. and Henriques, E. (2010) 'The role of science parks and business incubators in converging countries: Evidence from Portugal'. *Technovation*, *30*(4): 278–90.

Ratinho, T. (2011) 'Are they helping? An examination of business incubators' impact on tenant firms'. Unpublished PhD thesis. Available at: http://doc.utwente.nl/78235/1/thesis_T_Ratinho.pdf (accessed on 28 October 2014).

Romer, P.M. (1994) 'The origins of endogenous growth'. *Journal of Economic Perspectives*, *8*(1): 3–22.

Rutten, R., Benneworth, P., Boekema, F. and Irawati, D. (eds) (2014) *The social dynamics of innovation networks.* London: Routledge.

Schutte, F. (1999) 'The university-industry relations of an entrepreneurial university: The case of the University of Twente'. *Higher Education in Europe*, *24*(1): 47–65.

Smith, R.G. (2003) 'World city actor networks'. *Progress in Human Geography*, *27*(1): 25–44.

Solow, R. (1994) 'Perspectives on growth theory'. *Journal of Economic Perspectives*, *8*(1): 45–54.

Temple, J. (1998) 'The new growth evidence'. *Journal of Economic Literature*, *37*(1): 112–56.

Yeung, H.W. (2009) 'Situating regional development in the competitive dynamics of global production networks: An East Asian perspective', in H.W. Yeung (ed.) *Globalizing regional development in East Asia: production networks, clusters, and entrepreneurship.* London: Routledge.

Yigitcanlar, T. and Velibeyoglu, K. (2008) 'Knowledge-based urban development: The local economic development path of Brisbane, Australia'. *Local Economy*, *23*(3): 195–207.

Yigitcanlar, T. (2010) 'Making space and place for the knowledge economy: Knowledge-based development of Australian cities'. *European Planning Studies*, *18*(11): 1769–86.

4 Synergy management at knowledge locations

Willem van Winden and Luis Carvalho

4.1 Introduction

In recent decades, many cities and regions globally have developed 'knowledge locations': these can be defined as area-based initiatives aimed at agglomerating knowledge-based activities in designated city districts. Knowledge locations come in a variety of forms, the longest-established and studied being science and technology parks (*inter alia* Massey, Quintas and Wield, 1992; Castells and Hall, 1994), spatial concentrations of scientific research institutes and companies, often at or near university premises. In the last fifteen years, new forms have emerged including 'creative factories', 'science quarters', and 'open-innovation campuses'. Many are developed around thematic fields beyond 'high-tech', such as digital media or other creative industries (van Winden *et al.*, 2012; Carvalho, 2013).

The development of knowledge locations results from a variety of stake-holders' ambitions and actions including (local and regional) governments, universities and the private sector in different constellations (e.g., IASP, 2010; Evans, 2009). Local governments invest in knowledge locations to create new jobs, gain a reputation as a 'creative city' or 'knowledge city' and attract and retain talented workers and companies. Universities and knowledge institutes are also increasingly engaged in developing knowledge locations, seeking to promote links to business and research commercialisation. The list of stakeholders and interests could be easily extended (see Benneworth *et al.*, 2011 for a comprehensive analysis of the reasons why different public and private stakeholders invest in knowledge locations).

Notwithstanding the different interests involved, investments in knowledge locations largely reflect contemporary expectations, insights and fantasies regarding the effects of co-location upon innovation and economic development. Most importantly, knowledge locations hold the common promise to produce *synergy*, the interaction of multiple elements in a system to produce an effect greater than the sum of their individual effects. Positive synergies are expected through increasing efficiency in resource utilisation (e.g., infrastructure, skills and specialised services), creating image and reputation, and stimulating fruitful knowledge exchange and innovation networks between a location's tenants.

This chapter focuses on the important question of how synergies emerge, and whether they can actively be managed. Many proponents and managers of knowledge locations increasingly believe that developing buildings and co-locating companies is not enough for creating synergies and are increasingly active deploying synergy management strategies and tools (Carvalho, 2013; van Winden *et al.*, 2012). Such strategies are primarily deployed at the level of the location, but also open new perspectives from which to reflect upon regional innovation policies. Understanding types of synergy management in knowledge locations can contribute to specifying and unpacking those processes and policies underpinning the promotion of regional knowledge spillovers and innovation networks. Moreover, this foregrounds knowledge locations (and its managers) as players with agency within contemporary policy frameworks of 'smart specialisation' and building 'regional competitive advantage' (e.g., Boschma, 2014).

In order to consider the different methods of promoting synergy in knowledge locations, we first discuss and conceptualise the space-innovation nexus behind knowledge locations, alongside studies dealing with synergy management. We identify four types of synergy management strategies and tools:

1   designing for interaction;
2   managing the tenant mix;
3   sharing facilities; and
4   promoting networks and communities.

We explore these four tools in five European cities, namely Aachen (RWTH campus), Aarhus (IT City Katrinebjerg), Coimbra-Cantanhede (Biocant), Dublin (The Digital Hub) and Eindhoven (the High Tech Campus and Strijp-S). We illustrate how the four synergy management strategies are applied in our cases, and then analyse the research and policy challenges emerging, and in particular balancing between managed synergy and spontaneous creativity necessary for blossoming innovation ecosystems in urban knowledge locations.

4.2 Literature review

This chapter sets out to address two key questions. First, what do we know about the benefits/added value of co-location in knowledge locations, and second, how and to what extent can managers of knowledge locations increase this value (namely, through what types of synergy management tools?). The literature on territorial innovation models sheds light on the intricate linkages between innovation, networks and space, highlighting the type of synergies that may arise from co-location. However, moving beyond physical proximity, innovation studies shed light on innovation as a social process, and we therefore develop a model based on four synthetic synergy management tools.

4.2.1 Territorial innovation models

From a neo-regionalist perspective, knowledge locations can be seen as 'micro-agglomerations', where hyper-local characteristics influence knowledge and innovation networks' configuration and density. From a neo-Marshallian industrial district perspective, knowledge locations are places where positive externalities materialise; knowledge spillovers occur more easily, innovation may spread more rapidly and the area may develop a competitive and dynamic spirit. From an institutionalist and innovative milieu perspective, emphasising trust, shared culture and institutions as conducive to innovation networks, knowledge locations can be interpreted as 'trust enhancers': co-located firms are proximate and may develop personal relationships and shared frames that facilitate interaction, knowledge exchange and innovation (see e.g., Moulaert and Sekia, 2003, for a review of those perspectives).

The neo-regionalist perspective on knowledge locations is, however, problematic in several regards. First, most mechanisms and social relations exist at the regional level, rather than exclusively within the specific knowledge location. Second, the neo-regionalist position has come under increasing challenge recently for overemphasising geographic proximity and local/regional factors explaining innovation. Mounting evidence demonstrates that local networks' roles may be less important than often conceptualised (Garnsey and Hefferman, 2005; Malmberg and Maskell, 2006; Giuliani, 2007; Vale and Carvalho, 2013). Many innovative firms do not acquire knowledge from geographically proximate partners, but rather source internationally (Davenport, 2005; Drejer and Vinding, 2007; Broekel and Boschma's (2012) 'proximity paradox').

There have been several empirical enquiries recently into knowledge locations' added value, confirming the neo-regionalist approach's limitations. Most studies focus on science and technology parks, and estimate effects from on-park location on tenants' performance in terms of innovativeness, R&D productivity, survival, and growth (see van Winden *et al.*, 2012; Carvalho, 2013 for a review). They cast serious doubt on the physical proximity-innovation nexus. Despite some indications that firms within science parks have stronger relations with universities than other firms (e.g., Detwiller, Lindelöf and Löfsten, 2006; Chan and Lau, 2005) there is little evidence that they are more likely to collaborate or exchange information with local universities or neighbouring firms on-site (Quintas and Massey, 1992; Bakouros, Mardas and Varsakelis, 2002; Lindelöf and Löfsten, 2003; Fukugawa, 2006). Overall, knowledge locations are not the 'local innovation network catalysts' they often pretend to be, confirming a growing consensus of not overstating the importance of geographically-proximate knowledge networks.

4.2.2 Innovation as a social practice

The previous studies suggest that geographical proximity is insufficient to create synergy. Some studies ascribe the scarcity of interaction in science and technology parks to tenants not being complementary businesses, or lacking complementary resources incentivising collaboration (Lowegren-Williams, 2000; Chan and Lau, 2005). Kocak and Can (2013) studied the effects of management interventions in twelve science and technology parks in Turkey, finding that sector-specific science and technology parks enjoyed a greater prevalence of knowledge sharing, joint development and common client ties. These findings fit with Boschma's (2005) and Gertler's (2008) arguments, that geographical proximity is merely one relevant factor in innovation networks. As Doloreaux and Sheamur (2012) noted:

> According to Boschma (2005), there are multiple ways in which economic actors share proximity: (i) cognitive—sharing a common vocabulary and conceptual framework; (ii) organizational—the capacity to coordinate and exchange knowledge; (iii) social—micro-level ties of friendliness and trust; (iv) institutional—rules and regulations; and (v) geographical proximity.
>
> (p. 83)

Knowledge exchange and innovation networks are most likely where different types of proximity coincide. If knowledge exchange and innovation are social practices (e.g., Amin and Roberts, 2008) then building social capital among entrepreneurs is a critical function for knowledge location managers (e.g., Hansson, Husted and Vestergaard, 2005; Youtie and Shapira, 2008). In this vein, some studies hint at the central role played by highly connected individuals who by bridging networks inside and outside the site are central for that location's growth and innovation potential (Link and Scott, 2003; Hommen, Doloreux and Larsson, 2006). Graf (2011) argues that innovative clusters benefit from 'gatekeepers' and 'boundary spanners', actors that generate local novelty by combining local and external knowledge sources. Localised learning and innovation becomes increasingly reliant on local 'buzz' but also on selective multi-scalar and relational 'pipelines' to the outside world (Bathelt, Malmberg and Maskell, 2004). Taiwan's Hsinchu Science Park (e.g., Chen and Choi, 2004; see also Chapter 5 this volume) has been a leading model, nurturing local innovation communities in close interaction with other counterparts abroad (in California). Many contemporary event-promotion strategies, liaison clubs and mentoring initiatives in knowledge locations pursue a similar local-global nexus (Carvalho, 2013).

4.2.3 Management strategies for building synergies

The two previous sub-sections hinted at how co-location may produce synergies, and what the limitations are to this process. But they do not address the issue of the extent to which synergies can be managed. This sub-section presents four repertoires of synergy management strategy currently deployed for building synergies at extant knowledge locations.

Designing for interaction

Synergy may be enhanced by designing the knowledge location to foster interaction, as studies on relations between physical space, knowledge working collaboration and innovation hint that design matters (Heerwagen *et al.*, 2004; Rashid, Kampschroer and Zimring, 2006). A clever design for offices and public spaces can enhance (planned and unplanned) interactions between people (a key mechanism for Marshallian knowledge spillovers), which may lead to knowledge exchange and innovation. Therefore, knowledge locations (in terms of buildings, public spaces, and infrastructures) may be built in ways that facilitate and promote interaction and communication between individuals and firms.

Studies on the links between physical space and collaboration in knowledge work settings also agree that working space is an organisational resource that can be mobilised to support individual awareness, interaction and collaboration. Improved spatial layouts – offering better accessibility, visibility and short walking distances – affect the frequency of face-to-face interaction in both offices (Heerwagen *et al.*, 2004) and university research centres (Toker and Gray, 2008). Penn, Desyllas and Vaughan (1999) suggest that increased frequency leads to more 'useful' interactions over time. There is also an apparent relation between physical layouts, organisational culture and collective identity formation (Peponis *et al.*, 2007), which can impact on knowledge workers' creative performance over time (Dul, Ceylan and Jaspers, 2012). As a coda, we note that these studies refer to individual companies, buildings and research centres, and to our knowledge, no study has to date systematically validated these claims for entire knowledge locations.

Managing the tenant mix

Managing tenant mix can also be an effective management tool to promote knowledge locations synergies. A study of US science parks found that specialised parks grew more over time, hinting that specialisation contributed to unique resource formation (e.g., ecosystems of interactions among tenants), increasing park attractiveness (Link and Scott, 2006). This fits with Kocak and Can (2013), who found sector homogeneity to be closely related to higher degrees of knowledge sharing in science and technology parks. These findings fit with innovation geography literatures showing that people are more likely to collaborate when they are close to each other not only physically but also cognitively (e.g., Boschma, 2005).

Knowledge location managers may actively restrict admission to tenants from specific industries or technologies, or only allow a certain percentage of 'unrelated' firms on their premises. Careful tenant selection might help to increase the chance that tenants can work together and benefit from each other's presence, while a sufficient mass of similar tenants offers scope for common facilities, services or infrastructures, such as specific laboratories, machinery or design workshops.

Finally, a specific tenant mix may help to build the identity and reputation of the knowledge location as a 'place to be' for specific types of firms. This synergetic effect has been reported in the case of Arabianranta, Helsinki (van Winden *et al.*, 2012), a knowledge location built around the theme of art and design. The concept acted as a 'lighthouse', making the location very attractive to national and international companies. Conversely, when a location hosts tenants with different profiles and interests, the concept's clarity may be undermined (Stankiewitz, 1998).

Sharing facilities

The cluster literature (e.g., Gordon and McCann, 2000) shows that co-locating similar activities brings several positive externalities. One such key advantage critical to knowledge locations is providing scarce, cluster-specific services, infrastructures and facilities. Knowledge location managers – or groups of co-located tenants – may invest in specific facilities (labs, clean rooms, or other costly infrastructures) and rent them out. This may bring several synergetic effects: higher occupancy rates may drive down expensive facilities' average costs, improve small tenants' access to otherwise prohibitively expensive facilities (Feldman, 1994), and encourage exchange of knowledge and prac-tices. Beyond a sharing effect, some joint facilities' distinctiveness (e.g., state-of-the-art laboratories) may become closely linked with the knowledge location's image and reputation (Carvalho, 2013).

Promoting networks and communities

A fourth type of synergy management is actively promoting knowledge locations' networks, relations and communities. Knowledge location managers increasingly try to promote networking and community formation in several ways, underpinned by the notion that innovation is a social phenomenon, requiring trust, sense of togetherness and mutual understanding (e.g., Amin and Roberts, 2008).

Several studies link locations' success (e.g., wealth and job creation) and new synergy formation driven with explicit network and community enhancing strategies (such as network and platform building, mentoring, or brokerage). Link and Scott (2003) suggest that a location's growth over time relates to what they call entrepreneurial leadership: its managers' capacity to mobilise resources, projects and new networks. Once created, these synergies contribute to attracting more companies and tenants. Ratinho and Henriques (2010) suggest that science parks and incubators' success is closely connected to mentoring and network-enhancing strategies, within and outside the location. Such strategies or initiatives are also pivotal in giving voice to newcomers and prevent the formation of closed, locked-in 'clubs' (Carvalho, 2013).

Summing-up: enhancing the synergetic effects of co-location

We have argued that knowledge locations are hardly 'Marshallian utopias' (even if their public and private proponents may argue so). Due to the intricate social nature of innovation, co-location alone is insufficient for yielding such synergies as efficiency in resource sharing, reputation and image building, access to networks and knowledge exchange. Yet, the literature does suggest that synergy management strategies and tools (deployed by location's managers) may enhance co-location's potential synergetic effects. Figure 4.1 below summarises these stylised facts, suggesting a number of relationships between the four types of management strategies (the left-hand side) and the potential derived advantages of co-location (the right-hand side).

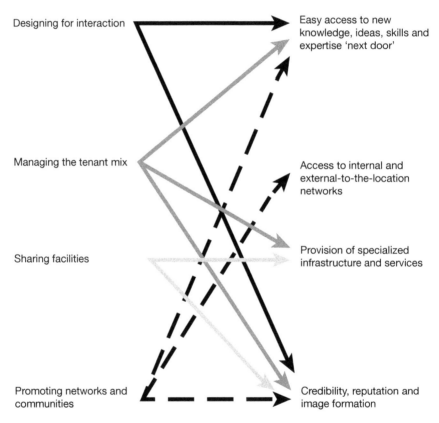

Figure 4.1 Potentially synergetic effects and synergy management
Source: Own elaboration.[1]

4.3 Introducing the case studies

In the remainder of the chapter, we illustrate how managers and tenants in different knowledge locations attempt to use the four types of synergy management strategies and tools to create the desired synergetic effects. In the following sections, we describe and analyse synergy management practices in six knowledge locations across Europe. Five are located in highly developed and knowledge-based economies, the exception being Biocant, located in an innovation-follower region (Coimbra-Cantanhede, Portugal), nevertheless close to an advanced scientific institution (University of Coimbra). All focus on one or more specific knowledge-based industries or technologies. Figure 4.2 depicts these cases' spatial distribution.

For each case, we studied policy documents describing plans, ambitions and achievements of that particular location. We visited each site on multiple occasions and held semi-structured discussions with developers, tenants, managers and policymakers, yielding insights into their 'synergy management' strategies, expectations and realities. Fieldwork was carried out between late 2008 and early 2012, as part of three different research projects.[2]

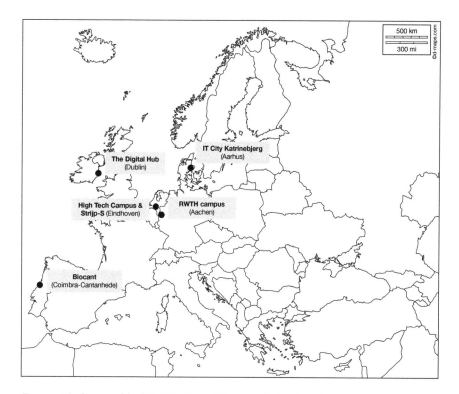

Figure 4.2 Geographical distribution of the knowledge locations
Source: http://d-maps.com/carte.php?num_car=13437&lang=en.

The RWTH campus in Aachen is a highly ambitious new campus concept of the RWTH University of Technology, led by the Vice-Rector for Industry and Business Relations at RWTH. Its distinguishing feature (involving €2bn total investment) is co-locating research groups, academic institutes and companies in specific multi-disciplinary themes (e.g., eco-friendly sustainable energy, photonics, or bio-medical engineering). The developers hope to achieve synergies by co-locating business and academic institutes in 'sub-clusters', nudging them towards co-operation. The sub-clusters are built on multi-disciplinary academic research strengths with sufficient critical mass. The university created a special vehicle, the RWTH Aachen Campus GmbH, to realise the project. At the time of writing, ninety-two firms had committed to locate at the campus, mostly firms not previously located in Aachen.

IT City Katrinebjerg (Aarhus, Denmark) is situated to the northwest of Aarhus' historic city centre, between the university campus and the city centre. It includes a run-down neighbourhood in full transformation towards a 'world class environment' for IT firms. The redevelopment started in 1999, when a handful of enthusiastic and influential people from the university and the corporate sector later involved the Municipality. The area is a multi-functional business district; more recently, it attracted the Alexandra Institute (2004), an IT research institute, the Department of Computer Science (2004) and INCUBA Science Park Katrinebjerg (2006), where around eighty mixed-sized firms are located, among others a Google R&D subsidiary. The university is expanding in the area to concentrate all IT research and education (more than 1,800 full-time IT students). Unlike the other case studies, IT City Katrinebjerg has no formal management body, with actions being co-ordinated by a working group of individual leaders working for key tenants, supported by the Municipality (who provides marketing and branding, sets legal parameters and undertakes master planning).

Biocant is a science and technology park exclusively dedicated to bio-technology, located in the rural municipality of Cantanhede, 25km from Coimbra, Portugal. Biocant resulted from a partnership between Cantanhede Municipality and the Centre of Neurosciences and Cell Biology (CNC, a leading research centre linked with the University of Coimbra), with the ambition to develop and commercialise life science in the region. The former CNC Vice-President is now Biocant's director, an active network broker inside and outside the location. Biocant opened in 2005 and now hosts eight specialised technology transfer centres, twenty dedicated biotechnology firms in start-up and early growth stages and a venture capital firm. Some entre-preneurs and lab directors are graduates of Harvard University, the University of Houston and Massachussets Institute of Technology (MIT). During 2011, despite the financial distress and overall economic crisis in Portugal and Europe, Biocant labs reported a 30 per cent increase in contract research volume (Biocant, 2012) and the park is still expanding.

Dublin's Digital Hub is located at a former Guinness brewery area, at the edge of Dublin's city centre, with brewery offices and other property converted into offices and labs for digital and new media firms. By 2011, around seventy firms were located there – including animation, design, learning, multimedia, e-commerce, software, gaming and mobile technology – providing 800 highly-skilled jobs. A key catalyst for the Digital Hub was the establishment in Dublin of the MIT Media Lab Europe in the early 2000s – the Hub's first anchor tenant (who left in 2005 due to business difficulties). In 2003, the State created a dedicated development organisation – the Digital Hub Development Agency (DHDA) – to enable the area's redevelopment and management, involving State agencies, the City Manager and the community association. One of the DHDA's key priorities has been to facilitate synergies between tenants in the location. As the city government did not want the Digital Hub to become an 'elitist island' within a deprived area (The Liberties), it took measures to link the Hub with its surroundings (e.g., for IT training in the surrounding schools).

Strijp-S, adjacent to Eindhoven's city centre, is a former manufacturing site of Philips being redeveloped as mixed creative quarter. The underlying idea is making Strijp-S 'the best practice of an historical important industrial complex [transformed] into a dynamic post-industrial city district, in which culture and technology play a key role' (KuiperCompagnons, 2007, p. 85). The plans envisage Strijp-S becoming a 'buzzing' district of designers, new-media companies and other creative businesses and education institutes. Strijp-S used to be a closed site that restricted access to Philips employees. The plans seek to give Eindhoven a stronger 'hip' urban image, and address the brain drain of creative young people to the Netherlands' larger cities. Strijp-S is managed by a management company, 'Strijp Park Beheer', owned by the Municipality and a real estate developer.

Also in Eindhoven, the High Tech Campus is a science and technology park situated at the city's southernmost edge and covering 103ha, although parts of it were in business use before the campus formally opened. Currently around 7,000 people work there, with Philips Research division as one its major tenants (1,800 employees) and 'launching customer'. There are single and multi-tenant buildings, a business accelerator and different knowledge institutes. The campus is owned by a private investor and actively managed to foster innovation. The campus management team provides operational management ensuring the 'open innovation' concept through tenant selection, liaison management and event organisation. A 'Technology Liaisons Office' maintains close contact with tenants and creates connections between them. The campus management also created an 'Intellectual Property and Standards office' to seek new patentable ideas among campus residents.

4.4 Synergy management practices

In this section, we describe and analyse how the four tools of synergy management (from Section 4.2) are applied and implemented in our case locations. Table 4.1 synthesises some (non-exhaustive) examples from the cases.

Table 4.1 Synergy management tools in knowledge locations

	Designing for interaction	Managing the tenant mix	Sharing facilities	Promoting networks and communities
RWTH campus (Aachen)	Public and semi-public meeting and working places Mixed-use buildings	Research 'sub-clusters' Long-term R&D framework contracts	Laboratories	'Matriculation': integrating firms in the university's activities
IT City Katrinebjerg (Aarhus)	Public and semi-public meeting and working places	Not enforced (self-selection for IT-related companies)	Advanced IT and broadband facilities (e.g., in R&D institutes and incubators)	Coaching, networking and experience sharing
Biocant (Coimbra)	Public and semi-public meeting places	Dedicated biotech firms (health, agro and environment)	Laboratories	Mentoring and tailor-made bio-brokerage
The Digital Hub (Dublin)	Public and semi-public meeting and working places	Digital value chains; new-media-related companies	Exhibition and piloting space, showrooms	On-demand, tailor-made brokerage Social-media tools (e.g., Digital Hub TV)
Strijp-S (Eindhoven)	Route and staircase design to foster encounters Cultural and consumption facilities	Cross-subsidising for small creative companies Market research for selecting and prioritising inhabitants	Experimentation spaces to link art and technology	Cultural events and festivals Bottom-up social-media profiling
High-Tech Campus (Eindhoven)	Enforced collective spaces, walking trails, mixed-use buildings	Five technological domains and types of companies (anchor, small and start-ups)	Clean rooms, laboratories and piloting spaces	Many social events (e.g., sports for expats) Technical seminars; liaisons club

Source: Fieldwork (derived from van Winden *et al.*, 2012; van Winden 2011; Carvalho, 2013).

4.4.1 Designing for interaction

All six knowledge locations are equipped with shared rooms, open public and semi-public spaces and meeting places designed to be inviting and welcoming, facilitating meetings between people working in the knowledge location. Buildings are often purposely made of transparent and light materials, to create an open atmosphere, open to outsiders and 'inviting' to collaboration, as exemplified by many of the facilities within Katrinebjerg. Other knowledge locations have specific design and architectural features to promote interaction. Eindhoven's Strijp-S's staircases are specially designed to encourage spontaneous meetings and interactions, while the location's cultural offering, including the first cafés and shops, have also been designed to optimise interaction between tenants and visitors.

Eindhoven's High Tech Campus is the most sophisticated case, explicitly and consciously designed to promote encounters. The spatial organisation of the campus is dominated by the centralised position of collectively-used facilities with a concentric zoning of different functions around it. In the campus heart, collective functions (a restaurant, shops and meeting rooms) are organised in one single building called 'The Strip'. Adjacent to that are buildings with shareable facilities, containing clean rooms, laboratories and other specialised spaces. Towards the campus edges are several collective parking facilities in between buildings with mixed functions and users. Cars are excluded from the site: walking trails are designed to maximise the chance of spontaneous encounters, and the site is carefully landscaped to encourage residents to walk, with maximum walking distance between the centralised shared facilities and other campus functions approximately eight minutes. Facilities for sports, children's day-care and a business accelerator (for start-ups) are also located at the campus. Within individual buildings the maximum meeting room size is eight persons, with larger facilities collectively offered within 'The Strip'. Lunchrooms or cafés are not permitted in individual buildings but in collective spaces. Even collective sporting facilities purposely focus on team sports over individual workouts.

4.4.2 Managing the tenant mix

We found different degrees of 'strictness' of tenant-selection practices. The High Tech Campus' management has a rather selective acquisition/admission strategy, with potential tenants required to be R&D-intensive organisations in one of five technological domains in which the campus wishes to profile itself (namely microsystems, life-tech, high-tech systems, infotainment and embedded systems). The campus management considers itself as defender of the park's concept, deciding which tenants are allowed to rent premises at the campus, and seeks to maintain a balanced mix of three types of potential tenants:

1   'triple-A' tenants: larger, established companies, for which the location's brand is important;
2   smaller technology firms for which access to specialized facilities – including prohibitively expensive specialised laboratories – is critical; and
3   technology start-ups, who can benefit from entrepreneurial and networking possibilities.

The process is similar at Biocant and at the Digital Hub; their respective management teams analyse company applications on a case-wise basis to judge whether applicants can benefit from (and contribute to) the location's atmosphere. Biocant only takes companies active in biotechnology, and preferably those activities able to benefit from the location's laboratories; all firms must have already a promising technology and business model, explicitly excluding incipient start-ups. The Digital Hub management board closely scrutinise tenancy applications and require tenants to be associated with IT and digital media solutions.

We also found knowledge locations that, despite their specialisation, do not apply or enforce any type of tenant selection. Aarhus' IT City Katrinebjerg is a case in point, where a self-selection mechanism has emerged with area predominantly attracting IT firms because so many other IT firms are already there, along with the availability of specific infrastructures and laboratories.

A particular type of tenant selection is applied in Aachen's RWTH campus. The Campus GmbH (the management body) invites industrial companies to locate near the academic institutes at the campus. But to be allowed at the campus, firms must sign a ten-year lease, base part of their research staff on-campus, enter into a long-term R&D framework contract committing them to contract research with the university in a particular cluster-field, alongside delivering lectures at RWTH. The concept aims to improve the quality, scale and relevance of research in the various fields by mixing the resources and knowledge of business and academia. The university also hopes to improve teaching quality by involving industrial partners as lectures transmitting the business world's latest insights to students. Employees of 'embedded' firms may take Master courses at RWTH at reduced rates. In parallel, any institute keeps the right to sign deals with other industrial partners who are not on the campus; new clusters may emerge, and spinning out is encouraged.

Some knowledge locations use cross-subsidising to achieve an appropriate tenant and functional mix. Strijp-S offers lower rent levels to dynamic but less wealthy tenants such as start-up companies or cultural institutes, justified in their presence's positive spillover effects, building the area's reputation and attracting specific audiences. A cultural fund was set up, offering financial support for organisations to organise events fitting with Strijp-S's desired creative-vibrant image; the management also subsidises the location of particular tenants (including a fashionable restaurant, an indoor skate park and other alternative sporting and cultural facilities).

4.4.3 Sharing facilities

Managers of knowledge locations develop and promote the use of shared facilities with an eye to enhance co-operation between tenants and supporting their R&D-testing-piloting activities with state-of-the-art equipment. IT City Katrinebjerg has special facilities for innovative IT firms. Its INCUBA institute built commercial premises to meet its tenants' specific requirements, including a switchboard and very fast broadband services. The High Tech Campus has clean rooms and many labs that can be rented by tenants, vital for smaller tenants who can't afford to have their own.

At the RWTH campus, lab sharing is an essential element. The campus is planned to evolve as a patchwork of thematic clusters, with each sufficiently large to allow for specific investments in shared facilities such as laboratories. New clusters may be set up only when particular and precisely defined levels of 'critical mass' are achieved, defined as at least 150 staff members (and a realistic growth perspective to have 350 staff in three years' time), ten research partners, two university institutes and 9000m^2 of rented property. In Biocant, the first lab facilities were developed upfront prior to any tenant's arrival. State-of-the-art labs provided a unique selling point and a magnet for new large and small bio-ventures; in Biocant (as with biotechnology in general), labs and adjacent spaces are privileged places for social interaction.

In other more 'creative-oriented' locations – such as the Digital Hub and Strijp-S – shared facilities have less of a high-tech, laboratorial dimension, but are places to nurture synergies among tenants. The Digital Hub has shared showrooms where new digital media solutions can be showcased and early tested together with larger audiences. Strijp-S is endowed with workshops and experimentation-oriented spaces, adjusted to the needs of smaller and big companies. Some anchor tenants in the area (e.g., Baltan Labs) offer experimentation facilities to connect art, design and technology.

4.4.4 Promoting networks and communities

In all sites analysed the management promotes the formation of professional communities, for example organising technical seminars and external lectures concerning themes interesting for the local knowledge community. In this way, a meeting arena is created where people can gather, exchange ideas and network. Seminars and events bridge between the knowledge location and the outside world. The location may become a kernel, living room or meeting place not only for the location's tenants but also for other firms and individuals working in similar activities.

Some studied locations add to seminars and events with other formal and informal community building interventions. High Tech Campus organises and facilitates non-work related events, for example sports tournaments or music shows, helping knowledge workers to gain new contacts and give them a sense of belonging to the park community, at a campus with thousands of expat workers from all over the world. Moreover, the Technology Liaison Office organises workshops, business meetings and network happenings to enhance knowledge diffusion. It has also initiated the 'Campus Technology Liaisons Club', a network organisation of decision-makers and 'influential people' on the campus. The office tries to build and maintain a sense of a community of practice, where people partly have the feeling of working on the campus instead of exclusively for an individual company.

Eindhoven's Strijp-S used bottom-up network management, with a tenant taking the initiative to promote networking: he opened a member-based website (strijp.is) where tenants upload their profiles, as a 'who-is-who' for the area. His aim is 'to bring the creative professionals closer to each other' (Eindhovens Dagblad, 2013). In Aachen's RWTH campus, the entire model seeks to form new communities of companies, universities and R&D institutes. The university uses the term 'matriculating', to refer to companies who are granted a special position: they influence coming years' research focus and obtain discounted access to R&D and education for their staff members. Dublin's Digital Hub's managers explicitly focus on fostering synergies between tenants, one of the location's main missions. However, there are no formalised or regular initiatives (apart from an internal Digital Hub TV): most brokerage is done in an 'on-demand' fashion.

In Biocant, community building is highly valued but also works in an informal, tailor-made fashion. Biocant's managers provide networking opportunities and actively support the relocation (and new firm creation) of international talented PhDs and star scientists, through the managers' own personal and professional networks. Biocant's brokerage and networking activities helped connect a peripheral bio-community to US-based advanced business and research networks. Biocant's managers often take seats in the advisory boards of new ventures, both acting as new company's mentors and linking up firms' and researchers' capacities to pave the ground for new partnerships. Recent examples include a new project for heart-disease solutions based on stem cells, as well as the joint commercial distribution of health kits. Over time, older entrepreneurs also mentor newer ventures, contributing to developing a supportive, problem-solving place-based ecosystem, highly valued by venture capitalists.

4.5 Conclusions and challenges ahead

This chapter described and analysed four contemporary management approaches to promote synergy at knowledge locations: designing for interaction, managing the tenant mix, sharing facilities and promoting networks and communities. We explored and exemplified how the managers of six European knowledge locations implemented these synergy management approaches in their sites. The extant literatures argue that knowledge locations should not be seen *a priori* as 'Marshallian utopias': as co-location does not automatically provide a fast track to synergy formation. Nevertheless, both recent studies and our evidence suggest that knowledge locations can offer synergetic effects and possibilities, and synergy management tools can enhance those synergies. In other words, while co-location is not sufficient, synergy management can help.

In this chapter we developed a framework connecting synergy management approaches to different types of synergetic effects. Managing the tenant mix and promoting networks and communities seem to be among the most relevant strategies; while the first is important to ensure learning potential and complementarities, the latter can be the 'glue' that binds the 'pieces' together. A location's physical design and the provision of shared facilities are also important supportive factors. The formation of image, credibility and reputation is a synergetic effect that largely stems – directly and indirectly – from our four synergy management strategies. Further research is needed to test this framework, and to better understand the different revealed effects of synergy management in different types of knowledge locations, their potential complementarities and interactions.

From a policy perspective, if creating synergies is among a location's most important *raisons d'être*, and if this at least partly depends on synergy management, the role of a location's managers is an increasingly important one. Managers must decide on the appropriate policy mix, and continually evaluate what works and what does not. The tools and strategies analysed in this chapter provide some first steps and hints, but there are many challenges ahead.

First, the 'right' tenant mix is far from easy to define or achieve. Tenant selection is difficult to maintain during difficult economic times; management may be tempted or urged to fill vacant spaces to generate rental incomes. Assessing whether a new tenant will add synergetic value to the area, or what that value might consist of, is not an easy process. Firms in similar or adjacent related technology fields or industries may be most likely to benefit from each other (Boschma and Frenken, 2011), but seemingly unrelated activities may also produce surprising combinations (Jacobs, 1969; Frenken, Van Oort and Verburg, 2007). Tensions may arise where a new tenant is a direct competitor of existing tenants. To ensure the tenant mix remains appropriate, tenant selection should perhaps be complemented with an 'exit' policy for tenants who lose their strategic value over time, for example in taking new strategic directions, becoming active in new technologies, or when taken over by another firm.

Second, the type of networking and community building strategies might differ between locations and activities. Innovation processes are notably different across industries (e.g., Asheim, Coenen and Vang, 2007), with management implications for knowledge locations. On the one extreme, knowledge networks in high-tech systems seem to be particularly structured; unplanned meetings within a park are not the way companies such as Philips or Siemens seek new technical knowledge nor innovate. Managers of these types of knowledge locations should focus less on creating random local networks but rather on offering shared labs/facilities and on highly specialised seminars and tailor-made brokerage. However, we find local spontaneous networking much more relevant in some creative industry segments, even to the point of being promoted by tenants themselves as witnessed in Strijp-S.

Third, and related with the previous, this chapter suggests that synergy management in knowledge locations can play an important role in contemporary regional innovation policies – whether under a 'smart specialisation' or a 'constructing regional advantage' framework (Boschma, 2014). Under the first, synergy management can contribute to the early identification and promotion of new regional innovation domains; under the latter, it can tackle innovation system failures by supporting connections between new and incumbent players, as well as between local and non-local actors. Moreover, by involving newcomers and fostering regional economic diversity, synergy management can ameliorate two critical bottlenecks in regional innovation policies, namely the risk of rent-seeking behaviour and regional lock-ins. In this vein, knowledge location's synergy managers become increasingly important actors in the design and implementation of regional innovation policies.

Fourth, there are newly emerging visions on the physical layout and spatial embedding of knowledge locations related to societal changes. The suburban model of the late 1980s (Massey *et al.*, 1992; Castells and Hall, 1994) is being challenged by several influences including: (a) the rise of open and networked innovation practices; (b) the blurring of boundaries between disciplines and emerging interplays between technology, design, finance, and behavioural science; (c) changing preferences of skilled people concerning their working environment; (d) changing balances between work and social life; and (e) a shift from hierarchical structures to networked and project-oriented ways of working. Influenced by these insights and trends, mono-functional hotspots and campuses are being redesigned to include more functional diversity (e.g., residences, amenities, cultural and consumption facilities, education alongside business and research), in city-centre locations with strong identity (as against anonymous suburban areas). A key challenge for the 21st century's knowledge locations and their synergy-searching managers will be to balance tensions between planning and spontaneous development, between functionality and serendipity, between uniformity and diversity, between creating a 'city in a city' and defining the knowledge location as part of a larger functional urban area.

Notes

1   We are grateful to Paul Benneworth for the suggestion of such a diagram.
2   These projects were called 'Developing Locations in the Knowledge Economy' (carried out by the European Institute for Comparative Urban Research and commissioned by the participating cities); 'EURODITE – Regional Trajectories to the Knowledge Economy' (EU FP6, consortium coordinated by the University of Birmingham) and 'REDIS – Restructuring districts into Science Quarters' (URBACT II). For detailed methodological procedures and interview protocol, please see van Winden *et al.* (2012) and Carvalho (2013).

Bibliography

Amin, A. and Roberts, J. (2008) *Community, economic creativity, and organization*. New York: Oxford University Press.

Asheim, B., Coenen, L. and Vang, J. (2007) 'Face-to-face, buzz, and knowledge bases: Sociospatial implications for learning, innovation, and innovation policy'. *Environment and Planning C: Government & Policy*, 25(5): 655–70.

Bakouros, Y.L., Mardas, D.C. and Varsakelis, N.C. (2002) 'Science park, a high tech fantasy?: An analysis of the science parks of Greece'. *Technovation*, 22(2): 123–8.

Bathelt, H., Malmberg, A. and Maskell, P. (2004) 'Clusters and knowledge: Local buzz, global pipelines and the process of knowledge creation'. *Progress in Human Geography*, 28(1): 31–56.

Benneworth, P., Hospers, G.J., Jongbloed, B., Leiyste, L. and Zomer, A. (2011) 'The "science city" as a system coupler in fragmented strategic urban environments?'. *Built Environment*, 37(3): 317–35.

Biocant (2012) *Annual report 2011*. Cantanhede: Biocant.

Boschma, R. (2005) 'Proximity and innovation: A critical assessment'. *Regional Studies*, 39: 61–74.

Boschma, R. (2014) 'Constructing regional advantage and smart specialisation: Comparison of two European policy concepts'. *Scienze Regionali – Italian Journal of Regional Science*, 13(1): 51–68.

Boschma, R. and Frenken, K. (2011) 'Technological relatedness and regional branching', in H. Bathelt, M. Feldman and D. Kogler (eds), *Beyond territory: Dynamic geographies of knowledge creation and innovation*. Abingdon: Routledge.

Broekel, T. and Boschma, R. (2012) 'Knowledge networks in the Dutch aviation industry: The proximity paradox'. *Journal of Economic Geography*, 12(2): 409–33.

Carvalho, L. (2013) *Knowledge locations in cities: Emergence and development dynamics*. ERIM PhD Series Research in Management, Rotterdam: Erasmus University Rotterdam.

Castells, M. and Hall, P. (1994) *Technopoles of the world: The making of 21st century industrial complexes*. London: Routledge.

Chan, K.F. and T. Lau (2005) 'Assessing technology incubator programs in the science park: The good, the bad and the ugly'. *Technovation*, 25: 1215–28.

Chen, S. and Choi, C.J. (2004) 'Creating a knowledge-based city: The example of Hsinchu science park'. *Journal of Knowledge Management*, 8(5): 73–82.

Davenport, S. (2005) 'Exploring the role of proximity in SME knowledge-acquisition'. *Research Policy*, 34(5): 683–701.

Dettwiler, P., Lindelöf, P. and Löfsten, H. (2006) 'Utility of location: A comparative survey between small new technology-based firms located on and off science parks – implications for facilities management'. *Technovation*, 26(4): 506–17.

Doloreux, D. and Shearmur, R. (2012). 'Collaboration, information and the geography of innovation in knowledge intensive business services'. *Journal of Economic Geography*, 12(1): 79–105.

Drejer, I. and Vinding, A.L. (2007) 'Searching near and far: Determinants of innovative firms' propensity to collaborate across geographical distance'. *Industry and Innovation*, 14(3): 259–75.

Dul, J., Ceylan, C. and Jaspers, F. (2011) 'Knowledge workers' creativity and the role of the physical work environment'. *Human Resource Management*, 50(6): 715–34.

Eindhovens Dagblad (2013) *Weblog Strijp: Strijp.is*, 27 June 2013. Available at: www.ed.nl/extra/strijp-s/weblog-strijp-s-strijp-is-1.3886925.

Evans, G. (2009) 'From cultural quarters to creative clusters–creative spaces in the new city economy'. In M. Legner (ed.), *The sustainability and development of cultural quarters: International perspectives*. Stockholm: Institute of Urban History.

Feldman, M. (1994) *The geography of innovation*. Dordrecht: Kluwer.

Frenken, K., Van Oort, F. and Verburg, T. (2007) 'Related variety, unrelated variety and regional economic growth'. *Regional Studies*, *41*(5): 685–97.

Fukugawa, N. (2006) 'Science parks in Japan and their value-added contributions to new technology-based firms'. *International Journal of Industrial Organization*, *24*(2): 381–400.

Garnsey, E. and Hefferman, P. (2005) 'High-technology clustering through spin-out and attraction: The Cambridge case'. *Regional Studies*, *39*(8): 1127–44.

Gertler, M. (2008) 'Buzz without being there? Communities of practice in context'. In A. Amin and J. Roberts (eds), *Community, economic creativity and organization*. Oxford: Oxford University Press.

Giuliani, E. (2007) 'The selective nature of knowledge networks in clusters: Evidence from the wine industry'. *Journal of Economic Geography*, *7*(2): 139–68.

Gordon, I.R. and McCann, P. (2000) 'Industrial clusters: Complexes, agglomeration and/or social networks?'. *Urban Studies*, *37*(3): 513–32.

Graf, H. (2011) 'Gatekeepers in regional networks of innovators'. *Cambridge Journal of Economics*, *35*(1): 173–98.

Hansson, F., Husted, K. and Vestergaard, J. (2005) 'Second generation science parks: From structural holes jockeys to social capital catalysts of the knowledge society'. *Technovation*, *25*(9): 1039–49.

Heerwagen, J.H., Kampschroer, K., Powell, K.M. and Loftness, V. (2004) 'Collaborative knowledge work environments'. *Building Research & Information*, *32*(6): 510–28.

Hommen, L., Doloreux, D. and Larsson, E. (2006) 'Emergence and growth of Mjärdevi science park in Linkoping, Sweden'. *European Planning Studies*, *14*(10): 1331–61.

IASP – International Association of Science Parks (2010) Annual statistcs. Accessed on 20 December 2011, at www.iasp.ws/web/guest/statistics.

Jacobs, J. (1969) *The economy of cities*. New York: Vintage.

Kocak, O. and Can, O. (2013) 'Determinants of inter-firm networks among tenants of science technology parks'. *Industrial and Corporate Change*, doi: 10.1093/icc/dtt015 (online first).

KuiperCompagnons (2007) *Bestemmingsplan Strijp-S*. Rotterdam: Kuiper Compagnons.

Lindelöf, P. and Löfsten, H. (2003) 'Science park location and new technology-based firms in Sweden – implications for strategy and performance'. *Small Business Economics*, *20*(3): 245–58.

Link, A.N. and Scott, J.T. (2006) 'US university research parks'. *Journal of Productivity Analysis*, *25*(1–2): 43–55.

Link, A.N. and Scott, J.T. (2003) 'The growth of research triangle park'. *Small Business Economics*, *20*(2): 167–75.

Lowegren-Williams, M. (2000) *Advantages of a science park location. Case studies from the Ideon Science Park*. Lund: University of Lund.

Malmberg, A. and Maskell, P. (2006) 'Localized learning revisited'. *Growth and Change*, *37*(1): 1–18.

Massey, D., Quintas, P. and Wield, D. (1992) *High-tech fantasies: Science parks in society, science and space*. London: Routledge.

Moulaert, F. and Sekia, F. (2003) 'Territorial innovation models: A critical survey'. *Regional Studies*, *37*(3): 289–302.

Penn, A., Desyllas, J. and Vaughan, L. (1999) 'The space of innovation: Interaction and communication in the work environment'. *Environment and Planning B: Planning and Design*, *26*(2): 193–218.

Peponis, J., Bafna, S., Bajaj, R., Bromberg, J., Congdon, C., Rashid, M. and Zimring, C. (2007) 'Designing space to support knowledge work'. *Environment and Behavior*, *39*(6): 815–40.

Quintas, P. and Massey, D. (1992) 'Academic-industry links and innovation: Questioning the science park model * 1'. *Technovation*, *12*(3): 161–75.

Rashid, M., Kampschroer, K. and Zimring, C. (2006) 'Spatial layout and face-to-face interaction in offices – a study of the mechanisms of spatial effects on face-to-face interaction'. *Environment and Planning D*, *33*(6): 825–44.

Ratinho, T. and Henriques, E. (2010) 'The role of science parks and business incubators in converging countries: Evidence from Portugal'. *Technovation*, *30*(4): 278–90.

Stankiewicz, R. (1998) 'Science parks and innovation centers'. In H. Etzkowitz, A. Webster and P. Healey (eds), *Capitalizing knowledge – new intersections of industry and academia*. Albany, NY: State University of New York.

Toker, U. and Gray, D. (2008) 'Innovation spaces: Workspace planning and innovation in US university research centers'. *Research Policy*, *37*(2): 309–29.

Vale, M. and Carvalho, L. (2013) 'Knowledge networks and processes of anchoring in Portuguese biotechnology'. *Regional Studies*, *47*(7): 1018–33.

Winden, W. van (2011) *Creating knowledge hotspots in the city: A handbook*. European Union: URBACT.

Winden, W. van, Carvalho, L., Tuijl, E. van, Haaren, J. van and Berg, L. van den (2012) *Creating knowledge locations in cities: Innovation and integration challenges*. Abingdon: Routledge.

Youtie, J. and Shapira, P. (2008) 'Building an innovation hub: A case study of the transformation of university roles in regional technological and economic development'. *Research policy*, *37*(8): 1188–204.

5 From technopoles to science cities

Characteristics of a new phase of science cities

David R. Charles

5.1 Introduction: the idea of the science city

The science city may be seen as a distinct form of, or as a sub-class of, the technopole and is not a new idea: a particular group of science cities were discussed in the original Castells and Hall (1994) book. However, the concept of the science city has broadened over the last twenty years, and hence a reassessment is overdue. *Technopoles of the World* identified the science city as a planned city, built for the purpose of concentrating science investment. These rarefied developments did not receive a very positive evaluation at that time (see also Lambert, 2000), but somehow aspects of this concept managed to find a favourable hearing elsewhere. A related idea was the Japanese technopolis programme (Tatsuno, 1986; Higashi, 1995) – science and technology developments integrated within existing cities – and this also has perhaps played a role in the evolution of the science city idea. Finally, some of the larger science parks have started to acquire something of an urban character and are stimulating a new round of very large-scale developments (Lin, 1997).

From these various beginnings, captured by Castells and Hall in 1994, the science city concept has subsequently developed in new ways. Some of the more recent claims for science city status are very different from the original planned city idea, and focus much more on networks of organisations associated with science development and exploitation within existing cities of varying sizes (Garner, 2006; Charles and Wray, 2010). Therefore, this chapter starts by developing a typology of science cities, in this case with a strong historical or evolutionary basis. Three main phases or waves of science cities are identified, each with particular characteristics, and these are explored in Section 3.2. The new departure, in the form of what might be termed the 'third wave' science cities, is the development of strategies applied to existing cities and metropolitan regions in which science is used as a core development factor both for high-tech industry growth and for wider business and community development. Specific property-based developments may often feature within these broader science city strategies, but they are only part of the strategy and sit alongside community participation processes and public science festivals, as well as new research centres and science commercialisation processes.

The new science city can be seen as a confluence of two policy dynamics: on the one hand the idea of the technopole has gained traction within a new generation of policymakers and moved beyond a focus on real estate and research labs, and on the other, urban brand-building[1] (Dinnie, 2010; Donald *et al.*, 2009) has taken up the idea of science as a distinctive resource. Many cities now seek to maximise their development opportunities by exploiting their science reputation in addition to culture and other resources, and have multiple identities as cities of science, and culture, and other things. In part this may also be attributed to the increasing obsession of cities in attracting talent or the creative class (Florida, 2002; Asheim and Hansen, 2009) and their positioning within international networks and rankings of knowledge cities (Yigitcanlar *et al.*, 2008).

Not all of these cities use the same label – science city or city of science – and in some cases, at least one of which is outlined in this chapter, the policy has been pursued without the label. In a sense this goes back to some of the ideas explored in another Peter Hall book, *Cities and Civilisation* (1998), of cities as centres of innovation – in this case those that specifically strategize to promote innovation and change through the development and application of science. Is a science city one that adopts the label, regardless of its success, or one that effectively implements the same policies without the branding?

In this chapter the idea of the science city is focused on both the use of the label and the implementation of the policy, either together or one without the other. The focus of the chapter then, having defined this new typology, is to explore the characteristics of some of this new generation of science cities in terms of a set of key attributes, related to four critical questions:

- What kind of vision has emerged and what is the process by which it has been developed (5.3.1)?
- What kinds of partnerships and governance arrangements have developed and are they determined by the nature of multi-level governance arrangements within the particular countries (5.3.2)?
- Are science cities taking an international orientation or focusing on domestic policy agendas (5.3.3)?
- How are science city projects being funded (5.3.4)?

These characteristics are explored through various examples drawn principally from the UK, but also other cases such as Brisbane and Barcelona.

5.2 Science city generations

From the original 'science cities' of Akademgorodok and Tsukuba (Castells and Hall, 1994) through to the re-imagining of old industrial cities such as Newcastle and Glasgow, the idea of the science city has evolved and changed:

from something focused primarily on the production of science, which had little resemblance to a city, to cities that sought to find new ways to exploit science. Anttiroiko (2004) extends the idea of the science city from planned new towns created by governments to cities with a science profile taking in larger science parks, and even to science museums and theme parks that adopt a science city label. Leaving aside the latter, Anttiroiko identifies three basic forms: the planned new town; local development strategies; and extended science parks. What has changed since 2004 has been the emergence of many more cities that can be categorised as having science-based development strategies, and these have specific characteristics that differentiate them from earlier attempts to create new science-based cities. Taking a chronological perspective, we can identify three generations of the science city concept as it has evolved through a form of policy imitation, mutation and adaptation.

5.2.1 First wave science cities

In the *first wave*, the term 'science city' emerged in the context of purpose-built, campus-based new towns, nationally instigated and hosting new public basic research. The classic examples are Akademgorodok in Siberia and Tsukuba in Japan, as described in some detail by Castells and Hall (1994), and also Daedeok in Korea (Park, 2004). The aim was to cluster a critical mass of science activity in spaces separated from the usual chaos and confusion of the city, in the hope of stimulating new ideas. However, as such new cities have been dominated by state-sponsored research units, the degree of local interaction has been disappointing. Links with industry have gradually developed but these have mainly been focused on corporate research units, rather than creating the kind of innovative ecosystem of Silicon Valley or Cambridge (Dearing 1995; Lambert, 2000; Anttiroiko, 2004).

A downside of the original science cities has been the absence of a strong urban character and cultural vibrancy, and even a disconnection from the history of the site (Traweek, 2004). While having the best national research centres means that the attraction of staff should not be a problem, the absence of other forms of urban attraction limits the real scope for creativity beyond the narrow vertical silos of government departmental labs. The centrally planned science city risks being a sterile environment far removed from the current focus on cross-discipline and socially embedded creative innovation, with Tsukuba, particularly, being subject to this criticism (González Basurto, 2007).

The Tsukuba experience fed into the wider technopolis programme in Japan in the 1980s in which small science city projects were linked with existing cities in each prefecture to stimulate technology-based development away from the main Tokyo to Osaka metropolitan corridor (Tatsuno, 1986). Similarly, there was an attempt to export this model internationally to Australia in what became termed the Multi-functional Polis to be located near Adelaide, although never built (Inkster, 1991).

5.2.2 Second wave science cities

The *second wave* of science cities, not always labelled as such, represents a step towards a greater focus on commercialisation. The science park concept, taken from the US, was developed into larger-scale projects funded by national governments, mainly in Asia, often on the outskirts of existing cities, heavily orientated towards national economic development, applied science and the attraction of multinational research centres, as well as supporting local and national industry. Here the national research labs, while present, were secondary to the main business that was commercial economic development based on high technology industry. While these may be seen as just large science parks, they are differentiated by having urban characteristics such as housing and other urban services. Examples include Hsinchu in Taiwan (Lin, 1997; Lee and Yang, 2000; Chou, 2007) and Guangzhou Science City in China (Anttiroiko, 2004). These developments started out as parks but have become more like cities, as motors of their national economy. Their scale was massively greater than the original science parks in the US and Europe – Hsinchu houses over 100,000 jobs and the park and nearby city have merged into a single urban zone. Cyberjaya in Malaysia has been developed as a new city, but with a focus on attracting high technology foreign direct investment (Bunnell, 2004a and b).

Some of the larger conventional science parks have also acquired some of the characteristics of these second wave science cities, such as Sophia-Antipolis in the South of France (Parker, 2010). Research Triangle Park in North Carolina also, despite a development model that has been extremely low density and focused only on workplaces, is now looking to develop housing and urban facilities at key nodes within the park (Research Triangle Foundation of North Carolina, 2011). In Sweden the high technology park at Kista on the outskirts of Stockholm has developed into a science city initiative as new urban functions have been added to the park and strategic connections made with the surrounding new town (Anttiroiko, 2005).

5.2.3 Third wave science cities

The *third wave* differs from the previous waves by the absence of major city-building activity. These more recent science city designations place science-based economic development within existing metropolitan areas. The focus is less on the attraction and construction of new research facilities (although this may be part of the strategy), but rather on leveraging existing science resources to meet the future developmental needs of the city. Greater emphasis is placed on soft infrastructure such as commercialisation programmes and networking. A notable feature of many of these initiatives is a broader social mandate concerned with social inclusion and public engagement with science, emerging from wider local partnerships constructed to develop the vision (Garner, 2006; Webber, 2008). The shift away from large-scale physical planning and government research labs also enables a more diverse range of forms of governance. Third wave science cities may be designated as such by government in some cases, but may also be locally initiated by state or city government, or even by local partnerships.

This idea of what we might call the third wave science city has become particularly popular in Western nations in recent years. The initial technopole interest in the West was primarily in the science park as a dedicated space for research and science-based business, usually attached to a university or research centre (Monck *et al.*, 1988). Often these developments were very small – in the UK the average science park is no more than a handful of buildings in a landscaped park on the edge of a university campus (Charles, Hayward and Thomas, 1995; Bruhat *et al.*, 1995) – very few have grown to be large centres of employment. After the initial explosion of science park developments in the 1980s there was something of a hiatus as the slow growth of many led to disappointment and criticism as high-tech fantasies (Massey, Quintas and Wield, 1992). In the UK, many failed and became incorporated into university campuses or became standard business properties. More recently, though, the science park has made a comeback, but often integrated into broader city strategies, and the university campus has been rethought as a more integrated space for innovation (Benneworth, Charles and Madanipour, 2010). At the same time there has been an increasing interest of cities and regions in science investment, with regional-level government taking a greater interest in building science and technology infrastructures as part of regional innovation strategies (Charles, Perry and Benneworth, 2004; Perry, 2007).

5.3 Explicit and implicit science city strategies

Many cities have taken up the science city label, or some variant of this, as a brand for their investment in economic development and science and innovation. In the UK, in the mid-2000s, the national government announced the designation of six English cities as science cities. The initial announcement of three in Northern England in 2004 (Manchester, Newcastle and York) was linked with a policy known as the Northern Way aimed at regenerating the North of England (HM Treasury, 2004). Three more were added in the Midlands and South West (Birmingham, Nottingham and Bristol) in 2005, but London and the South East with Oxford and Cambridge were left out, as the policy was about stimulating growth in the lagging regions only. Although a national designation, the English science cities were not allocated significant new funding for science – each was tasked with developing a local partnership to show how existing regional resources could be better channelled into science-based development (Charles and Wray, 2010, Garner 2006; OECD, 2008). Science cities in England were about rebalancing the country economically rather than recognising existing science strengths (May and Perry, 2011), although the cities had to have a credible science base. This policy domain had been devolved for Scotland, Wales and Northern Ireland, but these governments did not follow the English lead on science cities. However,

Glasgow has subsequently developed a city partnership, initiated by the universities, to pursue a 'City of Science' strategy,[2] while Edinburgh has a well-established 'Science Triangle' partnership to promote science-based development across the city-region.[3]

Other cities have pursued what might be called a science city strategy without overtly using the label. Barcelona, for example, has used science and innovation precincts as a key element in its regeneration of the former industrial area north east of the old city, around Poblenou (see Chapter 10). This area, rebranded '22@bcn', is a highly ambitious project involving large-scale urban development with new university campuses and technology centres (Ajuntament de Barcelona, 2009; Yigitcanlar *et al.*, 2008). The project is intended to be a focus for urban, technological and social innovation, but this is only part of a wider focus on science and innovation across the city with new regional government-funded research institutes elsewhere, cultural and public awareness programmes on science, and a strategy of attracting scientific talent from outside of Spain (OECD, 2010).

France is also currently pursuing a number of science city-type initiatives focused around new and relocated university campuses. This is particularly the case near Paris with the Plateau de Saclay in the south, which is developing as a major science hub with a cluster of universities, public research facilities and private R&D centres (Béhar, 2012). Elsewhere in France, Grenoble is a recognised centre for science-based development with a cluster of public labs and major corporate R&D centres (Lawton Smith, 2003) and Sophia Antipolis is a huge science park with an agglomeration of MNCs in the hills above Nice (Parker, 2010).

In Australia, Brisbane was the beneficiary of a state-led strategy during the 2000s that had all the hallmarks of a science city strategy yet without the name (Charles, 2011). Melbourne as well, with the support of its state government, has in recent years pursued an urban science strategy, with Australia's largest clusters in ICT and biotech and with a state government-funded synchrotron (Puukka *et al.*, 2010).

From 1998 until the 2012 change in state government, the Australian state of Queensland pursued a strategy under the title of 'Smart State', in part an economic development strategy for the state, but in part also a whole-of-government approach to modernisation and development (Queensland Government, 2000a). Smart State priorities and actions have varied over ten years, but a constant element was a belief that investment in science and innovation can help to transform the economic development of the state, and more particularly the main concentration of population in the south-east corner of the state based around the city of Brisbane, the state capital. Given the sheer concentration of population, economic potential and intellectual capital in the greater Brisbane area (Guhathakurta and Stimson, 2007), it was inevitable that investment focused in this area, and as the strategy evolved greater attention was placed on the physical proximity of knowledge production and exploitation activities. This led to the State Government labelling Brisbane as a Smart

City and the city displays similar kinds of policies and initiatives on the ground as in the UK science cities. The strategy encompassed new research facilities, investments in attracting talent, new degree programmes for high-tech industries, venture capital, science–industry partnerships, a series of knowledge precincts where research and industry are brought together within wider urban regeneration initiatives, and public science awareness and promotion campaigns (Charles, 2011). The new Liberal State Government has dropped the Smart State strategy since 2012, but many of the previously developed policies continue.

Elsewhere, science cities are more like festival cities and the designation, like European Capital of Culture, may only last for one year. In Germany, the *Stifterverband für die Deutsche Wissenschaft* (the Donors Association for German Science) awards the title of City of Science in an annual competition, with cities having to apply for the title.[4]

To limit discussion of science cities to just those places that use the label is problematic. Kista Science City, for example, is a new town in suburban Stockholm that adopted the title for its science park (Anttiroiko, 2005), whereas some of these larger city-wide strategies pursue the same mix of policies with or without using the title. What is interesting though is the way in which a number of cities are now using the idea of the science city in their strategies and their comparative experiences of similar policies.

5.3.1 Science city visions

At the heart of a science city strategy is the idea of a core vision or aim focused on science-based development. It is this vision that defines the science city, regardless of whether the label is used. Having a clear strategic vision is vital for the building of a partnership, often across different levels of government and different sectors of society: public and private sector, researchers and the wider community. In part the vision may identify the main areas of science to be developed, but also the wider social and economic aims of the strategy. Some visions are ambitious and utopian, while others are rooted in the realities of economic development, but invariably these visions have to be sufficiently ambitious to capture the imagination of the partnerships in the city and ensure the commitment to a project that might be expected to run for many years, if not for decades. Clearly some earlier rounds of science city projects sustained that vision and imagination over a period of many years, although it might be questioned whether a coherent vision was the reason for success, or whether success sustained the idea of the science city.

Visions can be developed in two ways. In some cases the vision was that of a single body, usually a level of government. In first and second wave science cities this was usually central government, but some of the third wave science cities were initiated by regional-level governments and their vision was the basis for animating a wider city partnership. In other cases the vision was developed through partnership: this was particularly the case for the UK science cities where national government had made an initial proposal and designation but provided no vision of what a science city might look like. It was left to the cities themselves to assemble partnerships that could develop the vision and strategy.

The initial announcement of science cities for England took the cities themselves by surprise (Webber, 2008). York already had a strategy called York Science City that had been developed by the City Council and University and which they had been promoting for several years. Manchester had a Knowledge Capital strategy that absorbed the science city idea (Garner, 2006), but for Newcastle it was a genuine surprise as there was nothing in place beforehand. Birmingham, Bristol and Nottingham also had no science city strategy in place prior to designation. Thus on designation, the first thing the cities needed to do was to establish a group that could develop the vision and strategy. In Newcastle's case this meant a three-way partnership between Newcastle University, Newcastle City Council and the regional development agency One NorthEast. These three lead partners assembled a board chaired by the chairman of the largest local technology company, Sage Group, with additional business participation, to develop the vision.

The Newcastle vision saw the city as:

> a major urban location where a critical mass of science related activity is concentrated, contributing significantly to the economic prosperity and growth of that location and its surrounding area. This economic prosperity and growth is generated by scientific research and teaching, the application of science, and supporting services.
>
> (Newcastle Science City, 2008, p. 2)

A key thrust of the vision was to stimulate translational research (translating between basic science and application, see Rubio *et al.*, 2010) around partnerships in selected science areas that became focused on ageing, sustainability, and stem cells and regenerative medicine. This involved new physical sites for research and commercialisation, but also a wider outreach to the local community. Education and the stimulation of an interest in science among young people was a key part of the vision. It is important to stress that the central role of the City Council reinforced a social dimension, especially when a major site became available on the edge of the city centre as a result of a closure of a large brewery, and was bought by the partnership for a science-led development. This site and an adjoining one is now being developed with a new business school, student housing and an incubator building (see Figure 5.1), but the position of the site next to some disadvantaged inner city neighbourhoods reinforced the City Council's view that the science city had to improve the lives of the wider population and had to help improve educational outcomes in the city.

Figure 5.1 The view into the Newcastle Science Central site
Source: Author's own photograph.

In the case of Brisbane, the origin of the Smart State strategy, within which Brisbane was to become focused on science-based development, was a State Government initiative, but stimulated by the University of Queensland. In 1998, following the election of a Labor administration under the leadership of Peter Beattie, he and his cabinet were at a community cabinet meeting to review policy when Professor John Maddock from the University of Queensland made a presentation on the need for investment in bioscience and innovation. This idea captured Beattie's imagination as innovation had been highlighted in his own election commitments (interview, 2008). The idea to make Queensland 'the smart state' became a whole-of-government strategy under the Department of Premier and Cabinet, with budget lines inserted in the 1999 budget specifically for research infrastructure. The vision for innovation was simple and clear, to 'establish Queensland as a national leader in innovation in 5 years and become a global leader in 10 years' (Queensland Government 2000b). In the subsequent implementation, a considerable amount of the investment was concentrated in the Brisbane city-region, given its dominance in the economic and population base of the state, and the existing concentration of research and technology-based industry. The early development of Smart State coincided with a Labor administration in Brisbane City, as well as a number of city-based initiatives such as a festival of ideas, and the planning of a series of university–research–business precincts. The precinct model subsequently became a core part of the vision of Brisbane as a smart city. Largely absent from the development of the Smart State strategy has been the Commonwealth Government in Canberra, although some of the precinct developments have included new premises for the Commonwealth funded CSIRO labs in the state.

In the Barcelona case, the Catalan government has pursued a vision of high R&D, high technology, knowledge economy (Generalitat de Catalunya, 2010), with Barcelona as the leading city in the Mediterranean. At the same time the City Council has sought to differentiate the city through festivals and image campaigns with a gradual shift from a focus purely on culture and tourism to a city of science and ideas (see Chapter 10). This also reflects a tradition from the late 19th century where Barcelona saw itself as a leader of new ideas in Spain.

5.3.2 Partnership building

Central to the development of the collective vision for the science city is the nature of the partnership and governance relationships. The third wave science cities have a complex and broad range of objectives and policy strands and as such need to assemble a diverse set of partners to deliver all of these. While these partners come together at the city scale, they are not all primarily city-oriented partners, and can involve regional and national government sector bodies, sectorally focused bodies such as the health service, business and industry organisations that happen to have a presence in the city, and of course a variety of research organisations including universities. Thus not only must the science city partnership link across different scales of governance, linking funding and other resources, but it must also link across policy domains connecting science with business development, urban planning, school education, health, environment, social services and potentially others. The precise nature of these policy domains will depend on the themes and specific research initiatives identified in the vision – sustainability and health-related themes are common as a result of the huge challenges facing the world in these areas, for example. This does not, however, mean that all science cities are pursuing the same agenda as the precise mixture of health or environmental research resources and business opportunities does vary between cities. Some of these domains also require participation from the voluntary sector alongside the public and private sectors. The ageing theme in Newcastle illustrates this perfectly in requiring collaboration and inputs from various charities concerned with the needs of the elderly and with specific diseases of ageing.

The precise form these partnerships take will vary by national context, according to different national governance structures. In strongly centralised countries science cities will inevitably have a strong national government direction, whereas in countries with a federal structure these strategies are more likely to be regionally led. Generally though, the variety of forms of partnership means they are specific to the local circumstances and in themselves influence the direction of the science city strategy. National governments are important, however, whether they act as the designator of a science city initiative or provide some form of endorsement, as a national status is important for external credibility. Even if leadership is taken by a state or regional government in a devolved system, national government is likely to have a role through its funding of national research programmes and key research organisations that may be based in the city.

At a local level the nature of partnerships will be influenced by the form of local and regional government, the respective powers of each level and the mapping of administrative boundaries onto city-regions. Where strong regional government exists alongside weaker city government, such as in Queensland and Cataluña, it is the regional level that dominates and shapes the form of the interventions. Elsewhere the city may take a leading role, although that also depends on the tradition of co-operation among urban authorities within a city region. Generally, though, a regionally-led science city project will usually emphasise more the relationship between the city hub and the surrounding region, whereas a city-led initiative may be more focused and inward looking.

In the UK science cities, national government did not play an active role, even though in the English cases they were designated by the then Chancellor, Gordon Brown. Science cities had to develop their own partnerships drawing on leadership groups, typically involving city councils, regional development agencies (RDAs) and one or more universities. While Newcastle and York had quite small leadership groups around these three partners, other cities had much wider partnerships, with groups of local authorities around city-regions (Manchester), health authorities (Manchester and Birmingham), business groups (Bristol and Birmingham) and science communication bodies (Bristol) (Charles and Wray, 2010). The nature of these partnerships influenced the geography of the initiatives with Newcastle being more focused on the central local authority area with little input from the rest of the city region, while Manchester and Birmingham were city-region oriented. The location of universities and other research organisations mattered here, as where there were universities in neighbouring authorities it was more important to ensure a broader city-region focus. A further level of partnership that was important was that between the English science cities as they exchanged experiences on what were quite experimental strategies. This took place through a formal Science Cities Development Group, learning from each other's insights into how this new concept of a science city could be made to work (OECD, 2008).

In the case of Brisbane the Smart State policy was a State Government initiative and as such was largely implemented by State Government departments with little need for formal partnerships in the design of policy. However, in looking at the Brisbane city dimension we have four elements of partnership that were important:

- There were partnerships around specific precincts where State Government collaborated with city and other partners in developing new spaces involving science investments and associated innovation support. This included a creative industries 'urban village' incorporating a new university campus (Beattie, 2000; QUT, 2010).

- The State Government worked closely with the main universities in Brisbane concerning Smart State investments in the universities and the broader strategies of the universities and their engagement with place (Dodgson and Staggs, 2012).
- Economic development strategies for SE Queensland and for individual councils such as Brisbane were framed in the context of the Smart State and other State policies, sometimes in close partnership and sometimes not (City of Brisbane, 2002).
- Finally, the State Government introduced a forum for discussing the evolution of the Smart State strategy with some representation from outside of the government, mainly from universities and high-tech industry but notably not including local government. The Smart State Council drew on a wider group in developing specific reports, but in the case of a Smart City report this did not involve Brisbane City Council (Queensland 2007).

Despite the need for collaboration around specific sites within the city of Brisbane, in the late 2000s there was no formal partnership between the state and city around Smart State matters. This appears to have been a consequence of party political differences. Prior to 2004 with a Labor Lord Mayor, and especially up to 2003 under Jim Soorley, the city worked positively with the State on a number of Smart State initiatives. Following the election of a Liberal Lord Mayor in 2004 and again in 2008, the relationship seemed to be more fraught and Brisbane City Council strategy paid little attention to Smart State, and indeed the Lord Mayor launched a 'City Smart' initiative focused on sustainability rather than innovation in a broader sense.

Brisbane also experienced structural difficulties in the relationship between the State Government and the universities, which were central to the Smart State initiative. Australian universities are largely funded by the Commonwealth government, although regulated by the state, but in this case their involvement in a state initiative was funded by additional resources from the State Government. Despite the fact that the states regulate the universities, Australian state governments find it difficult to effectively enrol universities behind state development priorities without additional funding, as the universities are primarily driven by national funding priorities and international student markets. There are often conflicting interests between universities and state governments, which can only be resolved by significant new funding to facilitate regionally oriented projects. Thus, effective partnerships may depend on the availability of financial resources to convince key institutions to play a full role.

5.3.3 International orientation

The development of science city strategies as seen above is primarily focused on the desire to bring together local actors and develop localised linkages between the science base, industry and society. However, this takes place within a context of intense globalisation of science and innovation in which successful innovative clusters are embedded in global networks (Bathelt, Malmberg and Maskell, 2004) and universities also operate in highly globalised markets and networks (Marginson, 2004). Success of science city strategies can thus be measured in terms of the extent to which the initiatives increase international investment and connections in the city, and by how the science cities are positioned in wider global circuits of people, capital and knowledge (Dicken, 2001).

All of the science city cases make considerable reference to globalisation and the need to tap into international innovation networks. In part this is driven by the desire to attract capital and investment, and all such cities are keen to attract international technology firms, especially R&D centres. In this sense the science city strategy connects with other initiatives to attract foreign direct investment (FDI), bolstering international investment campaigns with claims about the quality of the science base and the prospects for future development. Where specific science-based industries have been the focus of attention there has been particularly strong linkages. In seeking to promote the bioscience industry in Brisbane for example, the State Government supported a highly visible presence at international conferences and exhibitions. The former premier Peter Beattie was actively engaged in this and made a number of speeches at international biotech exhibitions and conferences, seeking to target international investors and influence the reputation and profile of Queensland. The English science cities have also emphasised the importance of attracting international firms, with the science city brands being used to support local inward investment strategies (Webber, 2008), although the opportunities have been limited in the period of the global financial crisis.

Another dimension has been the attraction of talent, with cities and regions competing to attract leading scientists who can build research groups and provide the stimulus for spin-offs. Barcelona has benefitted from Catalan policies to attract researchers and this has been particularly evident in the life sciences sector. Investment in research institutes and fellowships for leading international researchers have contributed to the attraction of biotechnology researchers to the city. Foremost in these developments has been the construction of the Barcelona Biomedical Research Park, a large ($55,000m^2$) building on the waterfront (see Figure 5.2), which houses eight research institutes and in which more than half of the 1300 staff are reported to be foreign (Ajuntament de Barcelona, 2011). The regional government's ICREA programme has provided funds to attract around 300 researchers to Catalonia since 2001 with a focus on scientific excellence and leadership – each of the ICREA fellows is supported by an average of 6.89 other staff.

5.3.4 Funding

Any policy requires funding of some form and ambitious plans to enhance science infrastructure and encourage science-based economic development are

Figure 5.2 The Barcelona Biomedical Research Park
Source: Author's own photograph.

likely to require access to considerable funds for research, economic development programmes, new buildings and also for community outreach activities.
However, much of these activities tend to be also funded by mainstream public
programmes, regardless of the existence of science city strategies. So the
question is partly one of how science city strategies acquire new financial
resources for additional activities, but also how existing funding is influenced
to favour the objectives of the science city leadership. Here the nature of the
science city leadership has an important influence. If the strategy is embedded
in government, such as the Queensland Smart State strategy, then some
additional funds may be identified from new programmes, but some activities
may be subsumed in normal budgets and difficult to disentangle. If there is a
new organisation set up to develop the science city strategy, then it may be
easier to identify the project funding obtained to develop that strategy. However, it is still likely to be the case that new funding sits alongside considerable
levels of normal investment in science and economic development within the
city – so what is, or is not, science city funding can never be fully defined as
science city strategies inevitably incorporate activities that would have taken
place anyway.

For those cases where science city strategies are being pursued by
strong and well-resourced regional governments, there is rarely a significant
national government contribution, although regions or states may seek some
form of matching funding from national government, or seek to use national

programmes to support specific projects. In the case of Catalonia, for example, the regional government has been given responsibility for university funding and has taken on a part of the research funding role. This has developed to the point where regional government funding for research in universities is on a similar level to that of national government funding and as a result Barcelona has much higher levels of public research funding than other regions of Spain. There has been significant additional funding for industry-oriented research centres also.

Queensland also is a case where the State has been the dominant funding body, despite a general principle of funding for HE and science being national. The State Government was able to devote AU$3bn into their Smart State initiative over the last decade or so. Not all of this has gone into science-city-type initiatives in Brisbane, but identifiable chunks of this amounting to several hundreds of millions each has gone into new university research facilities, new science precincts and related innovation projects in Brisbane. In the UK the situation was more complicated. Although designated by national government, no new funds were made available for science cities, although the existing Regional Development Agencies (RDAs) and a related programme for the Northern English regions, the Northern Way, did have available resources that could be dedicated to science city objectives. More particularly, local science city partnerships were expected to join up existing funding resources and also bid directly to government for additional funding (Science Cities Consortium, 2007), although the latter did not result in any new funds. The RDAs made considerable investment in science-based developments in each of the English science cities, including funding for the Science City secretariats, also in some cases drawing on European Regional Development Funds that had been devolved to the RDAs to manage. Since the abolition of the RDAs the science city teams have sought funding additionally from the Regional Growth Fund, administered by national government, and in some cases have been successful in winning funding for incubator buildings and grants for technology businesses.

5.4 Conclusions

This chapter has aimed to identify the key characteristics of what may be described as a third wave of science cities, a new set of strategic projects based in existing cities with a broad and diverse set of objectives and operational modalities. These are a step forward from the types of development described in *Technopoles of the World*, being an evolution from the idea of a planned city for scientists to a perspective on the branding of existing cities around their science and technology assets and city-wide strategies rooted in partnership and inclusion. There has been a key shift in emphasis from a focus on the production of science in laboratories and research centres to its exploitation and use across the city. Science cities are no longer just about using science to drive economic development but about its application in social and economic development for the wider benefit of the population. The crucial difference from earlier planned science cities and other forms of technopole strategy is the lower emphasis placed on property development and a greater focus on the community beyond the people working in the labs and high technology businesses.

While there are superficial similarities in the basic components of these new science city strategies – the nature of the vision, the kinds of activities supported, and the international orientation – there are considerable variations in their governance and funding (see Table 5.1). These differences are largely the consequences of differences in governance structures in the cities and their surrounding regions, as well as the role played by national government. The examples used in the chapter have all been primarily implemented by local or regional governments and their partnerships, even though the English science cities were designated by national government. Elsewhere, however, national strategies can also be seen, such as in Singapore, as well as in the ongoing development of the previous waves of science cities, which are themselves evolving and taking on new dimensions. The effective prosecution of these strategies depends on the financial resources available to the partnership and in this respect those strategies implemented by regional or national governments tend to have been better resourced than those developed at the city level. However, regionally-led strategies may not always have the full support of the city, as was the case in Brisbane. What emerges strongly is a sense of a place-based strategy in which cities and their regions develop approaches that fit their needs and their governance structures rather than adopting off-the-shelf solutions by imitation of the usual success stories.

One interesting aspect of the differences in approach is the question of the name or label. Not every science city fits with the broad model described here and there is still potential for hype around the title, as there was with science parks. Not every city that pursues a science and innovation-led strategy uses the term 'science city'. The label is not important and does not guarantee success, as has been seen in many of the so-called silicon landscapes of the past. It is the mix of policies that matter and it is argued here that a broader and more inclusive conception of science and city in a combined strategy may bring benefits. If the title is at all important then it is merely as a means of building partnerships and convincing both local and international organisations and firms to support the strategy.

Success in these third wave science city strategies depends on the kind of vision proposed and the timescale over which the strategies have operated, as well as the availability of funding. So while cities such as Brisbane and Barcelona have some significant achievements to show for their considerable expenditures, their objectives were also ambitious. Where resources were more modest, then incremental changes over a longer timescale have been anticipated. On this basis the UK examples may not have seen large science parks with rapid growth of science-based industry, but they have seen changes in the orientation of the existing science infrastructure towards local

Table 5.1 Characteristics of the three phases of science cities

	Vision	Governance and partnership building	International orientation	Funding
Phase 1	New city based on public research facilities, aimed at generating new science.	Central-government-led, top-down approach.	Links with global scientific community.	National government funding.
Phase 2	Large science park-based development aimed at national economic development through technology-based business.	Mainly central-government led, with limited range of partners, focused on attraction of FDI.	Focused on the attraction of FDI.	Mix of national and private funding.
Phase 3	Strategy to use science to benefit existing city through economic and social development.	Very diverse partnership usually led by city or regional government. Strong input from the private sector.	Seeking to build a global reputation, attracting firms and talent. Strong emphasis on brand-building.	Complex mix of funding, but often just small-scale networking funds. Usually led by state or regional funding rather than national government.

collaboration, alongside a wider support for science excellence. In this respect what is perhaps the most important lesson from these new science city projects is a shift in perspective of both science institutions and local stakeholders to recognise a greater interdependence and a willingness to pursue a future agenda of mutual engagement.

Acknowledgement

This chapter is based partly on research undertaken with funding to Newcastle University from the National Endowment for Science Technology and the Arts in the UK, which provided a scholarship for Dr Felicity Wray, supervised by Professor David Charles and Dr Paul Benneworth. The author wishes to thank Dr Wray for her thoughts and insights that have fed into this paper. Additional research has been undertaken through a variety of projects, notably a project funded by the UK Economic and Social Research Council's (ESRC) Science in Society programme on 'Building Science Regions in the European Research Area' (RES-151–25–0037). This was a collaboration between Newcastle University and the University of Salford that developed case studies of the North West and North East of England, Alsace (France), North Rhine Westphalia (Germany) and Catalonia (Spain). Additional research has been undertaken in Australia, especially in Brisbane, through a number of visits during the 2000s. The author also wishes to thank colleagues involved in Newcastle Science City and Glasgow City of Science for discussions about these initiatives.

Notes

1 Indeed the science city may be seen as one genus of branded cities (Donald, Kofman and Kevin, 2009), alongside knowledge cities (Yigitcanlar, Velibeyoglu and Martinez-Fernandez, 2008), cities of culture (Garcia, 2005), or of sport (Smith, 2005), healthy cities (Ashton, Grey and Barnard, 1986), smart cities (Caragliu, Del Bo and Nijkamp, 2011) and emerald (eco) cities (Fitzgerald, 2010).
2 www.glasgowcityofscience.com
3 www.edinburghsciencetriangle.com
4 Previous winners have included Bremen-Bremerhaven (2005), Dresden (2006), Brunswick (2007), Jena (2008), Oldenburg (2009), Mainz (2011), Lubeck (2012) and Munster (2013). See www.stadt-der-wissenschaft.de

Bibliography

Ajuntament de Barcelona (2009) 22@ State of Execution, Barcelona, December 2009, Barcelona. Available at www.22barcelona.com/documentacio/Estat_execucio_2009_ang.pdf (accessed on 10 January 2014).
Ajuntament de Barcelona (2011) The Biotechnology Sector in Barcelona, Barcelona. Available at www.biocat.cat/sites/default/files/Dossier_Biotecnologia_eng.pdf (accessed on 16 January 2014).

Anttiroiko, A.V. (2004) 'Science cities: Their characteristics and future challenges'. *International Journal of Technology Management, 28*: 395–418.

Anttiroiko, A.V. (2005) 'The saga of Kista Science City: The development of the leading Swedish IT hub from a high tech industrial park to a science city'. *International Journal of Technology Policy and Management, 5*: 258–82.

Asheim, B. and Hansen, H.K. (2009) 'Knowledge bases, talents and contexts: On the usefulness of the creative class approach in Sweden'. *Economic Geography, 85*: 425–42.

Ashton, J., Grey, P. and Barnard, K. (1986) 'Healthy cities – WHO's New Public Health initiative'. *Health Promotion International, 1*: 319–24.

Bathelt, H., Malmberg, A. and Maskell, P. (2004) 'Clusters and knowledge: Local buzz, global pipelines and the process of knowledge creation'. *Progress in Human Geography, 28*: 31–56.

Beattie, P. (2000) 'State Govt and QUT to develop creative industries precinct'. Ministerial media statement 6 July 2000 Queensland Government. Available at http://statements.cabinet.qld.gov.au/MMS/StatementDisplaySingle.aspx?id=31267 (accessed on 22 October 2013).

Bèhar, D. (2012) 'Saclay et le Grand Paris: Comment "faire cluster" en situation métropolitaine?'. In Ingallina, P. (ed.) *Universités et enjeux territoriaux: Une comparaison internationale de l'économie de la connaissance*. France: Presses Universitaires du Septentrion, Villeneuve d'Ascq.

Benneworth, P., Charles, D.R. and Madanipour, A. (2010) 'Building localised interactions between universities and cities through university spatial development'. *European Planning Studies, 18*: 1611–29.

Bruhat, T., Alderman, N., Hayward, S., Charles, D.R., Sternberg, R. and Escorsa, P. (1995) Etude Comparative des Parcs Scientifiques en Europe: Enjeux pour une Politique Communautaire d'Innovation, for the European Commission DG XIII.

Bunnell, T. (2004a) 'Cyberjaya and Putrajaya: Malaysia's "Intelligent Cities"', in Graham, S. (ed.) *The cybercities reader*. New York: Routledge.

Bunnell, T. (2004b) *Malaysia, modernity and the multimedia super corridor: A critical geography*. London: Routledge Curzon.

Caragliu, A., Del Bo, C. and Nijkamp, P. (2011) 'Smart cities in Europe'. *Journal of Urban Technology, 18*: 65–82.

Castells, M. and Hall, P. (1994) *Technopoles of the world: The making of 21st century industrial complexes*. London: Routledge.

Charles, D.R., Hayward, S. and Thomas, D. (1995) 'Science parks and regional technology strategies: European experiences'. *Industry and Higher Education, 9*: 332–9.

Charles, D., Perry, B. and Benneworth, P. (2004) *Towards a multi-level science policy: Regional science policy in a European context*. Seaford: Regional Studies Association.

Charles, D.R. (2011) 'The role of universities in building knowledge cities in Australia'. *Built Environment, 37*: 281–98.

Charles, D.R. and Wray, F. (2010) 'Science cities in the UK', Melbourne 2010 Knowledge Cities World Summit, Melbourne, 16–19 November.

Chou, T.-L. (2007) 'The science park and the governance challenge of the movement of the high-tech urban region towards polycentricity: The Hsinchu science-based industrial park'. *Environment and Planning A, 39*: 1382–402.

City of Brisbane (2002) *Economic Development Framework for Action, 2002–2005*. City of Brisbane.

Dearing, B.H. (1995) *Growing a Japanese science city: Communication in scientific research*. London: Routledge.

Dicken, P. (2001) 'Firms in territories: A relational perspective'. *Economic Geography*, *77*: 345–63.

Dinnie, K. (2010) *City branding: Theory and cases*. Basingstoke: Palgrave Macmillan.

Dodgson, M. and Staggs, J. (2012) 'Government policy, university strategy and the academic entrepreneur: The case of Queensland's Smart State Institutes'. *Cambridge Journal of Economics*, *36*: 567–85.

Donald, S.H., Kofman, E. and Kevin, C. (2009) *Branding cities: Cosmopolitanism, parochialism, and social change*. Abingdon: Routledge.

Fitzgerald, J. (2010) *Emerald cities: Urban sustainability and economic development*. New York: Oxford University Press.

Florida, R. (2002) *The rise of the creative class*. New York: Basic Books.

Garcia, B. (2005) 'Deconstructing the City of Culture: The long-term cultural legacies of Glasgow 1990'. *Urban Studies*, *42*: 841–68.

Garner, C. (2006) 'Science cities: Refreshing the concept for 21st century places'. *Town Planning Review*, *77*(5): i–iv.

Generalitat de Catalunya (2010) *Pla de Recerca i Innovacio de Catalunya (Research and Innovation Plan of Catalonia)*. Barcelona: Generalitat de Catalunya.

González Basurto, G.L. (2007) 'Tsukuba Science City: Between the creation of innovative milieu and the erasure of Furusato memory'. RCAPS Occasional Paper No.07–3, Ritsumeikan Center for Asia Pacific Studies, Ritsumeikan Asia Pacific University.

Guhathakurta, S. and Stimson, R.J. (2007) 'What is driving the growth of new "Sunbelt" metropolises? Quality of life and urban regimes in Greater Phoenix and Brisbane-South East Queensland region'. *International Planning Studies, 12*: 129–52.

Hall, P. (1998) *Cities and civilisation*. London: Weidenfeld and Nicholson.

Higashi, H. (1995) 'The technopolis in Japan: Its past and its future'. *Industry and Higher Education*, *9*: 357–64.

HM Treasury (2004) *Pre-budget report opportunity for all: The strength to take the long term decisions for Britain*. London: TSO.

Inkster, I. (1991) *The clever city: Japan, Australia, and the multifunction polis*. Sydney: Sydney University Press.

Lambert, B.H. (2000) 'Building innovative communities: Lessons from Japan's science city projects'. EIJS Working paper no. 107, European Institute of Japanese Studies, Stockholm, http://swopec.hhs.se/eijswp/papers/eijswp0107.pdf (accessed on 10 January 2014).

Lawton Smith, H. (2003) 'Knowledge organizations and local economic development: The cases of Oxford and Grenoble'. *Regional Studies*, *37*: 899–909.

Lee, W.-H. and Yang, W.-T. (2000) 'The cradle of Taiwan high technology industry development – Hsinchu Science Park (HSP)'. *Technovation, 20*: 55–9.

Lin, C.-Y. (1997) 'Technopolis development: An assessment of the Hsinchu experience'. *International Planning Studies*, *2*: 257–72.

Marginson, S. (2004) 'Competition and markets in higher education: A "glonacal" analysis'. *Policy Futures in Education*, *2*(2): 175–244.

Massey, D., Quintas, P. and Wield, D. (1992) *High tech fantasies: Science parks in society, science and space*. London: Routledge.

May, T. and Perry, B. (2011) 'Contours and conflicts in scale: Science, knowledge and urban development'. *Local Economy*, *26*: 715–20.

Monck, C.S.P., Porter, R.B., Quintas, P.R., Storey, D.J. and Wynarczyk, P. (1988) *Science parks and the growth of high technology firms*. London: Croom Helm.

Newcastle Science City (2008) 'Newcastle Science Central: Transforming tomorrow, transforming the city'. Options appraisal report: Stage 2, Newcastle Science City, Newcastle upon Tyne.

OECD (2008) *Reviews of innovation policy: North of England, United Kingdom*. Paris: OECD.

OECD (2010) *OECD Reviews of regional innovation: Catalonia, Spain*. Paris: OECD.

Park, S.-C. (2004) 'The city of brain in South Korea: Daedeok Science Town'. *International Journal of Technology Management*, *28*: 602–14.

Parker, R. (2010) 'Evolution and change in industrial clusters: An analysis of Hsinchu and Sophia Antipolis'. *European Urban and Regional Studies*, *17*: 245–60.

Perry, B. (2007) 'The multi-level governance of science policy in England'. *Regional Studies*, *41*: 1051–67.

Puukka, J., Charles, D., Hazelkorn, E., Piacentini, M. and Rushforth, J. (2010) *OECD reviews of higher education in regional and city development, State of Victoria, Australia, Peer review report*. Paris: OECD.

Queensland (Dept of Premier and Cabinet) (2007) *Smart cities: Rethinking the city centre. Report by the Smart State Council*. Brisbane: Queensland State Government.

Queensland Government (2000a) *The Smart State*. Brisbane: Queensland Government.

Queensland Government (2000b) *Innovation – Queensland's future*. Brisbane: Queensland Government.

Queensland University of Technology (QUT) (2010) *The QUT creative industries experience*. Brisbane: QUT.

Research Triangle Foundation of North Carolina (2011) *The Research Triangle Park masterplan*. Raleigh-Durham, NC: Research Triangle Foundation of North Carolina. Available at http://rtp.org/sites/default/files/Concise%20PUBLIC%20Master%20 Plan.pdf (accessed on 19 May 2014).

Rubio, D.M., Schoenbaum, E.E., Lee, L.S., Schteingart, D.E., Marantz, P.R., Anderson, K.E., Platt, L.D., Baez, A. and Esposito, K. (2010) 'Defining translational research: Implications for training'. *Academic Medicine*, *85*: 470–5.

Science Cities Consortium (2007) 'Transforming regions by building successful science cities', submission as a discussion paper to the Comprehensive Spending Review, Science Cities Consortium.

Smith, A. (2005) 'Reimaging the city: The value of sport initiatives'. *Annals of Tourism Research*, *32*: 217–36.

Tatsuno, S. (1986) *The technopolis strategy*. New York: Prentice Hall Press.

Traweek, S. (2004) 'Keizu to Nendaiki: Making history in Tsukuba Science City'. Available at www.sscnet.ucla.edu/history/traweek/MakingHistory.pdf (accessed on 10 January 2014).

Webber, C. (2008) *Innovation, science and the city*. London: Centre for Cities.

Yigitcanlar, T., Velibeyoglu, K. and Martinez-Fernandez, C. (2008) 'Rising knowledge cities: The role of urban knowledge precincts'. *Journal of Knowledge Management*, *12*: 8–20.

Section 3

Space, place and governance

6 Context matters

The English Science Cities and visions for knowledge-based urbanism

Beth Perry and Tim May

6.1 Introduction

The concept of the 'technopole' has captured a public imaginary, invoking a relationship between knowledge and place focused on the potential of technology-driven economic development for cities across the globe. *Technopoles of the World* (Castells and Hall, 1994) takes the pre-eminent success of Silicon Valley as its starting point, examining the interplay between structural transformations, factors of production in an informational age and the social, cultural and institutional conditions of new entrepreneurship. While the authors acknowledge that the success of Silicon Valley may 'ironically preclude the direct replication of its own experience' (p. 28), the proliferation of 'silicon-mania' is nonetheless noteworthy. Koepp (2002) notes that 'siliconisation' has reached to the Silicon Alps (Austria), the Silicon Tundra (Canada), Silicon Fen (England) and Silicon Polder (Netherlands). The focus tends to be on an instrumentally-driven, econo-centric perspective on cities and their contributions to national wealth creation, as these 'Silicon Somewheres' (Hospers, 2006) seek to make real 'high-tech fantasies' (Massey, Quintas and Wield, 1992).

On closer inspection, motivations and rationales for interventions in science, technology and innovation (STI), or knowledge more broadly, can be disaggregated according to sectors, departments and scales of governance. Differences in approaches, values and attitudes between knowledge and place can be distinguished, legitimised through reference to interdisciplinary perspectives. These 'divergent rationalities' (Benneworth *et al.*, 2011) may be strategically coupled through technopole projects that bring different interests and stakeholders together; they may alternatively point to different orientations and visions for how knowledge can be harnessed to transform urban fortunes.

Understanding these differences in initial orientation to the issues surrounding knowledge and place is important. All too often policies proceed in the absence of articulating underlying assumptions and presumptions – and how those relate to, or are disjointed from, expectations and desired outcomes. Drivers are assumed to be common between partners in the search for urban knowledge-based development; yet global dynamics are manifest in different ways as they are mediated through diverse governance, institutional, political and socio-cultural contexts. To develop more 'progressive, socially just, emancipatory and sustainable formations of urban life' (Brenner, Marcuse and Mayer, 2012, p. 5) requires greater sensitivity to the values, knowledges and social interests that produce and reproduce knowledge-based futures. Central to such an endeavour are questions of social inclusion, participation and the forging of discourses and approaches that transcend rather than replicate narrow technological or economic viewpoints (Perry *et al.*, 2013).

A wide variety of case studies are being constructed on how different cities are approaching the challenges of knowledge-based growth from Eindhoven, to Barcelona, to Holon and Singapore (Clua and Albet, 2008; Fernandez-Maldono and Romein, 2010; Ooi, 2008; Wong, Choi and Millar, 2006). Emphasis has been placed on different pathways to development, success factors, historical trajectories and the consequences and limitations of such approaches (Carillo, 2006). Dynamics have been illuminated in relation, for instance, to the conflation between creative, digital and knowledge economies, a narrow preferencing of particular forms of knowledge and the socio-cultural implications of dominant approaches (Chapain *et al.*, 2009). What is missing is a specific emphasis on the overall framing of debates and how the interplay between conceptualisation and governance frameworks de-limits the capacities and capabilities of city-regions to work towards alternative knowledge-based futures. Greater attention is needed not only on the governance of the knowledge economy, but on the alignment between national policies and local priorities (Winden, Berg and Pol, 2007), an issue that tended to be underplayed in Castells and Halls (1994) original work (see pp. 227–8).

The early development of the Science Cities initiative in England is a case in point. Heralded as a significant first step in recognising the potential relationships between 'science' and 'cities', this chapter highlights differences in initial orientation towards the 'science cities' concept from top-down and bottom-up perspectives. It then considers the implications for both national and sub-national science and urban policy and the broader questions this raises in comparative contexts. In so doing, it draws upon academic research carried out between 2002 and 2010 on building science regions and cities, which underpinned the provision of expert advice to and work for the Science Cities Policy Development Consortium between 2006 and 2007. This included documentary analysis, international comparisons and interviews within each of the six Science Cities and the production of a report that subsequently informed the Science Cities' own submission to the Comprehensive Spending Review in 2007.

Chapter 6 is divided into the following sections: first, it outlines different rationales to knowledge-based urban development with an emphasis upon how the 'urban' and 'knowledge' are conceptualised (6.2). Second, it turns to the English Science Cities initiative (6.3). It looks at pre-existing policy contexts, the genesis of the initiative and differentiates between interpretations within central and sub-national agencies (6.3.1). The consequences for action at the city-regional scale and the implications for national science and urban policy are discussed (6.3.2). Finally, the article considers the broader ramifications of this analysis in terms of the relationships between knowledge, space and public policy (6.4). It concludes with the need to adopt more context-sensitive approaches to understanding knowledge-based development as an antidote to the aspatiality of global knowledge capitalism.

6.2 Framing knowledge-based urban development

A wide range of perspectives are encompassed in the notion of 'knowledge-based urban development' (KBUD). A blurring of boundaries between science, knowledge, culture, society, geography and economy has given rise to a range of inter- and multi-disciplinary writings from a number of perspectives (Lyotard, 1984; Gieryn, 1999). Cutting across these literatures we can identify four economic, political, socio-cultural and scientific rationales for KBUD.

6.2.1 Rationales for knowledge-based urban development

An economic rationale is apparent in discourses that emphasise the relationships between knowledge and place in the context of globalization, localization, the knowledge economy and the relative importance of different factors for production. Debates around the rise of the post-industrial or post-Fordist economy are accompanied by a concern with the emergence of new networked and distributed forms of governance and multi-level arrangements that highlight the relevance of the 'city' – and more recently 'city-regions' – as appropriate units of analysis and action in both political and economic terms (Bache and Flinders, 2005; Brenner, 2004; Neuman and Hull, 2009; Storper 1997). The relationship between cities and knowledge is often understood through studies of 'innovation' and the city (Marceau, 2009). Here the emphasis is on theories of agglomeration, industrial districts, locational specific advantage, as well as innovative milieux, learning regions and economic advantage through systemic interactions (Uyarra, 2009). The concept of the 'technopole' fits neatly into this conceptualisation, in which particular forms of public–private partnerships are developed to build university–industry–partnerships through new 'growth machines' (Logan and Molotoch, 2007).

A second rationale is given by literatures relating to urban growth coalitions and the new urban entrepreneurialism (Macleod, 2002; Salet, Kreukels and Thornley, 2003). The roles of local governments and authorities have been re-cast in light of discourses of competitiveness and economic development with the result that city governance has become increasingly characterized through a focus on entrepreneurial activities and issues of production, rather than social welfare or consumption (Boddy and Parkinson, 2004; Wilks-Heeg, Perry and Harding, 2003). Barcelona's '22@bcn' project, characterized as a 'top-down redevelopment strategy to capture high-tech activities', has been held up as a central exemplar of urban policy strategy as an exercise in boosterism (Casellas and Pallares-Barbera, 2009, p. 1151). Cities have become more concerned with marketing, branding and global success and position, emphasizing the roles of creativity, innovation and knowledge in city futures (Hospers, 2008). Here 'science' is a label, utilized and valued for its ability to conjure up territorial images of the new, engaged, cutting-edge city. Through this focus, it tends to be the vision, rather than the strategy or action plan, that is seen to change urban fortunes.

A third rationale is provided by the debate on the 'creative city' or 'city of ideas'. In the UK this has found particular resonance with policy and practitioner communities through the concept of the 'ideopolis' as a means to capture the essential ingredients of a post-industrial city (Work Foundation, 2006). The ideopolis was initially seen to have three key elements: a set of key physical and economic features; a particular social and demographic mix and a specific cultural climate and set of commonly-held values (Canon, Nathan and Westwood, 2003). From a socio-cultural perspective the 'creative city' links clearly to Florida's (2002) notion of the 'creative class', concerned with attracting the right kind of knowledge workers, cultural feel and 'buzz', physical regeneration and connectivity, as well as the support networks necessary to develop as a smart and modern city. Human capital and the social, cultural and institutional conditions for growth take central stage (Archibugi and Lundvall, 2001). On the other hand, a more econo-cultural perspective emphasises the creative industries and the development of the creative economy (Collinge and Musterd, 2009). Here a hybridised discourse can be seen that links economic competitiveness with branding and positioning in the search for cultural capital at the urban level (Christopherson and Rightor, 2009). Science, knowledge, culture and creativity are conflated to produce particular ways of seeing the urban knowledge economy (Hutton, 2009).

A fourth rationale is provided through literatures relating to large scale changes in knowledge production (Nowotny, Gibbons and Scott, 2001). A number of shifts, including those outlined above, are said to both result in and be the result of a paradigmatic shift in how knowledge is produced, for what reasons, by whom, for whom and how it is subsequently judged. New modes of knowledge production emphasize interdisciplinarity, heterogeneity, distributed expertise, the need for user relevance, collaboration and an interactive process between research and practice and implicitly bring issues of scale into focus (Gibbons *et al.*, 1994; May, 2006). Local and regional stake-holders become important, not only in assessing impact and demonstrating engagement, but also in defining and co-funding research. This is reflected in increasing emphasis placed on impact assessment and innovative methodologies and action research approaches, based on the aspiration that excellence comes together with relevance through place to build localized systems for knowledge exchange (May and Perry 2010). Knowledge management literatures, drawing on business, critical management and organizational studies, are also reflected through this window in their focus upon tacit and embodied knowledge, codification and knowledge sharing.

Theoretically-grounded justifications for considering the relationship between knowledge and place are varied. Rationales are both exogenous and endogenous, stemming from within and outside epistemic communities (May with Perry, 2011). Embodied within each window are differing conceptualisations of knowledge, the urban and the roles of different actors (Perry, 2008). An econo-centric perspective emphasises products, outputs and particular forms of knowledge more amenable to codification. A narrow understanding of 'science' dominates with implications for those institutions (large research universities or big science industry) best placed to deliver on those agendas. This perspective emphasises the changing nature of the industrial fabric, for instance, in terms of knowledge-based industries and the linkages between universities and businesses as a precursor for commercialization and spin-offs, rather than to the redefinition of academics' research agendas and ways of working. The urban is then framed as container for or facilitator of 'innovation' with a reliance on trickle-down to achieve objectives of increased Gross Value Added (GVA).[1] Knowledge may alternatively be seen as a central element in the re-branding of places, as a tool in global positioning as much as urban regeneration. The acquisition of talent, research expertise, the development of assets and external symbols of success or marketing and image are critical as it is the symbolic value, rather than actual content, of knowledge that matters. It is large 'scientific emblems' and facilities, or stellar 'world class' academics that have the greatest potential for these kinds of representational effects. Universities are seen as tools, instruments, assets and status symbols to be acquired, harnessed and their benefits extracted. In an acquisition-driven view, universities are one among many participants, operating on an institutional basis within strategic alliances with little engagement with individual academics. In the context of the knowledge-economy, universities may be part of urban growth coalitions yet they may alternatively be absent – as it is their existence that is deemed important as assets, rather than the knowledge they produce. Alternatively, what is counted as 'knowledge' may be broader, taking in the sciences, social sciences, humanities and arts. The urban may be important through partnership between different actors within a locality in the definition of research priorities, or the involvement of institutional interests, including local authorities, business interests and city partners as potential users of, or participants in, research processes. On the other hand, it may be absent, as proximity and localized relationships are seen to take place without according any agency to the 'city' itself.

There is no linear relationship between these different issues and how they translate into policy frameworks and particular interventions. Policies for knowledge-based urban development or innovative urban environments tend to leave such underlying assumptions un-examined, without a clear understanding of the relationship between knowledge and place, intended outcomes and appropriate interventions. The assumption is often that 'doing something' about innovation and the knowledge economy is enough to result in transformation. Rationales for action in practice may relate to theoretical frameworks, but more commonly they have developed in policy and practice borne of experience or justified by necessity, with post-hoc justifications deployed to legitimise prior courses of action.

6.2.2 The multi-level governance of science and innovation

Economic, political, socio-cultural and scientific dimensions are not exclusive and may be in tension or even contradictory in terms of their spatial implications vis-à-vis, for instance, the concentration or distribution of resources and capacities. This is particularly the case given the increasing multi-level governance of STI in the contemporary era (Edler, Kuhlmann and Behrens, 2003; Perry and May, 2007). In multiple countries within Western Europe, Australasia, Asia and North America, an increasing percentage of national programmes are being delivered by regional and local actors in centralised, decentralised and federal contexts (Kitagawa, 2007; Salazar and Holbrook, 2007; Sotarauta and Kautonen, 2007). National programmes may have varied sub-national dimensions as regional actors become stages for the implementation of national policies; partners or co-funders in national/regional infrastructures or else develop independent sub-national policies for STI or knowledge-based growth (Perry and May, 2007).

Multiple actors at multiple levels are involved in STI policy and knowledge-based development. Yet institutional, governmental and departmental positions and attitudes vary. As our interviews with representatives in the European Commission in DG Research, Innovation, Enterprise and Regions revealed, acting as joint signatories on warmly-worded policy documents masks a range of different perspectives regarding the relationship between knowledge, scale and place. In practice, across a range of national and sub-national contexts, there is little cross-departmental discussion of any epistemological resonance, despite the seemingly endless re-organizations and re-naming of ministries for science, economics, business and higher education that have characterised government restructuring (Dresner and Gilbert, 2001).

Differences have been identified in what 'regionalisation' means in practice, as mediated through national economic and scientific systems (Fristch and Stephan, 2005). A common rationale behind the use of new instruments, such as clusters, technological districts and innovation poles, relates to the economic potential of science and technology. Yet in many countries an additional rationale shared between national and regional actors is a concern for balanced growth and the potential of STI to address regional disparities. In France, Germany and Italy examples can be seen of national policies with strong sub-national dimensions (Crespy, Heraud and Perry, 2007; Koschatzky and Kroll,

2007). These include initiatives to target specific regions and cities to build capacity, such in East Germany or Southern Italy, as well as open competitions to build excellence, in which all regions can participate, but only some will benefit. As we will argue below, these examples contrast strongly with the situation in the UK where regional economic development arguments have not traditionally been accepted at national level as legitimate rationales for influencing the contours of national policy, requiring sub-national actors themselves (the Devolved Administrations, English regions and Science Cities) to link STI and socio-economic development goals (Charles and Benneworth, 2001; Perry, 2007).

What matters is how pre-reflexive understandings about knowledge and space, informed implicitly or explicitly through different theoretical lenses, inter-relate with multi-scalar governance arrangements. As the quantity and quality of interactions across levels of governance increase, so too does the potential for differences in terms of the relationships between knowledge, space and place, with important effects on the capacities and capabilities of sub-national actors to build sustainable knowledge-based futures (Winden *et al.*, 2007).

6.3 The English Science Cities

English developments illustrate these dynamics in practice. The concept of the 'technopole' was re-imagined in the 2000s through the lens of the Science Cities initiative. This provides an appropriate focus for analysing how multi-level governance arrangements interact with assumptions regarding the relationship between knowledge and place to shape and re-shape the debate on the roles of cities in the knowledge economy.

6.3.1 Contexts and catalysts

The genesis of the Science Cities initiative can be seen against a history of policy developments in which 'science' had increasingly come to see 'cities' and, to a lesser extent, urban policy had begun to see 'science' (see Table 6.1). In the early 2000s national policies were being shaped by growing awareness of the economic importance of knowledge and science exploitation in wealth creation and competitiveness in light of global pressures, particularly from the emerging economies of Brazil, Russia, India and China. Awareness of the role of economies of scale, critical mass, agglomeration and proximity as a precondition for knowledge transfer and innovation was growing, which led to an increasingly sub-national dimension to policies for innovation and exploitation. Such shifts were reflected in policies for higher education, with a range of initiatives designed to achieve closer synergies between research and industry managed and facilitated through the Regional Development Agencies (RDA).[2]

Table 6.1 Technopoles at the interface of science and urban policies

The case for science	The role of cities	The case for cities	The role of science
Science and innovation are key drivers of productivity and national growth and competitiveness. The future wealth and economic development of the UK depends on better harnessing of science, technology and innovation for economic and social benefit.	Since 2000 there has been an increasing regional dimension to science and innovation policy in terms of the role of RDAs in knowledge transfer and developing HE–business links. However, recognition of the role of cities is limited and largely confined to narrow, linear notions of business-led innovation.	Regional disparities in prosperity are hindering the productivity of the UK as a whole. Cities are recognised as drivers of regional and national economic growth. Proposals for strengthened local government have also followed in the wake of the failed and deferred ERA referenda.	Innovation, skills and employment are essential to regional and national growth. Cities are increasingly emphasising their roles in contributing towards the knowledge-based society. However, initiatives tend to be bottom-up while Government urban policy focuses more on traditional 'urban' issues.
Challenges include: • Maintaining and improving current strengths in basic research to develop international excellence. • Enhancing knowledge transfer through university	Issues include: • A tendency in Government STI policy to see 'local' and 'regional' as synonymous without acknowledging the differential roles of actors at multiple spatial scales.	Challenges include: • Addressing regional growth gaps in prosperity as a foundation for national competitiveness. • Enhancing the role of cities in regional and national	Issues include: • Better understanding the role of science and innovation in local and urban growth. • Improving the 'innovation milieu' through relationships between universities, local

—business interactions, fostering innovation and commercialisation and leading to global competitiveness.
- Securing a supply of graduates in SET, including addressing science education in schools.
- Addressing issues related to educational aspiration, attainment and skills.
- Fostering excellence in teaching and learning across the educational spectrum.
- Improving the public understanding of and engagement with science and research.

- An emphasis on cities as 'containers' in which innovation takes place rather than seeing local authorities as agents of change or place shapers.
- Insufficient emphasis on the importance of cities in fostering knowledge transfer.
- Emphasis on the economic roles of HEIs to the exclusion of their wider social, community or environmental functions.
- Absence of recognition of the mutualities between actors' agendas, including international excellence, world-class competition and local relevance.

growth and productivity.
- Clarifying the governance of England's spaces and places and balance of responsibilities between cities, city-regions and regions.
- Improving the capacity of local actors to work strategically across administrative boundaries.
- Delivering the sustainable-communities agenda, including tackling deprivation, exclusion, neighbourhood renewal and quality of place.

government and businesses.
- Joining up regional and local science policies within and outside regions.
- Enlarging understanding of how HEIs can contribute to a range of science agendas beyond commercialisation, including skills and public understanding of science.
- Developing frameworks and appropriate structures for strategic partnership between key actors.

The roles conceived for RDAs were as implementers of national policy and 'containers' within which innovation could be managed. Economic-scientific rationales predominated with an emphasis on how achieving national objectives would be increasingly dependent on maximising returns on science, research and harnessing the capacity of different places in the interests of UK plc. The Department for Trade and Industry (DTI) and the Treasury were central departments, while urban strategies remained relatively untouched by knowledge- or innovation-based discourses. The rise of the sub-national agenda, in the context of the Labour Government's commitment to devolution, introduced a stronger political–economic rationale to concerns about science, innovation and place. National policy had tentatively begun to acknowledge arguments relating to regions, cities, innovation and knowledge transfer, yet 'space' remained a largely secondary consideration. In contrast, issues of spatial location, distribution and effect were central to regional and urban engagement with agendas around STI in the context of the knowledge economy. Decades of regional policy had failed to significantly impact on the gap in productivity and prosperity between England's region, with old industrial regions in the North of England deemed to be 'underperforming' or 'lagging'. Investing in the 'new' economy was not only seen to make economic sense but was seen by some as a 'last resort' for addressing long-term structural issues in regions outside London. Arguments about the increasing political and economic significance of cities and city-regions as motors of regional and national economies combined with a consensus over the need for knowledge-based growth to provide a fertile context for urban STI initiatives.

Legitimacy for cities to independently take actions in this terrain was built over time from the bottom-up, rather than accorded by central government. Science City York (SCY) had already been launched in 1998 as a close partnership between the University of York and York City Council to 'reposition York and North Yorkshire as a hub for R&D and enterprise in new technologies'. The emphasis was on business support in particular sectors, including bioscience, creative industries and information technology and digital industries. On the North-West side of England, Manchester's response to the challenges of knowledge-based growth was encapsulated through the Manchester: Knowledge Capital (M:KC) initiative, set up in 2002. While SCY was set up as a company limited by guarantee, M:KC was established as an unincorporated partnership body between the ten local authorities, four universities and public and private actors and developed a holistic vision for knowledge-based growth, drawing on the concept of the 'ideopolis' and underpinned by an aspiration to be a global pivot in the knowledge economy.

The early 2000s were marked by institutional and policy developments at the regional level. In 2002 the first Regional Science and Industry Council was established in the North West of England in response to the loss of a large-scale scientific infrastructure investment to the relatively prosperous South East. The debate over the location of the 'DIAMOND' synchrotron radiation source brought to the fore strong differences between, within and across national and sub-national actors. Two loose and temporary coalitions of interest emerged, both comprising national and regional, scientific and economic actors, which alternatively mobilised scientific-economic and political-economic rationales in support of different location decisions (Perry, 2007).

The legitimacy that the DIAMOND debate gave to the involvement of RDAs in science policy eventually led to the creation of new institutions and posts for science and innovation in all of the English regions. RDAs had already begun to acknowledge the central role of cities in driving regional economies and the two agendas combined at the regional level to provide a receptive context for the Science Cities initiative. At the same time, a re-framing of the rationale behind sub-national interventions in STI also took place. Through the complex inter-relationships, negotiations and dynamics of the DIAMOND debate and the subsequent forums that were established to discuss the future of the region, arguments about the relationship between science and economic policy and questions of re-distribution or equity were left unanswered.

In this absence, a dominant discourse emerged that emphasized the pre-dominance of a *national* science policy, supplemented by regional investments in STI and a responsibility for regions themselves to harness available scientific assets for regional economic and social benefit. National support for a regional dimension to STI was embedded in the recommendation in the ten-year Science and Innovation Investment Framework for regional science and industry councils (H.M. Treasury *et al.*, 2004) and national policy documents across the board began to more systematically reference regional developments, where they clearly added value to UK plc. A strong emphasis on the physical sciences, rather than knowledge more broadly, on the roles of research-intensive universities and big industries and on technological developments predominated.

The mid-2000s were marked by the redefinition of the objectives and appropriate scales of action for national regional policy. Following the Labour Party's manifesto promise to redress the democratic deficit in the English regions through the introduction of elected regional assemblies, referenda were planned for the North West, North East and Yorkshire and Humber regions (DTLR, 2002). In 2004 voters in the North East effectively vetoed further referenda, so resounding was the victory of the 'No' campaign (see Sandford 2009). This not only led to a shelving of plans for elected regional government but also a redefinition of roles and responsibilities, through the Sub-National Review of Economic Development (SNR) in 2007. The SNR increased the powers and responsibilities of local authorities in economic development and formally enshrined the variable geometry or multi-track nature of city-regionalism in England, through providing the basis on which some places could institutionalise multi-authority governance arrangements faster than others. In addition, the creation in 2004 of the Northern Way initiative, a partnership between the three Northern RDAs with funding of £100m from central government, sought to redress the fundamental structural problems facing the North, increasingly through an emphasis on the roles of science, technology and innovation (ODPM, 2004; Page and Secher, 2006).

6.3.2 Science Cities: national and sub-national perspectives

It is only against these associated developments that the initial shape, form and intent of the Science Cities initiative can be understood, in terms of fertile policy contexts, differential starting positions of city-regions, dominant science-based and technological discourses and the growing responsibilities and confidence of certain cities in relation to economic development and the city-regional debate. The first three Science Cities were announced in December 2004 by Gordon Brown (then Chancellor of the Exchequer) in his pre-budget report (Manchester, Newcastle and York). This was followed in the 2005 Budget by the announcement that a further three cities would be developed as Science Cities within their respective regions (Birmingham, Bristol and Nottingham).

The birth of the initiative and the criteria used to underpin the choice of cities reflected differing sets of rationales. A strong scientific–economic rationale for investing in science and technology was evident in the initial announcements and press release (see Table 6.2). The 2005 Budget report linked the value of Science Cities to their potential to increase investment in science and research, to enhance the ability to exploit excellent science and to compete in the global knowledge economy: 'the six Science Cities, along with other cities and regions, have a crucial role to play in meeting these *national* challenges' (emphasis added, John Healey, then Financial Secretary to the Treasury, *Times Higher Education Supplement*, 21 September 2005). National endorsement of an urban dimension to the challenges of knowledge-based growth, through support for Science Cities, was driven by globally-oriented, nationally-focused concerns with scientific-technological development and economic growth. A period of positive discussions between national and regional actors followed, with the Science Cities proudly announcing that they were to spearhead the UK's efforts to build clusters of scientific excellence in support of the knowledge economy.

The announcements did not, however, reflect the emergence of a spatially-sensitive STI policy or the development of an integrated or redistributive national agenda on the relationship between knowledge and place. There was no direct reference to differences in the distribution of scientific resources, assets and capacities across England or the structural deficiencies and problems of productivity facing the RDAs. While the conception of the initiative was strongly based on a scientific-economic rationale led by the Treasury and by those responsible for science and innovation, the implementation of the initiative was justified via the mobilisation of a political–economic rationale around regional development. The development of Science Cities was to be supported through the existing funding given to the Northern Way to close the gap in productivity between northern and southern regions. In other words,

A definition of 'Science cities'

'Science cities' are those with strong science-based assets, such as a major university or centre for research excellence – which have particular potential to use these assets as the basis for generating business success. Developing science cities requires a range of complementary policies to address the specific needs of research and development, to support university-business collaboration and to influence a wider spectrum of factors that contribute to the growth of knowledge-intensive industries, such as skills, transport, finance and infrastructure. By bringing these factors together in a concentrated space, science cities can attract a critical mass of innovative businesses and become drivers of regional growth.

While cities will need to tailor their strategies to their individual circumstances, successful science cities will typically emerge where world-class research capacity combines with successful knowledge-based industries in an environment with the physical infrastructure and supply of higher-level skills to support significant further investment. Strong local and regional leadership, in partnership with business, is also an essential factor for the growth of science cities.

Extracted from the UK Government, 2005 Budget,
Chapter 3: Meeting the Productivity Challenge

from a national point of view, the emphasis was on how cities could support science, technology and innovation, rather than how the latter could be harnessed as a tool in urban regeneration and development.

As a result of the juxtaposition between different rationales, no clear criteria for the choice of cities according to scientific or regional development targets emerged. Manchester and York were obvious first choices, given the developments that had already occurred from the bottom-up. The North East had been quick to follow the North West's lead in institutionalising regional science and innovation capacity and a spatial focus on Newcastle had quickly emerged within regional priorities. In the later designation of cities, an initial concern with regional balance can be seen to the extent that Bristol, Nottingham and Birmingham were all core cities within their respective regions and members of the Core Cities group.[3] No 'science city' was named in the East or South East of England or London, to the chagrin of some local representatives, which implied again a concern with the unbalanced distribution of STI assets and resources outside the Greater South East. York, however, offered a counter-balance as neither a 'core city' within the region, nor an area of significant overall economic deprivation.

Underpinning the above was little specificity about definitions or boundaries, either pertaining to 'science' or to 'cities'. 'Science city' was a loose label able to mobilise wide-ranging support from both national and sub-national actors, precisely because of its lack of precision. At the same time it was a matter for interpretation within national and sub-national circles as to whether the label was assumed or designated, driven by the RDAs or by developed by national government. In the initial press releases and documentation, responsibility for the initiative was initially unclear, which laid the seeds for the subsequent disappointment that followed within the cities themselves.

National endorsement did not subsequently materialise into concrete support. No additional funding was attached to the initiative from the science budget or elsewhere and ministerial sponsorship appeared variable depending on where (and with whom) responsibility for science and innovation lay. Warm words remained the currency of successive national representatives, who were keen to emphasise the necessity of cities and regions playing their part in the national race for knowledge-based success – but in a way that devolved responsibility without resource.This was further justified by acknowledgement that a national plan for Science Cities would be inappropriate and that the role of national government was not to 'dictate' or to 'micromanage local economic development' (Lord Sainsbury, then Minister for Science and Innovation, 2006).

The Science Cities were left with a challenge and apparent opportunity: on the one hand, the question of how to meet raised expectations and ambitions within the context of existing priorities and resource commitments; on the other, the chance to define and shape the meaning of 'science city' according to local priorities and contexts. The Science Cities Policy Development Consortium was established between the six Science Cities with a remit to share experiences, build an evidence base, interchange with all parts of central government, consider joint projects, develop the Science Cities brand and keep under review the possibility of extending the consortium to include other cities (Science Cities Terms of Reference, July 2006). Our research recommended a three-fold approach followed, comprised of representation, learning and development in which the Science Cities sought to influence and shape national government, share best practice through regular meetings and develop their individual approaches. A process of annual summits was instigated at which different elements of the above could be discussed and the Science Cities brand and profile effectively badged.

In what followed clear differences could be seen in the underpinning assumptions made about the relationship between knowledge and place – and the implications for policy. Following the second Science Cities summit in May in 2006 a cross-departmental meeting of the Treasury, Department for Trade and Industry (DTI), Department for Communities and Local Government (DCLG) and Department for Education and Skills (DfES) took place. The differences in orientation were clear: the DTI focused on knowledge exploitation and transfer; DfES emphasized science education and skills and DCLG expressed concern not to create an exclusive and privileged club. The latter, seen in the light of the absence of clear criteria, explains in part the reluctance of national departments to offer dedicated financial support for the initiative. For the Treasury, individual departments could choose how (or whether) to represent Science Cities in their submissions to subsequent spending reviews.

For the Science Cities emphasis then turned to how a cross-departmental case and justification could be made. We were commissioned by the Consortium to produce a report that looked across national policy contexts and departments and emphasised the potential for Science Cities to contribute to a range of agendas and public sector agreement (PSA) targets (see Figure 6.1) (May and Perry, 2007). This was to form the basis of the submission on behalf of the Science Cities to the Comprehensive Spending Review (CSR). Underpinning the submission was a debate between and within the Science Cities on its overall purpose, with some in support of directly requesting additional funds, while others supported moving away from the language of 'asks' towards an emphasis on dialogue and joint working, particularly in light of the difficulties in justifying, in terms of 'science' or 'cities', the choice of the six cities.

The CSR submission reflected a broader and more holistic view of the potential of Science Cities in the context of debates over the development of the knowledge economy. Spaces of potential were seen in the gaps between and across departments with local initiatives bridging agendas on innovation, skills, widening participation, higher and further education outreach, the creative economy and green and renewable technologies. For the Science Cities, the strength of the initiative may be characterized as not only symbolic, but also additive (in terms of resource and capacity) and transformative (May and Perry, 2006). An emphasis was to be placed not only on buildings and products, but also processes; not only upon 'science', but also 'knowledge'.

The Science Cities had differential starting positions and contexts. Within a shared set of understandings, distinct approaches to knowledge-based growth could be seen. Scientific, economic and cultural rationales were variously mobilised. York's largely business-focused emphasis could be contrasted with a broader vision expressed at senior levels for Manchester's knowledge-based growth (Garner, 2006). Bristol, for example, developed a strong emphasis on public understanding of science and engagement. The city's scientific and engineering history, through eminent figures such as Isambard Kingdom Brunel and Charles Darwin, were drawn upon to galvanise different publics, industry players and local and regional agencies around a common sense of purpose and potential. Similarly, heritage and community were central themes for Nottingham Science City alongside the commercial exploitation of science. Research alliances formed important elements of the Birmingham approach, through a collaboration between the Universities of Birmingham and Warwick. This also indicated further variation between the cities in their geographical scope and coverage, whether within existing administrative boundaries or reflecting more fluid city-regional or cross-urban

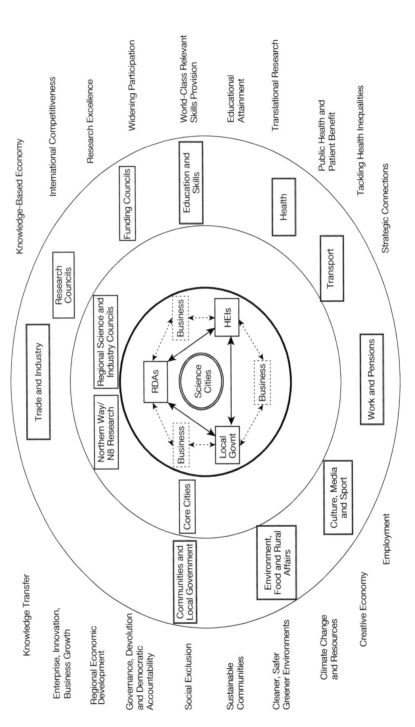

Figure 6.1 The UK context for Science Cities: organisations and issues, 2007

approaches. Levels of support from RDAs were varied, reflected in the centrality of the Science Cities within respective economic strategies, with Newcastle and Manchester appearing as central regional priorities (Couchman, McLoughlin and Charles, 2008).

The point is not to offer an in-depth, exhaustive analysis of differences across Science Cities nor to glibly pigeon-hole particular cities; rather, to identify how bottom-up perceptions of the scope and potential of Science Cities were reflected in the range and diversity of approaches to knowledge-based urban development. In comparison with national perspectives, a more joined-up view prevailed within the cities themselves, across urban, STI, skills, cultural and environmental agendas, bringing scientific excellence together with commercial and policy relevance and seeking to make connections with different communities and constituencies.

This holistic view was not shared across government departments reflecting different cultural views of the importance of place in policy conception and delivery (May and Marvin, 2009). National policy-makers have become more at ease with publicly acknowledging the place-based dimensions of innovation policy and the need for New Partnerships for Innovation (DIUS, 2008). The role of the National Endowment for Science, Technology and the Arts (NESTA) was influential in shaping this debate through its innovation and place programme and investments made in the Manchester city-region. Yet the discourse of innovation at the national level has remained predominately econo-centric and technology-based. Despite the wealth of initiatives within city-regions, examples that shape national policy tended to be those that emphasise commercialization, technology transfer or the development of new science parks, incubators or corridors (BIS, 2009, p. 44). Incentives and metrics for different organisations – RDAs, local authorities and universities – reflected and reinforced this dominant view.

Against this background the constant challenge for the Science Cities was to deliver on wide-ranging aspirations, in the context of existing governance responsibilities and resource constraints and their capacities and capabilities to deliver. The need to represent economic and technological potential to national organizations meant that representation externally tended to mirror, rather than challenge, dominant approaches to knowledge-based development, leaving the potential of alternatives largely unrecognized and unfulfilled at the local level. Although the cities were able to exploit certain cracks and fissures in hegemonic discourses (Holloway, 2010) in order to develop more context-sensitive approaches, the strength of the national polity and the broader context of national-urban relations in England de-limited the potential to go beyond the fantasy of the 'technopole' in practice.

6.4 Cities, knowledge and consequences

Existing studies of cities and knowledge-based development tend to examine specific case studies from within particular disciplinary perspectives. The discourse of 'technopoles' has become hegemonic, enshrined in particular kinds of public–private partnership in which some partners' knowledge is more valuable than others. This is recognised in writings on Silicon Valley since Castells and Hall's seminal work. O'Mara, for instance, notes that there is an often neglected story of Silicon Valley, 'a secondary definition of the city of knowledge, operating somewhat in tension with the first, that a scholarly community should use its scientific knowledge to improve society in general and urban life in particular' (O'Mara, 2005, p. 234). An emphasis on the overall framing of debates in different national contexts has been missing, along with sensitivity to how the interplay between conceptualisation and governance frameworks de-limits the capacities and capabilities of city-regions to work towards alternative knowledge-based futures.

Our analysis of the English Science Cities initiative provides some insight into this issue. Clear differences emerged between a 'national' and 'sub-national' view in terms of the mobilisation of different rationales for policy intervention and the implications for who was involved. Science Cities can be characterised as a peculiarly English initiative shaped by macro changes and the broader contours of the devolution/decentralization debate since 1997. A redistributive agenda for STI was quickly subsumed and forgotten within a discourse that successfully mobilized the acknowledgement that local actors were best positioned to determine local priorities and strategies in order to diffuse requests for a more balanced economic growth model. From behind the language of freedom and tailored solutions came a national devolving tendency that left responsibilities and commitments clear ('not ours'), but actual support far less apparent. Science cities, as a UK response to silicon-mania, were expected to emerge like phoenixes from the industrial contexts of English urban heartlands. Government policies sought to hold Science Cities to account according to measures that did not consider the relational space in which policy is enacted through, for example, targets and output-focused measures of effectiveness. Space was 'seen' according to its ability to live up to the abstract economic criteria of globalised competitiveness. In the case of the Science Cities it also explains why some places became invisible and others visible. The quiet but concerted privileging of particular places against the invisibility of other spaces is manifest in research and development expenditure and in terms of the politics of aspirations for the Science Cities. Expectations are high yet urban hierarchies result from a devolution of responsibility with neither power nor resource.

The Science Cities initiative is indicative of how too many unrealistic hopes can be pinned on limited understandings of 'science', rather than 'knowledge' without considering *how* expectations are to be realised. During a lecture early in 2010, the former Prime Minister Gordon Brown stated that it is to science that Government looks 'to provide new solutions, new technologies, new opportunities to further our common goals . . . it is science alone that can give us hope . . . challenges that only science can answer'

(Brown, 2009). He went on to compare the dangers of unregulated financial markets with the dangers of unregulated science, in which 'our progress can outstrip our humanity' (ibid.). This was indicative of an excess of expectations going hand in hand with the abdication of any general – or indeed specific governmental – responsibility for mediating change, harnessing potentials, distributing opportunity or creating enabling and supportive framework conditions. The emphasis has tended to be on quick fixes, shortcuts or technical solutions, rather than on the work of understanding and learning or on questions of appropriate empowerment. Science can deliver neither alone, while a broader concept of knowledge is needed to underpin the latter. Through the narrow deployment of concepts of scientific expertise and its relationship to place, science is being configured to transform the nature of democracy from a politics of sovereign citizens to a politics of diffused experts in which electoral struggle is replaced by expert bodies and specialised technical discourse is threatening democratic discussion (Turner, 2003). Gordon Brown's previous comments exemplify this assertion, as science is seen to provide unambiguous and disinterested technocratic 'solutions' to multiple areas of public policy.

Understanding the pre-cognitive assumptions made about 'knowledge' and 'place' is of central importance in providing an explanatory framework for the above state of affairs. This necessitates in turn an examination of how macro pressures are translated, mediated, magnified, refracted or transformed by meso-level institutions and structures and the people within them and with what effects for policies and outcomes at a micro level. The idea that there are 'global forces' over which states have no control frequently works to alleviate governments of responsibility through allusion to economic necessity. Instead we need an emphasis on the ways in which external pressures can be better managed to meet shared aspirations. Pressures for knowledge-based success are driven by a globalised ideology informed by a continual search for competitive advantage. A fundamental characteristic of this search is not to take context seriously – as to do so would undermine the pursuit of universal growth patterns. This tendency is replicated in the pursuit of scientific success as judged by peer review that focuses upon content through attention to international excellence (Lamont, 2009). Space becomes a passive entity in which things are enacted, but not co-constructed. Overall, what appears is an absolute sense of space according to the pursuit of the universal goals of globalization/ excellence.

Our analysis draws attention to a 'missing middle' between the multiple expectations of scientific knowledge and the extent to which it can – and should – deliver on a technocratic political agenda. Existing agendas tend to separate the 'what is being done' from 'how and using what resource and capacities and in what different contexts'. This is a central issue in reimagining the relationship between knowledge and place in the future requiring imaginative approaches to governance, participation and democracy and a willingness to think beyond the black box of the technopole imaginary.

Notes

1   Gross Value Added is a measure of the economic contribution of each individual producer, industry or sector in the United Kingdom.
2   Regional Development Agencies were first launched in 1999 with a mission to take a business-led approach to economic development and regeneration in the English regions.
3   The Core Cities group network comprises Birmingham, Bristol, Leeds, Liverpool, Manchester, Newcastle, Nottingham and Sheffield.

Bibliography

Archibugi, D. and Lundvall, B. (eds) (2001) *The globalising learning economy.* Oxford: Oxford University Press.
Bache, I. and Flinders, M. (eds) (2005) *Multi-level governance.* Oxford: Oxford University Press.
Benneworth, P., Hospers, G.-J., Jongbloed, B., Leiyste, L. and Zomer, A. (2011) 'The "Science City" as a system coupler in fragmented strategic urban environments?'. *Built Environment, 7*(3): 317–35.
Boddy, M. and Parkinson, M. (eds) (2004) *City matters. Competitiveness, cohesion and urban governance.* Bristol: The Policy Press.
Brenner, N. (2004) *New state spaces: Urban governance and the rescaling of statehood.* Oxford: Oxford University Press.
Brenner, N., Marcuse, P. and Mayer, M. (eds) (2012) *Cities for people, not for profit. Critical urban theory and the right to the city.* London: Routledge.
Brown, G. (2009) 'Science and our economic future'. Romanes Lecture, Oxford University, 27 February.
Business, Innovation and Skills (BIS) (2009) *Annual innovation report.* London: HMSO.
Canon, T., Nathan, M. and Westwood, A. (2003) *Welcome to the Ideopolis.* A Work Foundation Working Paper.
Carillo, F. (ed.) (2006) *Knowledge cities. Approaches, experiences and perspectives.* Oxford: Butterworth-Heinemann.
Casellas, A. and Pallares-Barbera, M. (2009) 'Public sector intervention in embodying the new economy in inner urban areas: The Barcelona experience'. *Urban Studies, 46*(5&6): 1137–55.
Castells, M. and Hall, P. (1994) *Technopoles of the world: The making of 21st century industrial complexes.* London: Routledge.
Chapain, C., Collinge, C., Lee, P. and Musterd, S. (eds) (2009) 'Can we plan the creative knowledge city?' *Special Edition of Built Environment, 35*(2).
Charles, D. and Benneworth, P. (2001) 'Are we realising our potential? Joining up science and technology policy in the English regions?'. *Regional Studies, 35*(1): 76.
Christopherson, S. and Rightor, N. (2009) 'The creative economy as "Big Business": Evaluating state strategies to lure filmmakers'. *Journal of Planning Education and Research*, March, 29: 336–52.
Clua, A. and Albet, A. (2008) '22@bcn: Bringing Barcelona forward in the information era', in T. Yigitcanlar, K. Velibeyoglu and S. Baum (eds) *Knowledge-based urban development: Planning and applications in the information era* (pp. 132–48). New York: Information Science Reference.

Collinge, C. and Musterd, S. (2009) 'Deepening social divisions and the discourses of knowledge and creativity across the cities of Europe'. *Built Environment*, *35*(2): 281–5.

Couchman, P., McLoughlin, I. and Charles, D. (2008) 'Lost in translation? Building science and innovation city strategies in Australia and the UK'. *Innovation: Management, Policy and Practice*, *10*(2–3): 211–23.

Crespy, C., Heraud, J.-A. and Perry, B. (2007) 'Multi-level governance, regions and science in France: Between competition and equality'. *Regional Studies*, *41*(8): 1069–84.

Crouch, C. (2004) *Post-democracy: Themes for the 21st century*. London: Polity Press.

Department for Innovation, Universities and Skills (DIUS) (2008) *Innovation nation*. London: HMSO.

Department for Transport, Local Government and the Regions (DTLR) (2002) *Your region. Your choice. Revitalising the English regions*. London: Cabinet Office.

Dresner, S. and Gilbert, N. (eds) (2001) *The dynamics of European science and technology policies*. Aldershot: Ashgate.

East of England Development Agency (2009) '£5m boost for Norwich as world-class science city'. Available at www.eeda.org.uk (accessed on 26 January 2010).

Edler, J., Kuhlmann S. and Behrens, M. (2003) *Changing governance of research and technology policy: The European research area*. Cheltenham: Edward Elgar.

Fernandez-Maldono, A. and Romein, A. (2010) 'The role of organisational capacity and knowledge-based development: The reinvention of Eindhoven'. *International Journal of Knowledge-Based Development*, *1*(1/2): 79–97.

Florida, R. (2002). *The rise of the creative class and how it's transforming work, leisure, community and everyday life*. New York: Basic Books.

Fritsch, M. and Stephan, A. (2005) 'Regionalisation of innovation policy – Introduction to the special issue'. *Research Policy*, *34*: 1123–7.

Garner, C. (2006) 'Building Manchester's Science City', in B. Perry (ed.) *Building science regions and cities. Regions Newsletter 263*, pp. 11–12.

Gibbons, M., Limoges, C., Nowotny, H., Schwartzmann, S., Scott, P. and Trow, M. (1994) *The new production of knowledge. The dynamics of science and research in contemporary societies*. London: Sage Publications.

Gieryn, T. (1999) *Cultural boundaries of science. Credibility on the line*. Chicago, IL: University of Chicago Press.

Harvey, D. (2007). *A brief history of neoliberalism*. Oxford: Oxford University Press.

Hirst, P. and Thompson, G. (2000). *Globalization in question: The international economy and the possibilities of governance* (2nd edn). Cambridge: Polity.

H.M. Treasury, Department for Trade and Industry and Department for Education and Skills (2004) *Science and innovation framework 2004–2014*. London: HMSO.

Holloway, J. (2010) *Crack capitalism*. London: Pluto Books.

Hospers, G.-J. (2008) 'Governance in innovative cities and the importance of branding'. *Innovation: Management, Policy & Practice*, *10*(2–3): 224–34.

Hospers, G.-J. (2006) 'Silicon somewhere? Assessing the usefulness of best practices in regional policy'. *Policy Studies*, *27*(1): 1–15.

Hutton, T. (2009) 'Trajectories of the new economy: Regeneration and dislocation in the inner city'. *Urban Studies*, *46*(5&6): 987–1001.

Kitagawa, F. (2007) 'The regionalization of science and innovation governance in Japan?'. *Regional Studies*, *41*: 1099–114.

Koepp, R. (2002) *Clusters of creativity: Enduring lessons on entrepreneurship from Silicon Valley and Europe's Silicon Fen*. Oxford: Wiley.

Koschatzky, K. and Kroll, H. (2007) 'Which side of the coin? The regional governance of science and innovation'. *Regional Studies*, *41*(8): 1115–28.

Lamont, M. (2009). *How professors think: Inside the curious world of academic judgement*. Cambridge, MA: Harvard University Press.

Logan, J. and Molotoch, H. (2007) *Urban fortunes. The political economy of place*. Berkeley, CA: University of California Press.

Lyotard, J.F. (1984) *The postmodern condition: A report on knowledge*, originally published in 1979, translated by G. Bennington and B. Massumi, foreword by F. Jameson. Manchester: Manchester University Press.

Macleod, G. (2002) 'From urban entrepreneurialism to a "revanchist city"? On the spatial injustices of Glasgow's renaissance', in N. Brenner and N. Theodore (eds) *Spaces of neoliberalism. Urban restructuring in North America and Western Europe*. Oxford: Blackwell.

Marceau, J. (ed.) (2009) 'Innovation in the city and innovative cities'. Special edition of *Innovation: Management, Policy and Practice*, *10*(2–3).

Massey, D., Quintas, P. and Wield, D. (1992) *Hi-technology fantasies*. London: Routledge.

May, T. (2006) 'Universities: Space, governance and transformation'. *Social Epistemology*, *20*(3–4): 333–45.

May, T. and Marvin, M. (2009) 'Elected regional assemblies: Lessons for better policy making', in M. Sandford (ed.) *The northern veto*. Manchester: Manchester University Press.

May, T. and Perry, B. (2006) 'Cities, knowledge and universities: Transformations in the image of the intangible'. *Social Epistemology*, *20*(3–4): 259–82.

May, T. and Perry, B. (2007) 'Realising the potential of science cities: Evidence, practice and policy lessons'. Submission to H.M. Treasury 'Comprehensive Spending Review' on behalf of the Science Cities Consortium. March.

May, T. and Perry, B. (2011) 'Urban research in the knowledge economy: Content, context and outlook'. *Built Environment*, *37*(3): 352–68.

May, T. with Perry, B. (2011) *Social research and reflexivity: Content, consequences and culture*. London: Sage.

Neuman, M. and Hull, A. (2009) 'The futures of the city region'. *Regional Studies*, *43*(6): 777–87.

Nowotny, H., Gibbons, M. and Scott, P. (2001) *Rethinking science: Knowledge and the public in age of uncertainty*. Cambridge: Polity Press.

Office for the Deputy Prime Minister (ODPM) (2004) *Making it happen: The Northern Way*. London: HMSO.

O'Mara, M. (2005) *Cities of knowledge. Cold War science and the search for the next Silicon Valley*. Princeton, NJ: Princeton University Press.

Ooi, C-S. (2008) 'Re-imagining Singapore as a creative nation: The politics of place-branding'. *Place Branding and Public Diplomacy*, *4*: 287–302.

Page, T. and Secher, D. (2006). 'The Northern Science Initiative (The N8)', in B. Perry (ed.) *Building science regions and cities, Regions Newsletter*, *263*, pp. 12–13.

Perry, B. (2007) 'The multi-level governance of science policy in England'. *Regional Studies*, *41*(8): 1051–67.

Perry, B. (2008) 'Academic knowledge and urban development: Theory, policy and practice', in T. Yigitcanlar, K. Velibeyoglu and S. Baum (eds) *Knowledge-based urban development. Planning and applications in the information era* (pp. 21–41). London: IGI Global.

Perry, B. and May, T. (eds) (2007) 'Governance, science policy and regions'. Special edition of *Regional Studies, 41.*

Perry, B. and May, T. (2010) 'Urban knowledge exchange: Devilish dichotomies and active intermediation'. *International Journal of Knowledge-Based Development, 1*(1/2): 6–24.

Perry, B., May, T., Marvin, S. and Hodson, M. (2013) 'Rethinking sustainable knowledge-based urbanism through active intermediation: What knowledge and how?', in H.T. Andersen and R. Atkinson (eds) *The production and use of urban knowledge: European experiences.* Dordrect: Springer.

Sainsbury, Lord (2006) *Thirteenth report of session 2006–07.* Great Britain: Parliament: House of Commons: Science and Technology Committee.

Salazar, M. and Holbrook, A. (2007) 'Canadian science, technology and innovation policy: the product of regional networking?'. *Regional Studies, 41*: 1129–41.

Salet, W., Kreukels, A. and Thornley, A. (eds) (2003) *Metropolitan governance and spatial planning: Comparative case studies of European city-regions.* Aldershot: E&FN Spon.

Sandford, M. (ed.) (2009) *The northern veto.* Manchester: Manchester University Press.

Sotarauta, M. and Kautonen, M. (2007) 'Co-evolution of the Finnish national and local innovation and science arenas: Towards a dynamic understanding of multi-level governance'. *Regional Studies, 41*: 1085–98.

Storper, M. (1997) *The regional world: Territorial development in a global economy.* New York: Guildford Press.

Times Higher Education Supplement (2005) 'UK designates six 'Science Cities' to spearhead economic growth'. *THES,* 21 September 2005.

Turner, S. (2003) *Liberal democracy 3.0: Civil society in an age of experts.* London: Sage.

Uyarra, E. (2009) 'What is evolutionary about "regional systems of innovation"? Implications for regional policy'. *Journal of Evolutionary Economics,* published online 18 February 2009.

Wilks-Heeg, S., Perry, B. and Harding, A. (2003) 'Metropolitan regions in Europe: Regimes, rescaling or repositioning?', in W. Salet, A. Kreukels and A. Thornley (eds) *Metropolitan governance and spatial planning: Comparative case studies of European city-regions.* Aldershot: E&FN Spon.

Winden, W. van, Berg, L. van den and Pol. P. (2007) 'European cities in the knowledge economy: towards a typology'. *Urban Studies, 44*(3): 525–49.

Wong, C., Choi, C.-J. and Millar, C. (2006) 'The case of Singapore as a knowledge-based city', in F. Carillo (ed.) *Knowledge cities: Approaches, experiences and perspectives* (pp. 87–96). Burlington and Oxford: Butterworth-Heinemann.

Work Foundation (2006) *Ideopolis: Knowledge city-regions.* London: The Work Foundation.

7 Territorial politics of collective provision in Hsinchu high-tech city-region

From a perspective of territorial structure of the state

Wei-Ju Huang

7.1 Introduction

Since the 1970s high-tech space developments, such as technology parks, science parks, science cities, technopolises, high-tech corridors and high-tech regions, have become a global phenomenon. For decades, a considerable number of studies have explored the relationships between technology policy, economy, society and space. Many studies aimed to explore the major factors associated with economic 'success' or 'failure' of technopoles (*inter alia* Carter, 1989; Keeble, 1989; Simmie, 1994, 2012; Sternberg, 1996a, 1996b); Komninos, 2002; Annerstedt, 2006; Kuchiki and Tsuji, 2005, 2008; and Lagendijk and Boekema, 2008). Despite the fact that the main focus differs across the studies, they share the same underlying assumption that knowledge and technological innovation can not only contribute to economic growth, but also be stimulated and induced by well-focused, supply-side policies.

In comparison, scant attention has been paid to the 'territorial politics of collective provision' in the development process of a technopole (Jonas, While and Gibbs, 2010). According to agglomeration theory within new economic geography, successful technopole developments create a circle of causation leading to growing varieties of goods and workers/people creating agglomeration forces (Fujita, 2008). Simultaneously, local demands on the provision of collective consumption increases, including workforce housing, transport, water, electricity, basic school, open space. Previous studies, such as While, Jonas and Gibbs (2004) and Jonas *et al.* (2010), demonstrated the endemic difficulty of internalizing the more localized, growth-related problems. Searching for a way to manage tensions between high-tech development and these more localised questions of collective provision therefore becomes a critical governance issue for long-term technopole development.

The long-standing tensions between the Taiwanese national government and the local governments in Hsinchu city-region resulting from the large externalities generated by the Hsinchu Science Park (HSP) development highlight this critical governance issue (Chen, 2001; Chou, 2007). Hsinchu high-tech city-region is considered the pre-eminent technology and innovation hotspot of Taiwan, due to its high economic performance in the ICT industry. The emergence of Hsinchu high-tech city-region followed the rapid development of HSP, which was established by the Taiwanese national government in 1980, aiming to drive national economic growth. The HSP not only achieved this national goal, but has also subsequently been recognised as one of the most successful technopoles in the world (see Castells and Hall, 1994).

Its output value in 2010 was €29.6bn, representing of 9.1 per cent of Taiwan's GNP. By 2011, more than 148,000 people were working in HSP with most of them living with their families in the Hsinchu city-region (SPA, 2012). The strong agglomeration forces created enormous pressure upon the supply of land and public investments in the surrounding area. Such external-ities have been a serious issue for local governance and since the 1990s have generated tensions and conflicts between the Taiwanese national government and the local governments in the city-region. These tensions and conflicts have, in turn, shaped state interventions in technopole development, spatial planning and infrastructure provision in Hsinchu city-region (Chen, 2001; Chou, 2007).

To further explore and illuminate the issue, this study examines various attempts by different branches of the state and different levels of government to create new governance spaces to manage the conflicts between the state-led science park development and the locally growth-related issues in the heartland of Hsinchu city-region. Section 7.2 examines a set of critical concepts in relation to high-tech development and the territorial politics as a reference for analysis. In Section 7.3, I briefly review the development of Hsinchu city-region in the past three decades and the tensions between the national state and the local governments upon the issues of collective provision, along with the rapid growth of HSP. Section 7.4 presents two case studies of two major governance initiatives in the city-region, namely Hsinchu Science City development plan and the Governor Forum, initiated at the beginning of the 1990s and 2000s respectively. By conducting the two case studies I investigate how the changing territorial structure of the state influence the results of the territorial politics of collective provision. Finally, I draw lessons from the experience of Hsinchu city-region to address the necessity to balance the national and local concerns in policy-making. I suggest that the necessary balance can be achieved by involving a variety of stakeholders at different levels in the governing coalition, and by setting up a common agenda that links various interests in relation to both high-tech development and local collective consumption demands.

7.2. The territorial politics of collective provision

The development of high-tech industries has very definite spatial dimensions (Castells, 1989). Alongside the rapid growth and agglomeration effects of high-tech industrial development, some cities and regions face a set of struggles in relation to the growth-related demands in two areas. First relates to the provision of production infrastructure and other policy inputs to retain high-tech industrial investment, to sustain high-tech industrial development and to serve high-tech industries. Second is the provision of local collective consumption goods[1], such as workforce housing, transport, and other basic infrastructure and facilities to secure local quality of life (While *et al.*, 2004; Jonas *et al.*, 2010). Governmental intervention is particularly important for such collective provision, because while it may seem unprofitable for capitalists, it is crucial for collective long-term capital accumulation.

Struggles for collective provision often take place between different levels of government situated in a territorial politics of high-tech economic growth and collective consumption to compete for the limited supply of land and public investment. The struggles may create issues of 'territorial non-correspondence' (Cox, 1993, p. 442) for local government, the situation where the local government's need or desire for control exceeds that of the local governments' territorial scales and competencies. Constructing a territorial coalition to create 'a space of engagement' is a common approach applied to the issue of territorial non-correspondence (Cox, 1998; MacLeod and Goodwin, 1999). The coalition may include both governmental and nongovernmental members. Investigating the mechanism the local government employed to create and organize new spaces of engagement in the politics of collective provision, requires paying special attention to the major reasons that motivate governmental and nongovernmental actors to join these coalitions, and the action situation of the local government to pursue external resources for resolving the growth-related issues. Two theoretical concepts can provide important insights into the investigation, namely spaces of dependence and the territorial structure of the state. I explain the connections between spaces of dependence and the motivations of actors, and between the territorial structure of the state and the action situation of the local government and different branches of the state as follows.

7.2.1 Spaces of dependence and motivations of the actors

Constructing a territorial coalition involves some socio-spatial relations that are considered to be not substitutable and always with respect to a particular territorial scale (Cox, 1993). This refers to:

> a space of dependence: a space within which it is possible to substitute one socio (-spatial) relation for another but beyond which such substitution is difficult if not impossible . . . Spaces of dependence occur at diverse scales. And for some agents there may be more than one.
>
> (Cox, 1998, p. 5)

The territory-bound relations in the development of a high-tech space – where technologically advanced industries and/or R&D firms and institutes gather –

may include the 'spatial fix' of capital accumulation (Harvey, 1982), the non-transferability of local knowledge and inter-firm linkages (Cox and Jonas, 1993), the accessibility to the 'raw material' for innovation activities (Castells, 1989), or the in situ accumulation of knowledge (Dicken, 2003). The concept of space of dependence shows the potential to invite lead high-tech firms, R&D institutes, universities, and/or other powerful actors, with shared interests in creating or securing territory-bound relations for high-tech development in a particular territory, to participate in the territorial coalition and bring resources necessary for pursuing their high-tech development agenda.

At the same time, local governments may also seek fiscal and regulatory support among higher levels of government to deal with the issues of territorial non-correspondence. This involves a politics of managing uneven development in the wider city-regional and national territory (While *et al.*, 2004; Jonas *et al.*, 2010): in other words, the coalition needs to be multi-scaled. The competition and conflict may occur not only between high-tech economy interests and other local interests within the particular territory, but also across different territorial scales of government.

7.2.2 Aspects to investigate the territorial structure of the state

The term 'the territorial structure of the state' refers to the relations between the state and territory. Cox (2003) suggests that territory is a bounded area where the state tries to influence the content of the area:

> But apart from the boundary of its own jurisdiction, the area within which it is supposed to enjoy sovereign power, there are numerous other bounded areas with which it is associated and which jointly define the territorial structure of the state.
>
> (p. 2)

However, it is not a one-way process – there are many other bounded areas also shaped by the territorial structure of the state; the degree to which the local governments encounter the issue of territorial non-correspondence, and the mechanisms they can employ to deal with the issue, relate considerably to the territorial structure of the state.

Cox (2003) provides three additional aspects to investigate the territorial structure of the state, including internal organization of the state, state inputs and states outputs. The internal organization of the state involves the state's division of responsibilities, the power relation between different levels of government, etc. The term 'state inputs' refers to 'the ways in which demands are made on the state, whether through legislators, pressure groups, corporatist structures, etc.' (p. 2) The aspect of 'state outputs' is relevant to the modes of state intervention, manifested in geographically selective infrastructure policies, for example, land use planning. These three aspects form a framework for this research to investigate how the territorial structure of the state shapes the action situations of the local government to create new spaces of engage-ment, and of different state's branches to organize new spaces of governance to manage the various growth-related struggles in the long-term development process of a technopole.

7.3 Development of Hsinchu high-tech city-region

The Hsinchu city-region is a functional city-region rather than an administrative division. Its formation was due to the development of Hsinchu Science Park (HSP), in operation since 1980. By observing dense flows of industrial activities, people and information between the HSP and its surroundings, some studies attempted to delineate the territorial scope of Hsinchu high-tech city-region, such as Hsieh *et al.* (2005), Hu, Lin and Chang (2005a, 2005b), and Chou (2007). The city-region identified in the respective studies does vary, but on their basis we can recognize an area consisting of the whole territory of Hsinchu city and some townships of Hsinchu county and Miaoli county along the national Freeway 1 and Freeway 3 as the core of Hsinchu high-tech city-region (see Figure 7.1). In order to set the scene for the case studies, I briefly introduce the development of Hisnchu high-tech city-region over the past three decades from the perspectives of socio-economic development and territorial governance.

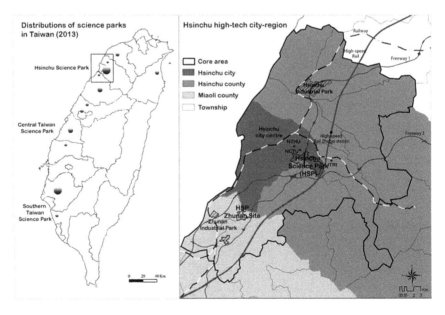

Figure 7.1 Hsinchu high-tech city-region.

Source: Author's own design, based on National Geographic Information System, Taiwan (http://ngis.nat.gov.tw).

7.3.1 Increasing socio-economic polarisation and housing demand

In the past three decades the success of HSP has attracted many knowledge workers to the city-region and thereby profoundly influenced local demographic structure. In 2011 employment in HSP reached 148,714 with 477 high-tech companies with total corporate sales of €25.9bn located in HSP (SPA, 2012), contributing 30.3 per cent of Taiwan's entire manufacturing sector's revenue. This contributes to the average household income of Hsinchu City and Hsinchu County, ranked respectively second nationwide since the mid-1990s and third nationwide since the beginning of the 2000s (CEPD, 2013, 2001, 1996), while in 1980 they were ranked seventh (CEPD, 1981).

However, as shown in Table 7.1, the gap between rich and poor in Hsinchu city is the biggest among the seven big cities of Taiwan (Taipei City Government, 2007). An increasing socio-economic polarisation, triggered by the HSP development, has been recognised since the end of 1990s. Moreover, from 1990 to 2012 the local population also underwent enormous growth, from around 700,000 to 950,000 (CEPD, 2013, 1991). This rapid growth pressured local governments to initiate spatial planning and land development projects to accommodate housing demand and to improve local public facilities.

7.3.2 An enclave institutional design of HSP and its governance implications

HSP was a state-led development aiming to promote industrial upgrading. It was intentionally designed as an enclave. This can be observed from two perspectives. The first is its physical design. HSP was designed as a new town, in which infrastructures and services were provided not only to satisfy the demands for production activities but also for creating a good environment to attract knowledge workers (Castells and Hall, 1994; Lin, 2010). Furthermore, the park was designed to have easy transport connections to Taipei area, while entirely bypassing the old town of Hsinchu (Castells and Hall, 1994). In fact, in its original plan the park had very little relationship with the old town.

The second refers to its institutional design. Based on the successful experiences of the exporting processing zone in Kaohsiung and Taichung during the 1960s and 1970s, HSP was planned as a free-trade zone, integrating elements of science and technology. Its development was based on the Act for the Establishment and Administration of the Science Park (EASP) in 1979. According to the Act, the Science Park Administration (SPA) was founded and budgeted by the central government under the supervision of National Science Council, Executive Yuan (the highest executive administration of the nation), as an independent authority to develop, operate and manage the park. The Act for EASP not only defined the duties of the SPA but also exclusively authorised a set of incentives, greater than for the exporting processing zones, to ensure HSP's successful development, including a five-year tax holiday, venture capital from the government, a low-interest loan, reduced land rent,

Table 7.1 Statistics of the seven biggest cities in Taiwan (2006)

Index		Taipei City	Kaohsiung City	Taichung City	Keelung City	Hsinchu City	Chiayi City	Tainan
Area (Km²)		272	154	163	133	104	60	176
Population (million)		2.63	1.51	1.04	0.39	0.39	0.27	0.76
Civilian education level above university (%)	2006	27.80	18.74	19.99	13.96	**22.22**	16.59	19.33
	2001	18.08	11.01	12.28	7.94	**13.90**	10.33	10.57
Average disposable income per household (Euro*)		31,560	24,252	24,231	19,561	**29,282**	20,017	21,299
Gap between rich and poor** (multiple)	2005	4.78	5.58	5.39	5.74	**7.35**	6.48	6.43
	2000	4.32	6	4.49	4.71	**6.91**	5.75	4.93

Note:* €M (Exchange rate: NT/euro=40); ** The average income of the richest twentieth of the population/The average income of the poorest twentieth of the population.
Source: Taipei City Weekly Statistics Report 2007; Urban and Regional Development Statistics 2007, available at www.cepd.gov.tw/dn.aspx?uid=4907 (accessed in May 2012).

no limit on foreign equity, ultramodern R&D facilities, on-the-job training programme, and so on (Castells and Hall, 1994; Chou, 2007).

Alongside financial incentives, HSP also provides tenant companies with one-stop services, including planning management and evaluation, talent cultivation, subsidies for R&D, investment services, labour affairs, medical and health care, civil engineering, environmental protection, land planning, landscape management, information networks, fire prevention and disaster relief, as well as security management (SPA, 2010). The one-stop services allow tenant companies to avoid complicated administrative procedures across different levels of government, hence reducing their operational risk and cost. However, this implies that via the SPA the tenant companies can bypass the supervision of local governments within the scope of the one-stop services. This further strengthens HSP's enclave characteristic and creates a divide in territorial governance (Chou, 2007).

7.4 Case studies of the politics of collective provision

The development of HSP has achieved the goal of leapfrogging national development, together with promoting local economic growth by attracting varieties of firms and workers/people to the city-region, but its surrounding areas also suffer large negative externalities, such as traffic congestion, environmental pollution, a shortage of local facilities and housing, which impacts upon local quality of life (Chang, Chiu and Tu, 2004; Chou, 2007; Huang, 2013). According to the division of responsibilities between different levels of the Taiwanese state, it is the duty of the local governments to deal with the large externalities, but due to the enclave design of HSP, the local governments have no authority to intervene and be involved in the decision-making of HSP's development.

When facing the issue of territorial non-correspondence, local governments, especially the Hsinchu city government, launched several initiatives, at either the urban or city-regional scale. These initiatives sought financial or other support from the national government, the SPA, the tenant companies located in HSP, the three major knowledge institutes located in Hsinchu city-region (including Industrial Technology Research Institute, National Chiao Tung University and National Tsing Hua University), and/or other local players. The initiatives, in turn, have shaped not only state interventions in Hsinchu city-region (Chen, 2001; Chou, 2007), but also the interrelationships between the local governments, the national government and the SPA. Some significant initiatives are listed in Table 7.2.

In this research the major focus is on the territorial politics at city-regional level, so I select Hsinchu Science City development plan and the Governor Forum as the basis for in-depth case study. I first briefly introduce the background and consequences of the two important territorial governance initiatives, which were launched in the 1990s and 2000s respectively, to explore the issue of collective provision in Hsinchu city-region. I then compare these

Table 7.2 Significant governance/planning initiatives in the city-region.

Initiative	Scale	Description	Major actors
Hsinchu science district plan (new city centre)	Urban scale	Hsinchu city government in 1999 initiated the redevelopment plan to make better use of the idle industrial land to provide spaces for convention, exhibition and other business services to support the development of HSP.	Hsinchu city government, and firms and land owners located in the planning area
Taiwan Knowledge-based Flagship Park development project	Urban scale	Hsinchu county government together with National Chiao Tung University (NCTU) in 1999 initiated the new land development project to provide new campus land for NCTU and industrial land for high-tech development, and to manage the enormous housing demand resulted from the HSP development.	Hsinchu county government and National Chiao Tung University
Hsinchu Science City development plan	City-regional scale	The plan was initiated by Hsinchu city government, the SPA and the three major knowledge institutes in Hsinchu area in 1986 with an aim to strengthen further the HSP's competitiveness by coupling with the increasing land demands for industry and housing and enhancing the quality of the business climate and living environment. Later on, Taiwan provincial government and Hsinchu county government also participated in the planning process.	Taiwan provincial government, the SPA, knowledge institutes, Hsinchu city and county governments
Governor Forum	City-regional scale	The SPA initiated the forum in 2002 and invited Hsinchu city and county governments, and Allied Association for Science Park Industries to participated in the forum in order to mitigate the increasing conflicts between the park and local governments.	SPA, Hsinchu city and county governments, and Allied Association for Science Park Industries

Source: Huang, 2013; Chou, 2007; Lin, 2006.

two cases by examining the implications of the changing territorial structure of the state in terms of the functional divisions between different levels of government and branches of the national state, the mechanisms employed by local governments to make demands on the national government alongside national state interventions in response to local demands.

7.4.1 Hsinchu Science City development plan in the 1990s

The Hsinchu Science City development plan was originally a bottom-up initiative aiming to enhance the high-tech development of Hsinchu city as a whole by resolving issues triggered by the rapid development of HSP. The issues include under-provision of collective consumption goods and land for accommodating a range of housing, transport, industrial, and commercial activities and relevant infrastructure and facilities. In 1986, the mayor of Hsinchu city government invited the SPA, the Industrial Technology Research Institute and the two national universities adjacent to the HSP to form the Hsinchu Science City Planning Steering Group to proceed with comprehensive development planning for the Hsinchu city (Chen, 2001). They later reported their draft plan to Executive Yuan to gain the national government's support. Executive Yuan instructed that

> it is necessary to address the study of science city at a regional level in order to enhance the development of Hsinchu Science Park, to increase the investment in high-tech industry ... and to develop together with nearby areas.
>
> (SPA and TPG, 1993, p. 1; author's own translation)

The instruction extended the concept of science city to a regional level and promoted the Hsinchu county government to participate in the planning process. The planning project thus became an umbrella to cover all participants' various interests. The major interests for the national government were to strengthen further the HSP development, as well as to use HSP as a growth pole to stimulate the development of nearby areas. For the SPA the plan could legitimate their land demands for future high-tech industrial development, while for local governments, it was a good chance to gain financial support from the national government to improve local public facilities and development. Thus, an economic space – the Hsinchu high-tech city-region – on behalf of an imagined community of economic interests, was demarcated through the 'spatial imaginary' (Jessop, 1997; MacLeod and Goodwin, 1999).

In 1990 the Executive Yuan brought the project into the eleventh Six-year National Development Plan and designated the National Science Council (NSC) and the Taiwan's provincial government in charge of the planning. In the planning process, the NSC and the Science Park Administration (SPA) played a leading role and the interactions between different levels of governments were so hierarchical that the comprehensive planning project thus became top-down in nature. Since the project was originally initiated by the city-region-based actors, this provided them with the chance to participate in the decision-making at the very beginning, but their proposals could be adopted only when the proposals were compliant with the major aim of the NSC and the SPA, namely to strengthen HSP's competitiveness and enhance its development. Their priority was clearly demonstrated in the planning concept, as the planned area was classified into two categories, a core area of the HSP development alongside the ancillary area of the HSP development (SPA and TPG, 1993, pp. 6–29). As shown in Figure 7.2, the science belt refers to the core area of the HSP development and the living belt and conservation belt are considered the ancillary areas of the HSP.

However, at the end of the 1990s the coalition collapsed because the two major executors of the regional science city plan, Taiwan's provincial government and the SPA, withdrew their roles from the plan. The withdrawal resulted from reorganization of governmental and fiscal structures, and alteration of national science park policy. In 1998 Taiwan's provincial government was downscaled:[2] while many of its competencies were ceded to the national government, some were devolved to the local level. The downscaling indicated that the Taiwan's provincial government would not have any competency to play a role in the planning process.

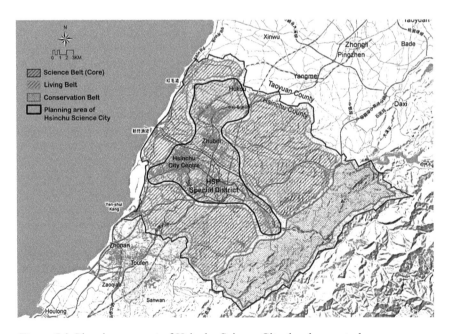

Figure 7.2 Planning concept of Hsinchu Science City development plan

Source: Author's own design, based on National Geographic Information System, Taiwan (http://ngis.nat.gov.tw).

At the same time, the national government altered its science park policy from a single technopole strategy to a 'technopolis' programme to gain political support from local factions and resolve the land demand pressure of high-tech industries (Hsu, 2010; Huang, 2013). The policy alteration let the SPA busy themselves with new science park developments and withdrew its role from the plan. For the SPA the priority of the plan was to search for new land to accommodate high-tech industrial activities, rather than to promote the development of the city-region as a whole. When the SPA could acquire new land for high-tech development in other cities and counties, Hsinchu city-region's regional science city plan thus became far less important than the new science park developments.

7.4.2 Governor Forum since 2002

After the collapse of the first collaboration in the form of comprehensive planning at the city-regional scale, the negative impacts of HSP's rapid growth on its surrounding area were becoming increasingly serious. Moreover, the major portion of the tax revenues generated by the HSP development and the administration fee paid by the firms in the park went respectively to the national government and the Operation Fund of the Science Park Administration. Local governments could gain only a very limited profit from the HSP development through obtaining land tax and building tax from the firms located in the park, and were left to deal with the negative impacts alone with their limited manpower and revenues (Chou, 2007). In this situation, the local governments were eager for compensation for the HSP development's negative impacts.

In 1999 the Local Government Act was promulgated. Together with the downscaling of Taiwan's provincial government, some administrative powers and responsibilities were devolved to local governments, including spatial planning and environmental protection. Previously, due to the full support of Taiwan's provincial government, decisions regarding environmental protection and spatial planning in the HSP special district were actually made by the SPA (Chen, 2001). After the reorganisation and devolution, local governments tried to utilise their new authorities to balance the power relation (such as the United Microelectronics Corporation event[3]). This increased the tensions and conflicts between local governments, the SPA and HSP's tenant companies. Nevertheless, it also alerted the SPA to the importance of collaborating with the local governments.

In March 2002 the Director General of SPA invited the mayor of Hsinchu City, the magistrate of Hsinchu County and the chairperson of the Allied Association for Science Park Industries (ASIP, the representative body of the industries located in the HSP), to hold the first Governor Forum. During the forum, they reached a consensus in favour of collaboration and agreed to strive for a budget from the national government (Lin, 2007). In 2003 the Legislative Yuan approved a new administrative regulation, the Principles for the Allocation of Science Park Subsidy for Local Development. This established an annual funding line based on the Operation Fund of the Science Park Administration to subsidize local development projects. Although the subsidy allocation indeed solidified collaborations (Jhan, 2008; Lin, 2007), it did not resolve the tensions and conflicts between the local governments and the SPA. This can be observed from the terms respectively used by the SPA and the local governments in referring to the same funding. For the SPA, the money it provides to the local governments is perceived as 'subsidies',[4] but the local governments perceive the money as 'community payments'.[5] In other words, for the SPA, the funding is a top-down mechanism to assist local development, while the local governments consider the funding as a form of compensation that they deserve to receive. This fundamental divergence of attitude is one symptom of the wider the tensions between the SPA and local governments.

Since the promulgation of the administrative regulation in 2003, negotiation of subsidy allocation has become the major focus of the Governor Forum. According to the principles, the SPA can only subsidize local projects in relation to transport infrastructure, public safety, water management, environmental protection, education and culture activities, and urban planning located within a geographical scale that extends three kilometres along the boundary of the HSP. Although NSC's subsidy allocation principles confine the space of engagement of the local governments to a narrow agenda and a localised geographical scale, the subsidy has been able to alleviate tensions and strike a temporary balance between the SPA and local governments. Consequently, the four participating parties have no urgent need to widen the scope of the agenda, to build up a common vision of this city-region, or to seek new possibilities of collaboration with other regional actors in developing the high-tech city-region as a whole.

However, since the late 2000s this collaboration form has faced a serious issue of the worsening financial situation of the SPA due to the technopolis programme. This approach not only overloaded the supply of high-tech industrial land but also significantly increased the financial burden on the Operation Fund of the Science Park. By the end of 2012, the debt had reached NT\$123.4bn (around €3.25bn). Although every year HSP have more than NT\$3.5bn net income for the investment in fixed assets and the repayment of the debt, HSP's debt will not be paid off until 2040 (National Science Council, 2011). Since its subsidy for local government is from the operational fund, consequently the subsidy is getting less and less. This has increased once again the tensions between the SPA and local governments.[6]

7.4.3 Territorial structure of the state and the politics of collective provision

The two governance initiatives were respectively launched in the 1990s and 2000s. The territorial structure of Hsinchu city-region meanwhile underwent some fundamental changes due to the reorganization of government system and the alteration of science park policy in Taiwan. This has created two major differences between the two initiatives. The first is the internal organization of the state regarding the institutional function of the primary actors in these two initiatives. The downscaling of Taiwan's provincial government at the end of the 1990s saw most of its competencies either ceded to national government or devolved to local government. No one succeeded its role in co-ordinating regional planning and development, and mediating intergovernmental disputes between national and local government, as well as between city and county governments. Its downscaling not only led to an end of the HSC development plan, but also increased the institutional barriers of intergovernmental co-operation to conduct spatial planning and development at city-regional level. Furthermore, since the alteration of science park policy, the SPA has had no need to seek new land in Hsinchu city-region to accommodate the growing high-tech industrial activities of the HSP, because five other sites in northern Taiwan have been successively designated as satellite parks of HSP (see Figure 7.2 and Table 7.3). In other words, the SPA's space of dependence has been enlarged and thus the SPA lost its motivation to promote high-tech-oriented spatial planning in Hsinchu city-region. The two primary actors thus withdrew from city-regional governance.

The second major difference between the two initiatives is the mechanisms employed by local governments to place demands on the national state. The alternation of science park policy implied a politics of managing uneven development in the wider national territory (for details see Hsu, 2010). Coming together with the withdrawal of the two primary actors, at the beginning of the 2000s local governments faced a very difficult situation in gaining support from the national government to deal with the issues of collective consumption arising as a consequence of the rapid growth of the city-region's high-tech industries. As a result, instead of employing the spatial imaginary to construct a local economic space that can crystallize different interests and build a common vision for the city-region as they did in the 1980s and 1990s, local governments turned to using their new powers, such as those relating to environmental protection, to influence the SPA's operation, and of its tenant companies. This reminded the SPA of the necessity of co-operating with local governments. The local strategy and its consequences demonstrate that although the SPA's space of dependence has enlarged, the local dependence of the SPA remains and becomes a bargaining chip for local governments to construct a space of engagement.

In addition to the two major differences, one significant similarity between the two governance initiatives can be identified regarding the underlying logic of the national state's response. In both cases, when the local governments tried to construct a space of engagement to make demands on the national state, the national state, in response to the demands, created new governance spaces, that defined 'the rules of engagement'. The rules of engagement expressed the major concern of the national government regarding the provision of local collective consumption, namely the reproduction of labour power of the HSP development.

Table 7.3 Summary of the two governance initiatives

	Hsinchu Science City Development Plan (1986–1994)	Governor Forum (since 2002)
Constellation of primary actor	– Before 1990 Hsinchu city government, Hsinchu county government, SPA, and the other three knowledge institutes – After 1990 NSC, SPA and Taiwan provincial government	SPA, Hsinchu city government, Hsinchu county government, and ASIP
Institutional function (internal organization of the state)	– National government: Global production and national collective provision of production infrastructure – SPA: HSP development – Taiwan provincial government: Coordinating and mediating regional development and collective provision – Local governments: Local collective provision	– National government: Global production and national/regional collective provision – SPA: Developing HSP Hsinchu site, Zhunan site, Tonguluo site, Biomedical site, Lontan site and Yilan site – Local governments: Local collective provision
The ways in which demands are made on the state (state inputs)	– Formation of the HSC planning steering group – Initiation of the HSC planning project	– From 2000 to 2002: Using new authorities to strive for collaboration with SPA and its tenant companies – After 2003: Asking for subsidies/community payments through Governor Forum
National state intervention (state outputs)	– Brought the project into the national development plan – Played a dominant role in determining the content of the HSC development plan – Investment of collective production infrastructure	– Initiation of the Governor Forum – Promulgation of the Principles for the Allocation of Science Park Subsidy for Local Development

In the case of the HSC project, the national government designated the National Science Council and Taiwan's provincial government as being in charge of planning. Consequently, planning emphasized strengthening the competitiveness of HSP rather than the competitiveness of the city-region as a whole. The HSC development plan mainly recognized as priorities the development projects that could contribute to the HSP development in the short term, including the land supply for high-tech industrial development, the housing provision for knowledge workers, the construction or improvement of production infrastructure and facilities, and the enhancement of business services and cultural amenities (SPA and TPG, 1993, pp. 10–16). The issues of social polarization, environmental protection and the provision of basic education and other basic facilities were either neglected or left to the long-term development list. The major challenge for the local governments to gain support from the national government and/or high-tech sectors is to convince them that to resolve local growth-related issues is beneficial for them. This chimes with what Jonas *et al.* (2010) noted, that too much emphasis on the specific preferences of the high-tech sectors may tend to neglect or impinge 'a range of other political and economic dimensions of "quality-of-life" that ought to be factored into the local spatial development milieu' (Jonas *et al.*, 2010, p. 186; emphasis in the original).

In the case of the Governor Forum, the national government promulgated the allocation principles to define the scope and the geographical scale of the subsidy. Specifically, only when the local development project had direct influence on the science park development, would the national government provide the subsidy to the local government. In comparison with the initiative of the HSC development plan, the initiative of the Governor Forum and the promulgation of subsidy allocation principles were more pragmatic for the local governments to resolve the issues of collective provision. Nevertheless, the bounds of the subsidy area have led to a situation in which it is difficult for the primary actors in the forum to draw attention to other issues concerning the wider socio-spatial impacts of the HSP development and the future development of the city-region as a whole.

There is no particular rule to define the scope of discussion subjects and the constellation of actors in the forum. Too much focus on the allocation of subsidy became the major obstacle to widening the scope of agenda and seeking new possibilities of collaboration with other regional actors. This implies that the primary actors in the city-region now lose sight of the spatial imaginary beyond their territories and at a higher scale. The mapping and naming of Hsinchu high-tech city-region in reality only exists in academic studies rather than in territorial politics. This may be the result of three factors: (a) the failed experience of the HSC development plan; (b) local governments' overemphasis on financial measures in dealing with the issues of collective consumption; and (c) national government neglect of the connections between the state-led science park development and locally based, growth-related issues in the city-region.

7.5 Concluding remarks

Considering other technopole developments throughout the world, such as around Cambridge UK and the Boston metropolitan area, the experience of the local governments in Hsinchu city-region in addressing high-tech growth-related problems is by no means unique (see Jonas *et al.*, 2010; While *et al.*, 2004). Although the mechanisms employed to resolve the problems might vary according to the place-specific territorial structures of the state, two interrelated lessons can be drawn from the territorial politics of collective provision in Hsinchu city-region. These are the importance of linkages between national and local interests, and the avoidance of overstating the specific preferences of high-tech sectors.

First, the case of HSC development plan shows the power of spatial imaginary in crystallizing local and national interests. By manipulating high-tech economic discourses – such as the importance of quality of life to attract knowledge workers – and the spatial imaginary, the local governments successfully constructed a space of engagement and linked the localized, growth-related issues of collective provision with the future development of HSP, which was nationally important, to gain national government's support. The spatial imaginary was animated and further consolidated by a series of spatial planning practices. However, in the case of the Governor Forum the new governance space defined by the national government has provided a more effective way to channel subsidies to assist in certain localized issues of collective provision. But at the same time both the SPA and the local governments have lost the motivation to seek a common vision for the city-region.

This has increased the fragmentation of governance in the city-region and decreased the institutional capacity to manage the tensions and conflicts between different sectors generated in the high-tech development process. The experience in Hsinchu city-region shows that it is problematic to consider only financial measures in managing the tensions and conflicts between high-tech economic development and the collective provision of social and physical infrastructure, but also to artificially separate the growth-related issues of collective consumption from high-tech development.

Second, in the process of crystallizing different interests, 'the task' is continuously redefined due to the changing actor constellations and their major concerns. The case of the HSC development plan indicates that there are some possibilities to link the provision of local collective consumption with the elements of high-tech development, but if in the process we overstate the specific preferences of high-tech sectors, it may be at the expense of certain local interests, such as environmental sustainability, social inclusion and spatial justice.

Nonetheless, the experience in Hsinchu city-region also demonstrates that redefining 'the task' is deeply influenced by the territorial structure of the state as well as the constellations of the primary actor in the governance spaces. It implies that the redefinition is a politics that involves different levels and branches of government as well as other actors, who are locally dependent.

In other words, involving various social organizations, which are locally based, in the redefining process may be a way to raise the level and widen the social bases of the technopole development, but also to avoid overstating specific preferences of high-tech sectors in the development process.

Notes

1   According to Castells (1977), collective consumption, which sometimes is referred to as the local 'quality of life', is associated with the reproduction of labour power, because production depends upon not only the existence of physical resources but also on a healthy workforce. However, in the past two decades, other wider social, cultural and environmental concerns, such as environmental sustainability and social inclusion, have gradually been taken into consideration and enrich the concept of local quality of life. Nowadays, the concept of collective consumption is associated with but not confined to the reproduction of labour power (Cox, 2011).
2   The constitution of Taiwan gave provinces the right of self-government, but the additional articles of the constitution promulgated in 1998 restricted the self-government right of provinces and let the provincial administration become an appointed body of the Executive Yuan rather than a local self-governing body. The additional articles are the revisions and amendments to the original constitution in order to meet current requisites and political status of Taiwan.
3   From 1996 to 2000, Hsinchu City Government launched a fundraising campaign for improving the local environment and transport system adjacent to the park and the old town. The local government also solicited the tenant companies of the park for sharing the cost of certain urban redevelopment projects, but the result was not so successful. In 2000, the United Microelectronics Corporation event occurred. The high-tech company, located in the park, accused Hsinchu city government of abusing the authority of the environmental impact assessment to squeeze the tenant companies to raise funds for urban redevelopment (for details please see Chou, 2007, p. 1393).
4   According to an in-depth interview with the Director General of Science Park Administration on 13 October 2011.
5   On the basis of in-depth interviews with several urban planning and development related officials of Hsinchu city government and Hsinchu county government in October 2011.
6   According to NOWnews, in 28 December 2010 at the eleventh Governor Forum, the Hsinchu County Government asked the SPA to revise the allocation principles in order to secure the amount of subsidy, but the Director General of the SPA responded that it was not reasonable for the SPA to borrow money for local subsidies, since the operational fund is deep in debt. He indicated that national government was considering asking local governments to share the costs of the science park development, because the science park development had positive effects for local economy. He further addressed that the local governments should alter their attitude. When the local governments proposed subsidy plans to the SPA, they should also take the science park development into account. (www.nownews.com/2010/12/28/11462-2677441.htm (accessed on 29 December 2010).

Bibliography

Annerstedt, J. (2006) 'Science parks and high-tech clustering', in *International handbook on industrial policy*. Cheltenham: Edward Elgar.

Carter, N. (1989) *Science parks: Development and management*. Abingdon: Taylor & Francis.

Castells, M. (1977) *The urban question: A Marxist approach*. Cambridge, MA: MIT Press.

Castells, M. (1989) *The informational city: Information technology, economic restructuring, and the urban-regional process*. London: Wiley-Blackwell.

Castells, M. and Hall, P.A. (1994) *Technopoles of the world: The making of 21st century industrial complexes*. London: Routledge.

CEPD (1981) *Urban and regional development statistics 1980*. Taipei City.

CEPD (1991) *Urban and regional development statistics 1990*. Taipei City.

CEPD (1996) *Urban and regional development statistics 1995*. Taipei City.

CEPD (2001) *Urban and regional development statistics 2001*. Taipei City.

CEPD (2013) *Urban and regional development statistics 2013*. Taipei City.

Chang, S., Chiu, H. and Tu, W. (2004) 'The silence of silicon lambs: Speaking out health and environmental impacts within Taiwan's Hsinchu Science-based industrial park', in *2004 IEEE International Symposium on Electronics and the Environment, 2004. Conference Record*. Presented at the 2004 IEEE International Symposium on Electronics and the Environment, 2004. Conference Record, pp. 258–63. doi:10. 1109/ISEE.2004.1299726.

Chen, L.C. (2001) 'High-tech fantasies: Hsinchu science-based industrial park and local development' (Master's thesis). Taipei City: National Taiwan Normal University.

Chou, T.-L. (2007) 'The science park and the governance challenge of the movement of the high-tech urban region towards polycentricity: The Hsinchu science-based industrial park'. *Environ. Plann. A 39*, 1382–402. doi:10.1068/a38200.

Cox, K. (2003) 'The territorial structure of the state: Some critical reflections', in *Territorial restructurings, comparisons and innovations*. Presented at the French–South African meeting on territorial innovation.

Cox, K.R. (1993) 'The local and the global in the new urban politics: A critical view'. *Environment and Planning D: Society and Space*, *11*: 433–48. doi:10.1068/d110433.

Cox, K.R. (1998) 'Spaces of dependence, spaces of engagement and the politics of scale, or: Looking for local politics'. *Political Geography*, *17*: 1–23. doi:10.1016/S0962–6298(97)00048–6.

Cox, K.R. (2011) 'Commentary. From the new urban politics to the "new" metropolitan politics'. *Urban Studies*, *48*: 2661–71. doi:10.1177/0042098011413947.

Cox, K.R. and Jonas, A.E.G. (1993) 'Urban development, collective consumption and the politics of metropolitan fragmentation'. *Political Geography*, *12*: 8–37. doi:10.1016/0962–6298(93)90022-Y.

Dicken, P. (2003) *Global shift: Reshaping the global economic map in the 21st century*. London: Sage.

Fujita, M. (2008) *The flowchart approach to industrial cluster policy*. London: Palgrave Macmillan/Ide-Jetro.

Harvey, D. (1982) *The limits to capital*. Chicago, IL: University of Chicago Press.

Hsieh, H.-N., Hu, T.-S., Ko, T.-C. and Hsueh, P.-P. (2005) 'A study of the spatial evolution of production activities around Hsinchu Science-based Industrial Park'. *Environment and Worlds*, *11*: 1–30.

Hsu, J. (2010) 'State transformation and regional development in Taiwan: From developmentalist strategy to populist subsidy'. *International Journal of Urban and Regional Research*, *35*: 600–19. doi:10.1111/j.1468–2427.2010.00971.x.

Hu, T.-S., Lin, C.-Y. and Chang, S.-L. (2005a) 'Role of interaction between techno-logical communities and industrial clustering in innovative activity: The case of Hsinchu District, Taiwan'. *Urban Studies*, *42*: 1139–60. doi:10.1080/030562405 00121230.

Hu, T.-S., Lin, C.-Y. and Chang, S.-L. (2005b) 'Technology-based regional develop-ment strategies and the emergence of technological communities: A case study of HSIP, Taiwan'. *Technovation*, *25*: 367–80. doi:10.1016/j.technovation.2003.09.002.

Huang, W.-J. (2013) 'Spatial planning and high-tech development: A comparative study of Eindhoven city-region, the Netherlands and Hsinchu City-region, Taiwan'. PhD thesis series on Architecture and the Built Environment. TU Delft.

Jessop, B. (1997) 'A neo-Gramscian approach to the regulation of urban regimes', in Lauria (ed.) *Reconstructing urban regime theory: Regulating urban politics in a global economy* (pp. 51–76). Thousand Oaks, CA: Sage.

Jhan, L.-W. (2008) 地方公共事務協力化管理之研究 - 以"科學園區等理局與新竹縣、市首長高層會議"為例 ['The research for collaborative management of local public affairs: The case study of science park administration, Hsinchu County, and Hsinchu City Heads meeting']. 中國地方自治 [*Zhong Guo Di Fang Zi Zhi*] *61*: 27–42.

Jonas, A.E.G., While, A.H. and Gibbs, D.C. (2010) 'Managing infrastructural and service demands in new economic spaces: The new territorial politics of collective provision'. *Regional Studies*, *44*: 183–200. doi:10.1080/00343400802662666.

Keeble, D.E. (1989) 'High-technology industry and regional development in Britain: The case of the Cambridge phenomenon'. *Environment and Planning C: Government and Policy*, *7*: 153–72. doi:10.1068/c070153.

Komninos, N. (2002) *Intelligent cities: Innovation, knowledge systems, and digital spaces*. London and New York: Spon Press.

Kuchiki, A. and Tsuji, M. (eds) (2005) *Industrial clusters in Asia: Analyses of their competition and cooperation*. Basingstoke: Palgrave Macmillan.

Kuchiki, A. and Tsuji, M. (2008) *The flowchart approach to industrial cluster policy*. New York: Palgrave Macmillan.

Lagendijk, A. and Boekema, F. (2008) 'Global circulation and territorial development: South-east brabant from a relational perspective'. *European Planning Studies*, *16*: 925–39. doi:10.1080/09654310802163710.

Lin, C. (2006) 城市空間治理的創新策略: 三個台灣首都城市案例評析: 台北·新竹·高雄 [*Innovative strategies for spatial governance: Case studies of three capital cities in Taiwan*]. Third Nature.

Lin, C.-Y. (2010) 'Planning and development of industrial land in Taiwan', in *Planning in Taiwan: Spatial planning in the twenty-first century* (pp. 164–95). London: Routledge.

Lin, Y.-W., 2007. 竹科回饋金制度探討-交易成本觀點 ['Exploration of the Hsinchu Science Park compensation mechanism: From the transit cost perspective']. Presented at the Local Autonomy and Democratic Development: Reflections on Taiwan experience, Taichung.

MacLeod, G. and Goodwin, M. (1999) 'Reconstructing an urban and regional political economy: On the state, politics, scale, and explanation'. *Political Geography*, *18*: 697–730. doi:10.1016/S0962–6298(99)00014–1.

National Science Council (2011) 101年度科學工業園區管理局作業基金附屬單位預算報告 [*2012 Annual Budget Report of the Operational Fund of Science Park Adminstration*].

Simmie, J. (1994) 'Technopole planning in Britain, France, Japan and the USA'. *Planning Practice and Research*, *9*: 7–20. doi:10.1080/02697459408722906.

Simmie, J. (2012) 'Learning city regions: Theory and practice in private and public sector spatial planning'. *Planning Practice and Research*, *27*: 423–39. doi:10.1080/02697459.2012.686223.

SPA (2010) *Hsinchu Science-based Industrial Park: Special issue for thirtieth anniversary*. Science Park Administration, Hsinchu.

SPA (2012) *2011 Hsinchu Science Park yearly report*. Science Park Administration, Hsinchu.

SPA and TPG (1993) 新竹科學城發展計畫：摘要 [Hsinchu Science City development plan: Summary].

Sternberg, R. (1996a) 'Regional growth theories and high_tech regions'. *International Journal of Urban and Regional Research*, *20*: 518–38. doi:10.1111/j.1468-2427.1996.tb00331.x.

Sternberg, R. (1996b) 'Reasons for the genesis of high-tech regions: Theoretical explanation and empirical evidence'. *Geoforum*, *27*: 205–23. doi:10.1016/0016-7185(96)00007-3.

Taipei City Government (2007) *Municipal statistics weekly report (No. 410)*. Taipei City: Taipei City Government.

While, A., Jonas, A.E.G. and Gibbs, D.C. (2004) 'Unblocking the city? Growth pressures, collective provision, and the search for new spaces of governance in Greater Cambridge, England'. *Environment and Planning A*, *36*: 279–304. doi:10.1068/a3615.

8 Suburbs in the cognitive-cultural capitalist economy

Limits to the suburban knowledge and creative strategies in Madrid and Lisbon

Mário Vale

8.1 Introduction

Since the influential work of Castells and Hall (1994) on the successes (and failures) of technopoles and science parks and the process of technological innovation in different regions of the world, virtually all European regions developed innovation policies targeting high-tech entrepreneurship and highly skilled employment creation. The ability to bridge gaps between new firms, universities and other science and technology public bodies has been a crucial element within the rationale underpinning technopoles and science parks policy. From the perspective of innovation as a social process, the interaction of myriad actors in the same geographical bounded space is the major fundamental factor favouring innovation dynamics (Moulaert and Sekia, 2003; Vale, 2011). However, the outcomes achieved by technopoles have been subject to strong scrutiny, to the point of being considered mere 'high-tech fantasies' (Massey, Quintas and Wield, 1992). Thus, it is quite understandable that technopoles and science parks remain a relevant research and policy research topic.

The typical location of technopoles favoured the periphery of large, dynamic urban areas, consisting of a series of low-density built-up areas providing a campus-like atmosphere (Castells and Hall, 1994). Suburban economies are also expanding their inventive and creative character, attracting creative workers, developing new social and political identities in the post-Fordist capitalist economy. Albeit imperceptibly within the strategies, policies and discourses of regions and cities in the knowledge economy, suburbs have come to be a relevant place for the location of not only ordinary economic activities but also advanced ones with significant creative and innovative content within their products and services.

The emergence of the knowledge and the creative economy illustrates clearly the intricate relations between cities and suburbs. Suburbs rightfully aim at attracting innovative and creative economic activities, thus contributing to the cognitive-cultural economic development of large metropolises (Scott, 2008). Yet, strategies for city core and suburbs respectively are often poorly coordinated at city-region level, hampering the overall outcome of public investments upon these advanced sectors of the urban and regional economies. Hence, the relations between city and suburb economies demand a more nuanced inquiry approach, which brings us in the context of this chapter to claim, in the same way Phelps (2012) did, that simplistic categorizations of the economies of city and suburbs are inaccurate in complex and large city-regions, particularly in the context of the cognitive-cultural capitalist economy.

The chapter's objective is twofold. First, it examines the emergence and development of the cognitive-cultural capitalist economy in the city-region (Scott, 2008), reviewing policy initiatives and outcomes in cities and suburban areas. Second, the chapter intends to shed some light on the current debate of (post)suburban development in the post-Fordist capitalist economy in the city-region context (European Commission, 2011, Carvalho, 2013). In order to develop the relationship between the cognitive-cultural economy and the suburban areas of large cities, this chapter articulates three different literatures, namely the literature on the innovation and knowledge locations, the literature on culture and creative economy and the literature on the suburban development.

In this chapter, I begin by discussing the emergence and development of the cognitive-cultural capitalist economy and how it relates to the city-region (see Section 8.2). I then examine why and how suburban areas evolve from a simple strategy of attracting businesses to more ambitious goals targeting high-technology firms and lately creative industries (Section 8.3). Subsequently, I discuss what have been the outcomes of such policies in suburban areas of Madrid and Lisbon, paying particular attention to how inner-city regeneration strategies challenge those suburban knowledge economy development strategies and how public investment decline as a result of the economic crisis has negatively affected suburban economic development (Section 8.4). Preliminary findings suggest that powerful competitiveness and creativity narratives go hand in hand with ambitious European and regional/local policies in what may be a case of policy circulation with some obvious constraints on suburban areas. This leads us to conclude that imitative strategies blind to specific place-capabilities are to say the least sterile and threaten suburban growth and that an integrated policy designed and delivered at metropolitan level is best suited to overcome limits to the suburban knowledge and creative development (Section 8.5).

8.2 Knowledge, cultural and creative economies and the city

The theoretical discussion articulates three different literatures to examine the relation between the knowledge-based economy, on one hand, and the culture and creative economy, on the other, in the context of the city-region. While these two literatures inform the discussion below, the following section incorporates these findings and the arguments from the literature on suburban development, with the aim of illuminating the complex relations between the knowledge, cultural and creativity economies and suburban development in large city-regions.

Despite the reduction of transport costs for goods, people and information and the various political agreements to form a global market, the truth is that the spatial concentration of people and activities remains an indelible feature of contemporary economic geography (Rodríguez-Pose and Crescenzi, 2008). Moreover, technological change and the importance of knowledge and innovation have somewhat paradoxically continued to strengthen urban agglomeration processes.

Over the last three decades, European regions have shifted toward adopting innovation policies targeting high-tech entrepreneurship and high-skilled employment creation. Technopoles and science parks stood out among other technological and innovation policy initiatives; they have been pivotal in bridging gaps among firms, universities and other science and technology institutions. Castells and Hall (1994) argued that cities – and clearly large metropolitan areas – are powerful new economic actors able to act in a more flexible and effective way in a globalized economy than national governments, which '. . . suffer from failing powers to act upon the functional processes that shape their economies and societies' (p. 7).

Although cities cannot rival state power, they are increasingly defining competitive strategies and targeting specific projects addressing markets, technologies, cultures (or a mixture of all of these), seeking to attract and secure new sources of income, wealth and prestige. Technopoles' formation occurred during a period of globalization, marked by the resurgence of cities and the rise of the information society, becoming very popular in cities across Europe and North America, trying to emulate the paradigmatic Silicon Valley in the San Francisco Bay Area. The focus on innovation led to several endeavours akin to technopoles, although most were unable to deliver the expected results, especially those in peripheral regions and some of them in developed regions that were mere real estate development projects.

After more than thirty years of technopole developments, cities and regions are facing new challenges associated with the rise of the cognitive-cultural capitalist economy. Certainly, many aspects are similar to those associated with the information society, but the focus on knowledge and creativity are powerful driving forces for cities' growth strategies. Some scholars have put forward new concepts aimed at analysing the new role of cities in the global economy, such as 'world cities' (Friedmann and Wolff, 1982), 'global cities' (Sassen, 2000; 2001) and 'regional motors' (Scott, 1998). Sassen (2000) claims that:

> [. . .] the combination of geographic dispersal of economic activities and system integration that lies at the heart of the current economic era has

contributed to a strategic role for major cities. Rather than becoming obsolete because of the dispersal made possible by information technologies, cities instead concentrate command functions.

(p. 22)

Cities' coordination ability relies on the spatial agglomeration of knowledge-intensive services, availability of high-quality information and communication (ICT) networks, concentration of large international corporations and a pool of highly skilled labour.

From a different perspective, Florida (2002) argues that creative professionals are increasingly relevant for the economic development of cities, which in turn should seek to provide an ideal 'atmosphere' for attracting and retaining highly skilled and creative mobile professionals. Moreover, cities' resurgence stems from the increasing importance of the intangible and symbolic dimensions of value creation, both fundamental in this new phase of cognitive-cultural capitalism (Scott, 2008). According to Hall (2000):

cities across Europe [. . .] have become taken with the idea that cultural or creative industries (a term that 20 years ago no one would have understood, and might even have thought offensive) may provide the basis for economic regeneration.

(p. 640)

Internationally successful cities provide quality, inclusive and safe public spaces, diversified services and retail, and a vibrant cultural environment. According to Florida (2002), 'jobs follow people', because more advanced activities require skilled labour, mainly located in big cities. Conversely, Glaeser, Kolko and Saiz (2001) argue that 'people follow amenities', which in any event continues to reinforce the city as a space of consumption and leisure.

Cities are not merely spaces that allow a reduction in transport costs; they are informational entities that exist to accelerate knowledge and learning processes, through technological innovation, knowledge spillovers and human capital externalities. Cities increase the possibility of occasional events that create new opportunities, particularly relevant in the innovative activities with a strong presence of SMEs and start-ups, giving them advantages of scale and range (Glaeser, 2000). In addition, Jacobs (1969) advocates that urbanization economies take place through the exchange of complementary knowledge across different economic agents. Indeed, knowledge spillovers are not limited to a specific technology (Jaffe, Trajtenberg and Henderson, 1992), meaning that the diversity of cities is important for innovation dynamics.

In any case, cities are privileged knowledge locations for the new phase of capitalism development. In Europe, the formation of a knowledge-based economy (KBE) has its foundations in large, competitive and innovative cities. The geography of the KBE is dominated by large cities (though different as they are), where knowledge is produced, processed, exchanged and marketed (Van Winden, Van Den Berg and Pol, 2007), benefiting from high-quality knowledge institutions, transport and communication infrastructures (airports, ICT networks), human resources and amenities and quality of life. Science parks are specially designed infrastructures to promote technological innovation at city level, although the role of integration of these knowledge locations in the urban fabric only recently become an object of study (Van Winden *et al.*, 2013), even if there is no stable conclusion on what kind of urban integration – vibrant inner-city atmosphere or quiet suburban green area? – might generate better urban knowledge and innovation outcomes (Carvalho, 2013).

8.3 Suburbia: towards a cognitive-cultural economy?

This section explores the relationship between the cognitive-cultural economy and suburban areas of large cities, seeking to examine the contemporary development strategies of city-regions. Creative and knowledge narratives, strategies and policies have a strong hold on city-regions, but there remains a lack of research regarding how different urban spaces – city core, former industrial sites, suburban areas, rural hinterlands – are articulated in this new economy. However, before exploring that main question, it is first necessary to more precisely specify the concept and meanings of suburbs and other related spatial categories as presented in the literature.

8.3.1 Defining urban, suburban and rural relations

There is, admittedly, a lack of study of urban-suburban-rural relations, although current assumptions state they can generate positive externalities and expand regional competitiveness (OECD, 2010). As an element of the Fordist capital accumulation process (Harvey, 1985), suburbs have been overlooked until very recently in terms of their economic relevance for growth and employment, innovation and knowledge territorial dynamics (Phelps, 2012). Despite residential functions predominant in the traditional suburbs, new forms of urban fabric have come to exist where important economic activities are located, creating new spatial concepts, such as 'technoburb' (Fishman, 1987), 'edge city' (Garreau, 1991), or 'exurbia' (Soja, 2000).

The interdependence between the centre and periphery may be applied to the city and hinterland in which a city disseminates innovations and capital flows towards rural areas, while the latter provide resources and labour to the urban core (Smetkowski *et al.*, 2011). However, the traditional urban-rural relation is changing and new spatialities are emerging enabled through more efficient transport and communication systems. Several authors have highlighted the existence of less hierarchical relations between the core and periphery in city-regions. Indeed, strong polarization effects and hierarchical relations are becoming less evident and new urban poles are growing along transportation and communication axes, thus exposing the fragility of the foundations of the modern metropolis organization theories. The typical daily commuter flows in a large metropolitan area reveal a concentration of jobs in the core, although lateral and inverse commuting movements are increasing at least in part due to a more complex location pattern of economic activities. At the same time, residential economies are developing at the edge of cities leading to an extension of travel-to-work areas, and possible 'increasing returns to scale' gains in post-suburban areas due to the clustering of economic activities.

The spatialities found at the edge of city-regions have been gaining new designations, such as outer-suburbs, exurbs or post-suburbs,[1] reflecting the new spatial configurations of the post-Fordist economy (Keil, 1994; Phelps *et al.*, 2006; Phelps, 2010). These spatial configurations strengthen the horizontal links between localities in a city-region, blurring the hierarchical and unidirectional relations between cities and their suburbs, particularly in commuting flows, caused by the delocalization of economic activities to the periphery and the location of new business initiatives in nodes of the metropolitan transport network. Indeed, smaller cities may have special meaning in a rebalancing city and suburban relations in city-regions, in relation to commuting, economic relations, collective services provision, cultural and environmental amenities (OECD, 2010). Certainly, the reconfiguration of urban-rural linkages is a clear matter for policy concern in city-regions (OECD, 2011).

8.3.2 Suburban cognitive-cultural economy

The rise of the cognitive-cultural economy has deep implications for the urban development process, both overcoming divides between industry and commerce on the one hand, and arts and culture on the other, of the Fordist city, as well as meshing production, work, leisure, the arts and the physical milieu (Scott, 2014). This phase of economic development demands a high level of cognitive and cultural skills, generically designated by some as creative competences. Along with the transformation of the economy,

> [. . .] significant rearrangements of intra-urban space have also come about. Among the more dramatic of these changes is the revitalization of selected areas in the city, most especially in and around the urban core.
>
> (Scott, 2014, p. 572)

Yet, suburban economies are changing too and become more aligned with the emerging cognitive-cultural capitalist economy, where regional governing structures lack appropriate responses from the lack of innovation and creative policy coordination at metropolitan level, hampering the potential development of city-regions.

Employment decentralization shaped the traditional urban-suburban-rural relations, reinforced by science and technological innovation policies, including the foundation of technological infrastructures on new 'greenfield' parks in urban peripheries seeking to boost firm formation and job creation in knowledge-intensive activities. A proportion of the cultural cognitive economy has been 'organised' into particular campus spaces (such as science parks and science cities), which have formed one key ingredient of the suburban matrix, and even according to some a new urbanity (O'Mara, 2005; Forsyth and Crewe, 2010; Mozingo, 2011). The case of technopoles' suburban location illustrates processes of high-tech employment decentralisation (Castells and Hall, 1994), even if these planned agglomerations lack in most cases strong linkages between universities and firms, and have been not even been very successful in stimulating innovation at the regional level (Cooke, 2001). These high-tech agglomerations, planned by public authorities (state or municipality), evolved over time, in many cases becoming more than exclusively spatial concentrations of new economic activities or new urban centralities in the outskirts of city-regions.

It is precisely in this context that suburban agglomerations in large metropolitan regions devised strategies and plans for exploring new opportunities in the emerging cognitive-cultural economy, often in competition with the metropolitan core. In fact, Phelps *et al.*, 2006) '[. . .] argue that these spaces are also socially and politically dynamic' (p. 13). Often, for a suburban local authority the issue is not so much installing innovative activities, such as simply attracting companies in more advanced sectors (even if not very innovative) to thereby create more skilled jobs and increase retention rates of the working population living in the local area. Hence, in the framework of pro-growth political coalitions (Phelps, 2010), a number of suburban (or post-suburban) authorities started to develop their own strategies and policies to create knowledge and creativity sites, often *in competition with* the metropolitan core and with other suburban localities, not always aligned with regional/national knowledge and innovation strategies and policies.

Despite suburban attempts to develop projects in cultural and creative sectors, cities' cores remain attractive locations too for knowledge-intensive firms and creative and cultural activities, combining important agglomeration economy effects and providing a suitable atmosphere for creation and innovation (Musterd and Murie, 2010). Moreover, city cores have benefited from the new cognitive-cultural economy, as one can observe in the revitalization of selected areas in and around the urban core (Scott, 2014). Thus, suburban economic development faces two major threats, both of which demand integrated metropolitan policies to deliver growth and well-being at city-region level.

The first is related to the spatial concentration of creative- and knowledge-intensive activities in the inner-city, linked particularly to large-scale urban regeneration interventions and central business district redevelopment (Scott, 2014), exploring Jacobs' economic diversity opportunities (Swyngedouw, Moulaert and Rodriguez, 2002). Obviously, peripheral science parks, technopoles, creative incubators and knowledge infrastructures in metropolitan non-core areas face competition from these inner-city knowledge and creativity location infrastructures. The second threat is a structural and pervasive one, originating from the financial crisis and increased difficulties in accessing cheap credit, resulting from the austerity crisis, particularly in the countries of Southern Europe. Overall, the crisis' effect on consumption has severely affected cultural and creative activities (Mendez, 2013; Ferrão, 2013), precisely those that have been supported by local authorities in the fringe of city-regions.

8.4 Madrid and Lisbon cognitive-cultural economies

The cases of the Madrid and Lisbon city-regions illustrate the tensions between city-core and suburban areas' development strategies in the emerging cognitive-cultural capitalist economy. In both cases, suburban economies evolved from a strong dependency upon the city-core towards more autonomous economic development, supported by ambitious local policies, alongside relevant urban regeneration interventions in city cores, focused on cultural and creative development. In analysing these two cases, we seek to shed light on the complex relations between suburbs and inner-city in large city-regions, aiming at better policy coordination underpinning the development of the cognitive-cultural economy in large city-regions.

8.4.1 Madrid and Lisbon: urbanization and infrastructure development of two European capitals

Madrid and Lisbon are the capitals of Spain and Portugal respectively. Madrid is the largest urban agglomeration in the Iberian Peninsula and the third largest in the European Union (after London and Paris). Its population reaches 6 million inhabitants with 54.2 per cent of the total population of the Madrid metropolitan area concentrated in the city of Madrid (Table 8.1). Lisbon is the largest Portuguese urban agglomeration, and the third in Iberian Peninsula (after Madrid and Barcelona), with 2.7 million inhabitants. Around 20 per cent of the total population of the Lisbon metropolitan area are located in Lisbon municipality.

Both Madrid and Lisbon benefit from national capital effects and are the major agglomerations of knowledge-based economy activities and creative activities in Spain and Portugal respectively. Madrid metropolitan region has a much larger creative economy sector, but Lisbon metropolitan region has a relatively higher share of creative economy employment at the national level (Table 8.2). This illustrates the differences between the national urban systems: in Spain the city of Barcelona is also challenging Madrid's leading role in the creative economy, whereas in Portugal, Lisbon's leading role remains unchallenged, despite recent efforts made by Porto supported by national and European Structural Funds. Interestingly the city of Madrid has a huge share of total metropolitan area creative sector employment (71.5 per cent), which compares with 47 per cent in Lisbon municipality. In both cases, the

Table 8.1 Madrid and Lisbon metropolitan areas

City-region	Number of municipalities	Population (000's)	% Population in the core municipality
Madrid	52	6,028	54.2
Lisbon	18	2,718	20.1

Source: Adapted from López Trigal (2013), p. 47.

Table 8.2 Employment in the creative economy in Madrid and Lisbon metropolitan areas, 2009

City-region	Employment (000's)	% of cultural and creative employment at national level	% of cultural and creative employment in core city
Madrid	207.1	29.3	71.5
Lisbon	54.6	56.6	47.0

Source: Adapted from Méndez *et al.* (2012); André and Vale (2012).

localization trend of these activities indicates a strong tendency to agglomerate in the city's consolidated central areas (Méndez *et al.*, 2012, André and Vale; 2012).

Since EU accession, the two capitals of the Iberian nation-states captured a large share of inward investment flows, concentrated important in-migration flows and built large infrastructures that supported urban growth and facilitated regional economies' internationalization processes. Madrid became a global city with very significant links to South America and a pivotal role in the Iberian urban system, in part a consequence of strategic decisions to expand Barajas airport and the development of the high-speed train system connecting large urban areas in Spain[2] (López Trigal, 2013). Madrid is the primary Iberian city-region for knowledge-intensive business services, financial services, corporations' headquarters and high-quality cultural facilities (Méndez *et al.*, 2012). Madrid witnessed a rapid demographic growth, as well as an intense urbanization process within the city-region fringe. The development of road and rail infrastructures (including the Atocha rail terminus, underground transport system, tunnelling of the M30 in the Manzanares, and the construction of the M40/M50 motorways) sustained the expansion of the built-up area, and made possible several flagship projects in the fringe of the city-region (Figure 8.1).

As a typical capital city, Lisbon city has a remarkable concentration of large companies' headquarters, administrative functions, financial system and knowledge-intensive business services. Similar to Madrid, national and local governments invested heavily in road and rail infrastructures, supporting both the internationalization process and the expansion of the city-region (including the CREL (outer) and CRIL (inner) ring roads, North-South connection, the Lisbon-Cascais A5 motorway, the widening of IC19 Lisbon-Sintra, the iconic *Vasco da Gama* bridge, and the introduction of railway to the *25 Abril* bridge) (Figure 8.2). The infrastructure development initiatives led to a population decrease in the city of Lisbon and to a rapid increase in suburban and outer metropolitan municipalities, in spite of large-scale urban interventions, such as the EXPO 98 on the Lisbon city waterfront (André and Vale, 2012). The absence of an administrative political power is still a major issue in the Lisbon city-region (Barata-Salgueiro, 2006), exacerbated by political fragmentation (eighteen municipalities in the Lisbon metropolitan area), hindering the design and implementation of a coherent development strategy.

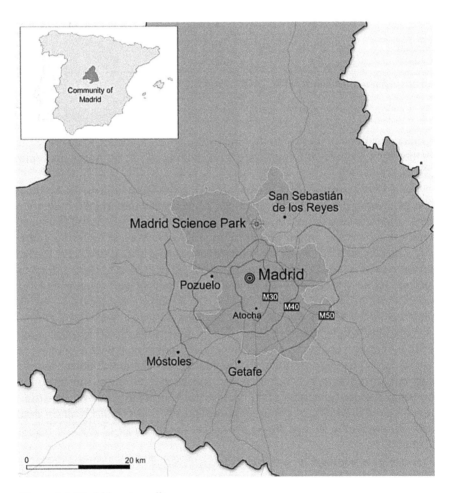

Figure 8.1 Madrid metropolitan area

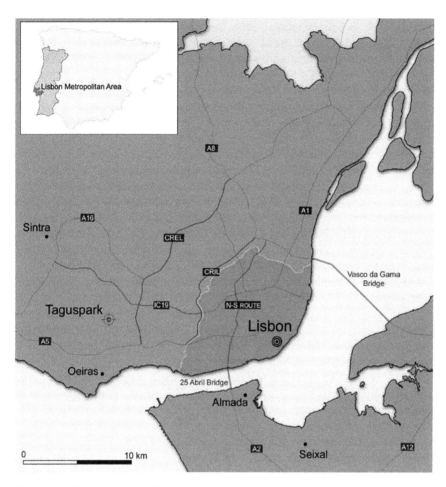

Figure 8.2 Lisbon metropolitan area

8.4.2 Inner-city and suburban cognitive-cultural economy in Madrid and Lisbon regions

The city of Madrid creates a strong polarization effect on the metropolitan region's knowledge and creative economy. As well as the inner-city–suburbs divide, there is also a north/west vs. south/east metropolitan divide, where low-density suburban sectors in the former have a higher social and environmental status compared to the lower standard housing and industrial past of the latter (Michelini and Méndez, 2013). It was only natural that this geographical metropolitan imbalance culminated in the formation of high-value-added clusters supported by technological infrastructures in the north sector of Madrid city-region, including several business parks and Madrid Science Park. A large number of firms from more intensive knowledge sectors settled there, taking advantage of the higher density and quality of infrastructure and facilities in the north and west of the Madrid agglomeration (Méndez *et al.*, 2012). Madrid's southern and eastern areas developed during the industrial Fordism period and have struggled during the deindustrialization period, finding it difficult to engage in new economic activities, especially those more intensive in knowledge and creativity (Michelini and Méndez, 2013).

A few suburban municipalities have tried to develop new strategies and actions to become important locations for knowledge-intensive firms and for cultural and creative activities. The metropolitan municipality of Pozuelo de Alarcón – the location of both Telemadrid and LaSexta (radio and television) networks and the premises of RTVE (the Antena3 network is based at San Sebastián de los Reyes) – stand out in the creative and cultural economy through an ambitious initiative dubbed *Ciudad de la Imagen*. This is a flagship project supported by the regional and municipality administrations, aiming to anchor new firms in the audio-visual sector (Michelini and Méndez, 2013).

Other good examples of suburban initiatives within the creative and cultural economy are the *Centro de Arte Dos de Mayo* at Móstoles and the *Centro de Arte de Alcobendas* (at Alcobendas), supported by both regional and local authorities and delivering traditional cultural functions to the local population (such as exhibitions and festivals). Also in Alcorcón, south of Madrid, the local authority promoted an ambitious cultural initiative – *Centro de Creación de las Artes* (CREAA) – aiming at integrating artistic creation, exhibition and cultural training activities. The *Matadero de Madrid*, at the southern edge of Madrid city, incorporates the large-scale urban intervention *Madrid Río*. *Matadero de Madrid* is a new ambitious centre for artistic creation, each of its industrial facilities specializing in areas such as theatre, cinema, music, or design (Sánchez and Méndez, 2012) – it is located in the former slaughterhouse of the city, following a rehabilitation of 80,000 m^2 supported by European and local investments and private funds (see Figure 8.3).

Like Madrid, Lisbon capital city has a strong concentration of employment in the activities of the knowledge-based economy and the creative sector. Grande Lisboa, the north sector of Lisbon metropolitan area, especially along the Lisbon-Cascais axis, has a higher socio-economic status. The south sector – Península de Setúbal – evolved as the most relevant Fordist metropolitan-industrial site specializing in chemistry, pharmacy, metallurgy, construction and shipbuilding, electronics repair and telecommunications (Vale, 1998), along with the suburbanization of working class and tertiary unskilled and semi-skilled workforce (Gaspar, Henriques and Vale, 1998; Barata-Salgueiro, 2006). The explosion of urban growth and the delocalization of enterprises from urban industrial belts to remote areas well-served by transport and communication networks has shaped Lisbon metropolitan area's spatial organization model, often encouraged by urban planning and territorial policies.

Figure 8.3 Matadero de Madrid

The case of the large inward investment in the automobile industry – *Autoeuropa* – in a 'greenfield' location at the municipality of Palmela, illustrates this de-concentration trend (Vale, 2004). Opposing views of metropolitan development strategies were evident during the last attempt made by the regional authority five years ago to draw a metropolitan spatial plan – while Lisbon municipality advocated a more dense and inner-city driven urban growth, suburban municipalities argued for, not always explicitly, actions that contributed to employment decentralization and the continuation of residential development model (André and Vale, 2012).

As in Madrid city-region, some suburban agglomerations in Lisbon metropolitan area planned new knowledge and cultural-creative sites. Probably the most visible and successful of those is the Science and Technology Tagus Park, supported by Structural Funds, located in Oeiras and stretching out to Cascais and Sintra. Currently this has around ninety high-tech firms including start-ups and seven R&D units, and has evolved into an important suburban centre, paving the way to office parks development projects (Feio and Ferrão, 2001). Other technological parks were established, namely Madan Park and Mutela Technology Park, both in Almada, in the south sector of the Lisbon metropolitan area.

Following similar strategies to the Madrid periphery, albeit with smaller budgets, suburban municipalities engaged in new strategies targeting knowledge and creative ventures, such as *DNA Cascais*, an infrastructure to promote entrepreneurship on innovative and creative sectors, or *Fabrica da Pólvora*, a cultural facility located in a former gunpowder factory in Oeiras. The competition to attract new institutions is growing in the region and a new round for the attraction of R&D units is underway, as evinced by the announcement of the relocation of the *Nova School of Business and Economics* from Lisbon to Carcavelos, within the municipality of Cascais. Located at the edge of Lisbon municipality, the *Champalimaud Centre for the Unknown*, a new R&D institution in the field of biomedical research, shows a clear trend of peripheral urban development favoured by knowledge-based economic activities.

Perhaps a better example of a development strategy based on the cultural and creative economy in the outskirts is provided by the Óbidos case, in the Lisbon and Tagus Valley region outside the formal metropolitan area border. The municipality launched a technology park dedicated to creative industries and is implementing a flamboyant cultural development strategy, which includes an intense and diversified events agenda. Finally, urban plans to re-urbanize former manufacturing production sites in the south sector of Lisbon Metropolitan Area – a total of 912ha, including the former Margueira shipyard at Almada, a steel industry site at Seixal and a former chemical complex at Barreiro – intend to attract high-value-added activities, including among them knowledge-based and creative activities.

8.4.3 Suburbs and inner-city tensions in the cognitive-cultural development of Madrid and Lisbon city-regions

The goal of this section is to highlight and debate the suburbs and inner-city tensions, comparing Madrid and Lisbon's cognitive-cultural development strategies and initiatives. Madrid and Lisbon's suburban knowledge-based and creative projects, with a few exceptions, have not delivered the expected results. These ambitious local development plans relied upon large facilities and infra-structures, which in turn were dependent upon cheap credit and public funding. In the aftermath of the 2008 world financial collapse, these two countries needed external help: as part of the International Monetary Fund, the European Union and the European Central Bank 'troika' bailout, Portugal and Spain agreed to implement a special adjustment plan (Vale, 2014). Overall, the current economic and financial crisis in both countries has brought with it severe austerity measures and public budget cuts, which hamper large public works, such as infrastructure and large social facilities. Thus, financial repercussions and the economic crisis have harshly hit these recent large-scale knowledge and creative suburban development plans, leaving some of them now incomplete, delayed or abandoned (including, for example, *CREAA – Centro de Creación de las Artes, Centro de Arte de Alcobendas, Arco Ribeirinho)*.

Madrid and Lisbon are no exceptions and both are developing diverse and significant successful initiatives to reinforce their status, both at national and international levels, and to a certain extent hindering suburban knowledge locations development. The outcome has been the strengthening of central areas in the formation of a new generation of technological spaces in metropolitan areas. Probably the most paradigmatic and flagship case is the *MediaLab Prado*, a laboratory for research, production and diffusion of digital culture in Madrid inner-city (Sánchez and Méndez, 2013), but other knowledge-based, creative and cultural initiatives can be found in both cities.

Madrid, for example, effectively consolidated as a cultural international city anchored in the prestige of *Prado*, *Reina Sofia* and *Thyssen-Bornemisza* museums, located in the *Paseo del Arte*, a two-mile axis between the squares Colón and Embajadores, stretching to *Madrid Río* (Sánchez and Méndez, 2013). Likewise, in the Cibeles Square, *Madrid Centro Centro* envisages promoting a cultural space for urban life (Michelini and Méndez, 2013). Likewise, Lisbon is concentrating investments in the riverside on tourism and culture, including a new National Coach Museum (yet to be inaugurated at the time of writing), the new cruise terminal, and on knowledge-based and creative industries close to the former International Exhibition site EXPO 98 (Parque das Nações).

However, Madrid and Lisbon's culture and creative strategies include small-scale neighbourhood interventions, aimed at promoting cultural and creative activities. Among them, it is perhaps worth mentioning several spaces for creative workers in old workshops and factories, such as co-working areas, collective creation and exhibition centres, incubators, and start-up facilities, spreading among Madrid and Lisbon's central neighbourhoods. A set of good examples can be identified, including:

*   Hub Madrid – a network of creative spaces targeting social innovation;
*   Madrid International Lab – an organisation located in the historical core city targeting talent and managing a network of incubators in the city limits (Michelini and Méndez, 2013) – in *Centro* district in Madrid;
*   LX Factory – a cluster of creative industries and professionals in Alcântara, at Lisbon (Figure 8.4), that promotes diverse events on fashion, design and architecture, communication, arts, music (Leandro *et al.*, 2013); and
*   Startup Lisboa – a creative business incubator in an historical building in downtown, approved by the Lisbon participatory budget process.

Even more socially relevant is the *Tabacalera* project in Madrid, located in the Lavapiés neighbourhood, which stands out as a paradigmatic case of collective management by artists and creative people; likewise Mouraria is becoming the new alternative cultural neighbourhood, rivalling Bairro Alto in contention for the title of the cultural district of Lisbon. More dependent on private investment, creative and cultural activities are also central to the urban regeneration projects of Príncipe Real and Colina de Santana, both in Lisbon inner-city, increasing gentrification, not without social protests from active social urban organizations and political dispute at municipal assembly.

Figure 8.4 The LX Factory, Lisbon

As shown by these recent developments in Lisbon and Madrid it is untenable to draw a simple distinction between city and suburban economies. The economies of suburban areas have been evolving towards more creative and innovative activities, despite facing some drawbacks linked to ambitious real estate and large-scale cultural facilities resulting from imitative strategies among local suburban elites. Simultaneously, cities remain important ingredients to sustain the cognitive-cultural economy, also strongly supported by city mayors, regardless of suburbs' own ambitions and strategies. What is true is that core cities and suburbs contribute in a complementary way to creativity and innovation in the city-region. Better policy coordination is required to avoid sterile competitive strategies to attract firms or develop large facilities in Madrid and in Lisbon.

The cognitive-cultural developments in Madrid and Lisbon illustrate that suburbs become socially active and politically involved in local and metro-politan economic development. These two cases also highlight a lack of cooperation between suburbs and city-core alongside the absence of coordination mechanisms at a city-region level. In both cases, suburban municipalities have put in place ambitious plans to develop stronger knowledge-based and creative local economies, fuelled by easy access to credit, alongside powerful actions to regenerate city-centres, often showing overlapping goals. Overall, the lack of metropolitan coordination and poor inter-municipalities cooperation hamper balanced cognitive-cultural development at city-region level.

8.5 Conclusion

After a process of delocalization of urban functions and the development of new centralities in suburban areas during the Fordist era, the inner city draws together excellent conditions to strengthen the knowledge-based and creative-cultural economy. Despite this, suburban economies have been evolving towards more creative and innovative activities, despite a few drawbacks linked to ambitious real estate and large-scale cultural facilities, and thus making simple distinctions between the economies of cities and suburbs no longer valid.

Suburban municipalities experienced past urban and economic growth based on new infrastructure and large facilities developments, which enabled the construction of large office parks, technological parks, logistics parks and leisure parks. Technopoles bring together relevant conditions to attract new firms from high-technology sectors, allowing for the development of suburban economies. In many ways, these crucial technological infrastructures pave the way for more ambitious suburban growth strategies, including the recent development of creative and cultural activities.

Often propelled by the powerful 'creative city' narrative, the attraction of highly skilled human resources and the development of high-quality urban amenities became the main target for suburban municipalities seeking to attract and to develop new ventures on the knowledge-based and creative-cultural economy. As major political entities, suburban local authorities have increasing autonomy and legitimately aspire to develop knowledge and creative-cultural sites (Carvalho, 2013). As shown in the Madrid and Lisbon cases, several initiatives emerged in suburban municipalities, benefiting from the decentralization from inner-cities and sustained by available public funding along with political ambition of suburban local politicians. Economic crisis and subsequent fiscal austerity measures have hampered the development of many of those ambitious projects, but suburbs are, in their own right, contributing to the creativity development of the city-region.

Limits to suburban knowledge and cognitive-cultural development stems from inner-city responses to the Fordist counter-urbanization process. Madrid and Lisbon have been very active in promoting new cognitive-cultural initiatives, regardless of the agents involved or the magnitude of the projects. Ranging from collective and social projects to private ones, from urban rehabilitation and social integration to urban regeneration and gentrification, inner-city dynamics are limiting suburban development in the cognitive-cultural capitalist economy.

Two main implications for further research and policy can be drawn from this chapter. In the interest of socially cohesive cities, suburban development must be coordinated with core-city redevelopment, for which policy coordination at metropolitan level, so far non-existent in Madrid and inefficient in Lisbon, is required. New governance forms and institutions are essential to overcome this problem and balance economic and social development in the inner city and suburbs, through integrated policy design at city-region level.

A second important implication is that policy action needs to move away from mega-project examples imported from elsewhere and to focus on place-based actions. In accordance, it needs to be better aligned with local economic structures and adjusted to the dynamics and the local institutions in the suburbs, otherwise they risk threatening suburban economic development. Nevertheless, suburban areas have developed new economic functions and in the process they have become more than simple functional spaces, since they have established their own social and political structures, in which the role of local governments is key element to understand suburban development.

Acknowledgements

A preliminary version of this chapter was presented in the International Conference of Regional Studies Association held at Delft in 2012. The fieldwork undertaken for this study was developed as part of the Luso-Spanish Integrated Actions (Refª E-43/10) *Tendências Económicas e Transformações Territoriais das Regiões Metropolitanas Ibéricas na Sociedade do Conhecimento*, supported by the Foundation of the Portuguese Universities. The author greatly benefited from the insights of Spanish colleagues involved in the aforementioned action – Ricardo Méndez, Simón Sanchez, José Prada and Juan Michelini – as well as from the support of the Portuguese team members Soraia Silva and Leandro Gabriel – the latter also provided the cartography for this chapter.

The author acknowledges the support of the research project RUCAS – *Utopias Reais em Espaços Socialmente Criativos* (PTDC/CS-GEO/115603/ 2009), funded by the FCT – Portuguese Foundation for Science, and Technology, coordinated by Isabel André.

Notes

1   In this chapter, post-suburbs are defined as settlements in a peripheral location in relation to a dominant core in a city-region that, in comparison with traditional suburbs, do have an increasing community identity and are embodied in a local government structure with autonomous development policy goals, albeit related with the city-region's development opportunities and strategies.
2   The high-speed train system in Portugal and its connections to the Spanish system have been postponed by the Portuguese government.

Bibliography

André, I. and Vale, M. (2012) 'Lisboa: Tensiones entre la ciudad y la metrópoli', in M. Balbo (ed.) *Europa: La Ciudad Central en el Sistema Urbano*. Quito: OLACCHI.
Barata-Salgueiro, T. (2006) *Lisbonne: Périphérie et centralités*. Paris: Harmattan.
Carvalho, L. (2013) *Knowledge locations in cities: Emergence and development dynamics*. Rotterdam: Erasmus Research Institute of Management (ERIM).
Castells, M. and Hall, P. (1994) *Technopoles of the world: The making of 21st century industrial complexes*. London: Routledge.

Cooke, P. (2001) 'From technopoles to regional innovation systems: The evolution of localised technology development policy'. *Canadian Journal of Regional Science*, *24*: 21–40.

European Commission (2011) *Cities of tomorrow – Challenges, visions, ways forward.* Directorate General for Regional Policy, Luxembourg: Publications Office of the European Union (p. 112).

Feio, P.A. and Ferrão, J.(2001) 'Taguspark: Gestão de expectativas num parque de criação recente', in C. Antonelli and Ferrão, J. (ed.) *Comunicação, conhecimento colectivo e inovação. As vantagens da aglomeração geográfica.* Lisboa: Imprensa de Ciências Sociais.

Ferrão, J. (2013) 'Território', in J.L. Cardoso and P. Maglhães (eds) *Portugal social de A a Z.* Paço de Arcos: Impresa Publishing, Expresso.

Fishman, R. (1987) *Bourgeois utopias: The rise and fall of suburbia.* New York: Basic Books.

Florida, R. (2002) *The rise of the creative class: And how it's transforming work, leisure, community and everyday life.* New York: Basic Books.

Forsyth, A. and Crewe, K. (2010) 'Suburban technopoles as places: The international campus-garden-suburb style'. *Urban Design International, 15*(3): 165–82.

Friedmann, J. and Wolff, G. (1982) 'World city formation. An agenda for research and action'. *International Journal of Urban and Regional Research, 6*(3): 309–44.

Garreau, J. (1991) *Edge city: Life on the new frontier.* New York: Doubleday.

Gaspar, J., Henriques, E. and Vale, M. (1998) 'Economic restructuring, social re-composition and recent urban changes in Portugal'. *GeoJournal, 46*: 63–76.

Glaeser, E.L. (2000) 'The new economics of urban and regional growth', in G. Clark, M. Feldman and M. Gertler (eds) *The Oxford handbook of economic geography.* Oxford: Oxford University Press.

Glaeser, E.L., Kolko, J. and Saiz, A. (2001) 'Consumer city'. *Journal of Economic Geography, 1*: 27–50.

Hall, P. (2000) 'Creative cities and economic development'. *Urban Studies, 37*: 639–49.

Harvey, D. (1985) *The urbanization of capital.* Oxford: Blackwell.

Jacobs, J. (1969) *The economy of cities.* New York: Random House.

Jaffe, A.B., Trajtenberg, M. and Henderson, R. (1992) *Geographic localization of knowledge spillovers as evidenced by patent citations* (no. w3993). National Bureau of Economic Research.

Keil, R. (1994) 'Global sprawl: Urban form after Fordism'. *Environment and Planning D, 12*: 131–6.

Leandro, G., Vale, M., Silva, S. and Azevedo, F. (2013) 'Formação de espaços criativos: o caso da LX Factory em Lisboa. IX Congresso da Geografia Portuguesa'. *Geografia: Espaço, Natureza, Sociedade e Ciência*, Universidade de Évora. Associação Portuguesa de Geógrafos: 290–6.

López Trigal, L. (2013) 'Estrategias de recualificación e innovación en las metrópolis ibéricas: Una revisión en tiempo de crisis'. *Ciudad y Territorio: Estudios Territoriales, 175*: 45–64.

Massey, D., Quintas, P. and Wield, D. (1992) *High-tech fantasies. Science parks in society, science and space.* London: Routledge.

Méndez, R. (2013) 'Crisis económica, vulnerabilidad urbana y desempleo en España'. *Ciudad y Territorio: Estudios Territoriales, XLV*: 649–67.

Méndez, R., Michelini, J.J., Prada, J. and Tébar, J. (2012) 'Economía creativa y desarrollo urbano en España: una aproximación a sus lógicas espaciales'. *EURE (Santiago)*, *38*: 5–32.

Michelini, J.J. and Méndez, R. (2013) 'Creative industries, spatial contrasts and urban governance in Madrid'. *Revista de Geografia e Ordenamento do Território*, *1*: 143–70.

Moulaert, F. and Sekia, F. (2003) 'Territorial innovation models: A critical survey'. *Regional Studies*, *37*: 289–302.

Mozingo, L.A. (2011) *Pastoral capitalism: A history of suburban corporate landscapes*. Cambridge, MA: MIT Press.

Musterd, S. and Murie, A. (eds) (2010) *Making competitive cities*. Chichester: Wiley-Blackwell.

O'Mara, M.P. (2005) *Cities of knowledge: Cold War science and the search for the next Silicon Valley*. Princeton, NJ: Princeton University Press.

OECD (2010) *Urban-rural linkages: Issues, measurement and policies in OECD countries*. Paris: OECD.

OECD (2011) *Assessing and monitoring rural-urban linkages in functional regions: A methodological framework*. Paris: OECD.

Phelps, N.A. (2010) 'Suburbs for nations? Some interdisciplinary connections on the suburban economy'. *Cities*, *27*: 68–76.

Phelps, N.A. (2012) 'The sub-creative economy of the suburbs in question'. *International Journal of Cultural Studies*, *15*(3): 259–71.

Phelps, N.A., Parsons, N., Ballas, D. and Dowling, N. (2006) *Post-suburban Europe: Planning and politics at the margins of Europe's capital cities*. Basingstoke: Palgrave Macmillan.

Rodríguez-Pose, A. and Crescenzi, R. (2008) 'Mountains in a flat world: Why proximity still matters for the location of economic activity'. *Cambridge Journal of Regions, Economy and Society*, *1*: 371–88.

Sánchez, S. and Méndez, R. (2012) 'La ciudad de Madrid en la economía del conocimiento'. *Barómetro de Economía de la Ciudad de Madrid*, *31*: 129–60.

Sánchez, S. and Méndez, R. (2013) 'La economía creativa en la ciudad de Madrid'. *Barómetro de Economía de la Ciudad de Madrid*, *37*: 121–50.

Sassen, S. (2000) *Cities in a world economy* (2nd edn). Thousand Oaks, CA: Pine Forge Press.

Sassen, S. (2001) *The global city: New York, London, Tokyo*. Princeton, NJ: Princeton University Press.

Scott, A.J. (1998) *Regions and the world economy. The coming shape of global production*. Oxford, Oxford University Press.

Scott, A.J. (2008) *Social economy of the metropolis: Cognitive-cultural capitalism and the global resurgence of cities*. Oxford: Oxford University Press.

Scott, A.J. (2014) 'Beyond the creative city: Cognitive–cultural capitalism and the new urbanism'. *Regional Studies*, *48*: 565–78.

Smetkowski, M., Gorzelak, G., Kozak, M., Olechnicka, A., Ploszaj, A. and Wojnar, K. (2011) *The European metropolises and their regions: From economic landscapes to metropolitan networks*. Warsaw: WN Scholar.

Soja, E. (2000) *Postmetropolis: Critical studies of cities and regions*. Oxford: Blackwell.

Swyngedouw, E., Moulaert, F. and Rodriguez, A. (2002) 'Neoliberal urbanization in Europe: Large-scale urban development projects and the New Urban Policy'. *Antipode*, *34*: 542–77.

Vale, M. (1998) 'Industrial restructuring in Lisbon Metropolitan Area: Towards a new map of production?', in T. Unwin (ed.) *A European geography*. London: Longman.

Vale, M. (2004) 'Innovation and knowledge driven by a focal corporation – The case of the Autoeuropa supply chain'. *European Urban and Regional Studies*, *11*: 124–40.

Vale, M. (2011) 'Innovation networks and local and regional development policy', in A. Pike, A. Rodríguez-Pose and J. Tomaney (eds) *Handbook of local and regional development*. Abingdon: Routledge.

Vale, M. (2014) 'Economic crisis and the regions: Towards alternative territorial development policies', in J. Salom and J. Farinós (eds) *Identity and territorial character. Re-interpreting local-spatial development.* Valencia: Publicaciones de la Universitat de València.

Van Winden, W., Carvalho, L., Van Tuijl, E., Van Haaren, J. and Van Den Berg, L. (2013) *Creating knowledge locations in cities: Innovation and integration challenges.* Abingdon: Routledge.

Van Winden, W., Van Den Berg, L. and Pol, P. (2007) 'European cities in the knowledge economy: Towards a typology'. *Urban Studies*, *44*: 525–49.

9 Urban innovation as urban redevelopment in Spain?

The Janus-face of Barcelona's science and technology parks

Antònia Casellas

9.1 Introduction

The emerging paradigm of the globalizing knowledge-based economy emphasizes the importance to national and regional economies seeking to survive and thrive in the competitive economic environments of producing, transferring and applying knowledge. Co-operation is central to territorial capacities, whether between businesses in decentralized organizational form and co-operative exchange (Saxenian, 1994) or between public sector, the business community and the universities via the triple-helix model (Etzkowitz and Mello, 1994). Within this context, science parks have become a broadly applied economic development strategy seeking to stimulate territorial competitiveness in the global knowledge-based economy (Massey, Quintas and Wield, 1992).

An emerging model of science-park driven development has materialized, stressing a number of key dimensions. First, there is an important role for the public sector in investing, leading and co-ordinating investments to create innovative territories (Zerbinati and Souitaris, 2005). Second, as new firms emerge and innovate, linkages to universities are critical, and indeed universities become an important growth seedbed (Castells and Hall, 1994; Audretsch, 2006). Third, mutual, reciprocal linkages between public and private actors need developing, particularly supporting innovative SMEs (Etzkowitz and Mello, 1994; Audretsch and Feldman, 1996). Fourth, there is a growing emphasis on constructing new kinds of utopian suburban/urban spaces attractive to scientific elites (Wakeman, 2003; Kaiser, 2004; Forsyth and Crewe, 2010). Finally, within a decentralisation of policy-making to the regional level, there is the imperative to focus regional innovation policy on building innovative networks (Koschatzky and Kroll, 2007).

What is striking about this heuristic is that it brings together a range of literatures from a very diverse array of disciplinary backgrounds, from management studies, innovation policy, regional studies, planning and economic geography. In particular, there is an elision between the imperatives of industrial and economic development (in terms of stimulating new forms of growth) and urban and regional development (creating new kinds of liveable places). This chapter focuses on this issue, asking the overall question of how these imperatives interplay in the creation of high-technology spaces in an existing context, Barcelona, a city with coherent urban form and identity; and in a country where real estate development has traditionally played a key role in economic growth. Studying the agents involved in promoting science parks, the policies implemented and the outcomes achieved in Barcelona, where science parks have a marked infill character, allows the dynamics between economic innovation and urban redevelopment to be explored.

The chapter calls the attention to the close relationship between science parks and urbanization in Spain, arguing that in the Spanish case there is a problem of conceptualization of what defines parks, which reflects the parks' problematic land development nature within the Spanish economic structure. Field research involving semi-structured interviews with public and private stakeholders and independent observers, together with the review of broad secondary data provided by parks' promoters and consultants, highlights that science parks are dependent in multiple ways on the public sector and closely interrelated with land urbanization seeking to deliver two goals – economic regeneration and real estate redevelopment. The chapter concludes that this dependency could generate problems in related economic innovation strategies. Conversely, the analysis of the structure of the Spanish productivity system, dominated by micro and small firms, thereby limited in terms of innovation and private investment, reinforces the broad and fuzzy character of parks, with the version that appears in marketing tools embracing many different realities.

9.2 Origins of Spanish parks and their fuzzy terminology

Compared to other European countries and regions, science and technology parks arrived relatively late in Spain. The first initiative was the 1985 establishment of the Technology Park of Bilbao, located in one of Spain's few old industrial regions, the Basque Country. Between 1985 and 1992, eight parks were created, a relatively low rate compared to elsewhere in Europe: in France, there were thirty technology initiatives sites (Wakeman, 2003), while Britain hosted forty science parks (Gower and Harris, 1994). In contrast to countries such as the UK and Belgium, where science parks were adopted from US practices bringing universities and firms together around commercialisation (Massey *et al.*, 1992; Debackaere and De Bondt, 2002), the establishment of the parks in Spain was not initially strongly rooted in co-operation between the parks and universities and associated research centres.

It is likewise important to note that science park policy in Spain emerged at a time of political consolidation towards a democratic system, with economic policy decisions being transferred from the central government to the regions. In this initial phase, regional governments took the initiative to define economic policies but were left to promote the parks in isolation, as neither universities nor private corporations showed any interest in getting involved (Ondategui, 2001 and 2003). In fact, it took more than a decade, until the late 1990s, to generate effective interactions between academic institutions and science parks, with the creation of the Barcelona Science Park, opened in 1999.

A further turning point occurred in 2000, in the context of a period of significant economic growth in Spain. The Spanish Ministry of Science and Innovation began providing direct grants to science and technology parks seeking to promote research and development (R&D) activities. The grants varied on an annual basis from the initial €189.5m (2000) to a minimum of €10.8m (2004), and overall represented a total investment in a ten-year period (2000–2010) of €2.3bn (APTE, 2010). This strategy translated into a significant growth in the number of parks in the country (see Chapter 10, this volume). By 2013, APTE (the umbrella organization of Spanish parks) had forty-seven full members and twenty-five affiliated members (cf. membership criteria is discussed in the following section).

Alongside the significant growing number of parks since 2000, a peculiar feature in Spanish science parks is the fuzzy terminology used to define and identify them. While parks internationally are often labelled as 'science parks', in Spain parks are labelled under a wide arrange of different terms, 'science and technology parks' being the most prominent. The effort to differentiate between parks' terminologies highlights a more widely-acknowledged need for academics, consultants and policy-makers to properly clarify the concept. Past efforts to provide definitions have faltered because of the lack of a well-established and broadly accepted concept, while also leaving open the possibility to generate new reformulations adapting the discourse to different park realities. The following three examples – from a consultancy study, an academic report and the Spanish science park representative body – illustrate the plasticity with which the term is used.

The first is the INFYDE (2011) consultancy study, evaluating Spanish parks' contribution to the Lisbon agenda (i.e., promoting competitiveness and cohesion among European territories through investment in R&D), while using a typology distinguishing between research, science and technology parks. In this report, the idea of *Research Parks* relates to basic research rather than development, and they are closely linked to and often co-located with universities. *Science Parks* may be promoted by universities, but their core aim is commercialisation, devoting a significant part of their space to research performed by university research groups and firms' R&D units. *Technology Parks* focus on applying knowledge-intensive production techniques to the production of services and products (INFYDE, 2011).

In a study commissioned by a local government from academics seeking potential concepts to base a redevelopment of a former military facility as a new park, Pié, Testar and Majoral (2102) identify four types of parks, differentiating Science Parks, Technology Parks, Science and Technology Parks, and Corporation Parks. To them, a *Science Park* has a strong dependency upon public sector financial support, here defined as with 40–60 per cent of activity focused on basic research with the remainder divided between incubator activities and scientific and technological support infrastructure. A *Technology Park* is oriented towards (>60 per cent activity) firm-based innovation and includes significant numbers of privately-funded start-ups and spin-offs firms. A *Scientific and Technology Park* is a hybrid, with neither R&D nor innovation accounting for more than 50 per cent of total activity. Last, a *Corporation Park* is one including corporations with no R&D functions, effectively the equivalent of technology business clusters.

Finally, the 2013 definition of the Spanish Science and Technology Park Association (Asociación de Parques Científicos y Tecnológicos de España – APTE – created in 1989 by six park managers) resembles the one established in 2002 by the International Association of Science Parks (IASP). The IASP defined a 'science park' as stimulating innovation and competitiveness by encouraging knowledge and technology flow among universities, R&D institutions, companies and markets, while facilitating technology entrepreneurship (IASP, 2011). Similarly, APTE defines a 'science and technology park' as a physical space with the following characteristics:

1 formal and operational dealings with universities, research centres and higher educational institutions;
2 designed to encourage the creation and growth of knowledge-based companies and other service sector organizations, with high value added; and
3 a stable managing body promoting technology transfer and fostering innovation between the companies and organizations using the park (APTE, 2013).

Adding to the fuzziness in the definitions of parks presented above, there is also the need to highlight the different spatial characteristics of Spanish science and technology (S&T) parks, which further underscores this identity problem. The concept of S&T parks covers a whole range of very broad types of spatial clustering of knowledge-based activities, ranging from a single facility or a cluster of diverse firms to a mix-land infill redevelopment, with diverse economic activities, housing and facilities. Different Spanish regions have their own specific territorial organization and classifications: in Catalonia, the region with most parks, its own S&T parks association, Xarxa de Parcs Científics i Tecnològics de Catalunya (XPCAT) defines parks within the network as a system of 'big spaces of production, transfer, diffusion and use of knowledge' (XPCAT, 2013), covering thirteen full and nine affiliated members by 2013. An analysis of Spanish and Catalan members associated to these respective organisations reveals further discrepancies between these classifications. This recurrent fuzziness and discrepancies with park classifications has been explained by the independent economic development observers and academics interviewed for this study with the argument that Spain had a historic interrelation between economic development and real estate redevelopment, which often prioritised land development over innovation policies. Viewed in such a light, the lack of specificity works as an advantage because it allows a gamut of different S&T park realities to be simultaneously embraced. The following sections explore these issues of diversity as a response to the dominance of land development interests through the analysis of the Barcelona case.

9.3 Multi-level public sector co-operation

As one of Spain's few industrialized areas in 2007 Catalonia was, together with Madrid (Spain's capital), Spain's most productive region, producing 18.7 per cent of Spain's total gross value added (GVA). Within Catalonia, Barcelona is the dominant concentration of regional population and economic activity, accounting for 74.1 per cent of Catalan GVA (Burdett, Colantonio and Myfanwy, 2010). Caught between the Mediterranean coast and the Collserola mountain range and due to historical urbanization factors (Casellas, 2009), the city is a compact urban space with high population density (102 sq. km, with 1.6m inhabitants in 2011, giving a density of 713 inhabitants/ sq. km). Historical political reasons precluded incorporating municipalities across the urban space, leaving the functional city spreading far beyond the city administrative limits, a continuously built-up environment constituting Europe's sixth-largest urban area by population.

The origins of one of Spain's first S&T park, Park Vallès Technology (Parc Tecnològic de Vallès, PTV), within Barcelona's metropolitan area, shows the complexity of public co-operation at different administrative levels and provides insights on creating consensus and mobilising public resources within Spain. The PTV idea was initially generated by a public land development agency in 1983, which explored the feasibility of building a park in the Barcelona city-region. In the following years, and involving co-operation with the neighbouring Cerdanyola municipality (on whose land the park would be built) public actors approved new zoning regulations. This process was not easy, taking two years to finalize. Once land availability was secured in 1985, in the following two years, the Catalan land development agency transferred project execution to the *Consorci de la Zona Franca*, a consortium specialized in economic development. The same year the consortium reached a co-operation agreement with the Catalan government's business development agency, creating a new ad hoc agency: PTV, Inc., 50 per cent of which was owned by the metropolitan economic development consortium and the other 50 per cent by the Catalan Government's own economic development agency.

This complexity in multi-level collaboration – between municipal, metropolitan and regional governmental agencies – was necessary to facilitate disagreement resolution and avoid poor public co-ordination (Burdett *et al.*, 2010); moreover, it highlights the public sector strategy of responding to the limited private interests in developing a park. As Castells and Hall assert (1994), regions and cities have less power than national governments but have a greater response capacity to generate targeted development projects. Fourteen years after its inception, and with specializations in telecommunications, biotechnology, chemistry, new materials, robotics and laser technology, by 2009 the PTV park had 150 members, with 2,910 employees and a total investment of €254m. By 2009, 45 per cent of the existing companies had relocated in the park from the surrounding area, 25 per cent were new start-ups, 14 per cent were expansions/relocations from Spain and 16 per cent were from abroad (Parc Tecnològic del Vallès, 2011).

Between 1985 and 1992, following the positive PTV experience, the Catalan regional government supported the creation of eight S&T parks in Catalonia. Although the underlying science park model emphasised linking science production and business execution in order to foster economic growth (Massey, *et al.*, 1992), the S&T parks were also promoted and supported by multi-level public administrations co-operation. Initially, these parks were dominated by micro and small companies with limited high-technology development capability, but by the late 1990s, public universities started to be involved, with the first scientific park link to Universitat de Barcelona, via Barcelona Science Park, operating from 1999.

Barcelona's metropolitan S&T parks illustrate a powerful attraction towards the city as a desirable site, a by-product of both the parks' origins linked to the city's importance as well as policy-makers' strategies seeking to capitalize upon previous existing institutions and development initiatives. Of the nine parks in Barcelona city, seven were articulated around universities and research centres by 2011, with the other two growing from previously existing public economic development agencies. Of the seven related to universities, the Barcelona Science Park served as a model for the rest. By 2011, it combined private and public institutions, including fifty research groups, three research institutes, a biotech enterprise incubator and thirty companies with 1,400 professionals. Of the two fostered by economic development agencies, the Barcelona North Technology Park exemplifies a single facility building upon a well-established municipal economic development agency (Barcelona Activa) created in 1986 to incentive endogenous growth. The park provides 10,000 sq.m. accommodation and common support services to its residents, as well as formal and operative relations with universities and research centres, seeking to help these companies to expand internationally.

Analyzing the different parks' evolution, we could argue that they are the direct result neither of national policies nor private initiatives, but rather from public municipal and/or metropolitan initiatives, in co-operation with the Catalan government, and often generating ad hoc institutional arrangements such as PTV. The process followed a pattern of multi-level public collaboration where private sector involvement emerges following the initiative being conceptualized, planned and initially financed by public partners. This type of governmental co-operation has been identified as a key feature of Barcelona's urban and economic development strategy, under the label of

'Barcelona model' originating in the 1992 Olympic Games (Blanco, 2009; Borja, 2010; Casellas, 2006).[1]

In 1986 the city council created the first municipal agency to develop the Olympic Village, combining administrative capabilities with private resources. It initiated its operations with 100 per cent public funding, acting as a limited firm and incurring debts independently outside the municipal balance-sheet (Nel.lo, 1997). The agency was later opened to private capital, creating a public-private partnership instrumental in arranging financing. The private-public co-operation in urban redevelopment subsequently permitted local policy-decision makers to claim that, while a majority of investment was private, its design and the management were largely public (Clusa, 1996). The model has been criticized for its lack of effective community participation and transparency (Borja, 2010; Capel, 2007; Casellas, 2006; Delgado, 2007), although allowing the public sector to maintain control over planning and regulations, and to provide initial capital funding while eventually working to attract private capital.

Alongside the leading role and multi-level co-operation of the public sector, a second key feature of Spanish S&T parks also becomes evident in these stories, namely their close relationship with land development with the 22@Barcelona project providing one of the best examples of this symbiosis; it is to this case that the paper now turns.

9.4 The symbiosis between innovation and urbanization

Unlike other countries where S&T parks have been a predominantly suburban phenomenon, distinctive to Spanish and Barcelona's S&T parks has been their close relationship to urban brownfield redevelopment, as exemplified by 22@Barcelona. This involved a close relationship between site development and economic development. The former manager of the 22@Barcelona, Piqué highlights this in asserting that: 'The 22@project emerged as a combination of both in-depth urban regeneration and an ambitious economic promotion strategy oriented to increasing the competitiveness of Barcelona' (Pareja-Eastaway and Piqué, 2011, p. 2).

The 22@Barcelona project is a zone of discontinuous land in Poblenou district covering 198ha, equivalent to 1.98m sq.m. In the 19th century its open land and water supply outside the city walls saw Poblenou become Barcelona's manufacturing heart. During the 20th century, though zoned as industrial land, Poblenou's urban fabric grew organically as an unplanned amalgam of factories, warehouses and housing. By the 1990s, after industrial production relocated elsewhere in the metro area, it had become a working-class neighbourhood with family-owned companies producing industrial subcomponents and warehouses (Dot, Casellas and Pallares, 2010). Although adjacent to the city centre, its inadequate connectivity with the city s urban fabric, obsolete buildings and industrial infrastructure hindered the area's development.

The idea for the 22@Barcelona project developed from the city council's efforts to sustain the post-Olympic development momentum for urban restructuring and city promotion efforts. By involving civil society agents (scholars, economic associations, among others) within a 'city of knowledge' concept, municipal leaders adopted a new economic strategy targeting high-tech industries for Poblenou (Clua and Albet, 2008). The first step involved commissioning an international best-practice study on science parks and high-tech clusters, analysing twenty-one case studies from Europe, the USA, Asia and Middle East (MPGM, 2000). The study concluded the need to consider two different kinds of spatial dynamics when designing Barcelona's strategy. Some high-tech industries emerged outside urban areas based on previous industrial parks or direct state interventions. Alternatively, the media sector sought the urban character of locations, requiring adequate infrastructure, incubators, flexible spaces and quality of life for potential residents.

The second step was modifying zoning regulations to foster both these kinds of new economic activities as well as the desired urban restructuring. This requiring amending the Barcelona General Metropolitan Plan (1976), under the MPGM (Modificación del Plan General Metropolitano de Barcelona) approved in 2000. The changes in the zoning regulations transformed the industrial zoning category (22a) into a high-tech park (22@) from whence is derived the project name. The new zoning established a mixed land development, providing for new economy activities alongside housing, services and recreational spaces. MPGM allowed the legal recognition of 4,614 pre-existing dwellings and approved 4,000 new state-subsidized housing units, with a minimum of 25 per cent rental. The MPGM regulation established a long list of economic development activities permitted within the targeted area (MPGM, 2000) and, while quite broad in defining knowledge production, forced a range of businesses either to relocate elsewhere in the metro area or close their economic activities (Dot *et al.*, 2010).

To create an initial critical mass of development to attract private investors, the PMGM identified six areas of redevelopment led by the public sector. These areas represented 47 per cent of total land targeted for renewal. The redevelopment of the remaining space was designed to be undertaken by private or public initiative guided by different planning tools. The initial plan sought to specialize each area in an economic sector to act as engine for the urban renewal alongside generating coherence, providing an identity and sense of location. This initial strategy failed to develop a critical mass of private investors, and did not succeed to materialise with only the media sector becoming a well-defined cluster (Casellas and Pallares-Barbera, 2009).

Following the Olympic governance model, the city created a public corporation, 22@bcn, S.A. to manage the project in 2000. Initially 100 per cent of share capital was held by the municipality, with the agency-combined administrative and corporate capabilities, including:

- the capacity to draft, process and approve planning instruments;
- the implementation of infrastructure through projects, finance, execution and management;

- the purchase and award of land from tenders;
- the collaboration with the town planning authorities with respect to licenses and permits; and
- the promotion of the area

The public agency later entered into ad hoc agreements in partnership with the private sector. Due to its inner-city location, pre-existing urban fabric and the mixed-use land redevelopment, the project was promoted as a new compact city model (22@Barcelona, 2011). By 2012, the project had arguably been successful in its scale of urban transformation, with 70 per cent of targeted renovation complete (by surface area), of which two-thirds were undertaken by the private sector. Private sector involvement was encouraged by the public sector's infrastructure provision alongside increasing the permitted density to 6,000 sq.m. surface area for a standard city block. To fully access these building rights, developers needed to allocate a minimum of 20 per cent of floor space to knowledge-related activities.

In the project, sectoral specialization evolved over time from the initially envisaged seven engines of economic activity: audiovisual, information and communication technologies, bioscience, new knowledge spaces (university and R&D centers), entrepreneurship, technology, and social cohesion. Detailed analysis of these speciality groupings reveals that they were primarily focused on capitalizing upon university, institutional and firms' relocation agreements, and rather less on social concerns initially included due to the existing urban and social fabric of the targeted area. Over time, the concept of specific sectors for zones was abandoned and the speciality groupings were reformulated as new constraints appeared and opportunities arose (Casellas and Pallares-Barbera, 2009). By 2005 the concept of clusters was introduced, identifying four key economic sectors: media, TICs, medical technologies, and energy. In 2011 they were reformulated to introduce the new cluster of design.

In 2006, 22@Barcelona joined the XPCAT association, becoming identified as a new S&T park. Detailed analysis of business data is difficult as, unlike other countries, neither Spain nor Catalonia have a strong statistical base with corporations, associations and organizations often reluctant to share their databases for academic purposes, making it necessary to rely on highly limited secondary sources. In 2009, the number of knowledge-intensive companies in the 22@Barcelona park was estimated at 1,114 firms, with the total number of workers at 32,300 employees (Pareja-Eastaway and Piqué, 2011). That would suggest that approximately 50 per cent of the total Catalonia S&T parks workforce was concentrated in 22@Barcelona: it was a significant outlier in the XPCAT group. There has certainly been a substantial increase in the number of intensive knowledge companies in 22@Barcelona. Data provided by the promoter shows a jump to 32.3 per cent of 7.329 resident firms and institutions in 2012 (i.e., 2,367 firms focused on knowledge economy activities) (Barcelona Activa, 2014). However, it must be noted that a lack of transparency, shifting definitions and accounting practices in data gathering methods, together with the aggregated character of the numbers provided generates fuzziness in the data, and makes difficult an impartial assessment of the parks.

However accurate the data may be, it is evident that the parks strategy in Spain tries to capitalize on the links between economic and land development. The construction sector still represented 10.2 per cent of Spanish GDP in 2010 (i.e., after the construction bubble had crashed) (UNECE, 2013). This data, taken together with information provided by independent observers, suggests that the Spanish S&T parks' strategy has been predominantly oriented towards land development schemes, which have the capacity to attract private capital, but at the same time can see a lesser emphasis placed on economic viability and failing to embed innovative policies based on solid economic assessments by being too reliant upon urbanization interests. This outcome could be understood as a policy-makers' adaptation to the limited capital investment of the private sector in Spain, together with the dominant role of micro-firms within the county's economic base.

9.5 Micro-firms' dominance and limited private capital investment

Despite the previously-mentioned restrictions to Catalan data, literature and statistics from the parks' promoters suggest that, in a little more than a decade, there has been a significant growth in the number of companies and institutions located in Catalan parks. At a national level, the total number of companies and institutions involved in the parks increased from 500 to 5,115 (1997–2009), with a corresponding increase in employment from 13,000 workers to 136,200 workers. It is necessary, however, to notice that not all this employment is exclusively in research and development: only 23,138 jobs (17 per cent of total employment) were classified as research and development in 2009 (APTE, 2011). In Catalonia, by 2009 the Catalan association asserted that 2,165 'knowledge economy' firms were located in the parks, employing 64,200 employees, although clearly not all of those are in research and development.

A second feature of the parks in Catalonia is the company size, dominated by micro and small firms (see Table 9.1). The number of micro and small companies reached a total of 81 per cent in 2009, with 92 per cent of total firms in S&T parks being SMEs in 2011. However, this is more skewed towards

Table 9.1 The size and location of ownership of Catalan S&T park firms

Size (emps)		Ownership	
>10	47%	Catalan	80.0%
11–50	34%	Other Spanish	15.4%
51–250	11%	International	4.6%
>250	8%		

Source: XPCAT, 2010.

large firms than Spain in general, where 93 per cent of all firms were micro-businesses, 6 per cent small, 0.8 per cent medium and 0.1 per cent large. In this sense, the companies in the S&T parks of Catalonia, although with an overrepresentation of small firms, show a shift towards a relative presence of middle-sized firms (11 per cent) compared to the total of Spain (0.9 per cent), and large firms (8 per cent and 0.1 per cent respectively). Nonetheless, the dominant structure of micro and small businesses influences the capabilities of the firms in terms of innovation and investments, which historically has been limited.

The limited capacity of capital investment and the dominance of small firms, together with the leading role of real estate development in the country's economic growth until 2007, could justify why there has been a tendency to invest in land rather than innovation and economic productive capacity. In the new crisis scenario, under draconian austere measures imposed on Mediterranean countries, limited public sector investment and restricted private capital, S&T parks face uncertainties as the planning gain foundations they are based on are no longer achievable. Within this constraint and in a creative policy twist, capitalizing on the idea that high-tech products are the products and symbols of the new economy (Castells and Hall, 1994), local policy-makers repackaged existing S&T parks with urban redevelopment projects to create new S&T park identities for marketing purposes. Under three labels, Park Alba, Delta Park and 22@Barcelona[2], these new S&T park marketing entities work as a promotional tool for a geographical area bigger than the city. The marketing expands to the metro area and targets the parks for image creation.

9.6 Metropolitan scale and parks as image creation

Barcelona has been able to achieve a dramatic urban transformation in recent decades, unmatched by non-capital cities. From the early 1980s to the late 1990s the city reinvented itself from being the capital of Catalonia, an old industrial town in the European periphery of Europe, to a fashionable metropolis and a model for urban renewal and city promotion (Gonzalez, 2010). The global financial crisis of 2007 hit Barcelona at a time when its policy-makers were redefining its urban and economic policies, shifting focus from the municipality to the metropolitan scale, following lengthy efforts by political, economic and social agents to invigorate and strengthen the metropolitan dimension (Borja, 2010).

The Barcelona metropolitan region had long suffered historical challenges and shortcomings regarding strategic co-ordination and service/infrastructure management. From 1974 to 1987 the most powerful administrative body in urban planning, public transit, water supply and waste treatment was the Metropolitan Corporation of Barcelona (MCB), comprising twenty-seven municipalities. Despite its functional role, MCB was abolished in 1987 by the Catalan Parliament as a result of party-political struggles. The abolition drove institutional fragmentation and the proliferation of voluntary co-operation tools between metropolitan municipalities that fell short of providing full co-ordination (Tomàs, 2010). Local political and economic agents' efforts to co-ordinate the metropolitan administration, management and governability and drive its economic development were invigorated in 2003, with the approval of Barcelona's first metropolitan strategic plan, refreshed in 2010 as *2020 Vision*. This plan built on and expanded the lessons and experiences from three previous strategic city plans (from 1990, 1994 and 1999 respectively), alongside Barcelona municipality's many strategic sectoral plans since the 1990s including tourism, culture and sports, among others.

In Barcelona, strategic planning's focus evolved from prioritising socio-economic and urban balance to a more entrepreneurial approach (Casellas, 2006). Nevertheless, strategic urban planning has consistently been successful as a tool for building broad consensus between political and economic agents (Santacana, 1999; Raventós 1998 and 2000). A total of 650 experts in different fields collaborated for more than a year in drafting the later plan to define a vision for the future of the city's metro area.

In this policy frame, innovation and technology appear as fundamental drivers of urban upgrading. *Vision 2020* prioritises the urban restructuring of the metropolitan scale to promote knowledge-economy activities, alongside international promotion and attracting investment capital, entrepreneurs and tourism. The other main goals are business development and export expansion, investment in infrastructure and interconnectivity. To provide institutional co-ordination, in 2010, the Catalan parliament approved (via Law 31/2010 of 3 August) the creation of Barcelona Metropolitan Area (BMA), a new metro-politan governance framework covering an extended territory of 636 sq.km, covering a population of 3.2m across thirty-six municipalities (Idescat, 2010). BMA has authority over five areas, namely economic development, strategic planning, administration and territory, environment, and transport and mobility (PEMB, 2010).

Within this context, S&T parks have become one of the emerging flagships of Barcelona's reformulated economic marketing policy. Under the label 'Barcelona Economic Triangle', in 2010 city and Catalan governments initiated the international promotion of the metro area. Central to this was the identification of three technological districts, which brought together existing science parks, urban redevelopment projects and facilities, all in different stages of development. The new technological marketing districts were presented as 'consolidated economic spaces with new projects underway'. Two of these new marketing/branding S&T districts are located near the rivers that have historically defined Barcelona's city limits, the Besòs in the northeast and Llobregat river basin in the southwest; while Park Alba is located across the Collserola mountain range, to the northwest of the Barcelona metropolitan area, where Park Vallès Technology was built in the 1980s.

'Park Alba' is an amalgam of different parks and projects that constituted Catalonia's largest land development by 2011, targeting 340ha. Its most emblematic infrastructure is the new generation ALBA Synchrotron, a strategic

Catalan development project that opened in 2010 with initial capital investment of €200m of a total planned €1.5bn (including €300m earmarked for infrastructure improvement). The park's implementation involved co-operation across different governmental agents, with significant participation by Cerdanyola municipality, alongside the Catalan government's land development agency. Surrounding universities' infrastructure and facilities including the Universitat Autònoma de Barcelona's 40,000 students, and pre-existing parks including Park Vallès Technology, added to this collaborative effort. The agency leading the Alba Park development is a public agency consortium jointly owned by Cerdanyola municipality and the Catalan government (50 per cent each). The consortium is similar to 22@Barcelona in that it possesses full competencies for project implementation, including planning, financing, implementing infrastructure, managing, and national/international promotion efforts, while co-ordinating its efforts with other public agencies.

Planned development is in almost 90 per cent publicly-owned land. As with 22@Barcelona this area was planned as a mixed-use land development, including housing and other related services. Public land ownership permitted 40 per cent of housing units to be social housing, and of these 50 per cent were rented units, alongside developing a network of open green space covering a total area of 150ha. The construction bubble that crashed in Spain in 2008 and the subsequent economic crisis hit this project hard, requiring substantial reformulation given austerity and economic uncertainties. By 2013 its scientific and technological character were substituted by a mega-shopping mall project (217,250 sq.m footprint) that if implemented would become Catalonia's biggest commercial centre (Espinosa, 2013). Grassroots and small business opposition alongside 43ha. of contaminated land requiring prior remediation adds to the project's uncertain future.

'DeltaBCN', located in the Llobregat delta, is close to two major logistic infrastructures, namely the port and airport. The area was an historical development for Catalan industry, especially related to paper and textiles. During the 20th century its development was driven by port and airport, alongside industrial activity located along the riverbanks. Although initially the river delta covered an area of 100 sq.km, construction of roads, airport, port docks, industrial parks and housing left only 5 per cent of the original wetlands remaining by the late 1990s. In 1994, local, Catalan and Spanish public authorities collectively approved a plan to redevelop the area as southern Europe's principal logistics hub.

The Delta Plan implied doubling the port's size to 1,300ha., a new airport terminal increasing annually capacity to 70 million passengers, improvement of roads and rail lines, a high-speed train line and railway station. The plan development implied diverting the river southwards by 4.8km. Although contaminated, the delta still represented an area of high ecological value, with multiple species of birds, reptiles and amphibians, therefore environmental and civil society groups actively opposed the project and its attendant environmental impacts. The plan's objective is to capitalize on expanding transportation hubs and restructuring old industrial parks, and to build a strong international profile for the district wider than the specific marketing of the park: plans are also afoot to attract international attention towards the port and airport expansions and related business opportunities.

Finally, uncertainties also affect the new and expanded district with the name 22@Barcelona project. The new concept includes the 22@Barcelona project previously presented earlier, as well as the Diagonal-Besòs Campus and the Sagrera high-speed train station (both these projects began construction in 2013). Diagonal-Besòs Campus builds direct links to higher educational centres, involving three different clusters of economic activity focused on energy, water and mobility. Covering a total footprint of 77,332 sq.m, it includes a floorspace of 174,112 sq.m of academic, research and business facilities. It plans to host 6,000 students and faculty members, 1,000 researchers and 5,000 business employees. The park initiative has been driven by a consortium of two Catalan universities, the Catalan government, and Barcelona's chamber of commerce, who have combined in the 'b_TEC' Foundation. At the same time, two of its key stakeholders are public universities who have suffered swingeing budget cuts since 2012.

A second regeneration project involves developing a new high-speed train station and associated economic district. The Sagrera station connects Barcelona with the European high-speed rail network via France. Located in a working-class neighbourhood, regeneration involves covering 3.7 km overground rail tracks, which will remove a key barrier fragmenting this neighbourhood. Of the total 164ha. planned development, the total envisaged footprint is 1.7 sq.m, including 812,000 sq.m residential space, 55,000 sq.m hotels (approximately 800 rooms), alongside 380,000 sq.m office/retail associated with 30,000 planned jobs. Re-urbanisation involves creating a compact-build environment of high-rise buildings within public space consisting of a 48ha. network of urban parks. Currently being developed, the plan's success will depend on creating synergies among consolidating the remaining urban redevelopment areas of 22@Barcelona, universities' knowledge transfer and start-up creation capacities, and completing both the high-speed train line to France and an airport linkage.

9.7 Concluding remarks: the challenges of a Janus-faced strategy

Spain has been a relative latecomer in implementing parks as a spatial and institutional organizational tool for economic development. Unlike elsewhere, these parks have often been associated with wider urban redevelopment and infill activities. The chapter has explored the relationship of science parks to urban regeneration and to city promotion using the case study of the Barcelona metropolitan region, paying attention to issues of governance and marketing re-scaling.

The confusing signifier 'science and technology parks' in Spain can therefore be understood as signifying the parks' nature as an amalgam of public-sector dependent agents, often interrelated with urbanization, seeking to create positive synergies between economic growth and real estate development to attract private capital. As Benneworth *et al.* (2011) argue, science projects materialize as an intersection of public and private different interests that ultimately have to meet all partners' needs in the long term. In the Spanish case, the narrow dependency of innovation on land redevelopment has made Spanish S&T parks excessively dependent on urban development schemes, which may jeopardize the economic viability of some parks in the long term.

The reliance on urban land development coalitions – and their intertwined interests – for achieving successful parks has made it difficult to implement innovative policies that are based on primarily economic assessments and assets. As such, what should be a strategic coupling between different agents and interest to implement innovation clusters (Yeung, 2009), turns into a Janus-faced coupling of innovation and land development. This Janus-faced coupling unintentionally generates a devious strategy that has not only made innovation investment dependent upon the capacity to be able to realise capital gains through urban redevelopment, but may also reinforce the shift from innovation investment towards land development investment. This has become particularly acute in the context of the latest economic crisis, and appears to have been – insofar as we can trust the rather fragmented data sources that we have to hand – associated with disinvestment processes within firms, leading to their under-capitalisation, a failure to invest in innovation, and ultimately threatening their ability to drive future economic productivity gains.

However, it is also necessary to highlight that the leadership of the public sector in the promotion of parks in Spain has been a natural consequence of Spain's peculiar business structure. In contrast to Europe as a whole, where around 92 per cent of businesses are SMEs, in Spain the figure is over 99 per cent: in comparison with the rest of Europe, Spanish SMEs have been extremely limited in terms of their capacity to invest in and yield the benefits from R&D. These features have clearly negatively influenced the capacities within the private sector to drive forward innovation and act as a motor of development, and therefore strong public intervention has been justified in terms of attempts to improve Spain's overall innovation performance, productivity growth and long-term economic growth levels.

The case studies of parks in the metropolitan region of Barcelona, one of the Spanish regions more advanced in park growth, show the sophisticated governance structure that has been associated with the development of S&T parks, involving different levels of public bodies. The strategy has been characterised by, on the part of the public sector, the co-operation of different departments or organizations within the same tier of government, as well as different levels of public government, including the local, metropolitan and regional governments to generate co-ordination. This has all been underpinned by a willingness to use innovative vehicles and consortia to plan and shape park development.

In the longer term, the S&T parks in Barcelona emerge as the centrepiece of an economic development strategy not just for the city, but for the wider metropolitan region. But even this must be understood through the lens of the dual logic of these parks – the metropolitan scale is evoked to attract international investment and to hence drive regional economic development, but at the same time it has also provided a means to invest in real estate and drive urban redevelopment. The strategy may work as an image creation strategy that extrapolates the reputation of the city of Barcelona to its metropolitan region, but reinforces the park's (at least partly problematic) fuzzy character, which in reality embraces many different features.

Acknowledgements

The author would like to thank Julie T. Miao, Paul Benneworth, Nicholas A. Phelps for their invitation to be part of this book. She also expresses her gratitude to Paul Benneworth for extensive discussions and helpful comments on previous drafts of the chapter.

Notes

1   Despite disagreements between scholars and policy-makers regarding whether a distinctive model exists, consensus exists that the 1992 Olympic Games catalyzed a new approach to Barcelona's urban policy-making. Only 9 per cent of total Olympic investments went into sport facilities (Brunet, 1993), and the Games provided the pretext for a comprehensive urban restructuring. To secure the necessary administrative, technological and material resources for both Games and urban restructuring, the city council enrolled public and private agents thereby initiating the first public-private partnership co-operation (Maragall, 1999; Nel.lo, 1997; Santacana, 1999).

2   It capitalizes on the well-known project studied earlier, but in addition it now includes new urban redevelopment projects such as those related to a new high-speed railway station and university research centres in a nearby municipality.

Bibliography

Association of Science and Technology Parks of Spain (APTE) (2010) *Science and technology park evolution*. Available at: http://ec.europa.eu/digital-agenda/events/cf/fi-ppp-1013/document.cfm?doc_id=25196 (accessed on 10 December 2013).

Association of Science and Technology Parks of Spain (APTE) (2011) *Association of Science and Technology Parks history*. Available at: www.apte.org/en/history.cfm (accessed on 7 September 2011).

Association of Science and Technology Parks of Spain (APTE) (2013) *Association of Science and Technology Parks directory 2013*. Available at: www.apte.org/es/documents/DIRECTORIO_APTE_2013.pdf (accessed on 2 February 2014).

Audretsch, D. (2006) *The entrepreneurial society*. Oxford, UK: Oxford University Press.

Audretsch, D. and Feldman, M. (1996) 'Research & development spillovers and the geography of innovation and production'. *American Economic Review, 86*: 630–40.

Barcelona Activa (2014) Power point presentation on 22@Barcelona District. 25 February 2014.

Benneworth, P., Hospers, G.-J., Jongbloed, B., Leiyste, L. and Zomer, A. (2011) 'The 'science city' as a system coupler in fragmented strategic urban environments?'. *Built Environment, 37*(3): 317–35.

Blanco, I. (2009) 'Does a 'Barcelona Model' really exist? Periods, territories and actors in the process of urban transformation'. *Local Government Studies, 35*(3): 355–69.

Borja, J. (2010) *Llums i ombres de l'urbanisme a Barcelona*. Barcelona: Biblioteca Universal Empúries.

Brunet, F. (1993) *Economy of the 1992 Barcelona Olympic Games*. Lausanne: International Olympic Committee.

Burdett, R., Colantonio, A. and Myfanwy, T. (2010) *Barcelona. Global repositioning of an emerging metro*. London: LSE Cities London of School of Economics and Political Science.

Capel, H. (2007) 'El debate sobre la construcción de la ciudad y el llamado "Modelo Barcelona"'. *Scripta Nova. Revista Electrónica de Geografía y Ciencias Sociales, XI*(233) www.ub.es/geocrit/sn/sn-233.htm (accessed on 5 January 2014).

Casellas, A. (2006) 'Las limitaciones del "modelo Barcelona". Una lectura desde Urban Regime Analysis'. *Documents d Anàlisi Geogràfica, 48*: 61–81.

Casellas, A. (2009) 'Barcelona's urban landscape: The making of a tourist product'. *Journal of Urban History, 35*(6): 815–32.

Casellas, A. and Pallares-Barbera, M. (2009) 'Public-sector intervention in embodying the new economy in inner urban areas: The Barcelona experience'. *Urban Studies*, May, *46*(5&6): 1137–55.

Castells, M. and Hall, P. (1994) *Technopoles of the world: The making of 21st century industrial complexes*. London: Routledge.

Clua, A. and Albet, A. (2008) '22@bcn plan: Bringing Barcelona forward in the information era', in T. Yigitcanlar, K. Velibeyoglu and S. Baum (eds) *Knowledge-based urban development: Planning and applications in the information era*. Hershey: Information Science Reference (IGI Global), pp. 132–47.

Clusa, J. (1996) 'Barcelona: Economic development 1970–1995', in N. Harris and I. Fabricius, *Cities and structural adjustments*. London: University College of London Press, pp. 203–37.

Debackere, K. and De Bondt, R. (eds) (2002) Leuven Research and Development: 30 years of breakthoughs and innovations towards an entrepreneurial university. Leuven: KUL Press.

Delgado, M. (2007) *La ciudad mentirosa. Fraude y miseria del 'modelo Barcelona'*. Madrid: Los libros de la Catarata.

Dot, E., Casellas, A. and Pallares, M. (2010) 'L'ambigüitat de la producció intensiva en coneixement: el nou espai econòmic del Poblenou'. *Documents d Anàlisi Geogràfica, 56*(3): 389–408.

Espinosa, M. (2013). 'Se inician los trámites para alzar un centro comercial de más de 200.000 metros cuadrados en Cerdanyola'. *La Vanguardia*, 25 November 2013.

Etzkowitz, H. and Mello, J.M.C.D. (1994) 'The rise of triple helix cluster: Innovation in Brazilian economic and social development'. *International Journal of Technology and Management & Sustainable Development, 2*(3): 159–71.

Eurostat (2011) *Key figures on European business – with a special feature on SMEs.* http://epp.eurostat.ec.europa.eu/cache/ITY_OFFPUB/KS-ET-08-001/EN/KS-ET-08-001-EN.PDF (accessed on 2 September 2011).

Forsyth, A. and Crewe, K. (2010) 'Suburban technopoles as places: The international campus-garden-suburb style'. *Urban Design International*, *15*(3): 165–82.

Gonzalez, S. (2010) 'Bilbao and Barcelona in motion. How urban regeneration models travel and mutate in the global flows of policy tourism'. *Urban Studies*, published online 10 September 2010. doi: 10.1177/0042098010374510.

Gower, S.M. and Harris, F.C. (1994) 'The funding of, and investment in, British Science Parks'. *Journal of Property Finance*, *5*(3): 7–18.

Idescat i Observatori del Treball (2010) *Generalitat de Catalunya*. Available at: www.idescat.cat (accessed on 8 June 2013).

INFYDE (2011) 'Estudio sobre la contribución de los Parques Científicos y Tecnológicos (PCT) y Centros Tecnológicos (CCTT) a los objetivos de la Estrategia de Lisboa en España'. Available at: www.madridnetwork.org/Info/Documentos/Pdf/Informe_Final_completo_Parques_13sept20116345695995061311.pdf (accessed on 12 April 2013).

International Association of Science Parks (IASP) (2011) Available at: www.iasp.ws/publico/index.jsp?enl=2 (accessed on 7 September 2013).

Kaiser, D. (2004) 'The postwar suburbanization of American physics'. *American Quarterly*, *56*(4): 851–88.

Koschatzky, K. and Kroll, H. (2007) 'Which side of the coin? The regional governance of science and innovation'. *Regional Studies*, *41*(8): 1115–27.

Maragall, P. (1999) 'El evento como estrategia del desarrollo urbano: Los Juegos Olímpicos del '92'. In P. Maragall (ed.) *Europa próxima. Europa, regiones y ciudades*. Barcelona: Edicions Universitat de Barcelona, pp. 249–54.

Martorell, J., Bohigas, O., Mackay, D. and Puigdomenech, A. (1992) *La Villa Olímpica: Arquitectura, parques, Puerto Deportivo*. Barcelona: Editorial Gustavo Gili.

Massey, D., Quintas, P. and Wield, D. (1992). *High-tech fantasies: Science parks in society, science and space*. London: Routledge.

Modificació del Pla General Metropolità (MPGM) (2000) Available at: www.22barcelona.com/component/option,com_remository/Itemid,750/func,select/id,6/orderby,1/lang,en/ (accessed on 23 March 2013).

Nel·lo, O. (1997): 'The Olympic Games as a tool for urban renewal: the experience of Barcelona '92 Olympic Village', in M. de Moragas, M. Llinés and B. Kidd (eds) *Olympic Villages: A hundred years of urban planning and shared experiences: International symposium on olympic villages, Lausanna 1996*. Lausanne: International Olympic Committee, pp. 91–6.

Ondategui Rubio, J.C. (2001) *Los parques científicos y tecnológicos en España: Retos y oportunidades*. Available at: www.madrimasd.org/informacionidi/biblioteca/publicacion/doc/ParquesCientificosTecnologicos.pdf (accessed on 7 September 2011).

Ondategui Rubio, J.C. (2003) 'Tecnología, industria e innovación: Los parques tecnológicos en España'. PhD Thesis. Universidad Complutense de Madrid.

Parc de l'Alba (2011) Available at: www.cerdanyola.cat/webapps/web/continguts_portal/menu_principal/nova_cerdanyola/inici/Parc_de_lalba/Parc_de_l_alba.html (accessed on 18 April 2013).

Parc Tecnològic del Vallès (2011) Available at: www.ptv.es/ (accessed on 5 September 2011).

Pareja-Eastaway, M. and Piqué, J.M. (2011) 'Urban regeneration and the creative knowledge economy: The case of 22@Barcelina'. *Journal of Urban Regeneration and Renewal*, 4(4): 319–27.

Pié, R., Testar, X. and Majoral, A. (2012) Evolució i tendències en el disseny urbanístic dels parcs científics i tecnològics espanyols. *Revista Econòmica de Catalunya*, November (66): 28–43.

Pla Estratègic Metropolità de Barcelona (PEMB) (2010). *Barcelona Visisó 2020.* Available at: www.pemb.cat/wp-content/uploads/2011/04/PEMB-2020-cat-WEB. pdf (accessed on 12 January 2014).

Raventos, F. (1998) *Més d'una dècada de planificació estratègica de ciutats. 10 Anys de Planificació Estratègica a Barcelona (1988–1998).* Barcelona: Associació Pla Estratègic Barcelona, pp. 17–28.

Raventos, F. (2000) *La Col.laboració Publicoprivada.* Aula Barcelona Barcelona.

Santacana, F. (1999) 'La planificació estratègica urbana: l experiència de Barcelona', in P. Maragall (ed.) *Europa próxima. Europa, regiones y ciudades.* Barcelona: Edicions Universitat de Barcelona, pp. 261–6.

Saxenian, A.L. (1994) *Regional advantage: Culture and competition in Silicon Valley and Route 128.* Cambridge, MA: Harvard University Press.

Strategic Metropolitan Plan for Barcelona (2000) *Vision 2020.* Available at: www.pemb.cat/en/2020-vision/ (accessed on 7 September 2011).

Tomàs, M. (2010) 'Gobernabilidad metropolitana, democracia y eficiencia. Una comparación Barcelona-Montreal'. *Revista Española de Ciencia Política*, 23: 16–24.

UNECE (2013) Share of construction in GDP, %, year 2010. Available at: http://w3. unece.org/pxweb/quickstatistics/readtable.asp?qs_id=8. (accessed on 10 November 2013).

Wakeman, R. (2003) 'Dreaming the new Atlantis: Science and the planning of technopolis, 1955–1985'. *Osiris*, second series, Vol. 18, Science and the City, pp. 255–70.

Xarxa de Parcs Cientifcs de Catalunya (XPCAT) (2010) *Memòria.* Available at: www.biopol.cat/docs/Memoria/Memoria%20Biopol'H%202009.pdf (accessed on 5 July 2011).

Xarxa de Parcs Cientifcs de Catalunya (XPCAT) (2011) Available at: www.xpcat.net/ index.php?idm=3&pagina=0&subpagina=0&parc=&a=&m= (accessed on 7 September 2011).

Xarxa de Parcs Cientifcs de Catalunya (XPCAT) (2013) Available at: www.xpcat.net (accessed on 25 May 2013).

Yeung, H.W. (2009) 'Situating regional development in the competitive dynamics of global production networks: an East Asian perspective', in H.W. Yeung (ed.) *Globalizing regional development in East Asia: Production networks, clusters, and entrepreneurship.* London: Routledge.

Zerbinati, S. and Souitaris, V. (2005). 'Entrepreneurship in the public sector: A framework of analysis in European local governments'. *Entrepreneurship & Regional Development*, 17(1): 43–64.

22@Barcelona (2011) *A new model of City.* Available at: www.22barcelona.com/ content/blogcategory/37/123/lang,en/ (accessed on 19 August 2012).

Section 4

Heterogeneity and technopoles' evaluation

10 Science and Technology Parks: does one size fit all?

The importance of park and firm heterogeneity

Alberto Albahari

10.1 Introduction

Science and Technology Parks (STPs) are a particular subset of policy interventions seeking to promote agglomerations (Huang, Yu and Seetoo, 2012), designed to encourage the formation and growth of on-site technology- and knowledge-based firms, which have a management function actively engaged in achieving park goals. The interest of scholars and policy-makers in the effects of STPs on firm innovation has grown due to the wide diffusion of STPs worldwide and the huge amounts of money being invested in their creation and growth. A census of existing initiatives is not easy; however, they are a worldwide phenomenon estimated by some at 1,500 STPs (Wainova, 2009). The highest concentrations are in the US, where the phenomenon originated more than sixty years ago at Stanford University, and in Europe.

However, despite their spread, there is vibrant debate, especially among academics, about the effectiveness of STPs as innovation policy instruments. Some authors argue that STPs do not help firms to achieve improved performance, and question the STP model (e.g., Macdonald, 1987; Massey, Quintas and Wield, 1992; Hansson, Husted and Vestergaard, 2005; Quintas, Wield and Massey, 1992); others claim that STPs create added value for technology- and knowledge-based firms by facilitating technology transfer, promoting firm growth and fostering strategic alliances and networks (Siegel, Westhead and Wright, 2003a; Hommen, Doloreux and Larsson, 2006; Del Castillo Hermosa and Barroeta, 1998).

Both views are supported by empirical evidence. Some studies find no significant differences between on-park and off-park firms in relation to inputs to the innovative process (Westhead, 1997; Colombo and Delmastro, 2002), outputs of innovation activity (Löfsten and Lindelöf, 2002; Colombo and Delmastro, 2002) and research productivity (Westhead, 1997). Conversely, some authors are of the view that on-park location can have a positive impact on the inputs to the innovation process (Fukugawa, 2006; Leyden, Link and Siegel, 2008; Yang, Motohashi and Chen, 2009), research productivity (Siegel,

Westhead and Wright, 2003b; Yang, Motohashi and Chen, 2009), likelihood of patenting (Squicciarini, 2008, 2009) and sales from new products (Vásquez-Urriago *et al.*, 2014a).

Despite the burgeoning literature on STPs, it is not conclusive about the role of parks for supporting technology- and knowledge-based firms. A possible reason for this contrasting evidence may be that studies on STPs, so far, have been mainly aimed at assessing the *homogeneous* effects of on-park location. Research typically focuses on assessing whether on-park firms outperform off-park firms, assuming implicitly that all firms benefit in the same way from on-park location and that all the parks have the same effects on their tenant firms.

We suggest adopting a perspective towards STPs of asking *when*, under what conditions, STPs have a positive effect on firm performance. The basic idea is that parks are heterogeneous – some work well and create added value for their tenants, others do not – and that not all the firms benefit in the same way from location in a park. In this view, analysis of park and tenant heterogeneity is required to determine whether parks provide effective support for firms and which firms benefit the most from being located inside a STP.

Heterogeneity is central to many scientific disciplines, including biology, which inspired Nelson and Winter's (1982) *An evolutionary theory of economic change*, in which heterogeneity of economic agents is a fundamental feature (Castellacci, 2011). STPs are not an exception. Although park heterogeneity is not a new concept (more than two decades ago the United Kingdom Science Park Association stated that 'no two science parks are alike' (Grayson, 1993, p. 119)) there have been no attempts to empirically analyse the effect of parks' and tenants' heterogeneity, arguably due to the lack of appropriate data. In this chapter, we report the results of work on STPs carried out by our research group[1], aimed at questioning the homogeneity hypotheses. The rest of the chapter is organised as follows: Section 10.2 provides theoretical arguments of why parks' and tenants' heterogeneity should be taken into account when assessing parks' effects on innovation performance of tenants; Section 10.3 presents some statistics on the level of development achieved by the STP system in Spain; Section 10.4 presents an overview of the data and methodology used in the study. Section 10.5 reports findings from our studies of the respective importance of park and tenant heterogeneity. Section 10.6 presents some conclusions and Section 10.7 suggests directions for further research.

10.2 Theoretical framework

STPs are not homogenous organisations. For instance, some parks have been in operation for many years, while some are very young parks, some may have large numbers of tenants and some only a few firms. There are parks that provide business services to firms, and parks which do not, parks that are located in economically and technologically advanced regions and parks that are located in lagging regions, parks that are owned and managed by universities and parks with no relations at all with any university. Thus, we can say that STPs are heterogeneous. Similar considerations can be made for tenant companies: for example they have different age and size, may belong to different industrial sectors and differ for their internal R&D capabilities.

Nonetheless, to our knowledge no attempts have been made to empirically analyse whether STPs with different characteristics have different impacts on tenants' innovation performance, and which park characteristics help tenants to achieve better results. Similarly empirical evidence on the effects of tenants' heterogeneity on the return of the on-park location is very limited.

In this section we provide some theoretical arguments on why park and firm heterogeneity should be considered in empirical studies on STPs.

10.2.1 Are STPs all the same? The importance of park heterogeneity

From a theoretical point of view, there are arguments that support both a positive and a negative impact of many park characteristics on tenants' innovation performance.

The first characteristic we may consider is park age. On the one hand, park age may have a positive impact on tenants because STP managers are more likely over time to accumulate knowledge (Decarolis and Deeds, 1999) and to improve their understanding of tenants' needs (Gower, Harris and Cooper, 1996), allowing more effective business support. Time is also required to establish and nurture mutual trust (Mayer, Davis and Schoorman, 1995) between park management and tenants. Also, park age may have a positive effect on the results for links between tenants, which likely will increase with their duration (Izushi, 2003; Barge-Gil and Modrego, 2011). On the other hand, older parks might suffer from ossification of routines, non-learning processes, blindness and conservatism (Durand and Coeurderoy, 2001), which would have negative consequences for firms.

Another park characteristic that can affect tenants' performance is the size of the STP where they are located. We can expect that the positive externalities generated by co-location with other firms within the park will increase as the number of tenants increases (Arthur, 1990), for example, because of the increased stock of available knowledge on site (Beaudry and Breschi, 2003). By contrast, firms in larger parks might suffer diseconomies of agglomeration related to tougher competition in input and output markets (Prevezer, 1997), available space (Chen and Huang, 2004), specialized workforce (Zucker, Darby and Brewer, 1998) and utility services (Folta, Cooper and Baik, 2006).

The location of the park is another characteristic that may affect the return for firms of the on-park location. As we already know, STPs are not spontaneous agglomerations and their geographical location is often a policy decision. The intention of policy-makers is often for parks in less-developed regions to act as innovation enclaves (Felsenstein, 1994), to compensate in these regions for lack of appropriate inputs to the innovation processes compared to more-developed regions where STPs could become poles of excellence (Chorda, 1996). Given that STPs raise growth potential in more-developed and in lagging regions, we are interested in analysing whether STPs work better and have different impacts on firms if they work as enclaves of innovation or poles of excellence.

We can refer to this first set of park characteristics (age, size and location) as *structural characteristics* of the STP. But there are also some park characteristics, more related with the management of the park, that we can call *managerial characteristics*, which will likely play an important role in determining the effectiveness of the business support provided to tenants. In fact, one of the main differences between STPs and other types of agglomerations is the existence of a management team: STPs have a management function that is active in encouraging the formation and growth of on-site technology and knowledge-based firms (IASP, 2015).

The existence of a management team is believed to provide a more secure basis for firm development (Westhead and Batstone, 1999) and to help young firms to overcome the problems they typically suffer (Storey and Tether, 1998a; Löfsten and Lindelöf, 2002), mainly through the provision of business advice and services related to financial and marketing support (Westhead and Batstone, 1998; Storey and Tether, 1998b; Heydebreck, Klofsten and Maier, 2000). However, some studies point out that many firms choose an on-park location based on the site's prestige (Monck *et al.*, 1988; Westhead and Batstone, 1998) rather than expected business support. In this case, the park's management function will play a marginal role in firm innovativeness. In our research we study how the size of the management team and the provision of services affect tenants' innovation results.

Another important source of parks' heterogeneity within the managerial characteristic is the local university involvement in the park's management. The importance of universities as sources of external knowledge for firms has been acknowledged widely in the scientific literature (Etzkowitz and Leydesdorff, 1997; Bozeman, 2000; Chesbrough, 2003), along with the problems related to efficient flows of knowledge, technology and skills from academia to industry. Policies, including STPs, have been implemented to facilitate academic-industry relations aimed at facilitating and managing flows of knowledge and technology among universities, R&D institutions and firms. For this reason, the business model of many parks includes the presence or some input from a university. However, the reality is that different development patterns and a wide variety of shareholders and founders of STPs (Phan, Siegel and Wright, 2005) have resulted in very heterogeneous organizations (Westhead, 1997), with a frequent important difference being the level of university involvement in the park. In our research we are interested in analysing how this source of heterogeneity affects tenants' innovation results.

10.2.2 Are all tenants the same? The importance of firm heterogeneity

In Section 10.2.1 we have provided the theoretical argument for considering the heterogeneity of the supply-side of a STP. However, given that STPs are primarily business-support institutions, it is also possible that heterogeneity in the demand-side, that is, the different characteristics of tenants, affects the returns from on-park location.

There are several critics of the tacit assumption made in most papers on industrial districts and economic geography regarding the relative homogeneity of firms (Lazerson and Lorenzoni, 1999; Maskell, 2001). There are theoretical arguments and empirical evidence supporting the effect of firm characteristics on the advantages derived by firms from location in an innovative environment and, more specifically, proximity to other firms and R&D institutions (Caniels and Romijn, 2003; Giuliani, 2007; Hervas-Oliver and Albors-Garrigos, 2009; Hervas-Oliver, 2011). What remains still to be debated is whether higher or lower internal R&D capabilities enable firms to benefit more from an innovative environment. Firms with higher internal capabilities have higher absorptive capacity (Cohen and Levinthal, 1990) which enables them to recognize the value of new knowledge and to assimilate and use it. On the other hand, firms with lower levels of internal capabilities will be more motivated to access external knowledge (Shaver and Flyer, 2000; Barge-Gil, 2010) in order to innovate (Rammer, Czarnitzki and Spielkamp, 2009). Given that knowledge spillovers are often geographically localized (Feldman and Kogler, 2010), such firms should benefit from location in an innovative environment.

Despite the evidence on the role of firm characteristics in determining the returns from location in an innovative environment such as an STP, the heterogeneity of firms is mostly ignored in studies on STPs. To our knowledge, the only relevant exception is Huang, Yu and Seetoo (2012). They investigated 165 Taiwanese manufacturing firms using regression analysis and linear interaction terms between the on-park location and firms' characteristics. They found that smaller firms benefit more from location on-park than larger firms, measured in terms of innovation performance based on patent applications. They explain this finding as due to smaller firms being more able to demonstrate credit worthiness in order to raise capital to conduct innovation activities, attract specialized skilled workers, and access technology from other park firms. Also, larger firms are less likely to acquire external knowledge and technology from third parties within the park, explaining their reduced benefit from on-park location compared to smaller firms (Huang, Yu and Seetoo, 2012).

We contribute to this issue by assessing whether on-park location is more beneficial for firms with higher or lower internal capabilities.

10.3 The Spanish experience

The first parks, promoted by regional governments, appeared in Spain in the late 1980s. Since then their number has increased and, at the end of 2012, there were forty-eight operative STPs, in fifteen different Spanish regions, hosting approximately 6,200 firms and employing 146,000 people[2] (APTE, 2013). Without doubt, one of the reasons for this rapid diffusion has been the strong commitment of central government, which has implemented sets of policies specifically designed to support STPs (Albahari, Catalano and

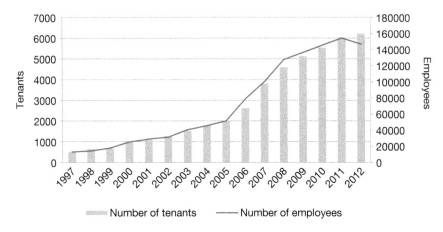

Figure 10.1 Evolution of the number of tenants and employees in APTE's park
Source: Adapted from APTE, 2013.

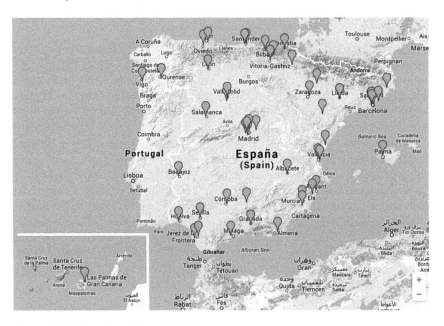

Figure 10.2 Location of Spanish STPs
Source: Google, 2014. Map data GeoBasis-DE/BKG (2009). Google, based on BCNIGN España.

Landoni, 2013) and whose STP investment is estimated at over €1,600 million (COTEC, 2011). Based on the size of this investment, STPs can be considered one of the main innovation policies implemented by central government in Spain.

Figure 10.1 provides an overview of the level of development of STPs in Spain, showing the evolution in numbers of tenants and employees; Figure 10.2 shows the locations of Spanish STPs and their geographic spread across the territory.

The high number of STPs, their heterogeneity and the availability of reliable data make Spain an ideal case for this research.

10.4 Data and methodology

Lack of systematic data collection is a common problem in research on STPs (Phan, Siegel and Wright, 2005). In our research, we rely on the Community Innovation Survey (CIS) for Spain. The Spanish CIS is managed by the National Statistics Institute (INE), is mandatory,[3] and collects very detailed information on the innovation behaviour of firms. Since 2007, the survey has included a question about on-park location and name of park. The responses to this question allow us to study how the innovation results of tenants are affected by the characteristics of STPs and how firms' characteristics affect the return of the on-park location.

Information on parks' characteristics come from the *Survey 2009 on the characteristics and results of science and technology parks*, which is an annual survey, introduced in 2008, by the Ministry of Economic Affairs and Competitiveness[4] of the Spanish Government, administered to Spanish STP management entities. Response is mandatory for receipt of government financial aid (Albahari, Catalano and Landoni, 2013).

These data sources constitute a strength of our research. Full microdata sets are not publicly available and access to this information was enabled by research contracts with INE and with the Ministry of Science and Innovation of the Government of Spain. Use of CIS data allows us to employ a wide set of co-variates and to achieve much higher heterogeneity across STPs than in previous quantitative studies, many of which are based on only a very few parks (e.g., Yang, Motohashi and Chen, 2009; Malairaja and Zawdie, 2008; Chan, Oerlemans and Pretorius, 2011; Bakouros, Mardas and Varsakelis, 2002; Felsenstein, 1994). Compared with other works (e.g., Squicciarini, 2008, 2009; Fukugawa, 2006; Colombo and Delmastro 2002; Westhead, 1997; Westhead and Storey, 1995; Siegel, Westhead and Wright, 2003b; Löfsten and Lindelöf, 2002), we rely on a much higher number of firms. For example, in the 2009 CIS survey the sample is composed of 37,201 firms, 849 of which are located on one of the twenty-five STPs included in the study.

We have used different methods to carry out our research. To obtain empirical evidence on how STP *structural* and *managerial* characteristics affect the innovation performance of tenants we employ multiple linear (OLS) and non-linear (Tobit) regressions with controls. The dependent variable we use to measure the innovation performance is the volume of sales of new-to-the market products.[5] This variable is used frequently in studies of innovation (for a review see, e.g., Vásquez-Urriago *et al.*, 2014a). When the effect of university involvement is analysed we also used the number of patents[6] as dependent variable. Controls include firm size, age, exports, industrial sector, innovation effort and perceived obstacle to innovation. We test the robustness of results to different definitions of the dependent and some of the independent variables.[7]

To assess whether on-park location is more beneficial for some types of firms compared to others we estimated the average treatment effect, which has been often used to analyse the causal effects of programmes or policies (so-called 'treatment effects'), with STP location being, in our case, the 'treatment'.[8]

10.5 Results

In this section we present the results of our research. First we focus on the effect of park *structural* characteristics (i.e., park age, dimension and location) and *managerial* characteristics (i.e., number of full-time equivalent employees in the management company, provision of services by park management and involvement of university in the park) on innovation. Then the focus shifts to tenants' heterogeneity to show whether on-park location is more beneficial to some types of firms than others.

10.5.1 Effect of structural characteristics

We found that the park age has a non-linear effect on sales of innovative products: firms located in younger and older parks out-perform those in mid-aged parks. We interpret this finding as the result of a twofold impact of on-park location. There is an initial short-term positive impact on the firm generated by marketing aspects such as increased visibility and higher reputation, and a long-term positive effect that is likely due to the accumulation of knowledge and trust, organizational learning, experience of interacting and better understanding of tenants' needs. This interpretation reconciles the two contrasting views in the literature: the short-term effect confirms the arguments that STPs are prestigious locations for innovative firms, and the long-term positive effect supports the idea of STPs as innovation policy instruments. This result strengthens Castells and Hall's opinion, who claim that quite a long period, between twenty and thirty years, is needed for STPs to fully show their effects on tenants (Castells and Hall, 1994, p. 236).

In relation to park size, we found a positive effect of size on tenants' innovation performance. This finding is indicative of economies of agglomeration, probably due to a larger stock of knowledge in larger parks, which facilitates knowledge spillovers. We found no evidence of congestion effects, although we cannot discount the parks in our sample being of insufficient size to exhibit them.

Using different measures for the level of technological development in the region[9] we found that STPs have a higher impact on tenants' performance in areas with lower levels of technological development. This finding supports the role of STPs as instruments of innovation policy in less-developed regions, where parks constitute enclaves of innovation that counters the lack of valuable inputs that more developed regions provide for their firms.

10.5.2. Effect of managerial characteristics of STPs

Where managerial characteristics are concerned we first analysed the effect of management team size and provision of services on the innovation results of tenants; then we studied how the different level of university involvement within the park affects tenants' performance.

Where the size of the park management team is concerned we found that it positively affects innovation performance: the larger the team is, the better for tenants. A possible explanation for this result is that a larger management team helps firms to achieve better results, for example, by enhancing the entrepreneur's network, augmenting firms' reputations and helping to create an environment conducive to innovation. However, this positive effect cannot be ascribed to the provision of services by park management: services to foster internationalization were not found to have a statistically significant effect, while the effect of general consultancy services on innovation performance is negative. These latter results can be explained by the likely lower quality of the services provided by management compared with those available in the market.

To analyse how the different levels of formal involvement of universities in STP initiatives affects the innovation performances of tenant firms, we identified four types of park according to level of formal university involvement: a) parks owned and managed by a university; b) parks where the university is a minority shareholder; c) parks where the university is not a shareholder, but has some formal research facilities or personnel on-park; and d) parks with no formal connections with universities. We studied whether and how tenants' innovation performance and also tenants' links with universities are affected by the location of the firm in the different types of park. We found that higher involvement of a university negatively affects turnover from new-to-the-market products: firms on parks with no relations with universities out-perform firms on parks managed by universities on this measure. By contrast, higher levels of university involvement positively affect the propensity of firms to apply for patents. These results can be explained by the difficulties experienced by Spanish universities keen to commercialize their research (Testar Ymbert, 2012), which seems also to be translated to the parks they manage. We found also that the involvement of a university in a STP does not seem to affect the propensity of tenants to co-operate with universities nor affect the amount of R&D bought from the university. Table 10.1 summarises main findings.

Table 10.1 Effects of park characteristics on tenants' innovation performance

Characteristics	Effect on tenants' innovation performance
Structural characteristics	
Age	Non-linear effect. Firms in younger and older parks outperform firms in mid-aged parks
Size	Positive effect. No evidence of congestion effects
Location	On-park location has higher impacts in less developed areas
Managerial characteristics	
Management Team Size	Positive effect
Services	General consulting services have a negative effect. Services to foster internationalization have a statistically non-significant effect
University Involvement	Negative effect on innovation sales. Positive effect on patenting activity

10.5.3 Are all tenants the same? The importance of firm heterogeneity

We analysed the heterogeneous effect of STPs on firms' innovation results, contingent to two tenant dimensions: size and innovation effort.

We found that the effect of the on-park location on firms' innovativeness decreases with increasing firm size, that is, smaller firms benefit more than larger ones from a location in a park. One possible explanation for this finding is that smaller firms are quick and flexible enough to recognize and take advantages from opportunities generated in the environment (Rogers, 2004; Rammer, Czarnitzki and Spielkamp, 2009).

In relation to innovation effort, the effect of on-park location on the innovativeness of tenants seems to be higher for firms with lower levels of innovation effort compared to more R&D-intensive firms. However, it should be noted that tenants who do not perform innovation activities scarcely benefit from being on-park. This last finding suggests that some level of absorptive capacity is needed to benefit from the on-park location.

These findings suggest that smaller firms with lower internal R&D capabilities benefit more from location in a STP, confirming Huang, Yu and Seetoo's (2012) findings (see Section 10.2.2).

10.6 Conclusions

At the Laboratory for Analysis and Evaluation of Technical Change at the Instituto de Economía in the Universidad Carlos III de Madrid, we have created a multidisciplinary team, with members from various Spanish universities that have been researching STPs since 2007. In this chapter we have presented our most recent research results for how STPs work and under what conditions they have more positive impacts on firms.

The STP phenomenon has attracted the attention of policy-makers, practitioners and academics. This interest is justified by the increased importance of STPs in the technology and innovation scenarios of many countries around the world. Many studies focused on assessing the effect of on-park location on tenants' performance, typically comparing on- and off-park firms. However, these studies overlook the fact that STPs are not all the same, and that by being somehow 'better' they provide firms with greater advantages. Similarly, the on-park location could be more beneficial for some firms than others. In other words, we were interested in studying the effects of supply- and demand-side heterogeneity respectively. Heterogeneity is thus at the core of our research on STPs.

Our research has implications at the theoretical, managerial and policy levels. From a theoretical perspective we have shown that heterogeneity of both parks and tenants should be considered when assessing the added value of on-park location for firms' innovativeness. Thus, future quantitative studies of STPs should include supply- and demand-side characteristics as control variables. The implications for managers apply to both tenants and prospective tenant firms, park managers and university decision-makers. When deciding about location on an STP, firm managers should be aware of the different comparative advantages provided by an on-park location for a series of firm and park characteristics. In particular, firms should consider park age, size, characteristics of the management company, level of technological development in the region where they are located, and the level of university involvement within the park. Our research suggests that the management of firms located in parks should obtain services from the best provider, which may not be the park's management. At the same time, they should be aware that on-park location provides different advantages for different firms, with smaller and less R&D-intensive firms benefiting the most from a location in a park. For park managers, our advice would be to provide services that compete with those that can be obtained from external providers. More generally, our work suggests ways that park management could increase the added value for tenants. In particular, a larger number of park firms and a larger management team seem beneficial for tenants.

For university managers, our research suggest that university involvement in park ownership/management allows firms to benefit from the knowledge created in the university, as shown by the higher levels of patenting activity, but that more effort is needed to transform this knowledge into commercial outputs. So far, Spanish STPs have not enabled strong co-operation links between university departments and firms.

At policy level, the existence of a long-term effect of parks on firms' innovation performance and the fact that on-park location is more beneficial for firms in less-developed regions, support the view of STPs as technology and innovation policy instruments. The heterogeneous effects identified suggest that policy-makers should avoid indiscriminate financial support for STPs, since we show that some STPs operate better than others. Taking account of the heterogeneity of STPs could help policy-makers to design more effective support schemes.

10.7 Directions for further research

Finally we suggest some directions for further research.

Our work is based on CIS data for Spain and, thus, focuses on Spain. It would be interesting to extend it to other countries, especially those characterised by a different entrepreneurial culture. We analysed the effect on firms of a level of formal involvement of a university in the STP. An interesting extension of this may include measures of university and university department quality.

Overall, we believe that more studies of park heterogeneity would add to knowledge in this area. For example, studying STP ecology and demographics might be an interesting research line. Also, despite heavy data requirements, a joint analysis of firms' and parks' heterogeneity might allow the development of more context-specific strategies to foster innovation through STPs.

Acknowledgments

The authors want to thank the Spanish Institute of Statistics for access to the data, and acknowledge funding from Spanish Department of Science and Innovation under the project 'Evaluación del Impacto de los Parques Científicos y Tecnológicos Españoles'.

Notes

1   The research was carried out at the Laboratory for Analysis and Evaluation of Technical Change at the Instituto de Economía, Universidad Carlos III de Madrid, and funded by the Ministry of Science and Innovation of the Government of Spain, through the project 'Data analyses of the Survey on Spanish Science and Technology Parks'.
2   These figures refer to APTE (the Spanish Association of Science and Technology Parks) members only. To our knowledge, the only sizeable (in terms of numbers of employees and tenants) park that is not a member of APTE is the Parque de la Innovación de Navarra.
3   Infractions attract fines of €60 to €30,000.
4   Formerly the Ministry of Science and Innovation.
5   Operationally, the dependent variable is the logarithm of the sales from new-to-the-market products/services per employee (see Albahari *et al.*, 2013a,b and Vásquez-Urriago, Barge-Gil and Modrego, 2014b).
6   Operationally, the dependent variable is the logarithm of the of number of patent applications per employee (see Albahari *et al.*, 2013b).
7   More details on the methodology followed can be found in Albahari *et al.* (2013a,b).

8   More details on the methodology followed can be found in Vásquez-Urriago, Barge-Gil and Modrego (2014a).
9   I.e., number of patents per million inhabitants in the province, gross domestic provincial product per capita, number of patent applications in the region, and regional R&D effort.

Bibliography

Albahari, A., Catalano, G. and Landoni, P. (2013) 'Evaluation of national science park systems: A theoretical framework and its application to the Italian and Spanish systems'. *Technology Analysis and Strategic Management, 25*(5): 599–614.

Albahari, A., Barge-Gil, A., Pérez-Canto, S. and Modrego-Rico, A. (2013a) 'The influence of science and technology park characteristics on firms' innovation results'. *MPRA Paper 48829*, University Library of Munich, Germany.

Albahari, A., Pérez-Canto, S., Barge-Gil, A. and Modrego-Rico, A. (2013b) 'Technology parks versus science parks: Does the university make the difference?'. *MPRA Paper 49227*, University Library of Munich, Germany.

APTE (2013) *Memoria APTE 2012*. Malaga: APTE, Association of Science and Technology Parks of Spain.

Arthur, W.B. (1990) '"Silicon Valley" locational clusters: When do increasing returns imply monopoly?'. *Mathematical Social Sciences, 19*(3): 235–51.

Bakouros, Y.L., Mardas, D.C. and Varsakelis, N.C. (2002) 'Science park, a high tech fantasy? An analysis of the science parks of Greece'. *Technovation, 22*(2): 123–8.

Barge-Gil, A. (2010) 'Open, semi-open and closed innovators. Towards an explanation of degree of openness'. *Industry and Innovation, 17*(6): 577–607.

Barge-Gil, A. and Modrego, A. (2011) 'The impact of research and technology organizations on firm competitiveness. Measurement and determinants'. *Journal of Technology Transfer, 36*(1): 61–83.

Beaudry, C. and Breschi, S. (2003) 'Are firms in clusters really more innovative?'. *Economics of Innovation and New Technology, 12*(4): 325–42.

Bozeman, B. (2000) 'Technology transfer and public policy: A review of research and theory'. *Research Policy, 29*(4): 627–55.

Caniëls, M.C.J. and Romijn, H.A. (2003) 'Firm-level knowledge accumulation and regional dynamics'. *Industrial and Corporate Change, 12*(6): 1253–78.

Castellacci, F. (2011) 'Theoretical models of heterogeneity, growth and competitiveness: Insights from the mainstream and evolutionary economics paradigms', in M. Jovanovic (ed.), *International handbook of economic integration, volume II* (pp. 90–118). Cheltenman, UK: Edward Elgar.

Castells, M. and Hall, P. (1994) *Technopoles of the world: The making of 21st century industrial complexes*. London, UK: Routledge.

Chan, K.Y.A., Oerlemans, L.A. and Pretorius, M.W. (2011) 'Innovation outcomes of South African new technology-based firms: A contribution to the debate on the performance of science park firms'. *South African Journal of Economic and Management Sciences, 14*(4): 361–78.

Chen, C.J. and Huang, C.C. (2004) 'A multiple criteria evaluation of high-tech industries for the science-based industrial park in Taiwan'. *Information & Management, 41*(7): 839–51.

Chesbrough, H.W. (2003) *Open innovation. The new imperative for creating and profiting from technology*. Boston, MA: Harvard Business School Press.

Chorda, I.M. (1996) 'Towards the maturity stage: An insight into the performance of French technopoles'. *Technovation*, *16*(3): 143–52.

Cohen, W.M. and Levinthal, D.A. (1990) 'Absorptive capacity: A new perspective on learning and innovation'. *Administrative Science Quarterly*, *35*(1): 128–52.

Colombo, M.G. and Delmastro, M. (2002) 'How effective are technology incubators? Evidence from Italy'. *Research Policy*, *31*(7): 1103–22.

COTEC (2011) *Análisis de la evolución de los parques científicos españoles*. Madrid: Fundación Cotec para la Innovación Tecnológica.

Decarolis, D.M. and Deeds, D.L. (1999) 'The impact of stocks and flows of organizational knowledge on firm performance: An empirical investigation of the biotechnology industry'. *Strategic Management Journal*, *20*(10): 953–68.

Del Castillo Hermosa, J. and Barroeta, B. (1998) 'The technology park at Beocillo: An instrument for regional development in Castilla-Leon'. *Progress in Planning*, *49*(3–4): 241–54.

Durand, R. and Coeurderoy, R. (2001) 'Age, order of entry, strategic orientation, and organizational performance'. *Journal of Business Venturing*, *16*(5): 471–94.

Etzkowitz, H. and Leydesdorff, L. (1997) *Universities and the global knowledge economy: A triple helix of university-industry-government relations*. London: Pinter.

Feldman, M. and Kogler, D. (2010) 'Stylized facts in the geography of innovation', in B.H. Hall and N. Rosenberg (eds), *The handbook of the economics of innovation, volume 1* (pp. 381–410). Amsterdam: Elsevier.

Felsenstein, D. (1994) 'University-related science parks – Seedbeds or enclaves of innovation'. *Technovation*, *14*(2): 93–110.

Folta, T.B., Cooper, A.C. and Baik, Y.S. (2006) 'Geographic cluster size and firm performance'. *Journal of Business Venturing*, *21*(2): 217–42.

Fukugawa, N. (2006) 'Science parks in Japan and their value-added contributions to new technology-based firms'. *International Journal of Industrial Organization*, *24*(2): 381–400.

Giuliani, E. (2007) 'The selective nature of knowledge networks in clusters: Evidence from the wine industry'. *Journal of Economic Geography*, *7*(2): 139–68.

Google (2014) *Map data GeoBasis-DE/BKG (2009)*. Google, based on BCNIGN España. Available at: https://mapsengine.google.com/map/edit?mid=znXntMfue8Yc.kuw0ZeaYiYew (accessed on 16 May 2014).

Gower, S.M., Harris, F.C. and Cooper, P.A. (1996) 'Assessing the management of science parks in the UK'. *Property Management*, *14*(1): 30–8.

Grayson, L. (1993) *Science parks: An experiment in high technology transfer*. London: The British Library Board.

Hansson, F., Husted, K. and Vestergaard, J. (2005) 'Second generation science parks: From structural holes jockeys to social capital catalysts of the knowledge society'. *Technovation*, *25*(9): 1039–49.

Hervas-Oliver, J.L. (2011) 'When and why companies benefit from collocation in clusters?'. Paper presented at the *DRUID 2011: Innovation, strategy, and structure – organizations, institutions, systems and regions*. Copenhagen Business School, Denmark, 15–17 June.

Hervas-Oliver, J.L. and Albors-Garrigos, J. (2009) 'The role of the firm's internal and relational capabilities in clusters: When distance and embeddedness are not enough to explain innovation'. *Journal of Economic Geography*, *9*(2): 263–83.

Heydebreck, P., Klofsten, M. and Maier, J. (2000) 'Innovation support for new technology-based firms: The Swedish Teknopol approach'. *R&D Management*, *30*(1): 89–100.

Hommen, L., Doloreux, D. and Larsson, E. (2006) 'Emergence and growth of Mjardevi Science Park in Linkoping, Sweden'. *European Planning Studies*, *14*(10): 1331–61.

Huang, K.F., Yu, C.M.J. and Seetoo, D.H. (2012) 'Firm innovation in policy-driven parks and spontaneous clusters: The smaller firm the better?'. *The Journal of Technology Transfer*, *37*(5): 715–31.

IASP (2015) Available at www.iasp.ws/the-role-of-stps-and-innovation-areas (accessed on 4 February 2015).

Izushi, H. (2003) 'Impact of the length of relationships upon the use of research institutes by SMEs'. *Research Policy*, *32*: 771–88.

Lazerson, M.H. and Lorenzoni, G. (1999) 'The firms that feed industrial districts: A return to the Italian source'. *Industrial and Corporate Change*, *8*(2): 235–66.

Leyden, D., Link, A.N. and Siegel, D.S. (2008) 'A theoretical and empirical analysis of the decision to locate on a university research park'. *IEEE Transactions on Engineering Management*, *55*(1): 23–8.

Löfsten, H. and Lindelöf, P. (2002) 'Science parks and the growth of new technology-based firms – academic-industry links, innovation and markets'. *Research Policy*, *31*(6): 859–76.

MacDonald, S. (1987) 'British science parks: Reflections on the politics of high technology'. *R&D Management*, *17*(1): 25–37.

Malairaja, C. and Zawdie, G. (2008) 'Science parks and university-industry collaboration in Malaysia'. *Technology Analysis & Strategic Management*, *20*(6): 727–39.

Maskell, P. (2001) 'The firm in economic geography'. *Economic Geography*, *77*(4): 329–44.

Massey, D., Quintas, P. and Wield, D. (1992) *High tech fantasies: Science parks in society, science and space*. London: Routledge.

Mayer, R.C., Davis, J.H. and Schoorman, F.D. (1995) 'An integrative model of organizational trust'. *Academy of Management Review*, *20*(3): 709–34.

Monck, C.S.P., Porter, R.B., Quintas, P., Storey, D. and Wynarczyk, P. (1988) *Science parks and the growth of high-technology firms*. London: Croom Helm.

Nelson, R. and Winter, S. (1982) *An evolutionary theory of economic change*. Cambridge: The Belknap Press of Harvard University Press.

Phan, P.H., Siegel, D.S. and Wright, M. (2005) 'Science parks and incubators: Observations, synthesis and future research'. *Journal of Business Venturing*, *20*(2): 165–82.

Prevezer, M. (1997) 'The dynamics of industrial clustering in biotechnology'. *Small Business Economics*, *9*(3): 255–71.

Quintas, P., Wield, D. and Massey, D. (1992) 'Academic-industry links and innovation – Questioning the science park model'. *Technovation*, *12*(3): 161–75.

Rammer, C., Czarnitzki, D. and Spielkamp, A. (2009) 'Innovation success of non-R&D-performers: Substituting technology by management in SMEs'. *Small Business Economics*, *33*(1): 35–58.

Rogers, M. (2004) 'Networks, firm size and innovation'. *Small Business Economics*, *22*(2): 141–53.

Shaver, J. and Flyer, F. (2000) 'Agglomeration economics, firm heterogeneity, and foreign direct investment in the United States'. *Strategic Management Journal*, *21*(12): 1175–993.

Siegel, D.S., Westhead, P. and Wright, M. (2003a) 'Science parks and the performance of new technology-based firms: A review of recent UK evidence and an agenda for future research'. *Small Business Economics*, *20*(2): 177–84.

Siegel, D.S., Westhead, P. and Wright, M. (2003b) 'Assessing the impact of university science parks on research productivity: Exploratory firm-level evidence from the United Kingdom'. *International Journal of Industrial Organization, 21*(9): 1357–69.

Squicciarini, M. (2008) 'Science parks' tenants versus out-of-park firms: Who innovates more? A duration model'. *Journal of Technology Transfer, 33*(1): 45–71.

Suicciarini, M. (2009) 'Science parks: seedbeds of innovation? A duration analysis of firms' patenting activity'. *Small Business Economics, 32*(2): 169–90.

Storey, D.J. and Tether, B.S. (1998a) 'New technology-based firms in the European Union: An introduction'. *Research Policy, 26*(9): 933–46.

Storey, D.J. and Tether, B.S. (1998b) 'Public policy measures to support new technology-based firms in the European Union'. *Research Policy, 26*(9): 1037–57.

Testar Ymbert, X. (2012) Informe CYD 2011. *Monografía. La transferencia de tecnología y conocimiento universidad-empresa en España: estado actual, retos y oportunidades*. Barcelona: Fundación Conocimiento y Desarrollo.

Vásquez-Urriago, A.R., Barge-Gil, A. and Modrego, A. (2014a) 'Which firms benefit more from being located in a Science and Technology Park? Empirical evidence for Spain'. *MPRA Paper 55130*, University Library of Munich, Germany.

Vásquez-Urriago, A.R., Barge-Gil, A., Modrego, A. and Paraskevopoulou, E. (2014a) 'The impact of science and technology parks on firms' product innovation: Empirical evidence from Spain'. *Journal of Evolutionary Economics, 24*(4): 835–73.

Wainova (2009) *Wainova atlas of innovation: Science/technology/research parks and business incubators in the world*. Cheshire: Ten Alps Publishing.

Westhead, P. (1997) 'R&D "inputs" and "outputs" of technology-based firms located on and off science parks'. *R&D Management, 27*(1): 45–62.

Westhead, P. and Batstone, S. (1998) 'Independent technology-based firms: The perceived benefits of a science park location'. *Urban Studies, 35*(12): 2197–219.

Westhead, P. and Batstone, S. (1999) 'Perceived benefits of a managed science park location'. *Entrepreneurship & Regional Development: An International Journal, 11*(2): 129–54.

Westhead, P. and Storey, D.J. (1995) 'Links between higher-education institutions and high-technology firms'. *Omega-International Journal of Management Science, 23*(4): 345–60.

Yang, C.H., Motohashi, K. and Chen, J.R. (2009): 'Are new technology-based firms located on science parks really more innovative? Evidence from Taiwan'. *Research Policy, 38*(1): 77–85.

Zucker, L., Darby, M. and Brewer, M. (1998) 'Intellectual human capital and the birth of US biotechnology enterprises'. *American Economic Review, 88*(1): 290–306.

11 Stories behind science parks

Resources and networking in Optics Valley of China, Wuhan

Julie Tian Miao

11.1 Introduction

A search for the term 'Science Park' on Google Scholar returns over 80 per cent of publications focusing on developed economies, led by North America. The world's first university science park, Stanford, was established over sixty years ago, and now more than 170 university research and science parks are located in the USA. While the world has paid much attention to this productive land for inspiration and lessons, developing countries have increasingly been adopting, and more importantly adapting, this model to suit their own contexts and development targets. China, for example, was home to eighty-eight science and technology industry parks (STIPs) at the national level by 2011, almost quadruple the number two decades ago. These STIPs hosted over 57,000 companies in 2011, accounting for a total industrial value added of 2715.2 bn RMB ($US435m) (MOST, 2012).

Given the rising popularity of the concept of technopole in developing countries, it is therefore timely to revisit, and possibly update, the archetype classification advanced by Castells and Hall (1994), especially their second and third types of technopoles, i.e., science cities and technology parks. Castells and Hall profiled science cities as those 'strictly scientific research complexes, with no direct territorial linkage to manufacturing' (p. 10), while technology parks referred to those spaces that mainly targeted:

> inducing new industrial growth, in terms of jobs and production, by attracting high-technology manufacturing firms to a privilege space. Innovation functions are not excluded from such projects, but they are mainly defined in terms of economic development.
>
> (ibid., pp. 10–11)

In terms of their potential added value, Castells and Hall (1994) warned that for science cities, 'spatial concentration of research activities has little effect on scientific innovation in the absence of a deliberate program to favour synergy', and without such programmes, 'old scientific vices', (i.e., a lack of interaction between academia and industry), 'are simply reproduced in the new science cities' (p. 81). For technology parks' success, they emphasized the importance of interactions between public research centres and universities, large firms, and small and medium-sized firms. But judged against the strongest definition of providing a fertile innovation milieu, few of the technology parks they examined were successful.

Their cautious attitude towards these dominantly 'top-down' innovation complexes finds its echoes in other studies (see, for example, Massey, Quintas and Wield, 1992; Phillimore and Joseph, 2003; Westhead and Storey, 1994). Although Castells and Hall (1994) adopted a history-friendly and multi-dimensional analytical framework, most recent science park literature tends to carry an implicit model of unidirectional knowledge transfer from research institutions to companies and then into the market (see, for example, Chen and Kenney, 2007; Hong 2008). In the case of China, the lack of trust and interactions between knowledge institutions and private sectors has led many scholars to focus exclusively on either research institutions or companies as if they were operating in a vacuum. Furthermore, Chinese case studies have been overwhelmingly focused on science parks located in the coastal regions, notably around Beijing and Shanghai. The reality is that almost every Chinese province now hosts at least one national level STIP (Torch Center, 2009), but what is less understood is how effective this model is in promoting economic growth in China's hinterland.

To address above these research lacunae, I argue for moving beyond linear knowledge transfer and paying greater attention to science parks' system dynamics. While Castells and Hall (1994) already pointed out the importance of interactions between the various park components for cultivating an innovative milieu, they did not offer an opinion on whether the characteristics of different park actors could influence interactive processes. Therefore, in this chapter, the research questions I will focus upon are the following:

1   What are the contributions of science parks in inland China?
2   How do the different characteristics of on-park companies make a difference to their contributions?

I will address these questions drawing upon a case-study region from inland China, where science parks are playing an increasingly important role, and explore the different ways in which the multiple innovation elements interact to create new configurations of industrial complex. Specifically, I use a detailed case study on Optics Valley of China (OVC) in Wuhan, Hubei Province to contend that in China, companies' ownership could influence their international resources, external relations, and ultimately their economic performance.

11.2 Science parks and innovation systems

Studies of science parks have long tended to be primarily empirical-descriptive rather than theoretical-explanatory. When the first generation of science parks appeared in the 1950s and 1960s, scholars often interpreted these as property developments (Carter, 1989; Gower and Harris, 1994; Massey and Wield, 1992) and later suburban expansion (Forsyth and Crewe, 2010). Geographically the focus was predominantly on western countries, given their pioneer experiences, such as the US and UK. As the scope of science park practices expanded in the 1990s (AURP and Battelle, 2007), researchers correspondingly broadened their attention to cover various kinds of interactions both within and outside science parks (Phillimore, 1999). Lindelöf and Löfsten (2002, 2003, 2005), for example, compared on- and off-park firms in Sweden. Their quantitative analysis not only identified performance differences between these two groups of firms, but also found that firms' characteristics, such as motivation, management competencies and academic background, were all highly relevant for their innovation and marketing activities.

Some shortcomings can be distinguished in these earlier studies. First, the most innovative studies tended to focus predominantly on firms (McAdam and McAdam, 2008; Watkins-Mathys and Foster, 2006), overlooking the wider institutional environment within which these actors and science parks exist. Institutional factors may play a crucial role in the operation, function and growth prospection of such industrial complexes (Huang, see Chapter 7 in this volume).

Second, the bulk of science park literatures are based on the experience of more developed economics. It is not uncommon to see bottom-up initiatives in shaping the path and performance of these industrial complexes, as illustrated perhaps most clearly by the case of Silicon Valley (see Chapter 1, this volume). In contrast, science parks in developing countries and in Asian regions are often top-down initiatives from the central state, creating perceivably different underlying dynamics and innovative ecosystems. Castells and Hall's (1994) original account of 'science cities' and 'technology parks' needs urgently upgrading to reflect the growing popularity of this approach in these emerging economic areas.

Finally, and related to that, current studies on science parks are quite often an ad hoc analysis of their performance without reference to a systematic, comparable framework. In order to understand the contemporary features of science parks, especially those mushrooming forms in developing countries, a better structured theoretical framework is urgently required, which takes into account the systematic nature and institutional environment of science parks.

To address this issue, in this chapter I adopt innovation systems theory (OECD, 1997). Lundvall (1992), for example, suggested that the 'core' of the innovation system is private companies. Its 'supporting infrastructure' includes institutions directly involved in producing, diffusing and using knowledge, such as universities and financial departments; as well as the much wider socioeconomic system. The interactions within companies and institutional actors, as well as between them, in turn determines how efficiently knowledge and innovation can be created, transferred, utilised and multiplied. Figure 11.1 below illustrates a simple innovation system, highlighting the most important institutional infrastructure factors.

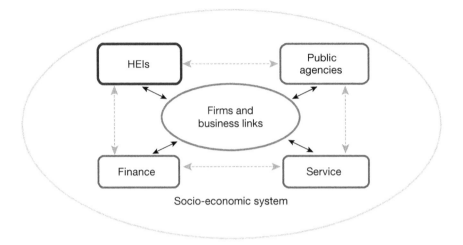

Figure 11.1 The simple structure of an innovation system
Source: The author.

Since its first appearance, the innovation system (IS) approach rapidly gained popularity both politically and academically. The OECD published many case studies on national innovation systems across European countries (OECD, 1999). Since the 2000s, studies on regional innovation systems (RIS) have also gained momentum (e.g., Cooke, Heidenreich and Bracyck, 2003). Although Mothe and Paquet (1998) have claimed the IS framework as one of the most comprehensive explanations regarding the innovation process and its dynamic characteristics it nevertheless tends to sacrifice micro-level characteristics for providing longer-term, macro-level accounts. More particularly, the over-emphasis of IS theory on the linkages *among* firms and *between* firms and institutions (Capello and Faggian, 2005) weakens its depth of investigation on what is going on *inside* firms and the institutions. This ignorance reflects a current tendency in innovation studies towards telling 'happy family stories', an overwhelming focus on how wider coalitions have been able to work together to create linkages between firms and institutions, without examining the potential barriers within what drives individual decision-making institutions (including firms) (Lagendijk and Oïnas, 2005).

A failure to fully understand companies' decision-making processes and motivations substantively undermines discussions of the whole system's dynamics and growth. To address this problem, I incorporate the resource-based view (RBV) of companies into the framework in this chapter, to offer a 'resource-based view of innovation', especially drawing on the RBV's distinction between companies' international resources and external interaction. There are four basic arguments of this eclectic framework. First, organizations are collections of unique resources and capabilities (Conner and Prahalad, 1996;

Penrose, 1959). Internal resources may generate sustained competitive advantages if they are rare, valuable, difficult to imitate and without equivalent substitutes (Barney, 1991, p. 99). Second, along with the increasing intensified market divisions and growing resource specification, it is neither possible nor feasible for a company to acquire all necessary resources and capabilities internally, but rather firms must establish external relationships and outsource complementary resources. Third, positive regional environments help companies to both harness their own capabilities proactively, such as providing training programmes and access to seed capital, and access external resources more easily, via marketing, capturing mobile capital, and improving physical and virtual infrastructures. Finally, these three factors are clearly inter-related: companies' internal resources influence their capabilities in accessing and absorbing external resources.

In terms of companies' internal resources, their size, age, skills of employees and R&D resources are most commonly discussed. One of China's most distinctive institutional features is the mixture of state/collective controlled and private companies. Previous studies documented strong relations between companies' ownerships and their economic performances (Jefferson *et al.*, 2003; Pyke, Farley and Robb, 2002; Xu and Wang 1997), as well as their capabilities in obtaining other resources (Li, Zhang and Zhou, 2005). Since few papers on Chinese STIPs have dealt with the role played by companies' ownership, this chapter aims to fill this gap, specifically testing whether companies' ownership influences their capabilities in mobilizing internal and external resources within a given system, and hence their economic and innovation performance.

11.3 STIP in China and OVC

In China, the equivalent industry complexes to science parks have been labelled by the State as science and technology industry parks (STIPs). Compared to the 'science city' and 'technology park' archetypes identified by Castells and Hall (1994), the Chinese STIPs could be seen as taking the functions of both, a dual role hinted at by the wide range of definitions provided by the China Torch High Technology Industry Development Centre (hereafter the Torch Centre).[1] These include:

1   a base to develop the high and new technology industries;
2   a node for diffusing high technologies and products to traditional industries;
3   an experimental zone for institutional reform and innovation;
4   a demonstration centre for linking science, technology, and industry;
5   a new community that embodies modern socialism;
6   a school for cultivating high-tech enterprises and entrepreneurs;
7   an exhibition window to other countries.

The science park model was recognized by the Chinese government in the 1980s, relatively late compared to developed countries. The first national-level STIP was Zhongguancun in Beijing, approved by the State Council in 1988, followed by the upgrade of twenty-six provincial level science parks in 1991 and twenty-five more in 1992. The following two decades nevertheless only saw two more national STIPs open their doors, with Beijing taking a pause to see the effect of this particular growth model.[2] Nevertheless, at the end of 2010 and early 2011, fifty-nine local STIPs were upgraded to the national level, reflecting Chinese Government belief in STIPs as an effective way of leveraging its productivity. According to a senior MOST official, 'China considers science parks to be central to its efforts to build capacity for innovation' (SciDev.Net 2006). But the data constraints in China (Watkins-Mathys and Foster, 2006), and a lack of individual data for STIPs in particular (Zhang and Sonobe, 2011) means only a handful of studies were available to explore the contribution of these knowledge facilities: this section is reliant upon secondary data to address the first research question.

Table 11.1 below shows that the economic contributions of these forty-one STIPs were already significant by 2006. For example, the total number of on-park companies was 45,800, 15 per cent of China's total number of industrial companies; on-park employees reached 5.74m, 3 per cent of China's total industrial employment. With this relatively small share of companies and employees, STIPs in China contributed 13.8 per cent of industrial revenue, 14 per cent of China's exports and 34.8 per cent of industrial production in 2006. Furthermore, twenty-one STIPs generated more than 30 per cent of their host cities' industrial added value, including Yanling (94.2 per cent) and Xi'an (62.2 per cent), both in Shaanxi Province, and Wuhan in Hubei Province (30.5 per cent). In terms of GDP contribution, in 2006 eleven STIPs generated over 20 per cent of their host cities' GDP, including Zibo in Shangdong Province (48.9 per cent) and Zhongguancun in Beijing (27.9 per cent).

Notwithstanding their overall economic significance and wide geographical coverage,[3] Chinese STIPs' contributions to their host regions varied greatly. The coastal regions, for example, took unbeatable leading positions (as shown in Table 11.1) – in 2006, the total high-tech industrial outputs of the six STIPs in the Yangtze River Delta and Pearl River Delta were US$138.4bn and US$82.4bn, respectively. In contrast, the nine STIPs in Central China only generated US$70.7bn industrial outputs, with their average industrial output of STIPs around half of that in the Pearl River Delta and less than one third of that in Yangtze River Delta (Torch Center, 2007).

Given this regional diversity, this research has focused on one STIP in Central China, the Optics Valley of China (OVC), in Wuhan, Hubei Province, for three reasons. First, even with the regional disparities between China's STIPs, existing studies have overwhelmingly focused on those in the most developed coastal regions. Therefore, it is highly desirable to shift our attention to inland China, especially Central China, where economic and political ignorance has been highlighted as an important reason in its lagging economic

Table 11.1 Economic performance of STIPs in different regions of China, 2006 (unit: US$0.1bn)

	No	Total revenue	Industry output	Industry added-value	Net profit	Tax/fees turned over	Export
1) Yangtze River Delta	6	1586.89	1383.75	280.47	75.33	49.34	628.4
Average		264.48	230.63	46.75	12.56	8.22	104.73
2) Pearl River Delta	6	880.31	824.11	166.45	33.80	24.68	305.2
Average		146.72	137.35	27.74	5.63	4.11	50.87
3) Northeast	7	796.30	703.09	188.54	33.72	50.59	39.7
Average		113.76	100.44	26.93	4.82	7.23	5.67
4) Central	9	784.16	706.61	210.63	41.46	56.62	30.2
Average		87.13	78.51	23.40	4.61	6.29	3.36
5) West	13	863.63	705.79	203.65	46.68	45.88	61.6
Average		66.43	54.29	15.67	3.59	3.53	4.74
Total STIPs	41	6942.07	5752.84	1365.49	341.09	316.83	1360.9
Average		169.32	140.31	33.30	8.32	7.73	33.19
National industrial total		50253.62	16531.85	14632.70	3125.61	6211.34	9689
STIPs/national total		13.81%	34.80%	9.33%	10.91%	5.10%	14.05%

Source: Torch Center (2007).

position (Zhongguo jingji, 2009). Second, among the existing STIPs in Central China, OVC stood out prominently as an innovation hub, specialized in optical electronic-related products, a fact acknowledged by the Central Government at the end of 2010 in awarding OVC the 'National Self-Innovation Model Zone', the second STIP to win this accolade after Zhongguancun. Finally, OVC was the first group STIP recognised by Beijing in 1991, but its physical construction and operation actually started in 1988. Given that twenty years are normally required for any science park to take shape (Castells and Hall, 1994), OVC's long-term operational existence ensures a meaningful performance evaluation is possible compared to other STIPs.

This study concentrated on the single largest sector within OVC, namely optoelectronics. Names of companies and their contact details were obtained through the Directory of Photonics Industry (2010), Wuhan East Lake High-Tech Development Zone (OVC, 2009), Guangzhou Optics and Optoelectronics Manufacturers Association (GZOEMA, 2010), and Wuhan Laser Association of OVC (WLA, 2008). Cross-matching these different directories identified 203 optoelectronic-related companies registered in Hubei province. Two rounds of telephone and website checking reduced the number to 184, of which 147 were registered in OVC. Face-to-face interviews with the 147 on-park companies achieved 138 usable questionnaires, corresponding to a response rate of 93 per cent. Interview questions followed three themes: their internal resources, external networks, and performances. The questionnaire was tested in three rounds to reach the clearest and simplest design, with results recorded and analysed using SPSS software.

11.4 OVC from a systematic view

The official name for OVC is 'East Lake High-tech Development Zone', and has a relatively leading economic performance within China. Table 11.2 reports its economic position based on the available indicators. Among China's fifty-six STIPs in 2009, OVC ranked among the top ten in all indexes except exports, an impressive achievement given Hubei province's lagging economic position, a situation largely resulting from China's 1980s and 1990s reform policy and unbalanced regional development strategy (Miao and Hall, 2013). The relatively gloomy picture of OVC's export levels was understandable with companies in OVC not dominantly export-oriented compared to those in coastal regions. Among the various sectors present in OVC, the optoelectronic industry is the most competitive. According to the 2009 Annual Report of OVC (2011), its total revenue was RMB 226.1bn (US$36.32bn), and it ranked tenth among fifty-six national-level STIPs. A total of 37.2 per cent of revenue came from the optoelectronic and communication industry (RMB 83.56bn/ US$13.56bn), leading its second-largest revenue generator, the Modern Equipment Manufacturing Industry, by RMB 48.56bn (US$7.8 bn).

OVC's construction reflected the local authority's purpose of cultivating a 'growth pole' for the region. OVC's overall economic performance has shown

Table 11.2 Economic performance of OVC (unit: US$0.1bn)

	OVC 2009	Compared to 2008	National ranking 2009	National ranking 2008	Regional total 2009	OVC/ Region 2009
Total revenue	363.25	28.55%	10	10	2435.87	14.91%
Industry product	317.32	25.64%	8	9	969.9	32.72%
Added-value	107.19	25.86%	2	3	832.65	12.87%
Net profit	21.27	27.27%	8	8	175.48	12.12%
Tax and fees turned-over	19.51	36.40%	7	9	168.5	11.58%
Export	25.18	128.08%	21	29	99.79	25.23%

Source: OVC (2011) and National Bureau of Statistics (2011).

positive signs of transforming the province's industrial structure from heavy industries to lighter, high-tech industries. However, it is not immediately evident that these on-park companies were making similar contributions and being innovative, particularly given the Chinese context, where a mix of ownership could potentially influence companies' capabilities in utilising their internal resources, assessing and obtaining external resources, and networking with other system partners. All these capabilities, in turn, greatly influence the system's synergy and dynamics, and it is to this issue that this section now turns.

11.4.1 Companies' ownership patterns

Among the surveyed companies, twenty-two were state controlled and ten were collectively owned (together accounting for 23.2 per cent of the sample), ninety-nine companies were privately owned, and the remaining seven companies were foreign-owned. Comparing this ownership distribution with other data sources, state-owned companies were over-represented in the optoelectronic sector with respect to OVC's overall company profile (9.76 per cent as state-owned), as well as the national average (4.97 per cent as state-owned). This is to be expected because of the optoelectronic sector's strategic importance, which in turn results in the dominance of the state capital. Moreover, the lack of foreign investment in OVC compared with the national average reflects the position that Central China is still in an inferior position in competing for foreign investment (Broadman and Sun, 1997).

A closer examination of companies' ownership and other features reveals more interesting relationships: first, significant age differences existed between the optoelectronic companies with different ownership – all the long-established companies (older than 25-years) were state-owned, while all seven foreign companies were established less than 10 years ago. Second, both state- and foreign-owned companies tended to be larger (more than fifty employees), whereas three-quarters of private companies would be ranked as SMEs with less than fifty employees.

11.4.2 Emerging patterns

This section explores the influence of a company's ownership on three factors, namely its internal R&D resources, external linkages and innovation performance. Companies' R&D resource was approximated by their R&D spending against their annual revenues. For companies' external linkages, surveyed companies were asked to rank the relative importance of different actors in contributing to their innovation performance, the result of which would be seen as reflecting their external networks with different partners, as well as their evaluation of these networks. For companies' innovation performance, their revenues and industrial outputs were chosen as proxies to their general economic performance, while their high-tech product sales and new product sales were used as indicators for their innovation competitiveness.

Companies' ownership and R&D resources

Figure 11.2 below shows the relationship between companies' ownership and their R&D resources. Most strikingly, a significant higher percentage of state-owned companies had higher R&D input than both private or foreign-owned firms, contradicting the common wisdom that state-owned companies in China are burdened with out-of-date technologies and equipment, and are generally less keen on R&D. For foreign companies, there was a noticeable diversity within the group. While one-third had no R&D inputs at all, another third had 21–40 per cent of their revenues devoted to R&D, and a further sixth had over 80 per cent R&D spending ratio, both significantly higher than the average level. Private-owned enterprises, in contrast, were least interested in R&D

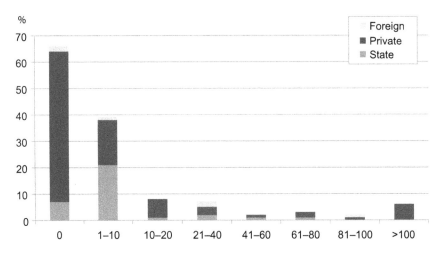

Figure 11.2 Firm R&D expenditure as percentage of turnover, by ownership
Source: The author.

spending, with 60.6 per cent having no R&D budget at all. As R&D activities are generally regarded as the pre-conditions for companies to build up their own innovation capabilities and absorbing external knowledge, this implies that companies with different ownership in OVC would very possibly develop different innovation capabilities and networks. But a cautionary note must be sounded at this point: with the state- and foreign-owned companies in the sample tending to be larger than private companies, the directionality of the relationship between companies' ownership and R&D resources was not immediately clear.

Companies' ownership and their external networks

The relationship between companies' ownership and their external networks was captured by asking companies to evaluate the relative importance of different actors in leveraging their innovation capabilities. This was done on a five-point Likert scale, with '0' referring to 'least important' and '5' to 'most important' (see Figure 11.3), with 'innovation capability' captured by general descriptions of any innovation-related activities in the questionnaire.

For most companies, 'customers' emerged as the single most important partners for their innovation activities, implying the prevalence of 'learning-by-doing' in OVC. Second, state-owned companies gave a higher ranking to all six partners than private companies, possibly reflecting their better external networks than the private companies. In particular, the importance allocated to 'Public Agencies' was highest among the state-owned companies, echoing previous findings that the Chinese governments tend to cultivate more favourable conditions to their owned companies.

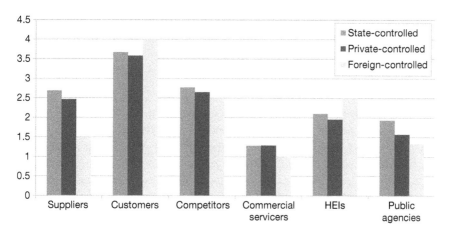

Figure 11.3 External relationships of companies with different ownerships
Source: The author.

Foreign companies, in comparison, ranked highly their relationships with customers and higher education institutes (HEIs), and were the only kind of firms to regard higher education institutions as important, perhaps explained by the fact that overseas companies are more used to co-operating with research institutions than the domestic ones. Chinese enterprises, education institutions and research institutions in the pre-reform era used to be vertically managed and organised, which minimized their co-operation capacities (OECD, 2008). An alternative but equally plausible explanation could be found in foreign-owned companies' higher absorption capabilities, Eun, Lee and Wu (2006) observing that one of the most substantial obstacles for industry-research collaborations in China was the its domestic firms' low absorption capabilities. Finally, private companies tended to view most of the actors listed here as less important for their innovation capabilities (scored lower than '4'), possibly reconfirming their relatively low R&D activities, but also possibly reflecting internal deficiencies in establishing outside connections. This observation was in line with the theoretical modelling proposed earlier in this chapter, where companies' internal resources and external networking capabilities are mutually intertwined and, together, they could impact companies' innovation capabilities as well as whole system synergy.

Companies' ownership and economic performance

The relationship between companies' ownership and economic performance, in terms of their general economic index and innovation capabilities, is summarised in Table 11.3.

Contrary to common wisdom, state-owned companies on average out-performed other ownership categories in all four economic indexes. This pattern was explicable given their previously noted relative higher R&D investment and better networking capabilities. Private firms, although not so committed to R&D, were ranked second in terms of their average performance. Nevertheless, their lower median figures meant significant divergences among the private companies' economic performances. Foreign-owned companies, conversely, showed the worst performance on average among the three groups, puzzling if one recalls that more than a third of the foreign companies showed a high involvement in R&D activities. However, as the medium figures reveal, half of foreign-owned companies had neither R&D activities nor new product sales, these companies possibly only functioning as satellites for their head offices, with R&D mainly oriented towards adopting products to China's specific local markets. Furthermore, these companies' low efficiency and reluctance to transfer their knowledge, might limit their external network and their economic performance. These speculations will be cross-checked by the focused case studies below.

Table 11.3 Summary of companies' performance with different ownership

Ownership	Economic performance (Million YMB)								
	Revenue		Industry output		High-tech product sales		New product sales	
	Median	*Mean*	*Median*	*Mean*	*Median*	*Mean*	*Median*	*Mean*
1. State/collective	78.39	779.17	97.47	770.14	24.50	644.83	0.32	181.48
2. Private	3.87	40.15	2.81	44.07	0.0	17.34	0.0	6.90
3. Overseas	14.50	22.98	14.50	22.39	0.0	4.29	0.0	2.96
Total	9.28	216.00	8.74	216.60	0.0	166.73	0.0	48.45

Note: One-way ANOVA test showed all four between-groups-mean differences were significant on 95 per cent level.

Source: The author.

11.5 'A tale of three companies'

This section uses three company case studies to explore further the relationship between companies' ownership and their systemic capacities. Based on OVC's 2010 economic survey data, the most competitive company in each category (state-owned, private-owned, foreign-owned) was chosen as a case study. The main sources of information were obtained through multi-media reports cross-referenced with face-to-face interviews with these companies' senior managers.

11.5.1 Company 1: Fiber Home

The first case study is Fiber Home, an archetypical state-owned company in OVC. Fiber Home emerged as the direct consequence of the research institutes (RIs) reform in China in the early 1990s. Its predecessor was Wuhan Post and Telecommunication Research Institute (WRI), widely regarded as the 'cradle' of China's optoelectronic industry (Guang, 1995). When the 'Decision on Accelerating Technology Progress' was published by the Central Government in 1995 (The State Council 1995), WRI quickened its reform process and restructured completely into a joint venture called Fibre Home in 1999, with the state as the dominant shareholder (China IT Industry Net 2006). In reality, WRI and Fiber Home are one unit using two titles, and as a research institute WRI has managed to retain its industry-leading position – WRI engaged in almost all the National Key Technology Projects related to optical fibre communications, contributing to more than 500 R&D projects. It had been awarded over 170 prizes by the central and local governments for its tech-nology contributions since the reform and opening-up of China (Baidu, 2011).

   The joint effect of technology leadership, the optoelectronic industry's huge market potential, and favourable instituitonal environment locally and nationally, resulted in Fiber Home's absolute dominant position in the optoelectronics sector in OVC and China. According to an OVC internal company survey, Fiber Home's total revenue and industrial outputs in 2009 were double those of the second-largest company. Moreover, Fibre Home established many holding companies specialized in different branches, including communication technologies, communication equipment and opto-devices. All these sub-branches benefitted from WRI's internal knowledge, putting them at the leading edge of technology advance and strengthening their profit-making capabilities. These tradable advantages of WRI all contribute to its excellent performance in industrial output and innovation capabilities.

   More intangibly, the market reform of WRI also brought another change to this company's external relationships. When WRI was owned by the former National Bureau of Post and Telecommunication, local authorities could hardly benefit from the WRI's location, as all profits, along with its personnel, organization and external affairs were controlled by the Central Government. When WRI was gradually reformed into a share-holding company in the 1990s, the tie between this company and Beijing was loosened, and the importance of this company to the local economy was increasing significantly. This deepening of local embeddedness, in turn bonded Fiber Home more tightly to the local government. As the R&D Director of this company related:

> Regarding our relationship with the local authority, we have some 'hard' advantages: first of all we are among the earliest research institute in the area of opto-communication, and we have now transformed into an enterprise, therefore our contribution to the overall local industrial chain and other related sectors is considerable. Secondly we have promoted local HEIs to establish relevant courses on optoelectronics. Therefore we have a benign relation with the government, who reacts to our needs quickly – as we say, 'key enterprise, key attention' . . . we have established R&D centres around China, but we are not going to move the core of our enterprise out of OVC, as it is not necessary.
>
> (Interview: 8 July 2010)

Fibre Home's story partly explains the above-average performance of state-owned companies and their outstanding networks with external partners. First, many of OVC's state-owned companies were the marketization results of former research institutes, which developed a substantial technology capability and research personell. Second, these reformed companies retained, and even strengthened their relations with, local authorities. The security brought about by public ownership won state-owned companies a better bargaining position with other system components, such as banks, land developers and knowledge institutes. Conversely, as the direct beneficiaries, the governments were also more willing to back up their holding enterprises. Together, these internal and external advantages contributed significantly to the superior performance of OVC's state-owned companies.

11.5.2 Company 2: Chutian Group

Among the three laser companies in OVC generating over RMB100 (US$16.06m) sales by 2008, Chutian Group was the only company with private ownership. Chutian was created by a number of technicians from the Laser Research Group of Huazhong University of Science and Technology (HUST), one of China's most prestigious higher education institutes (HEIs) with a historical research strength in laser technologies (China Computer, 2005). Together with Wuhan Optics Research Institute and Wuhan Optical Device Factory, HUST established Chutian Laser in 1985 on the site of the Wuhan Optical Device Factory, which later moved into an incubator. After graduating in the early 1990s, Chutian's CEO successfully transformed this state-owned company into a limited liability company. It has now developed into the OVC's largest private enterprise and also is a leading company in China, specializing in industry laser, medical laser and laser processing technologies (Chutian Laser, 2011).

Although it possessed almost half of the domestic market share in the industrial laser sector, Chutian faced two main challenges in accessing external resources. The first was technology input: the company had been mainly relying on internal R&D capabilities, an exception to private companies' generally low R&D profiles. The reason for its self-reliance, as compared to collaboration with RIs, was explained by the Sales Manager of Chutian: 'the HEIs are mainly dealing with theoretical research, whereas the application feasibilities are tested out in our enterprises'. More specifically, I was told that

> Chutian has to devote to different recourses in its three market areas. For medical laser, China has no established technologies yet, so we have to rely on import. One example here is that we have bought in technologies from an Israel company. For laser processing, China has some technology base, so we tend to cooperate with our partners. For industrial laser, China again lacks technology foundation but we have nowhere to buy. This is because western countries, such as the US, block their technologies export to China, so it is impossible to buy-in but to self-develop.
>
> (Interview: 28 July 2010)

Besides this tangible difficulty, Chutian also experienced disadvantages in intangible linkages with the public sector. Although my interviewee was confident in their higher efficiency in using public funds, he nevertheless complained that it was very difficult to get funding from the government, who preferred to invest in research institutes, HEIs and HEI-owned companies. Falling behind these government-backed enterprises in accessing research funding and other resources, Chutian wished for 'a farer competition environment which enables every company to start at the same line'.

Therefore, although a variety of ownerships is now legally permitted and encouraged in China, the large number of private companies may in reality still face a less-favourable competitive environment. Besides the general park services, such as office space, infrastructure, administration and consultation, private companies in OVC tended to be on the margin of public attention, unless they could reach a threshold scale (Chutian was one of the limited cases) or partner with state-owned companies. This may explain why the performances of private companies here generally lagged behind those state-owned firms.

11.5.3 Company 3: Wuhan NEC

Foreign-invested companies were traditionally under-represented in OVC, but their numbers began to grow from the 1990s, thanks to energetic promotion work by the local government. The Director of OVC's Investment Promotion Bureau of OVC noted that:

> The starting of this development zone was burdened with economic targets, because the government evaluation system in China was primarily

based on the economic indexes, such as the economic scales of your industry and the amount of foreign investment. Therefore, the previous authorities of OVC had made attracting FDI their top priority, and had tried their best effort to attract foreign investment.

(Interviewed: 12 August 2010)

Attracted by these government promotions as well as OVC's industrial growth, by 1995 the number of foreign-invested companies had increased to 281, reportedly accounting for over half of the total number of enterprises in OVC (Zhong and Liang, 1995). One conspicuous investment in optoelectronics included Wuhan NEC in 1992, a joint venture between Yangtze Communication Enterprise Group, NEC Japan and Sumitomo Japan, engaging mainly in optical fibre production, sales and technology services. Its arrival was claimed as finally completing OVC's optical communication sector (Feng, 1994).

Notwithstanding these high expectations, Wuhan NEC's performance was disappointing. Its industrial output and revenue in 2009 did not rank within the top ten of OVC's 285 registered optoelectronic companies, while Wuhan NEC's technological sophistication, as well as its willingness to diffuse its technologies, is questionable. For example, a former engineer working in Wuhan NEC's joint venture with a local company[4] noted that 'the cooperation between China and Japan was not very smooth most of the time ... The Japanese were highly sensitive to technological issues and it was almost impossible for us to learn their technologies through the cooperation' (interview: 30 June 2010). An anonymous interviewee provided more evidence on this point:

> The activities in Wuhan NEC are limited to system installation and packaging. All the core parts are manufactured somewhere else, especially in Japan. Speaking of system installation, I do not think there are any technologies involved. What we do is to plug in the mobile phone with the computer, download the pre-written systems to the phone, turn the phone on, test it, or should I say play around with it, and then pass on to the packing department. However, the staff working on the assembly line suffer seriously from the computer radiation, and you will have your eyesight decreasing quickly if you work for a long time. NEC chose Wuhan as its assembling factory all because of the cheap labour here. I work in Wuhan NEC and the majority of us are college interns. We only earn a mean salary of RMB 800 (approximately US$130) per month and no insurances.

(Interview: 5 July 2010)

The limited number of foreign-invested companies in OVC has brought both benefits and costs. Certainly, the investment of the influential MNCs in the optoelectronic industry strengthened some sectors, especially the optical communication sector. Second, their appearance significantly increased OVC's international exposure and raised global market awareness of endogenous companies. However, their contribution to OVC, and to Central China in general, should not be overemphasized: the relatively small amount of FDI and their reluctance to diffuse advanced technologies all constrained their economic and innovation performance and their contributions to OVC. This is not a particularly unsurprising finding and suggests that OVC was still a 'technology follower', not a 'place to be' for accessing cutting-edge technologies, but rather a production complex with some R&D elements.

11.6 Conclusion

This chapter has addressed two questions (see Section 11.1):

1   What are the contributions of science parks in inland China?
2   How do the different characteristics of on-park companies make a difference to their contributions?

Following Castells and Hall's (1994) emphasis of the importance of system synergy for the success of any technopole, this chapter adopted an innovation system approach, augmented with a resource-based view of innovation and in particular including the variable of firm ownership as a potential determinant. The justification for that is, while in Western countries such as Spain, companies' sizes and ages are regarded as influential factors in their innovation performance (see Chapter 10, this volume), in China's context, companies' ownership is a noteworthy factor, but few studies on science parks have yet explicitly taken that focus.

Official data on the economic contributions of national STIPs in China noted their overall significance, but highlighted the existence of reasonably strong regional differences, with STIPs in West and Central China being less productive than their peers in the coastal regions. From a systematic perspective, STIPs' regional divergence is clearly related to the different economic conditions of their embedded regions. This divergence would also have been observed within Central China, as OVC was certainly emerging as a promising innovative hub, and contributing a great proportion of wealth to its host region.

Focusing on the OVC, the chapter further explored the influence of companies' ownership on their engagement with the system dynamics. Survey results of the optical electronic companies revealed some interesting yet puzzling findings. First, state-owned companies were more willing to devote internal resources to R&D activities, and also valued their relations with public agencies more. Their superior resource mobilizing and networking capabilities corresponded to their leading position both in their economic performance and innovation achievement. These findings were contrary to the literature, which suggested state-owned companies would have both lower productivity and innovation capabilities. As the case of Fibre Home makes clear, state-owned companies in OVC were dominated by companies transformed from knowledge institutes. These companies inherited the knowledge reserves, technology achievements and even human capital of these institutes, and therefore boasted rich internal resources. Moreover, their intimate linkages with local authorities made public funding easier to secure. In some cases, the local government was even willing to tailor their policies for the needs of the 'star' companies.

Second, the private firms in OVC were in a relatively inferior position both in terms of their R&D resources and their external networks. But their average performances were in the middle range – better than those of foreign-owned firms. Nevertheless, there were increasing numbers of companies realizing the importance of in-house R&D and were building on their research capabilities quickly, as shown by the example of Chutian Group. Their efforts in building up their internal resources could to some extent compensate for their inferior position in securing external resources, and this might explain why the private companies were in the middle range of economic and innovation performance.

Third, the foreign-owned firms in OVC were quite diverse in terms of their R&D commitments, potentially reflecting the mixture of genuine investors and branch-plants in OVC. Performance of these foreign-owned companies was least strong, despite the supposedly preferential policies many of them enjoyed. The dilemma for foreign-owned companies could be tentatively explained by the story of Wuhan NEC, who were reluctant in sharing their internal resources, especially technologies. It follows that many foreign-invested enterprises had devoted their main effort into product adapting or improvement. Nevertheless, their less-active internal resource organisation and utilisation was further aggravated by their relatively passive requirements for external linkages and co-operation. The joint result saw foreign-owned companies having the lowest R&D performance outcomes among the three categories.

Drawing a general conclusion based on a single case study is always dangerous. Bearing this in mind, the chapter does allow a number of tentative suggestions to be made. First, it seems reasonable to suggest that these interactions between companies' ownership and their innovation capacities might have something to do with China's specific context. When Castells and Hall (1994) visited the technopoles of the world twenty years earlier, only the former Soviet Union showed some similarity to China. But its 'shock therapy' means that there was no such mixed-ownership profile emerged either before or after 1991. In China and particularly its inland regions, however, this phenomenon of mixed ownership still plays a role, and arguably influences the added value of a science park's location. This particular finding can be generalised to explore the micro-based functioning of innovation systems. In particular, the strongest message was that a systematic view of science parks based on firm-level analysis will bring in new insights into the assessment of these knowledge facilities. This applies not only to China but also other countries that are eager to pursue this science park model. A more comprehensive understanding of the situation could be revealed by better taking into account other variables besides companies' ownership, such as their locations and organization structures. A wider evaluation on the impacts of firms' ownership towards their contributions to the regional innovation system, and hence to the added value of the technopoles, is therefore also very much desirable.

Notes

1   Torch is the administration bureau of STIPs in China under the supervision of the Ministry of Science and Technology (MOST).
2   Interview with an officer in the Torch Centre, June 2010.
3   Each province has at least one national-level STIPs now, except Tibet.
4   This joint venture, NEC Zhongyuan Electronics, had already witnessed the divorce between its parent companies in 2000.

Bibliography

AURP and Battelle (2007) 'Characteristics and Trends in North American Research Parks: 21st Century Directions'. Association of University Research Parks, pp. 1–14.

Baidu (2011) *Wuhan Post and Telecommunications Research Insitute* (5 July 2011). Available at: http://baike.baidu.com/history/21538926 (accessed on 12 October 2011).

Barney, J.B. (1991) 'Firm resources and sustained competitive advantage'. *Journal of Management*, *17*: 99–120.

Broadman, H.G. and Sun, X. (1997) *The distribution of foreign direct investment in China*. London: Blackwell (pp. 339–61).

Capello, R. and Faggian, A. (2005) 'Collective learning and relational capital in local innovation processes'. *Regional Studies*, *39*(1): 75–87.

Carter, N. (1989) *Science parks: Development and management*. London: Estates Gazette.

Castells, M. and Hall, P. (1994) *Technopoles of the world: The making of 21st-century industrial complexes*. London: Routledge.

Chen, K. and Kenney, M. (2007) 'Universities/research institutes and regional innovation systems: The cases of Beijing and Shenzhen'. *World Development*, *35*(6): 1056–74.

China Computer (2005) 'Crucial events over the last twenty years'. Available at: www.qikan.com.cn/Article/jsjb/jsjb200595/jsjb20059502.html (accessed on 30 June 2011).

China Economic Net (2005) 'Analysis of the economic development trend of central region in the new century'. Available at www.ce.cn/kfq/KFQSY/lt/200508/23/t2005 0823_4501114.shtml (accessed on 6 July 2010).

China IT Industry Net (2006) 'FiberHome Technology Group. Wuhan Post & Telecommunication Research Instutute Introduction' (8 June 2006, in Chinese). Available at: www.cnii.com.cn/20060529/ca356094.htm (accessed on 5 March 2011).

China Optics and Optoelectronics Manufacturers Association (2010) *Firm directory of photonics industry*. Available at: http://coema.org.cn/news (accessed on 3 May 2010).

Chutien Laser (2011) *History of Chutian Laser*. Available at: www.chutianlaser.com/ gyct-ls.asp (accessed on 30 June 2011).

Cooke, P., Heidenreich, M. and Bracyck, H.J. (2003) *Regional innovation systems: The role of governance in a globalised world* (2nd edn). London: Routledge.

Conner, K.R. and Prahalad, C.K. (1996) 'A resource-based theory of the firm: Knowledge versus opportunism'. *Organization Science*, 7(5): 477–501.

Eun, J.H., Lee, K. and Wu, S.G. (2006) 'Explaining the "university-run enterprises" in China: A theoretical framework for university-industry relationship in developing countries and its application to China'. *Research Policy*, 35: 1329–46.

Feng, L. (1994) 'Optical communication industry in OVC is leading in China', *Hubei Daily*, 28 July 1994.

Forsyth, A. and Crewe, K. (2010) 'Suburban technopoles as places: The international campus garden suburb style'. *Urban Design International*, 15: 165–82.

Gower, S.M. and Harris, F.C. (1994) 'The funding of, and investment in, British science parks: A review'. *Journal of Property Finance*, 5(3): 7–18.

Guang, C. (1995) 'Exert the advantages of universities and research institutes, develop the economy of Wuhan', *Yangtze Daily*, 1 December 1995.

GZOEMA (2010) *Firm directory*. Available at: www.lighting86.com.cn/company/ index.html (accessed on 6 May 2010).

Hong, W. (2008) 'Decline of the center: The decentralizing process of knowledge transfer of Chinese universities from 1985 to 2004'. *Research Policy*, 37: 580–95.

Jefferson, G., Hu, A., Guan, X. and Yu, X. (2003) 'Ownership, performance, and innovation in China's large- and medium-size industrial enterprise sector'. *China Economic Review*, 14(1): 89–113.

Lagendijk, A. and Oïnas, P. (2005) 'Towards understanding proximity, distance and diversity in economic interaction and local development', in A. Lagendijk and P. Oïnas (eds), *Proximity, distance and diversity, issues on economic interaction and local development*. Chicago, IL: Ashgate (pp. 307–32.)

Li, H., Zhang, W. and Zhou, L.A. (2005) 'Ownership, efficiency, and firm survival in economic transition: Evidence from a Chinese science park' (no. 70025201). *Journal of Comparative Economics*, September, 1–37.

Lindelöf, P. and Löfsten, H. (2002) 'Growth, management and financing of new technology-based firms: Assessing value-added contributions of firms located on and off Science Parks'. *Omega*, 30(3): 143–54.

—— (2003) 'Science park location and new technology-based firms in Sweden – Implications for strategy and performance'. *Small Business Economics*, 20(3): 245–58.

—— (2005) 'Academic versus corporate new technology-based firms in Swedish science parks: an analysis of performance, business networks and financing'. *International Journal of Technology Management*, 31(3–4): 334–57.

Lundvall, B. (1992) 'National systems of innovation: Towards a theory of innovation and interactive learning'. London: Pinter.

Massey, D. and Wield, D. (1992) 'Evaluating science parks'. *Local Economy*, 7(1): 10–25.

Massey, D., Quintas, P. and Wield, D. (1992) *High-tech fantasies: Science parks in society, science and space*. London: Routledge.

McAdam, M. and McAdam, R. (2008) 'High-tech start-ups in University Science Park incubators: The relationship between the start-up's lifecycle progression and use of the incubator's resources'. *Technovation*, 28: 277–90.

Miao, J.T. and Hall, P. (2013) 'Optical illusion? The growth and development of the Optics Valley of China'. *Environment and Planning C: Government and Policy*, 31.

MOST, China (2012) *China high-tech industry statistics*. Available at www.sts.org.cn/sjkl/gjscy/data2012/data12.pdf (accessed on 17 April 2014).

Mothe, J.D. and Paquet, G. (1998) *Local and regional systems of innovation*. Norwell, MA and Dordrecht, the Netherlands: Kluwer Academic Publishers.

National Bureau of Statistics, China (2011) *Statistics database of China*. Available at: www.stats.gov.cn/tjsj/ndsj (accessed on 12 September 2011).

OECD (1997) National Innovation Systems, OECD Publications: Paris. Available at: www.oecd.org/science/inno/2101733.pdf (accessed on 8 July 2010).

—— (1999) The National Innovation Systems (Phase I & II). Available at: www.oecd.org/sti/inno/thenationalinnovationsystemsphaseiii.htm (accessed on 4 February 2014).

—— (2008) *OECD Reviews of Innovation Policy: China*. France: OECD Publications (pp. 1–648).

OVC (2009) *Enterprises directory*. Available at: www.wehdz.gov.cn/structure/QYFW/qyml/lb (accessed on 17 September 2009).

OVC (2011) *Annual statistics report of East Lake High-tech Development Zone 2009*. Available at: www.wehdz.gov.cn/jsp/zwgk/browser/content.jsp?id=384 (accessed on 11 September 2011).

Penrose, E. (1959) *The theory of the growth of the firm*. New York: John Wiley.

Phillimore, J. (1999) 'Beyond the linear view of innovation in science park evaluation. An analysis of Western Australian Technology Park'. *Technovation, 19*: 673–80.

Phillimore, J. and Joseph, R. (2003) 'Science parks: A triumph of hype over experience?', in L.V. Shavinina (ed.) *The international handbook on innovation*. Kidlington, Oxfordshire: Elsevier Science (pp. 750–57).

Pyke, D., Farley, J. and Robb, D. (2002) 'Manufacturing technology and operations in China: A survey of state-owned enterprises, private firms, joint ventures and wholly-owned foreign subsidiaries'. *European Management Journal, 20*(4): 356–75.

SciDev.Net (2006) 'China to build 30 new science and technology parks'. Available at: www.scidev.net/global/capacity-building/news/china-to-build-30-new-science-and-technology-parks.html (accessed on 15 August 2014).

The State Council (1995) 'Chinese Communist Party Central Committee and the State Council on the decision to accelerate technology progress'. Xinhua Net (07/01/2006). Available at: http://news.xinhuanet.com/misc/2006-01/07/content_4021977.htm (accessed on 10 May 2010).

Torch Center (2007) 'Development analysis of the national science parks in 2006', Available at: www.chinatorch.gov.cn/kjb/tjnb/list.shtml (accessed on 5 July 2013).

Torch Center (2009) 'National Science and Technology Industrial Parks (STIPs)'. Available at: www.ctp.gov.cn/ctp-eng/areas_two.htm (accessed on 3 July 2010).

Watkins-Mathys, L. and Foster, M.J. (2006) 'Entrepreneurship: The missing ingredient in China's STIPs?'. *Entrepreneurship & Regional Development, 18*(3): 249–74.

Westhead, P. and Storey, D.J. (1994) *An assessment of firms located on an off science parks in the United Kindom: Main report*. London: HMSO.

WLA (2008) 'Firm directory'. Available at: www.laser.org.cn/enterprise.asp (accessed on 6 May 2010).

Xu, X. and Wang, Y. (1997) 'Ownership structure, corporate governance, and firms' performance: The case of Chinese stock companies'. *Policy Research Working Paper No. 1794* (The World Bank, May 1997): 1–55.

Zhang, H. and Sonobe, T. (2011) 'Development of science and technology parks in China, 1988–2008'. *Economics*, 5(6): 1–27.

Zhong, P. and Liang, X. (1995) 'Foreign-invested companies have accounted for half of the enterprises in East Lake'. *Yangtze Daily.*

12 Neither special nor diverse

Contradictions in the economic logic of technology parks in Malaysia

Sharifah R. S. Dawood and
Nicholas A. Phelps

12.1 Introduction

Science and technology parks have been an important vehicle for organising scientific and high technology industry as part of concerted efforts by developing countries to 'move up the value chain' to improve national economic structures and productivity and ultimately achieve higher national income levels. They represent a peculiarly spatial or geographically-defined attempt to develop industry with the thinking that companies can benefit from Marshallian externalities of industry specialisation and that these advantages are better fostered in particular places where resources and institutional support can be co-located. However, in their seminal exploration of such planned high technology spaces – *Technopoles of the World* – Castells and Hall (1994) noted an important contradiction: that although such technopoles had been widely used as vehicles to promote the decentralisation of innovative activity as part of regional policies, major metropolitan areas remained the most important sources of industrial innovation globally. That is, science and technology park policy and the local economic development contributions of parks are windows onto broader analytical questions over the relationship between regional economic development via Marshallian industry specialisation, on the one hand, and via the industrial diversity or 'related variety' described by Jacobs (1969) and Boschma and Frenken (2011), on the other hand (see also van der Panne, 2004 for a discussion of Marshallian and Jacobs externalities). This chapter draws on original research designed to explore the extent to which technology parks in Malaysia leverage externalities related to Marshallian specialisation and externalities related to industry diversity or related variety.

In Malaysia, the contributions of technology parks in promoting regional economic development may reflect the position they have occupied as just one – and not the most important – ingredient within deliberate national planning geared towards promoting a structural transformation to a knowledge-based economy. Indeed, the ambiguous position of technology parks reflects the uncertainty with which national planning has had an explicitly spatial or geo-graphical orientation in light of domestic, ethnically-inflected, political considerations, which we discuss at greater length elsewhere (Phelps and Dawood, 2014).

In this chapter we focus instead on comparing and contrasting the character of industry corralled into such parks focusing on the two most successful technology park cases of Technology Park Malaysia (TPM) in the greater Kuala Lumpur area and Kulim High Tech Park (KHTP) in Kedah. As enclaves for development of high technology industry they differ significantly and offer a means of comparing and contrasting the role played by Marshallian externalities (of industry specalisation) or Jacobs externalities (of industry diversity). TPM signalled the origins of technology parks within Malaysian science and technology policy and its location in the greater Kuala Lumpur metropolitan area ought to enable it to benefit from the urban diversity and related variety of the capital city region economy. With an eye on bolstering political support for the major *Barisan Nasional* ruling party in an ethnically segmented economy and polity, KHTP was designed as a specialised site to promote innovation away from the capital city region. In this chapter, we draw upon original empirical findings from questionnaire surveys of tenants located on the two parks and interviews with policy-makers and the business community at local, state and Federal levels to explore the success of these two parks as exemplars of industry specialisation in isolation, in the case of KHTP, and related variety in the case of TPM. The story we have to tell is one of technology parks failing to make a significant contribution to local innovative activity; as yet, they represent neither new specialised collections of industry generating Marshallian externalities nor are they able to leverage to any great extent on the synergies of related variety – that is between specialisation and urban industrial diversity.

12.2 Technology parks and the advantages of specialisation and related variety

We somehow know a 'real' science park when we see one. It is a highly successful real estate development in which the property and facilities on offer have contributed positively to the attraction and innovative performance of high technology activities. This, of course, is a retrospective archetype we have in mind – some kind of hybrid of internationally successful examples more often than not drawn from the United States. Indeed, so powerful has this archetype been that it has promoted what Forsyth and Crewe (2010) refer to as an 'international garden suburb-campus' model. However, it is important to recognise that most science and high technology parks are unlikely to match up to this archetype.

The definition offered by the International Association of Science Parks (2011) affirms the value-added nature of science parks as a location for high technology business.

A Science Park is an organization managed by specialized professionals, whose main aim is to increase the wealth of its community by promoting the culture of innovation and the competitiveness of its associated businesses and knowledge-based institutions. To enable these goals to be met, a Science Park stimulates and manages the flow of knowledge and technology amongst universities, R&D institutions, companies and markets; it facilitates the creation and growth of innovation-based companies through incubation and spin-off processes; and provides other value-added services together with high quality space and facilities.

(IASP, 2011)

The generality of the first part of this definition, however, makes it clear that it might be wise to view science parks as particular industry park offerings on a continuum in which 'ordinary' trading estates exist at one end of the spectrum, while what we might regard as the fullest meaning of a science park exists at the other end of the spectrum. This is an important point to consider as there are hundreds of trading, industry, technology and science parks in every national setting and some of those 'ordinary' trading and industry parks will have transformed over the years to accommodate more high technology activities either by accident (of changes in the likes of national planning regulations) or by design. Thus, some evolution is to be expected in the population of parks and individual parks in any given national setting – a feature relevant to understanding the Malaysian experience of science and technology parks.

As the quotation above also suggests, as spaces with specialised resources devoted to innovative activities, science parks have been designed to promote a high degree of specialisation in particular activities (notably R&D) or industries. While the two are different, they have often been conflated in policies that have sought to decentralise innovative activity within nations. Doubtless science parks as specialised spaces seek to generate Marshall's industrial atmosphere or what Storper (1995) has termed the untraded interdependencies of innovation associated with specialised industry/activity clusters. However, it is unclear whether and to what extent science parks can come to embody significant new clusters of high technology industry bound together by such localised untraded interdependencies or knowledge flows.

To the extent that science parks accommodate particular parts of the division of labour such as R&D they have been predicated on a linear model of scientific and corporate inventive behaviour in which conception of new products and services has tended to be separated from production and sales as the scale of industry has expanded. Indeed, the logic of the division of labour in economy and society is a powerful one and has led to the fine slicing of activities within global value chains orchestrated by the likes of MNEs (Rugman, Verbeke and Yuan, 2010) with the implication being that ever more specialised research laboratories are created as a result of the division of labour *within* conception stages. Such high levels of specialisation surrounding the innovative activities of companies appears to have led to Science Parks having mixed results in terms of their local economic development contributions. These specialised spaces have contributed significantly to the dynamism of outer suburban and metropolitan economies in the United States, given the scale of corporate industrial research and government research (O'Mara, 2005). The more modest scale of both corporate and governmental research in the United Kingdom have meant that science parks have rarely generated the activity and industry specialisation to form distinct new industry clusters and have also been rather detached from the urban and regional economies of which they are a part (Massey, Quintas and Wield, 1992).

However, specialisation based on Marshallian externalities has ambiguous implications for regional economic development since Marshallian agglomeration based on industry specialisation is argued to represent sterile divisions of labour (Jacobs, 1969). Instead, sustained high levels of innovation are found to be a product of the synergies between Marshallian specialisation and the industry diversity of larger urban economies, or what Boschma and Frenken (2011) refer to as related variety.

It is also an economic logic that has begun to shape both corporate dynamics and science and technology policy, including that relating to science parks. Thus, the division of labour is not an inexorable unidirectional process and it is clear that recently companies have been seeking out the possibilities for a re-synthesis of the division of labour. There is some evidence to suggest that corporations have sought to improve their innovative capacities by co-locating conception, production and sales and marketing, not least due to shortening product-to-market times and time-based competition (Schoenberger, 1997) and in recognition of the interactive and iterative nature of innovation involving the value of close articulation of upstream and downstream activities (Von Hippel, 1988).

It may be possible to speak of a further round of innovation in thinking regarding the location and design of science parks as the connection between creativity and urbanity has been re-created and experimented vigorously in some urban contexts – notably Singapore. The city itself has been rediscovered as a locus of innovative activity with universities playing a key role in some settings (Haar, 2011). This view is commensurate with scientific activities being simply part and parcel of the economy more broadly and in particular benefitting from the sorts of diversity of economic activity that Jacobs (1969) saw as present in heavily urbanised regions.

National science and technology park policies have reflected these contradictory logics and variations in the character and success of individual science and technology parks are bound up with these twin logics. On the one hand, the advantages of specialisation have tended to be associated with the idea that science parks could help promote shifts in industrial structures nationally, and in lagging regions particularly, and have therefore often been seen as a key part of 'regional policy' strategies to decentralise economic development by corralling particular parts of the value chain into prescribed locations, irrespective of their location relative to major concentrations of population and employment in metropolitan regions. This has been a line of policy thought apparent in our country of study, Malaysia. On the other hand, the central importance of industry diversity to promoting innovation suggests that science parks may be at their most efficacious within or close to major urban areas. This is certainly one of the conclusions of Castells and Hall's (1994) *Technopoles of the World* and recent research that affirms the role the very largest urban agglomerations play as arenas for businesses to access international sources of knowledge (Simmie, 2001). Here, one could argue, science and technology parks and the companies within them benefit from the possibilities presented by the 'related variety' (Boschma and Frenken, 2011).

Important questions remain, then, regarding the relationship between science and technology parks and existing urban agglomerations, both in terms of the contributions that the support infrastructure and real estate offer specific to those parks and the economic relationships to the wider urban economic environment make to the performance of companies in the parks. The research reported in this chapter was designed to explore the extent to which technology parks in Malaysia have been able to leverage externalities related to Marshallian externalities of industry and activity specialisation, on the one hand, and externalities of related variety on the other hand. We explore these two competing economic logics in relation to Malaysia's two most notable technology parks.

12.3 Science and technology policy and high technology parks in Malaysia

The context in which science and technology parks in Malaysia have emerged is one in which there has been significant national planning of economic activity as part of the post-Colonial state desire to modernise society. A series of national plans in Malaysia have focused on speeding up the process of industrial transformation with some success as the nation transformed from an economy centred on raw materials, such as rubber and tin, into a manufacturing economy within twenty years. Inspired by the speed of such economic transformation, the 2020 Vision of 1991 looked to a further transformation towards higher technology and knowledge-intensive industrial structure. According to Tidd and Brockleshurst (1999) there is evidence of a coherent policy to increase value added and promote structural change in Malaysia, but the implementation of policy has been less successful such that this particular economic transformation has proved much harder to effect.

Outward- and inward-facing politics surrounding science and technology policy in Malaysia have been in near-constant tension and this tension is reflected in some of the key planks of science and technology policy, such as the Multimedia Super Corridor (MSC) (Bunnell, 2004; Lepawsky, 2009) and the creation of high tech parks (Phelps and Dawood, 2014). The outward-facing politics have mobilised science and technology policy as international diplomacy of sorts when seeking to position Malaysia's modernisation in reference to a shifting set of international horizons (see Phelps and Dawood, 2014). The inward-facing politics of science and technology policy is inextricably intertwined with the politics of ethnic cleavages in participation in the Malaysian economy. *Bumiputera* (indigenous Malay) enterprises, Malaysian Chinese and Malaysian Indian enterprises occupy significant and often particular historical niches in the Malaysian economy (Trezzini, 2001; Bowie and Unger, 1997). In particular, it is the former interests that have been privileged through various affirmative action policies developed and retained by successive Malaysian governments. Such niches of participation have tended to have a spatial or regional expression, such that economic policy – including science and technology policy – has also tended to be framed in spatial terms as an accommodation to *bumiputera* interests.

In this way, 'government policy has contributed to the industrialization of sectors of the Malaysian economy, but it is less evident whether this industrialization has been accompanied by the transfer of technological and market know-how from foreign to domestic organisation' (Tidd and Brockleshurst, 1999, p. 252). Malaysia has benefited from important foreign direct investment (FDI) flows for some time but R&D employees are few and expenditures very modest (Mani, 2002), while R&D centres associated with the likes of Japanese FDI have taken a long time to arrive. Moreover, they suggest that indigenous expertise and absorptive capacity are insufficient to exploit benefits from the co-presence of FDI. Perhaps as a result, although not without some spillovers through the development of local industrial linkages (Driffield and Noor, 1999; Harianto and Safarian, 1997), the added value of FDI into Malaysia has been limited. Here a number of factors appear to have conspired. FDI flows have been significant with some suggestion that this has led to a less selective approach to screening of potential projects (Bowie, 1994; Felker, 2001). Organised input from the business sector has been relatively passive into industrial and science and technology policy in the context of the sensitive national political bargain struck in relation to different ethnic groups. The end result is what Felker (2003) has referred to as 'contingent clusters' centred on FDI, though it is noticeable that major MNEs have remained in Malaysia despite widespread predictions of relocation to China (Edgington and Hayter, 2013).

12.3.1 The emergence of high technology parks in Malaysia

To date, five technology parks have been set up throughout the country by the Federal and State governments, these are the Technology Park Malaysia in Kuala Lumpur, Kulim Hi-Tech Park in the northern state of Kedah, Selangor Science Park (SSP) and UPM-MTDC Incubation Centre in Selangor state, located in University Putra Malaysia (UPM), and Technovation Park based at the UTM Campus in Skudai in the state of Johor (Malairaja and Zawdie, 2008). Apart from science parks, technology incubation centers have also been set up within local universities to nurture the growth of small high tech companies and start-ups.

The history of science and technology parks in Malaysia started with the establishment of an incubation industry in 1988 through the establishment of an implementation unit called *Taman Teknologi Malaysia* (Technology Park Malaysia) under the Ministry of Science, Technology and Environment (MOSTE, now renamed the Ministry of Science, Technology and Innovation (MOSTI)). Since then, several incubators were spawned by various agencies and departments all over the country. However, the connection between the origins of technology parks in the creation of Technology Park Malaysia (TPM) as one of a number of incubation units, and the generalisation of this approach into a series of technology parks in Malaysia, has been more by accident than design since they are highly uneven in their attributes – such as areal coverage, numbers of tenants, supporting services, land and property tenure, quality of real estate and industry orientation (see Phelps and Dawood, 2014). After the creation of TPM, Federal government has only been involved with the upgrading of an industrial park at Kulim to form Kulim High Tech Park (KHTP) and most recently a new biotech park in Johor. Instead, science and technology parks have emerged as the product of competitive state governments.

Of the technology parks across Malaysia, Technology Park Malaysia (TPM) is perhaps the most successful. It was established in 1995 under the Ministry of Science, Technology and Innovations and has the task of stimulating indigenous technology development to spur Malaysia's drive towards industrialisation. TPM is a technology-based centre established to promote, stimulate, support and commercialise innovative concepts drawn for R&D activities (Dawood, 2002). TPM was established with the objective to promote private-sector collaboration to provide support in marketing, management and technical fields; support innovation; and to help create a knowledge-based society. The main objective of TPM is to be able to commercialise the research output and innovation that is generated by private and public research organisations in Malaysia. The focus is mainly on high technology industries and active collaboration between industries, government agencies, research institutions and academic institutions towards promoting technology transfer. Activities located on the park must be high technology by falling into one of four subsectors: biotechnology, ICT, engineering and education.

12.4 Research methods

This paper draws on original research designed explicitly to explore the manner in which the efficacy of technology parks in Malaysia leverage Marshallian and Jacobs externalities – that is the advantages of industry and activity specialisation or diversity. The research examined the contrasting cases of Kulim High Tech Park (KHTP) and Tecnology Park Malaysia (TPM) by way of questionnaire surveys of tenants and interviews with experts from the policy and business community. Figure 12.1 shows the location of KHTP in the north of Malaysia, which is some distance from the capital city region and from the major regional urban economic agglomeration of Penang. We examined KHTP, therefore, as it offered us the opportunity to examine a technology park predicated on the idea of attracting ostensibly a new specialised Marshallian agglomeration of high technology industries and activities in a less-developed state of the Malaysian federation.

Figure 12.2 shows TPM located in the greater Kuala Lumpur area and within the original designation of the Multimedia Super Corridor (MSC) where it was assumed in this research that character of the companies on the park and the success of the park would reflect the confluence of industry specialisation and diversity of the Kuala Lumpur metro economy.[1]

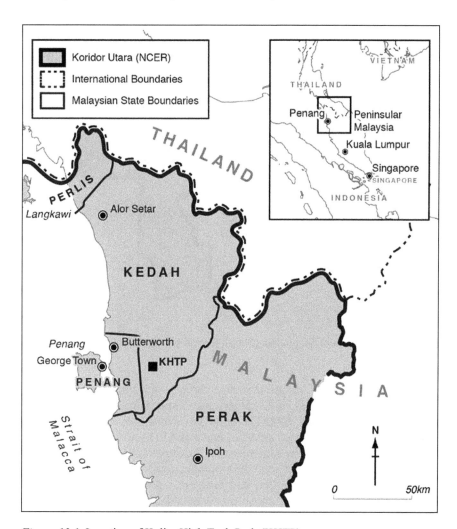

Figure 12.1 Location of Kulim High Tech Park (KHTP)

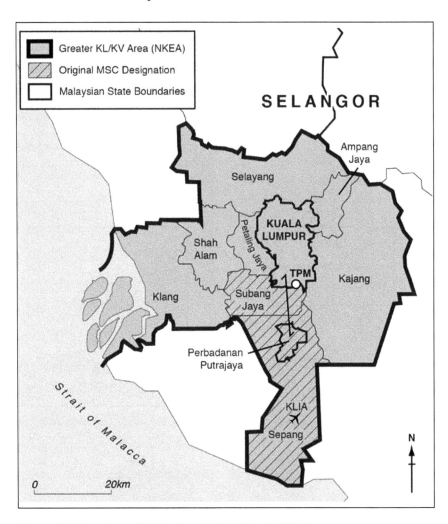

Figure 12.2 Location of Technology Park Malaysia (TPM)

The research consisted of questionnaire surveys of companies located on the two parks and a series of interviews with experts from Federal government ministries (notably MOSTI), state government economic planning boards, investment promotion agencies (such as MIDA and Invest KL), park management, quasi-government research institutes and authorities overseeing industry recruitment and development (such as MDEC, MIMOS, SIRIM and Biotech Corporation) and business representative bodies (such as MICCI) and private-sector consulting companies, conducted in 2011–13. The survey of companies on TPM was conducted in 2011 and the survey of companies on KHTP in 2013.

In the case of KHTP, out of a total population of seventy-one tenants located on the park at the time of the survey, we obtained responses from twenty-seven after three rounds of contact. In the case of TPM, there was a total of 151 tenants, from which we received a total of sixty-three questionnaires after three rounds of contact. The response rates were broadly similar for both parks despite some big differences in the complexion of the tenants and their industries, which we describe below. As we also describe below, however, it is likely that the different complexion of the tenants on the two parks, combined with some of the politics associated with the designation and development of the parks themselves, did appear to affect the responses to questions.

12.5 Neither special nor diverse: Malaysia's high technology parks

Drawing on aggregate responses from our questionnaire survey of tenants on TPM and KHTP, we compare and contrast the character of the two parks and the relationship of these activities to processes of urbanisation and the economic advantages of industrial specialisation and diversity. We also draw upon interviews to underline some of the conclusions that can be drawn from the survey data.

12.5.1 High technology?

Table 12.1 indicates major differences between the two parks in terms of the overall scale of employment, the size of companies operating there and the composition of the workforces in terms of the intensity of white-collar staff (managerial), R&D and indigenous workers. The contrast between KHTP and TPM is striking in terms of the company size of the tenants and the employment they generate. Whereas TPM is populated by micro and small businesses, KHTP is populated by some extremely large multinational companies undertaking manufacturing alongside any knowledge-intensive activities. Designated on greenfield land at some distance from the established city of Penang with its booming industrial base, KHTP struggled to attract tenants in its early years of development and several elements of an original master plan (such as the commercial centre), for what was envisaged to be a self-contained high tech community, have not materialised. An international school to service expatriate families operated for a time but closed recently.

Perhaps as a result, while KHTP is designated to accept tenants from a specified list of high technology industries and can only offer incentives to industries associated with this restricted list, the companies in these industries could not at present be described as focused exclusively or even mainly on knowledge-intensive activities as the much lower figures for the proportion of managerial and R&D workers suggests. As one interviewee argued,

Table 12.1 Indicators of character of employment on TPM and KHTP

	Number of surveyed companies	Total Employment	Mean company employees	Managerial, sales, research and development and technical staff	Managerial, sales, research and development and technical staff that are Malaysian	% R&D employees
TPM	63	902	14.3	851 (94.3%)	671 (78.8%)	196 (21.7%)
KHTP	27	11,681	432.6	2865 (24.5%)	2690 (93.9%)	346 (3.0%)

Source: Authors' survey.

The business ecosystem in Kulim is not there yet. Currently, at KHTP they are relatively still an industry-driven park meaning to say purely manufacturing. The ideal aim we have for KHTP is for them to move to an industry research park . . . Basically there is still a lack of R&D focus in Kulim and we can't blame the investor as there is not enough to support their growth [. . .].

(Interview: Senior Executive (Manufacturing),
NCIA Technology Development Centre
(NTDC), 10 April 2012)

Nevertheless KHTP is now clearly a major employment site within the Kedah region providing jobs primarily for local people. The numbers of large manufacturing enterprises attracted to the park in recent years reflect a process of industry relocation from Penang's congested and constrained economy.

Without possession of the freehold, the management company of TPM leases premises or plots of land to tenants, which has precluded the further development of the park and also posed problems for the attraction of larger corporate, multinational, operations seeking purpose-built facilities with freehold. As a consequence only half of the 680 acres at TPM has been developed.

On the other hand, this has meant that TPM has continued to focus on the incubation of smaller companies, providing subsidised space for start-up companies for a period of three years. Some measure of its success in this regard is that the fourteen buildings are almost fully occupied. Nevertheless, the constraints on future development of TPM are severe; with reduced funding from government, with virtually all existing space occupied and without freehold of the land there are major obstacles to the development of new revenue streams.

TPM itself and all other technology parks in Malaysia fall some way short of some of the international best practice. TPM itself has made study visits to Boston and San Diego in the US. One point of comparison that stands out from these study tours is the relative lack of integration between higher education institutions and property and facilities offered at technology parks in Malaysia, resulting in weaknesses in getting idea to market. The TPM College initiative is an attempt to forge links with overseas universities to offer training programmes at TPM. Some characteristics of the innovation process on science parks in the US have also proved challenging in the Malaysian context. This is particularly the case with shared facilities where 'I am still not able to convince the locals because they want to hide what they do, they want their own assets. The sharing of assets mentality is not there yet' (Interview: Vice President, Business Development and Corporate Services, TPM, 15 September 2011).

12.5.2 The advantages of TPM and KHTP

In the questionnaire survey tenants were also asked for the three main advantages of a location on their respective parks. The advantages cited by tenants on both parks barely extended into those sorts of factors that are taken to be the hallmark of a successful science park. This much was confirmed in a recent study into industrial parks in Malaysia sponsored by Federal government (EPU, 2012). Commenting on technology parks in Malaysia in general, an interviewee at TPM highlighted how 'It has become a property business instead of the economic growth of a more defined sector' (Interview: Vice President, Business Development and Corporate Services, TPM, 15 September 2011).

In the case of KHTP, tenants cited advantages that barely extend beyond the basic ingredients of accessibility (defined in terms of it being a strategic location) and infrastructure (such as purpose-built roads and highways to Penang and the port of Butterworth), which are very closely related. KHTP fared particularly poorly with respect to other benchmark parks across South East Asia in the recent government-sponsored review (EPU, 2012, p. 96). However, a proportion of tenants did cite the facilities such as training centres as an important advantage, while two companies also cited proximity to suppliers, suggesting that KHTP may make some qualitative contribution to processes of innovation at companies based there. Surprisingly incentives were mentioned by just two tenants. Nevertheless, the factors cited appear to be very much those demanded by manufacturing operations seeking low cost but accessible locations.

Tenants of TPM also appear quite attuned to factors that reflect the bottom line of costs (such as MSC status, which confers financial incentives). Sizeable proportions of tenants did at least recognise aspects of the physical and business environment that are specific to the park. However, even in TPM only nine of sixty-three tenants responding cited the sorts of factors (the specialised facilities, access to similar companies) that are supposed to be the hallmark of a successful science park as defined earlier. In this respect, the recent survey and report on industrial parks in Malaysia found that TPM compared favourably with benchmark parks elsewhere in South East Asia (EPU, 2012, p. 103). Our interviewees from the park itself were concerned that it did not match up with standards internationally, though this may also be an effect, as much as a cause, of the sorts of responses in Table 12.2, since it was also argued that business culture in Malaysia was, as yet, not oriented towards the sharing, or collective use, of facilities for innovation, upon which the whole idea of science and technology parks is to some extent predicated (Interviews: Vice President, Business Development and Corporate Services, TPM, 15 September 2011; Senior Manager, Marketing and Business Development Park Management and Services Division, TPM, 30 September 2011).

The industry complexion of TPM actually remains quite skewed towards ICT industries as a result of the cybercity status it enjoys within the MSC – with something in the region of two thirds of all tenants falling in this sector according to lists supplied at interview. The biotechnology, engineering, research and development and business consulting industries are represented in much smaller numbers, while TPM is also keen to diversify further by attracting start-up companies in the nanotechnology, stem-cell and solar-power industries (Interview: Senior Manager, Marketing and Business Development Park, Management and Services Division, TPM, 30 September 2011). Nevertheless, TPM seeks to attract companies from other sectors and has dedicated subsidiary companies to do so. It is notable that there may be reasonably common pressures facing technology parks in Malaysia with both TPM and Kulim High Tech Park trying to diversify themselves in terms of the industries attracted (Senior Manager, Marketing and Business Development, Park Management and Services Division, TPM, 30 September 2011). The complexion of TPM itself has evolved as part of this context and some of the contradictions of it and limits of Malaysian science and technology policy. TPM has come to represent a relatively high cost source of business premises for manufacturing activities to exist alongside research and development, managerial and sales and marketing functions. And so as companies have been incubated or have grown they have relocated elsewhere, within the region depicted in Figure 12.2, TPM has been retained as something of a prestige address from which to operate the managerial and sales and marketing functions of businesses.

Even fewer tenants cited the importance of proximity to Kuala Lumpur, which could be read as an indication that they draw little competitive advantage from any Jacobs externalities found within the diversified urban economy of the capital city region in which TPM is located. In this respect, Kuala Lumpur is itself a relatively small capital city region by international standards, both in terms of total population and economic activity, so that in terms of the incubation business 'the country does not have a big enough cake for everyone' (Interview: Senior General Manager, Group Strategic Planning Department, SIRIM Berhad, 15 September 2011).

Table 12.2 The advantages of a location on the park cited by tenants of TPM and KHTP

Advantages of TPM (n=63)		Advantages of KHTP (n=27)	
MSC status	35 (55.6%)	Infrastructure	21 (77.8%)
Attractive environment	23 (36.5%)	Accessibility to port/airport	20 (74.1%)
Quality of real estate	19 (30.2%)	Facilities and services	6 (22.2%)
Accessibility	15 (23.8%)	Location	5 (18.5%)
Facilities and services	9 (14.3%)	Incentives	2 (7.4%)
Low rents	9 (14.3%)	Others	3(11.1%)
Proximity to Kuala Lumpur	5 (7.9%)		
Presence of other companies	2 (3.2%)		
Other	12 (19%)		

Source: Authors' survey.

12.5.3 Tenant perceptions of technology parks and the politics of economic modernisation

Tenants on the two parks were asked to indicate the extent they agreed or disagreed with a series of statements on a four-point Likert scale. The results are presented in Table 12.3, that, in order to simplify presentation, collapses responses along this four-point scale into two (agree and disagree), but which also presents the mean score for each statement. The responses make for intriguing reading and they are the opposite of what might be expected given the location and business complexion of the two parks discussed above and, in the case of KHTP, could be read as contradicting the responses given by tenants in Tables 12.1 and 12.2. In the case of KHTP, populated mainly by very large companies with little in the way of knowledge-intensive activities, opinions on both the park and its surrounding economy are uniformly positive. TPM is, as we saw, a little closer to an idealised science park with a larger collection of small, knowledge-intensive companies, yet respondents provide a much more mixed view of both the park and its surrounding economic environment.

Scores refer to a four-point Likert scale in which respondents were asked if they strongly agreed (4), agreed somewhat (3), disagreed somewhat (2), or strongly disagreed (1) with a series of statements.

Despite the failings of KHTP that have been acknowledged in a recent survey of all industrial and high tech parks and in interviews with park management, all companies responded in an almost uniformly positive way on the statements put to them and indicate a role for both Marshallian and Jacobs externalities in the development of industry on the park. The responses from tenants on KHTP are difficult to interpret. One possible answer is that they reflect the politics of the creation and industry recruitment surrounding this park. As a symbol of national economic modernisation with a specific location, reflecting an accommodation to the ethnic political base of the *Barisan Nasional* party, KHTP benefits from unique advantages in terms of the incentives on offer and the efficiency of various administrative processes. Tenants are doubtless aware of its unique status in this regard and may not wish to be seen to be openly critical. On the other hand, it is hard to believe that the mainly large multinational companies operating there would not be forthcoming with such criticisms. Given these almost completely uniformly positive responses from KHTP tenants, the fact that the greatest level of criticism of the park environment relates to the level of R&D collaborations among tenants provides just a glimpse of its limitations in terms of stimulating processes of innovation. The responses from tenants on TPM appear at least to be more realistic, especially in terms of comparisons made between international benchmarks that are asked for in some of the statements.

It is possible that the level of inputs sourced from other tenants within the park could be low in the case of TPM with its large number of specialised competitor companies when compared to the possibilities for production complex-type (Gordon and McCann, 2000) inter-linkages among related companies in

Table 12.3 Likert-scale responses from companies based on TPM and KHTP

	Agree		Disagree		Mean	
	TPM	KHTP	TPM	KHTP	TPM	KHTP
Interaction among company staff in park is strong	47 (78.3%)	27 (100%)	13 (21.7%)	0 (0%)	3.00	3.44
Level of inputs sourced from within park is considerable	24 (43.6%)	24 (92.3%)	31 (56.4%)	2 (7.7%)	2.39	3.35
The business service inputs of the park compare favourably with S&T parks internationally	28 (52.8%)	23 (88.5%)	25 (47.2%)	3 (11.5%)	2.58	3.31
Products and services of companies on park are world leading	33 (55.9%)	25 (92.6%)	26 (44.1%)	2(7.4%)	2.88	3.33
The level of R&D interactions among tenants within the park is considerable	33 (58.9%)	22 (81.5%)	23 (41.1%)	5 (18.5%)	2.61	3.19
Reputation of the park as a business location compares favourably with S&T parks internationally	39 (68.4%)	25 (96.2%)	18 (31.6%)	1 (3.8%)	2.93	3.46

KHTP. However, responses to this statement from KHTP tenants surveyed hardly seem credible. Companies surveyed on TPM and KHTP were asked for the per cent by value of their sales and purchases destined for their three biggest clients and suppliers and for their location. Unfortunately, response rates for this specific question were low and data was not always captured in a form that was accurate or reliable. Seven of eighteen KHTP tenants responding to this question indicated that they had clients based in KHTP itself, while none from nine responding had suppliers based there. In the case of TPM three from twenty-one surveyed tenants had clients based also within the park and none from nine responding had suppliers based there. These data, although very imperfect, hardly support the very positive responses given by KHTP tenants nor the very different responses between KHTP and TPM tenants, presented in Table 12.3 above.

12.6 Conclusions

Technology parks in Malaysia have not been accorded a particularly prominent role in Federal government industrial and science and technology policy when compared to other developmental state nations. From the outset their role has not been clearly defined at the national scale when set against other more substantial policy vehicles such as the MSC. Instead, a small number of technology parks have emerged as a result of disparate initiatives of Federal, state and university sectors with widely differing characteristics. Indeed, such is the lack of clarity regarding the distinctive contribution of these parks that our study takes place against the backcloth of a major evaluation of all trading, industry, science and technology parks in Malaysia (EPU, 2012). If the fortunes of the two leading examples of technology parks in Malaysia considered in this chapter are anything to judge by, the policy surrounding technology parks in Malaysia has stimulated neither new specialised agglomerations of high technology industries or knowledge-intensive activities, nor leveraged effectively on urban diversity to stimulate indigenous innovative capacity.

There are likely to be several ingredients here, including: the limits of science and technology policy to act as regional policy – including through single major developments like KHTP – especially when these policies have been inflected with political concerns to steer economic opportunities to particular ethnic populations; the lack of scale and associated diversity of the national, capital city-region and other urban centre economies upon which the two parks might leverage, and; the unco-ordinated development of high technology parks and incubator facilities as part of national science and technology policy.

In TPM, as an enclave of high technology, innovative activity exists within a series of other territorially defined policies (such as the MSC, the Kuala Lumpur/Klang Valley Key National Economic Area) that have a bearing on the types of activities found within it, and the sort of role it plays in the wider economy as a result. Yet it appears not to represent a significant and specialised industry agglomeration in and of itself, but rather a diverse collection of businesses and business functions – including those not directly concerned with innovation but with administration and marketing and sales. While it takes its place in the wider economic spaces of the MSC and greater Kuala Lumpur, neither of these economies appears to have the scale as yet to offer the sorts of industry diversity upon which specialised clusters of industries or activities can leverage the advantages of related variety. While the accessibility and other physical infrastructural advantages of the greater Kuala Lumpur economy compare favourably (Bunnell *et al*, 2002; Ramasamy, Chakrabarty and Chea, 2004) with comparable capital city-regions internationally, the suggestion remains that the business-service infrastructure and 'intangibles' are lacking (Ramasamy *et al.*, 2004). Moreover, administrative arrangements for the time being leave a commercially successful operation such as TPM and its cluster of tenants unable to leverage further on its location within a growing capital city-region and one on which national resources are scheduled to be concentrated from now until 2020. The prospects of TPM, as an exurban campus within the greater Kuala Lumpur area, coming to thrive on the sorts of advantages enjoyed by its counterparts in many metropolitan economies of the United States, seems to rest in part on resolving some of these obstacles to further development.

KHTP as a high-profile attempt to steer economic development opportunities and a structural transformation towards knowledge-intensive activities, specifically away from the capital city-region at present, can leverage neither the advantages of localised industry specialisation on the park itself nor really on the scale of the Penang economy. Industry has relocated from the booming high technology economy of Penang to Kedah and to KHTP – rather like manufacturing operations have relocated to Johor from Singapore in the south of Malaysia. However, those companies and operations moving seek lower costs rather than any external economy advantages that a technology park such as KHTP was designed to foster. It remains to be seen whether KHTP will be able to leverage upon this stream of relocations in a way that sees the industries congregating there effect a significant move up the value chain, and the sorts of innovation and untraded interdependencies the park was designed to foster. Rather, it appears at present this is a case of what Jacobs (1969) would regard as sterile divisions of labour cascading or diffusing down the urban system.

The examination of these two contrasting technology parks in Malaysia underlines several aspects of theory regarding the location of innovative activity and the efficacy of policy designed to steer away from the largest urban centres. KHTP struggled for years to attract tenants and, although now much more successful in this regard, its story highlights the difficulties of fostering a new innovative agglomeration of industry with a significant industrial atmosphere away from established urban economies. Despite the major federal investment in and political favour for KHTP, its progress as a collection of high technology industries poses a significant question over the possibility of fashioning new Marshallian externalities away from major urban centres. The cases of both TPM and KHTP highlight the importance of the scale of industry and investment in innovation at the national and sub-national level within nations needed for science and technology parks to be able to thrive – as specialised spaces.

Note

1   The MSC is another key plank of the Malaysian government's strategies to effect a structural transformation in the national economy by promoting the development of high technology industry (see Bunnell, 2004 for a complete historical context). Companies of a defined set of preferred industry sectors locating in the MSC area enjoyed 'cybercity' incentives. The cybercity status associated with the designated MSC area was subsequently extended to a series of other locations across Malaysia (see Lepawsky, 2009; Phelps and Dawood, 2014).

References

Boschma, R. and Frenken, K. (2011) 'Technological relatedness and regional branching', in H. Bathelt, M.P. Feldman and D.F. Kogler (eds) *Dynamic geographies of knowledge creation and innovation.* Routledge, London.

Bowie, A. (1994) 'The dynamics of business-government relations in industrializing Malaysia', pp. 167–194 in A. MacIntyre (ed.) *Business and government in industrialising Asia.* Sydney: Allen and Unwin.

Bowie, A. and Unger, D. (1997) *The politics of open economies. Indonesia, Malaysia, the Philippines and Thailand.* Cambridge: Cambridge University Press.

Bunnell, T. (2004) *Malaysia, modernity and the Multimedia Super Corridor: A critical geography of intelligent landscapes.* Routledge, London.

Bunnell, T., Barter, P.A. and Morshidi, S. (2002) Kuala Lumpur metropolitan area: A globalizing city–region'. *Cities, 19*(5): 357–70.

Castells, M. and Hall, P. (1994) *Technopoles of the world: The making of 21st century industrial complexes.* London: Routledge.

Dawood, S.R.S. (2002) 'The globalisation of economic activities and the dynamic growth of an industrial region in Pacific Asia: The linkages between transnational firms in the manufacturing sector and engineering services in Klang Valley, Malaysia'. Unpublished PhD, School of Geography, University of Leeds.

Driffield, N. and Noor, A.H.M. (1999) 'Foreign direct investment and local input linkages in Malaysia'. *Transnational Corporations 8*: 1–24.

Economic Planning Unit (EPU) (2012) *Study on industrial estates development in Malaysia.* PwCAS Sdn Bhd. Kuala Lumpur. Available at: www.epu.gov.my/study-on-industrial-estates-development-in-malaysia (accessed on 27 February 2013).

Edgington, D. and Hayter, R. (2013) 'In China's shadow: The locational dynamics of Japanese electronic firms in Malaysia'. *Economic Geography. 89*: 227–59.

Felker, G. (2001) 'The politics of industrial investment policy reform in Malaysia and Thailand', in K.S. Jomo (ed.) *South East Asia's industrialisation: Industrial policy, capabilities and sustainability.* Basingstoke: Palgrave Macmillan.

Felker, G. (2003) 'Southeast Asian industrialization and the changing global production system'. *Third World Quarterly, 24*: 255–82.

Forsyth, A. and Crewe, K. (2010) 'Suburban technopoles as places: The international campus-garden-suburb style'. *Urban Design International, 15*: 165–82.

Gordon, I.R. and McCann, P. (2000) 'Industrial clusters: Complexes, agglomeration and/or social networks'. *Urban Studies, 37*: 513–32.

Haar, S. (2011) *City as campus: Urbanism and higher education in Chicago.* Minneapolis, MN: University of Minnesota Press.

Harianto, F. and Safarian, A.E. (1997) 'MNEs and technology diffusion: A Southeast Asian experience', pp. 189–219 in P.J. Buckley and J.-L. Mucchielli (eds) *Multinational firms and international relocation.* Cheltenham: Edward Elgar.

Harvey, D. (1985) *The urbanisation of capital.* Oxford: Blackwell.

International Association of Science Parks (IASP) (2011) Available at: www.iasp.ws/publico/index.jsp?enl=2 (accessed on 30 September 2012).

Jacobs, J. (1969) *The economy of cities.* London: Jonathan Cape.

Lepawsky, J. (2009) 'Clustering as anti-politics machine: Situating the politics of regional economic development and Malaysia's multimedia super corridor'. *Regional Studies, 43*: 463–78.

Malairaja, C. and Zawdie, G. (2008) 'Science parks and university–industry collaboration in Malaysia'. *Technology Analysis and Strategic Management, 20*(6): 727–39.

Mani, S. (2002) *Government, innovation and technology: An international comparative analysis.* Cheltenham: Edward Elgar.

Massey, D., Quintas, P. and Wield, D. (1992) *High tech fantasies: Science parks in society and space.* London: Routledge.

O'Mara, M.P. (2005) *Cities of knowledge: Cold war science and the search for the next Silicon Valley.* Princton, NJ: Princeton University.

Panne, G. van der, (2004) 'Agglomeration economies: Marshall versus Jacobs'. *Journal of Evolutionary Economics, 14*: 593–604.

PEMANDU (2010) *Economic transformation plan: A roadmap for Malaysia.* Available at: http://etp.pemandu.gov.my/Download_Centre-@-Download_Centre. aspx (accessed on 18 March 2013).

Phelps, N.A. and Dawood, S.R.S. (2014) 'Untangling the spaces of high technology in Malaysia'. *Environment and Planning C: Government and Policy, 32*(5): 896–915.

Ramasamy, B., Chakrabarty, A. and Chea, M. (2004) 'Malaysia's leap into the future: An evaluation of the multimedia super corridor'. *Technovation, 24*: 871–83.

Rugman, A., Verbeke, A. and Yuan, W. (2010) 'Re-conceptualizing Bartlett and Ghoshal's classification of national subsidiary role is the multinational enterprise'. *Journal of Management Studies, 48*: 253–77.

Schoenberger, E. (1997) *The cultural crisis of the firm.* Oxford: Blackwell.

Simmie, J. (ed.) (2001) *Innovative cities.* London: Spon.

Storper, M. (1995) 'The resurgence of regional economies, ten years later: The region as a nexus of untraded interdependencies'. *European Urban and Regional Studies, 2*: 191–221.

Tidd, J. and Brockleshurst, M. (1999) 'Routes to technological learning and development: An assessment of Malaysia's innovation policy and performance'. *Technological Forecasting and Social Change, 62*: 239–57.

Trezzini, B. (2001) 'Embedded state autonomy and legitimacy: Piecing together the Malaysian development puzzle'. *Economy and Society, 30*: 324–53.

Von Hippel, E. (1988) *The sources of innovation.* Cambridge: Cambridge University Press.

13 Science parks and their contribution to regional development

The example of the Campus Tulln Technopole

Simone Strauf and Roland Scherer

13.1 Introduction

From the perspectives of certain scientific and political communities, knowledge and innovation are considered crucial factors for economic development of both nations and regions. The exploitation, transfer and use of knowledge play a decisive role in the way to build the knowledge-based economy and society. Regions are important actors within the knowledge-based economy that have to take advantages and use their potentials. Regions are very heterogeneous, differing in terms of resources (human capital, social capital, technological and financial capital) as well as with respect to their competitive ability, including local spillover effects and other multiplier effects. To gain advantages, regions have to construct it by integrating different developmental directions, including the knowledge-creating sector, the market and the government (Cooke and Leydesdorff, 2006). Within the last decade several measures have been undertaken by many regions to promote the knowledge-based economy.

Technopoles are assumed to have positive effects on innovation and knowledge-based regional development. They are often promoted by government and based on public-private partnerships (Castells and Hall, 1994). Especially university-industry linkages are expected to be one of the success factors for the promotion of knowledge transfer and innovation (Trippl and Tödtling, 2008). This chapter analyses what drives knowledge-based development in technopoles and what contribution technopoles can make to regional development. Against the background of the scientific discussion on knowledge-based regional development, five factors were defined that, as a hypothesis, will allow statements on positive effects of technopoles, especially on the transfer of knowledge and the effects of regional embeddedness.

A set of examples of six European technopoles or science parks was chosen to analyse their contribution to knowledge-based development related to the mentioned five factors. In addition to these examples, a newly-founded university and research centre located in Austria will be discussed in detail.[1] Based on these empirical data we will gain insights into whether and in which fields technopoles contribute to knowledge-based regional development and whether the defined factors can provide useful information.

The paper will start with the contribution of knowledge and innovation to regional development from a theoretical point of view (13.2). Referring to the literature and the experiences of technopoles and their effects on regional development, five variables will be defined to show the contribution of technopoles and knowledge transfer to knowledge-based regional development. Section 13.3 compares six European institutions based on the mentioned five factors. In Section 13.4 the characteristics of the case study of the 'University and Research Centre Tulln (UFT)' in Austria and its objectives are discussed. Subsequently, the method of networked thinking will be used to draw a regional interdependent network to show which interdependencies exist between different factors, how the five variables contribute to regional development and how they can be visualised in this diagram. Based on this diagram, indicators for regional impact monitoring are derived. In the last section the results are summarised and conclusions are drawn.

The study is based on different methodological tools. Existing studies, reports and concepts were evaluated. In addition, qualitative interviews were conducted on two levels: with decision makers of the institutions and with key stakeholders of the UFT. The interviews were necessary for a better understanding of the underlying objectives and initiated activities and the existing networks of the institutions. The development of the interdependent regional networks for the UFT in Section 13.4.3 has been made on the basis of this information with regard to the networked-thinking approach. This method has its origin in a systemic approach based on cybernetic principles. Stafford Beer is regarded as the founder of management cybernetics (Beer, 1959). In the 1980s, pragmatic methods were developed for dealing with complex systems. The applied method in this paper goes back to studies by Frederic Vester, who saw the properties of a system as a networked interactive structure (Vester, 1974).

13.2 Knowledge and innovation and their contribution to regional development

In regional science, the questions of which factors have a positive effect on a region's success, along with how and why regions develop as they do, have long been discussed. Recent theories no longer examine classic production factors (such as capital, labour, resources) – today knowledge diminishes the significance of material factors (e.g., Yigitcanlar, 2010). Productivity and competitiveness are seen as a function of knowledge generation and information processing (Castells, 1996).

Thus the balance between knowledge and resources has shifted so far towards the former that knowledge has become by far the most important factor determining standards of living—more important than land, capital, or labour.

(Cooke and Leydesdorff, 2006: 7)

With the focus upon knowledge as one of the central drivers of economic development, endogenous factors gain more importance. The capacity of regions to support learning and innovation processes, as well as their ability to learn, has been identified as providing key sources of competitive advantage (Cooke, 1998; Lundvall and Johnson, 1994; Storper, 1997).

Although the success of a region depends on its ability to learn by creating and transferring knowledge to gain advantages, this alone does not satisfactorily explain which factors positively affect and promote innovation, a transfer of knowledge and spillover effects. Economic geographers and regional theorists have advanced a number of overlapping concepts, e.g., 'learning regions' or 'social capital' that emphasize the importance of knowledge and learning (Amin and Thrift, 1994; Cooke and Morgan, 1998; Morgan, 1997; Putnam, 1993; Storper, 1997).

Asheim (1996: 15), for example, with respect to the approach of innovative milieus, argues that the largest problem consists of identifying the impact mechanisms and processes that promote innovation in some regions more successfully than in others or, in other words, 'why localization and territorial specificity should make technological and organizational dynamics better' (Storper 1993: 14). Also, the lack of comparative empirical data, which would allow for explaining different development paths, is emphasized (e.g., Westeren, 2008; Russ and Jones, 2008). Other critics have suggested that the theoretical vitality of contemporary work in regional science is matched by a worrying lack of empirical rigour and an increasing policy irrelevance (Markusen, 1999; Martin, 1999).

To promote knowledge transfer and innovation in regions, networks and institutional conditions play an important role (e.g., Grabher, 1993; Rösch, 2000). Alongside high and medium tech firms and other knowledge-intensive branches, research institutions are of particular importance. Universities play a central role as a source of knowledge. Universities increase the significance for technological and economic progress, especially because they have been encouraged to enter into relationship with the industry in order to stimulate the production of more practical, applied research outputs. Universities could contribute in various ways, for example as knowledge providers in university-industry linkages or as incubators for academic spin-off companies (e.g., Trippl and Tödtling, 2008).

To foster co-operation between the private and public sector within a region, to intensify the transfer of knowledge and to contribute to innovation and knowledge-based regional development, so-called technopoles were established. Findings from some successful examples (e.g., Silicon Valley) leads to the assumption that proximity helps generate and transfer knowledge more effectively (Yigitcanlar, 2010). Raspe and van Oort (2008) also emphasise the role of the spatial context of the knowledge economy. Their definition of a knowledge region rests on several dimensions stressing the importance of knowledge workers and high and medium tech firms, a high share of R&D employees, and high levels of technical and non-technical innovation.

Since 2000 regional policy focused increasingly on innovation and knowledge (e.g., European Commission, 2006). Technopoles are promoted by governments, often in association with universities and private companies. Technopoles result from three historical processes: (1) technological revolution based on information technologies; (2) increasing globalization of capital, management, labour, technology, information, or markets; and (3) the emergence of a new form of economic production and management called 'informational' (Castells and Hall, 1994: 3). The term 'technopole' includes different forms and focus such as science parks, technology parks, science cities and the like. Besides the terminology, all of them have in common 'a specific form of territorial concentration of technological innovation with a potential to generate scientific synergy and economic productivity' (Castells and Hall, 1994: 8).

Within recent decades, the number of technopoles has increased rapidly and became a worldwide phenomenon. The creation of research parks is often seen as a means to create dynamic clusters that accelerate economic growth and international competitiveness around the world. Specifically, research parks of various sizes and types are widely perceived as an effective policy tool to realise larger and more visible returns on a nation's investment in research and development (Wessner, 2009: 2). Technopoles or science parks are expected to provide locational and economic advantages as well as image carriers, which can affect the locational quality of a region.

The interest of policymakers and the growing number of technopoles and science parks has led to numerous academic analyses. However, regarding their contribution to technology development science parks have been viewed sceptically as relying on a linear model of innovation, which assumes that scientific knowledge can be transferred very easily from research organisations to firms located nearby. In recent approaches more attention has been paid to the factors that lead to interactions and networking among firms and innovation support organisations (Phillimore, 1999; Cooke, 2001).

According to the experiences and the evaluation of the performance on science parks, an evolution can be observed. The first generation of science parks promoted the science push from universities into spin-off companies moving into surrounding dedicated industrial areas. The second generation of science parks was driven by industry's science pull, with major firms locating around leading research environments to extract scientific discoveries. The emerging third generation of science parks operate interactive models of innovation, embedded in diverse urban environments. In such areas, networks and systems of trust, the development of respective public, private or scientific partners, cultures of interpretation, and degrees of public or institutional participation, as well as the availability of financial/legal instruments, all form an integral part of the innovation environment's global function. Location embeddedness is no longer just a feature, but a key success factor (Haselmeyer, 2004). Technopoles or science parks could contribute to regional innovation if they absorbed the lessons learned of interactive innovation systems, by enhancing social capital, networking and intermediating activity (Cooke, 2001).

Science parks' key success factors reflected by the literature focus mainly on location factors, property-management skills and a quality management team (Saublens, 2007: 63). According to Seymour (2006) other relevant attributes of successful science parks exist, e.g., the advantage of single shareholders, a clear separation between ownership and management, involvement of higher-education institutions and the existence of a clear vision and strategy.

Whether a science park is successful or fails depends (besides the mentioned criteria) on the specific conditions of the global, national and regional framework (e.g., political system, technological uncertainty and rapid changes in consumer demand) (Sternberg, 2000). The performance of a science park is therefore related to its vision and strategy, as well as to external factors.

The aim of this chapter is to analyse the drivers of knowledge-based regional development by technopoles. Although each technopole has its unique aim as well as its specific implications, we elaborate a set of factors that allow a comparable analysis regarding their contribution to knowledge-based regional development. These factors focus on different aspects of knowledge transfer and regional embeddedness. This analysis was undertaken to gain insights whether and in which fields technopoles can contribute to regional development.

Summarising the aforementioned arguments the following criteria could be defined to indicate the contribution of technopoles to regional development by promoting knowledge transfer and regional embeddedness:

- links between academic and extra-faculty research;
- promotion of the knowledge transfer;
- entity co-ordinating the knowledge transfer;
- promotion of start-ups;
- co-operation with regional enterprises.

The regional embeddedness can be seen as a synoptic factor for the co-operation with regional actors and a result of the mentioned five factors.

Besides the universities as a node of knowledge to promote innovation and regional development, the university-industry linkage is quite important (Tripp and Tödtling, 2008). The transfer of knowledge between universities and firms and innovation does not automatically result from proximity. This is one of the main arguments to point out the failure of science parks (Capello and Morrison, 2009). It has to be promoted by the research institutions as well as by the firms.

An entity co-ordinating and fostering the transfer of knowledge could gain advantages. Knowledge and technology transfer organizations are crucial nodes connecting suppliers and users of knowledge that support the endogenous potential of innovation in firms (Landry *et al.*, 2013). One of the main tasks of this intermediary organization should be – together with research institutions – to promote start-ups and spin-offs.

The existence of regional networks of knowledge development is also an important asset to circulate knowledge outside the science park and spread it to regional firms (Russ and Jones, 2008). Within a global world international networks are a matter of course and a competitive factor, particularly for research institutes. On the other hand the regional anchorage and the knowledge exchange with regional partners could be one of the success factors for institutions within the science parks, as well as for the development of the region (Asheim and Isaksen, 2002).

An empirical basis of six European sciences parks was chosen for a comparative analysis relating to the five factors above, which indicate their contribution to regional development. The evidence of these analyses can lead to a benchmark for the case study of the newly established science park 'Campus Tulln technopole' presented in Section 13.4.

13.3 Effects of regional embedding: findings from six European examples

To provide information on how knowledge and technology transfer takes place and how institutions are linked to regions and beyond, a comparative analysis of six science parks was undertaken. Thus, the contributions such institutions can make to a region's locational quality are systematically described. The following institutions were selected as reference projects: Karlsruhe Institute of Technology (KIT), Karlsruhe (D); Science and Technology Park Adlershof, Berlin (D); SP Technical Research Institute of Sweden, Boras (SE); Institut Poytechnique de Grenoble (F); Tecnoparco del Lago Maggiore, Verbania (I); and Science City Davos, Davos (CH).

13.3.1 Link between academic and extra-faculty research

In the case of some of the institutions (KIT, the Science and Technology Park Adlershof and the Institut Polytechnique de Grenoble) universities belong to their core constituents. For them research and, in particular, its quality plays a key role. With their research they pursue the goal of gaining international recognition and a leading position in their field. Apart from basic research, applied research is an important element for the aforementioned institutions – plus the SP Technical Research Institute of Sweden. Especially the KIT and the SP Technical Research Institute of Sweden are very much engaged in applied research.

13.3.2 Promotion of knowledge transfer by a co-ordinating entity

The facilitation of a transfer of knowledge is a goal in all cases reviewed. However, there are distinct approaches– they range from common projects to commissioned research and consulting services to offers of further education. Across institutions, the transfer of knowledge is not always institutionalised and structured to the same extent. The KIT, the Science and Technology Park Adlershof, the Institut Polytechnique de Grenoble and the Tecnoparco del Lago Maggiore all have organisational units or bodies that establish a connection between academic research results and companies. The bodies offer services to both scientists and researchers of the institution in question, as well as to interested companies or external organisations. They see themselves as liaison offices and intermediary bodies between the interests of science and business.

13.3.3 Promotion of start-ups

The promotion of start-ups is one of the core tasks of the Science and Technology Park Adlershof and the Tecnoparco del Lago Maggiore. They explicitly aim at establishing companies on their premises. In the case of the institutions with a research focus, e.g., KIT or SP Technical Research Institute of Sweden, the promotion of spin-offs is welcome, but not necessarily a top priority.

13.3.4 Co-operation with regional enterprises

Co-operation with companies from the region depends, on the one hand, on the regional embeddedness of an institution and, on the other, on how co-operation is organized. Moreover, the thematic focus of the institution is important. Co-operation with media companies from the region plays an important role for the Science and Technology Park Adlershof. Co-operation between companies based on the Adlerhof's premises is also encouraged. As for the SP Technical Research Institute of Sweden and the Institut Polytechnique de Grenoble, the co-operation with companies from the region is not as advanced, due to those institutions' high degree of specialization.

13.3.5 Regional embededdness: co-operation with regional actors

Close co-operation with regional actors, especially public authorities, is usually the more intense the more closely they are involved in the institution's funding body. In the cases of Science City Davos, Tecnoparco del Lago Maggiore and the Science and Technology Park Adlershof, local and, in some instances, regional public authorities have a financial stake in the institutions. In the case of the KIT, regional embeddedness is achieved through a body made up of representatives of the municipality, the region and the KIT. This body tries to take advantage of synergies between the KIT and the region. The regional embeddedness of the analysed institutions can be described as a synoptic factor for its regional activities and the co-operation with different regional actors.

The following table provides an overview of the six institutions and their performance concerning the considered factors:

Table 13.1 Comparison of six European science parks

	Karlsruhe Institute of Technology (KIT)	Science and Technology Park Adlershof, Berlin	SP Technical Research Institute of Sweden, Borås	Institut Polytechnique de Grenoble	Tecnoparco del Lago Maggiore, Verbania	Science City, Davos
Link between academic and extra-faculty research	XXX	XX	XX	XX	XX	X
Promotion of knowledge transfer	XXX	XXX	XX	XX	XX	XX
Coordination centre for knowledge transfer	XXX	XXX	X/–	XXX	XX	XX
Support of spin-offs	XX	XXX	X	XX	XXX	–
Cooperation with firms from the region	XX	XXX	X/–	X	XXX	X/–
Regional embeddedness: cooperation with regional actors	XXX	XX	X	X	XX	XXX

Note: One 'X' was given for a low and three for a high performance, '–' means the institution currently underperforms.

Source: Scherer and Strauf (2011).

Overall, the effects on the host region and the regional embedment and the promotion of knowledge transfer vary across institutions, depending on their respective mission. Nevertheless, the considered factors provide valuable hints in understanding the contribution to regional development of science parks. These results will offer a benchmark for the case study of the UFT, and help to answer the question about whether areas of the host region's development will potentially be affected by the UFT and how those effects can be measured through a regional impact monitoring system.

13.4 The case of the University and Research Centre Tulln (UFT)

As in other countries, public programmes for the promotion of knowledge and innovation to improve the competitiveness of regions were introduced in Austria. In 2000, the Federal state of Lower Austria started a technology initiative aimed at the development and conversion of its technopole programme. The intention is to develop locations with public and semi-public R&D institutions as places of 'technology-oriented economic activity', to connect them with enterprises and to increase the economic power of Lower Austria. The government of Lower Austria envisages its technopoles as locations with a critical number of R&D institutions, whose research emphasises one or more key aspects, and which have built an appropriate infrastructure for that purpose. Furthermore, the direct local links to academic training are essential in order to connect research with teaching.

The 'Technopol Tulln for agrobiotechnology and environmental biotechnology' is one of four sites singled out for development by the technopole programme of the Federal state of Lower Austria.[2] The Department for Agrobiotechnology (IFA-Tulln), the University of Applied Sciences Wiener Neustadt/Tulln branch, the Technopark Tulln Ltd, the local technical school of agriculture, Zuckerforschung Tulln Ltd and the city of Tulln all co-operate within the framework of the Tulln technopole. Furthermore, there are additional co-operation agreements with industrial companies. Modern bioanalytics, environmental technology, plant breeding and the development of renewable natural resources are core issues the Tulln technopole is working on.

Before the UFT started, there were 236 high-tech jobs in technology fields, twenty-one university departments were represented at the technopole and 145 students were enrolled in courses of the University of Applied Sciences Wiener Neustadt/Tulln branch. Eight companies from the field of agricultural and environmental technology had their offices on the campus, employing thirty-one people (cf. Ecoplus, 2011).

The technopole attains critical mass with the aid of the UFT because the research centre improves the external perception of the location and the region, and contributes to identity-building on the campus. Representatives hope that enhanced co-operation will lead the partners to initiate more joint projects, to promote spin-offs and the creation of new firms on the campus.

13.4.1 The UFT's goals

The University of Natural Resources and Life Sciences Vienna (BOKU) and the Austrian Institute of Technology (AIT) are the main occupants. The two institutions' teams in Tulln focus on bioanalytics, renewable natural resources and biotechnologies. The BOKU has been active in Tulln since 1994 and co-operates with the Vienna University of Technology and the University of Veterinary Medicine Vienna within the framework of the Department of Agrobiotechnology (IFA-Tulln), which employs around 100 people. The AIT is Austria's biggest extra-faculty research institution with more than 1,100 researchers spread across various branches across the country. The AIT's main research areas are the infrastructure issues of the future, including health and the environment, safety and security, as well as energy and mobility.

The UFT, as an interdepartmental and interdisciplinary body, is designed to stimulate the co-operation between BOKU and the AIT and to produce a strategic partnership between the two institutions. Ideal working conditions and well-equipped laboratories lay the infrastructural foundation of the work at the UFT. Its focus will be on research; however, the modern laboratories are also available for lectures, particularly Master's and PhD courses.

To improve the links between academic and extra-faculty research is one of the UFT goals. An enhanced knowledge transfer between basic and applied research is to be produced by bundling the faculty and extra-faculty competencies of the two partners. The research's quality can be improved and new knowledge produced through co-operation within the scope of joint projects. The research's focus on a few issues, its presumably high quality and the improved exploitation of the common projects' results can contribute to a better positioning of both institutions. The specialization and the coverage of the entire chain of innovation from basic research to the marketable product should improve the prospects in the international competitive environment for both partners.

In a memorandum of understanding the state of Lower Austria, BOKU, the AIT and the city of Tulln agreed upon co-operation in the fields of science and technology in 2005. The document outlined the following goals:

- A 'Center of Excellence' with critical mass is to be created. It shall strengthen a common profile through its focus on 'green and white' biotechnologies.
- BOKU shall pursue further development of its Department of Agro-biotechnology (IFA) in Tulln.
- BOKU and the AIT can expect to obtain facilities including basic equipment. Space for establishing new businesses is to be found in the centre's immediate surroundings.
- The research and technology network is characterised by the fact that, on the one hand, from the first day of its operations there is the option to attract companies interested in R&D to the site. On the other hand, the

potential of BOKU and AIT students should allow for research spin-offs and the establishment of new businesses (promotion of start-ups).

- The city of Tulln is to offer a financial incentive package to companies during the first five years, amounting to the equivalent of the municipal tax (regional embededdbess: co-operation with actors from the region).
- The Campus Tulln Technopole is a flagship project for the state of Lower Austria. Up to 400 new jobs are to be created out of its academic potential. The attraction of companies to the region and the creation of spin-offs in the state's heartland should stimulate the technological and economic development of the city of Tulln and the federal state as a whole.

The campus' resident institutions, the city of Tulln and the state of Lower Austria expect an upgrading and strengthening of the campus Tulln from the presence of the UFT. The specialization in a few key research areas and the greater competency at the location are supposed to improve the image of the city as a place to do business and to undertake research. As an integral part of the Campus Tulln Technopole, the UFT plays an important role for the whole location. The city expects the UFT to create new high-quality jobs and more options to offer its youth a future-oriented education. The UFT should lead to the attraction of companies to the region and stimulate the local economy (co-operation with regional enterprises).

The availability of highly-qualified graduates should increase the attractiveness of the city for companies. The transfer of knowledge and technology between the UFT and (regional and supra-regional) firms is a crucial element to secure the competitiveness of local companies (promotion of knowledge transfer). The UFT is seen as a continuation of the strategic thrust towards the conversion of Tulln into a place of research and science that contributes to the completion of structural change in the city. Tulln expects positive effects on its image and positioning within the Vienna Region. Through the participating institutions' projects Tulln also hopes for more international links.

13.4.2 Characteristics of the UFT

The state parliament of Lower Austria decided to invest €45m into the establishment of the UFT in 2007. The construction and operation of the UFT are financed by Lower Austria and the city of Tulln, supported by the Austrian government with funds from the performance agreement. The total cost of establishing the UFT amounted to €64m. The two-storey university and research centre was constructed on a 6-hectare site. It has floor space of 15,000 square meters. Moreover, there is a 45-hectare testing ground and well-equipped greenhouses and laboratories, seminar rooms for up to 150 people and a 70-seat restaurant. After the construction period of two years, the UFT was formally inaugurated in September 2011. At the beginning of the winter semester 2011, approximately 250 researchers were employed at the UFT (maximum capacity 350). In April 2014 the Campus Tulln Technopole provided 700 high-tech jobs.

The addition of the UFT invigorated the campus Tulln, which is also reflected in its renaming from 'Technopole Tulln' to 'Campus Tulln Technopole'. To this end, a word mark and logo were created. The participating institutions' commitment to the Campus Tulln Technopole probably varies. While the IFA has had its own identity for many years, which it also demonstrates by using its own logo, the other departments of BOKU and the UFT will continue focusing on their close links to their respective headquarters in Vienna. The AIT, for its part, might grant more autonomy to the Tulln branch.

13.4.3 UFT's contribution to selected areas of regional development

If the UFT pursues the goal of establishing co-operation with regional actors, to co-operate with firms from the region and to promote knowledge transfer, in addition to the five factors mentioned in Chapter 2, the following aspects are crucial and could be seen as preconditions to fulfil its goals:

- The institutions that constitute the Campus Tulln Technopole and the regional actors need a common understanding of a shared vision in order to be able to assume their responsibility for the region together.
- The quality of the research and teaching are pivotal for the positioning of Tulln as a place to do research. It is the only way the Campus Tulln Technopole can gain international recognition, as well as have a positive effect on the region.
- In order to achieve critical mass and to create regional effects, the Campus Tulln Technopole must be perceived as a whole by both the internal and external actors involved.

The UFT is – just like the reference projects analysed in this paper – an actor in its regional network. Furthermore, a number of other actors contribute to the development and the attractiveness of the host region. The UFT's contribution to and involvement in different areas of regional development could be illustrated in diagrams that demonstrate the relation between different factors and how they can contribute to regional development.

In the diagram of the regional network below, connections and interdependencies between single elements (influencing factors) within the network can be seen. The diagram is based on the network-thinking approach. This method allows for the description of complex issues as dynamic networks. For the analysis of the UFT networks in the fields of 'research and teaching', 'knowledge and technology transfer' and 'location quality' were deemed to be the most relevant.[3] Figure 13.1 shows which factors concerning the UFT have a positive impact on its location's attractiveness and how they are composed.

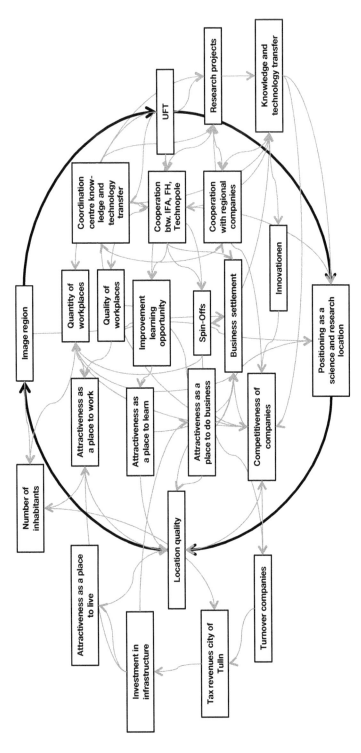

Figure 13.1 Interdependent regional network 'location quality'

Research and teaching

Along with the UFT, infrastructure that lays the basis for high-quality research was created on the campus. Apart from the excellent technical infrastructure, which could attract qualified employees, good appointment policy is needed to attract highly-skilled scientists. The co-operation between BOKU and AIT should create synergies in the fields of basic and applied research. The research projects the Campus Tulln Technopole's resident institutions undertake and the degree courses they offer play a central role in the field of research and teaching. The services influence the perception and attractiveness of Tulln as a location for science and higher education. The quality of research and teaching is an important factor to create positive effects in those fields. High quality of research can be achieved through co-operation projects and qualified employees. Also the *co-operation between academic and extra-faculty research* can lead to an increase in research quality. Cutting-edge research, in turn, can attract (international) attention; the positioning of both participating institutions and the location is improved and the quality of students rises, which could lead to an increase in companies' demand for graduates.

Knowledge and technology transfer

For the analysis of the UFT's effects on the field of knowledge and technology transfer, the centre's contributions to companies' competitiveness and capability in innovation are assessed. There is the underlying assumption that the UFT can offer advantages to companies through applied research projects, as firms need innovation to stay competitive. The resulting demand for research results can be met with projects by the UFT. Co-operation and exchange between companies and the Campus Tulln is crucial for the technopole to have a positive impact on the transfer of knowledge and technology within the region (promotion of the knowledge transfer).

In this context, the co-operation between the campus's resident companies is also important. Only if synergies and common offers can be created, will the technopole be able to satisfy the needs of companies and to become an attractive partner in the innovation process. In order to identify companies' research needs on the one hand and to transfer knowledge from research institutions to companies on the other hand, a co-ordinating centre should serve as a gateway between scientists and businesses.

To promote the transfer of knowledge is one of the Campus Tulln technopole's goals. The preconditions are present but to achieve this goal, a co-ordinating entity, a centre, is crucial. The centre for knowledge and technology transfer Campus Tulln technopole, a co-ordinating body, would be an eminent port of call. The centre's task is, first, to facilitate (regional) companies' access to products, processes and services of the research institutions on the campus and, second, to find adequate partners for companies according to their innovation and research needs. For the knowledge and technology transfer to be fruitful for both sides, a co-operation between all of the campus' resident institutions is necessary. The promotion of start-ups is mentioned as another role the co-ordinating entity has to play.

There already exist two institutions that are actively involved in knowledge and technology transfer: on the one hand, the technopole management plays an important role as a facilitator between the scientific and the economic systems (www.tfz-tulln.at). On the other, the BOKU departments on the campus have a common research co-ordinator who assumes a co-ordinating and mediating role in their scientific work. The rest of the scientific community in Tulln is not served by that co-ordinator so far, so a need for a common centre could provide advantages for all institutions involved.

Location quality

In our analysis of the field of location quality, various relevant factors were taken into consideration. Not all factors are separately listed and some are aggregated to maintain clarity in spite of the high degree of complexity.

The UFT and the entire campus are important factors in the process of positioning the city of Tulln as a place to do (scientific) research. High attractiveness of the location improves the city's image that, in turn, has a positive impact on the UFT, for example to attract highly-qualified scientists.[4] Location quality is composed of various factors, such as a location's attractiveness as a place to live, work, learn and do business. All components of Tulln's location quality are directly or indirectly affected by the UFT. The courses on offer there raise the city's attractiveness as a place to learn. The attraction of companies and competitive firms help to improve the attractiveness of the location as a place to do business. Also, the co-operation with regional enterprises strengthens the competitiveness of the location. In addition, the city's investments in its infrastructure raise its attractiveness as a place to live, which leads to an increase in the number of inhabitants. The close co-operation with regional actors, such as the city of Tulln, is important to ensure that the formal framework conditions are as good as possible to set the basis for the development of the UFT.

13.4.4 Regional impact monitoring

On the basis of the interdependent regional networks described above, regional impact monitoring was developed to collect empirical data about the technopole's performance. A monitoring system is not primarily of scientific interest but allows for statements on the regional relevance of a project or a (public) infrastructure measure. On the one hand, the impact monitoring is an internal control instrument that aims to contribute to the effective execution of a measure. On the other hand, the monitoring also has a more comprehensive function, namely to support external communication. With reference to the interdependent networks of the fields of 'research and teaching', 'knowledge and technology transfer' and 'locational quality', cause-effects chains can be constructed, on which the development of the impact-monitoring system was based (cf. Hummelbrunner, 2005: 6). They illustrate what outcome and what impact can be expected considering the relevant objectives in a field.

The impact-monitoring system is aimed at allowing for an estimation of the regional impact on the basis of the outcome and impact indicators,[5] which are summarised in the following two tables. The indicators relate to the so-called intangible effects that are responsible for a positive contribution of the UFT to its host region in the long term. In addition, the tangible effects can also be measured for the UFT. They include monetary effects, which the UFT generates for regional economic actors. In our view, it is sufficient for this purpose to identify and regularly measure the UFT's expenditures within the borders of the city of Tulln (or a somewhat larger spatial perimeter). In addition, the spatial distribution of wages and the cost of equipment and services are analysed and the appropriate share of the expenditure is attributed to the city of Tulln. The expenditures represent an outcome indicator in their own right, since there is a direct causal connection with the activities of the UFT.

The continuing collection of relevant data of the UFT's regional impact serves different objectives. First and foremost, it makes a contribution to the transparency of the UFT's activities. Second, transparency enables regional stakeholders to reflect on the observable regional effects, which creates the possibility of strategic control.

The monitoring system and the survey of the above-mentioned outcome and impact indicators also allow some statements on whether and how the UFT contributes to regional development. Some of the indicators could provide statements concerning the mentioned five factors and the aspect of regional embededdness:

- Links between academic and extra-faculty research: Number of joint projects by BOKU and AIT; degree of integration of relevant enterprises.
- Promotion of knowledge transfer: Number of conferences and seminars; number of event participants; degree of integration of relevant enterprises; amount spent on R&D; number of patents.
- Entity co-ordinating the knowledge transfer: Number of employees at UFT and campus; own business activities; number of attracted and newly incorporated companies.
- Promotion of start-ups: Spin-offs and start-ups from the UFT.
- Co-operation with regional enterprises: Degree of integration of relevant enterprises.
- Regional embeddedness: UFT's expenditures at the location of Tulln; trend in the number of overnight stays; percentage of workers with residence in Tulln.

Some of the indicators could contribute to several factors. Although a direct causal relationship will not be detectable in all cases, the indicators collected allow statements about the contribution of knowledge and knowledge transfer

Table 13.2 Outcome indicators

Quantitative	Qualitative
UFT's expenditure at the location of Tulln	Companies' awareness of bio-resources
Number of conferences and seminars	Own business activities
Number of event participants	Degree of integration of relevant enterprises
Percentage of workers with residence in Tulln	
Percentage of equity financing of a cluster	
Number of degree and training courses	
Number of students	
Number of employees at UFT and campus	
Employment ratio for graduates	
Number of joint projects by BOKU and the AIT	

Table 13.3 Impact indicators

Quantitative	Qualitative
Trend in population figures	Innovation activities by SMEs
Trend in the number of overnight stays	Integration into (international) networks
Trend in the real-estate value	
Number of attracted and newly incorporated companies	
Additional turnover for regional SMEs	
Spin-offs and start-ups from the UFT	
Number and quality of publications	
Number of (international) research projects	
Amount spent on R&D	
Number of patents	
New products and processes by regional SMEs	

and the embededdness of the science park in the region to development of the location region. This is an on-going project so it will need more time to get enough data to evaluate its impacts on regional development and its targets achieved.

13.5 Conclusions

Within the recent years scientific as well as political approaches have focused on knowledge and innovation as crucial factors to promote economic growth and development. Even on the regional level, the ability to generate, transfer and use knowledge is seen as one of the most important competences to compete and gain advantages. Accordingly, many countries build their regional-development policies around technology promotion. Part of these policies is the so-called technopole. Technopoles are assumed to have positive effects on regional development by initializing and supporting technological innovation and, as a result, leading to economic growth (Castells and Hall, 1994).

The experiences with technopoles have shown that the high expectations could not always be met. Critics relate, for example, to the assumed technological innovation that is automatically generated by spatial proximity, or the missing empirical data to explain causal relationships between technopoles and regional development (e.g., Cooke, 2001, Capello and Morrison, 2009).

This chapter has contributed to the discussion about knowledge-based regional development and the contribution that can be made by technopoles. Whether and what the contribution of technopoles could be depend on different aspects and preconditions. We assume that proximity, regional embededdness and well-organised and established knowledge transfer are crucial success factors for technopoles. Based on this hypothesis five factors were elaborated to analyse the fields of contribution.

- Links between academic and extra-faculty research;
- Promotion of the knowledge transfer;
- Entity co-ordinating the knowledge transfer;
- Promotion of start-ups;
- Co-operation with regional enterprises.

A comparison between six European technopoles or science parks shows that the performances of the institutions concerning these factors differ. In order to benefit from a region's economic growth potential, for example by attracting technology-oriented enterprises or by encouraging growth of existing companies, a well-functioning transfer of knowledge and technology is a necessary condition. The appropriate organizational structure to encourage the transfer of knowledge and technology is therefore a crucial factor to co-ordinate and promote knowledge transfer. A well-structured, well-established and widely accepted management of the technopole seems to be one of the key success factors, as also emphasised by Castells and Hall (1994).

For initiating a new technopole or science park – as, for example, the 'University and Research Centre Tulln' in Austria – the knowledge transfer and its promotion need to be established actively. The support by well-organised management is as important as the innovative environment created by the region. The embededdness of the technopole in regional activities on different levels could be seen as an important requirement that has to be met.

Several analyses mention the need for embededdness and the integration of technopoles in social networks (e.g., Russ and Jones, 2008; Asheim and Isaksen, 2002). The co-operation with regional enterprises and with other actors from the region – as shown by the comparison of the examples – is also an important precondition that the region can benefit from the technopole.

Besides aspects of regional development, the success and performance of technopoles has to be assessed according to their explicit and implicit goals (Castells and Hall, 1994). The existence of a shared vision by all actors can help and produce commitment to the goals of the technopole as the case study of the UFT has shown. Whether and to what extent technopoles contribute to regional development, and whether a causal connection could be identified, has to be established. A set of indicators defined in a monitoring system can be a useful tool to measure the direct and indirect impacts of the technopole. A monitoring system for technopoles can also improve the data availability and gives instructions on whether the performance is the expected one and relates to the defined goals.

Notes

1   The findings of this paper stem from a project that was carried out by the Institute for Systemic Management and Public Governance (IMP-HSG) at the University of St Gallen (CH) on behalf of NÖ Forschungs- und Bildungsgesellschaft m.b.H., a publicly-owned research and education company, in 2011.
2   The other sites are: Technopol Krems for medical biotechnology, Technopol Wiener Neustadt for medical and materials technology and Technopol Wieselburg for bioenergy, agricultural and food technology.
3   Their correspondence with the five factors identified above will be illustrated in Section 4.4.
4   About 700 high-tech jobs in tech fields are provided at the Campus Tulln Technopole, including 600 researchers that are involved in 150 projects (www.tfz-tulln.at/d/page.asp?tt=TZT_R2 Accessed on 27 April 2014).
5   Outcome indicators describe and measure the direct benefits that are generated by the intervention's results for a defined target group (direct effects of the project). Impact indicators describe the actually intended effects of an intervention/measure (the wider effects on the organization or the society).

Bibliography

Amin, A. and Thrift, N. (eds) (1994) *Globalization, institutions and regional development in Europe*. Oxford: Oxford University Press.
Asheim, B.T. (1996) 'Industrial districts as 'learning regions': A condition for prosperity?'. *European Planning Studies*, *4*: 379–400.

Asheim, B.T. and Isaksen, A. (2002) 'Regional innovation systems: The integration of local "sticky" and global "ubiquitous" knowledge. *Journal of Knowledge Transfer*, 27(1): 77–86. Kluwer Academic Publishers.

Beer, S. (1959) *Cybernetics and management*. London: English Universities Press.

Capello, R. and Morrison, A. (2009) 'Science Park and local knowledge creation: A conceptual approach and an empirical analysis in two Italian realities'. In C.H. Karlsson, A.E. Andersson, P.C. Cheshire and R.R. Stough (eds) *New directions in regional economic development* (pp. 221–45). Berlin Heidelberg: Springer.

Castells, M. (1996) *The rise of the network society*. Oxford: Blackwell.

Castells, M. and Hall, P. (1994) *Technopoles of the world – The making of 21st century industrial complexes*. London: Routledge.

Cooke, P. (2001) 'Regional innovation systems, clusters, and the knowledge economy. *Industrial and Corporate Change*, 10(4): 945–74.

Cooke, P. (1998) 'Regional innovation systems – origins of the concept'. In H.-J. Brazyck, P. Cooke and M. Heidenreich (eds) *Regional innovation systems. The role of governance in a globalised world*. London: UCL Press.

Cooke, P. and Morgan, K. (1998) *The associational economy: Firms, regions and innovation*. Oxford: Oxford University Press.

Cooke, P. and Leydesdorff, L. (2006) 'Regional development in the knowledge-based economy: The construction of advantage'. *The Journal of Technology Transfer*, 31(1): 5–15.

Ecoplus. Niederösterreichs Wirtschaftsagentur GmbH (2011) *Der Technologiestandort Niederösterreich, Tulln*: Technopol Tulln.

European Commission (2006) 'Community strategic guidelines on cohesion', *Official Journal of the European Commission*, L 291/11 (21 October 2006).

Grabher, G. (1993) 'The weakness of strong ties. The lock-in of regional development in the Ruhr area'. In G. Grabher (ed.) (1993) *The embedded firm: On the socio-economics of industrial networks* (pp. 255–77).

Haselmayer, S. (2004) 'Why science and technology parks go urban: Towards embedded innovation environments'. *Urbanistica Informazioni*, 10(2): 35–46.

Hummelbrunner, R. (2005) Process monitoring of impacts. Towards a new approach to monitor the implementation of Structural Fund Programmes. ÖAR Regional-beratung: Vienna.

International Organization of Science Parks (2012) *Official definition of science park* (IASP International Board, 6 February 2002). Available at www.iasp.ws (accessed 13 April 2012).

Landry, R., Amara, N., Cloutier, J.-S. and Halilem, N. (2013) 'Technology transfer organizations: Services and business models'. *Technovation*, 33(12): 431–49.

Lundvall, B.Ä. and Johnson, B. (1994) 'The learning economy'. *Journal of Industry Studies*, 1(2): 23–42.

Markusen, A. (1999) 'Fuzzy concepts, scanty evidence, policy distance: The case for rigour and policy relevance in critical regional studies'. *Regional Studies*, 33(9): 869–84.

Martin, R.L. (1999) 'The "new economic geography": Challenge or irrelevance'. *Transactions, Institute for British Geographers* (24): 387–91.

Morgan, K. (1997) 'The learning region: Institutions, innovation and regional renewal'. *Regional Studies*, 31(5): 491–504.

Morgan, K. (2007) 'The learning region: Institutions, innovation and regional renewal'. *Regional Studies*, 41(S1): S147–S159.

N.A. (2005) Memorandum of Understanding between the State of Lower Austria, BOKU, AIT and the City of Tulln. St. Pölten.

Phillimore, J. (1999) 'Beyond the linear view of innovation in sciene park evaluation: An analysis of Western Australian Technology Park'. *Technovation*, *19*(11): 673–80.

Putnam, R. (1993) *Making democracy work*. Princeton, NJ: Princeton University Press.

Raspe, O. and van Oort, F. (2008) 'Localized knowledge exernalities in regional economic development and firm growth'. *The Journal of Regional Analysis & Policy* (special issue on knowledge economy), *38*(2): 100–17.

Rösch, A. (2000) 'Kreative milieus als kaktoren der regionalentwicklung'. *Raumforschung und Raumordnung*, (2/3): 161–72.

Russ, M. and Jones, J. (2008) 'Regional economic development indicators for a knowledge-based economy in a knowledge-deprived region'. *The Journal of Regional Analysis and Policy*, *38*(2): 189–205.

Saublens, C. (2007) 'Regional research intensive clusters and science parks'. European Commission Report, Brussels.

Scherer, R. and Strauf, S. (2011) *Regionales Wirkungsmonitoring für das Universitäts- und Forschungszentrum Tulln, Institute for Systemic Management and Public Governance*. St Gallen: University of St Gallen.

Seymour, S. (2006) *Micro agglomerations of technology: A typology of ownership and implications of success*. Helsinki: IASP XXIII.

Sternberg, R. (2000) 'Innovation networks and regional development – Evidence from the European Regional Innovation Survey (ERIS): Theoretical concepts, methodological approach, empirical basis and introduction to the theme issue'. *European Planning Studies*, *8*(4): 398–407.

Storper, M. (1997) *The regional world: Territorial development in a global economy*. New York: Guilford Press.

Storper, M. (1993) 'Regional "worlds" of production: Learning and innovation in the technology districts of France, Italy and the USA'. *Regional studies*, *27*(5): 433–55.

Trippl, M. and Tödtling, F. (2008) 'From the Ivory Tower to the Marketplace: Knowledge organisations in the development of biotechnology clusters'. *Journal of Regional Analysis & Policy* (special issue on knowledge economy), *38*(2): 159–76.

Vester. F. (1974) *Das kybernetische zeitalter. Neue dimensionen des denkens*. Frankfurt: Fischer.

Wessner, C. (ed.) (2009) *Understanding research, science and technology parks: Global best practice: Report of a symposium 2009*. Washington: The National Academies Press.

Westeren, K.I. (2008) 'How to define and measure knowledge for the analysis of competitiveness'. *Journal of Regional Analysis and Policy*, *38*(2): 138–44.

Yigitcanlar, T. (2010) 'Making space and place for the knowledge economy: Knowledge-based development of Australian cities'. *European Planning Studies*, *18*(11): 1769–86.

The following internet sources were accessed:

www.wissensstadt.ch (22 October 2011)
www.grenoble-inp.fr (21 October 2011)
www.tecnoparco.it (22 October 2011)
www.solyndra.com (22 October 2011)

www.kooperation-international.de/countries/themes/international/clusterlist/grenoble-lyon-high-tech-cluster. (20 October 2011)
www.sp.se (21 October 2011)
www.kit.edu (22 October 2011)
www.technopark-tulln.at/de/site_de.php?site=technoparktulln (21 October 2011)
www.tk-adlershof.de (23 October 2011)
www.fv-berlin.de (23 October 2011)
www.adlershof.de (23 October 2011)
www.iasp.ws (15 April 2012)

Section 5

Conclusions

14 Old and new lessons for technopoles

Paul Benneworth, Julie Tian Miao and Nicholas A. Phelps

14.1 Introduction

In this concluding chapter, we wish to reflect on the future lessons for technopoles in the context of the new knowledge economy. In Castells and Hall's (1994) original volume, the penultimate chapter (Chapter 9) was entitled 'Distilling the lessons', and it was indeed this chapter that helped to provide the concept with a degree of momentum. Re-reading their Chapter 9 today, one is struck both by the far-sightedness and perspicacity of their analysis. But at the same time, there are also clear lacunae that were not evident or obvious at their initial time of writing. Our aim in this volume has been to reinvigorate and revive the technopole concept by re-situating it in the context of the contemporary social knowledge economy. And therefore, in this final chapter, our ambition is at least partly to distil some lessons from the range of case studies that our authors have presented. But at the same time, we also wish to blend that reflection with Castells and Hall's original observations to try to synthesise a contemporary technopole concept in the hope that the idea will retain its salience for another two decades.

In Chapter 1 we noted that in re-reading the original volume we were struck by the relatively limited attention it paid to the questions of governance that have moved to centre-stage in the intervening period, with the book devoting just one of its 250 pages to the matter. By contrast, what we have seen in the four case studies of Section 3 is the increasingly important role of governance in shaping the evolution of technopoles. What was perhaps unforeseen at the time of writing was that the idea of technopoles would become so popular that policy-makers would flock to the concept, with the result that part of the success or failure of policy was a consequence of the relative co-ordination between levels of government in meeting the needs of businesses. While the idea of a public sector body might have been something at the fringes of the original volume, across the case studies presented today, governance has become increasingly central. Technopoles are sites where so many different interests meet and interact, with the consequence that a better understanding of governance is perhaps unavoidable if we are to advance these ideas further.

Likewise, the issue of the corporate milieu has changed almost unrecognisably. With a few notable exceptions, the process observed by Charles and Howells in 1992 has reached its logical conclusion, with even large knowledge-intensive multinationals outsourcing considerable chunks of their R&D activities. The idea of 'open innovation' (Chesbrough, 2003) was a step on this journey, with global high-technology companies making some of their more peripheral discoveries open to a wider community of smaller innovative businesses. Multi-nationals found it economically advantageous to re-appropriate that knowledge when smaller firms and academics had brought it closer to market, and by creating open innovation ecologies they could reduce the costs and riskiness of their R&D efforts while maintaining their innovation positions. What we have seen in the last twenty years is the internalisation of the concept of open innovation in the spatial form of campuses. In parallel with this, the idea of synergy management as identified by Castells and Hall around links between R&D and manufacturing is also evolving to involve dynamic firm ecologies.

In this chapter, we provide a more systematic reflection on these original lessons, and reflect on how they can be updated to retain their contemporary salience. We begin by summarising the original set of technopole lessons under three main categories, an integrated milieu, a meeting-place of actors, and as a developing set of processes connected to other related processes. We then turn to provide a synthesis of the lessons emerging in the case studies following the framework provided in the introduction, namely synergy management, governance and evaluating these complex constellations. We then attempt to sensitively blend the old and new messages to produce a common understanding of how these coherent spaces can remain relevant for promoting innovation in increasingly globalised networks. We finally conclude by reflecting on the policy implications of these findings, and in particular their integration into contemporary regional policy approaches based around constructing regional advantage and smart specialisation (Asheim *et al.*, 2011; McCann and Ortega-Argilés, 2013).

14.2 The original distillate

The original volume included a total of ten lessons in the synthesis chapter. To avoid repeating them verbatim we have grouped them into three similar areas under three headings. 'Three faces of the technopole', 'Synergy and the innovative milieu' and 'The corporate milieu' all relate to the way that technopoles function as ways of bringing different actors in integrated innovation milieux. 'The state and innovation', 'University and technology generators' and 'Finance, institutions and the innovative milieu' all relate to the particular needs of stakeholders whose support is vital for innovative firms – the engine of any technopole – to be successful in that location. 'The social organisation of technopoles', 'Some implications for regional development', 'The importance of time' and a 'Winning formula' underscore the nature of the diverse processes involved in building technopoles, and for which simultaneous attention is required.

14.2.1 Technopoles as integrated innovation milieux

In 'Three faces of the technopole', Castells and Hall pointed to the fact that there were, at the time of writing, three different rationales for building technopoles. Some of these were related to strategies of re-industrialisation and helping to stimulate the growth of new industries and sectors to replace those that were being lost in the de-industrialisation that was at the forefront of policy-makers' considerations in 1994. A second group were seeking to promote regional development, and in particular to provide a stimulus to regions that had been so badly hit by processes of re-industrialisation that they had entered into a downward negative spiral, which appeared almost impossible to address. The third rationale related to the creation of synergy between actors and to create the necessary critical mass by ensuring cross-fertilisation between sectors, what some have belatedly referred to as Jacobs externalities (Paci and Usai, 1999). Although these three aims were often related, to stimulate re-industrialisation and regional growth through stimulating new combinations, attention was necessary for the context specificities of particular technopoles.

With 'Synergy and the innovative milieu', Castells and Hall drilled down further into this idea of building synergy, highlighting in particular the importance of

> networks connecting individuals in many different organisations – public and semi-public and private, not profit and for profit, large-scale and small-scale, within a system that encourages the free flow of innovation and through this, the generation of innovation.

> (p. 224)

The corollary of this was that large metropolitan areas were where the networks would be the strongest, and so they would be most propitious for the development of new industries. They pointed to the idea of technopoles functioning as neo-Marshallian industrial districts, promoting what economists refer to as Marshall-Arrow-Romer externalities (cf. Henderson, 1997) creating shared knowledge pools. Thus, technopoles needed not only to be creating path-breaking connections linking different technologies to break developmental trajectories, but also to be developing strong specialisation. They further argued that part of developing that expert knowledge demanded building close links between R&D and manufacturing, both to infuse R&D with production-side knowledge but also to accelerate the launch of the product into the market.

The focus of 'The corporate milieu' was the argument that synergies were complicated by the issue of the corporative milieu, *viz.* for any company, the point of R&D was almost always related to corporate aims, with few companies for whom undertaking R&D was a business in its own right. R&D activities always took place within conditions imposed by the corporate centre, and in many cases large vertically integrated businesses in the US sought to keep their knowledge hidden from other firms (and potential competitors), and only available to their internal clients within the corporation. Thus, these places had no real interest in a technopole milieu, but rather sought primarily a prestigious location in a greenfield science park. Conversely, in Japan the reliance of firms on their banks and the Ministry of International Trade and Industry (MITI) meant that it only made sense for Japanese firms to locate their R&D activities in metropolitan Tokyo. Likewise, they argued that the Île-de-France and the M4 Corridor in the UK were both related to a stronger dependence on a capital-city-located public client group than to controls from the corporate centre.

14.2.2 Technopoles as a meeting place of diverse actors

The second element of the conclusions dealt with the fact that technopoles derived their strength not only from the cohesion and synergy, but also from the heterogeneity of the actors involved. But at the same time, the desirable level of heterogeneity could create unexpected problems that could best be dealt with at the earliest possible opportunity to optimise technopole success. The point that Castells and Halls made in 'The state and innovation' was that it was impossible to understand the rise of technopoles without understanding a parallel increase in the levels of public investments in promoting technology to drive economic development. They argued that the form these took, often with relatively protected long-term contracts between the state and innovative firms, were a key influence on technopole success. The commitment of the state to long-term stable investments could increase firms' interest in pre-competitive research that was amenable to close location with other public and private sector R&D laboratories. They conversely noted that the state was not a 'monolithic entity', perhaps slightly anticipating the discussion about multi-level governance that dominates the contemporary policy landscape, highlighting that there could be different agendas between these different levels and even competition between actors within a single level. The nature of the relationships created opportunities for strategic alliances, as they highlight in pointing out how a coalition of municipalities and Cambridge University had overcome the traditional central government view that industrial location should be channelled away from East Anglia.

The second set of diverse actors with interests in technopoles that were not those of the innovating businesses were the 'University and technology generators'. Indeed, Castells and Hall acknowledged that

> universities have played a fundamental role in the development of some of the most innovative technological milieu, such as Stanford at the origin of Silicon Valley, Cambridge University or MIT starting the

spin-off process in their areas of influence, or the catalytic function of the *Ecole Nationale des Mines* in the birth of Sophia Antipolis.

(p. 230)

They noted that universities may play three quite distinct roles in technopoles, all three being grounded in their autonomy for producing general-universal knowledge that could be transformed and embedded in economic activities. First was in providing the raw material for technopoles in the form of new innovative knowledge. Second, universities also played a training function in creating the workforce for the technopole industries, particularly critical in the case of building a new industry where the workforce would not automatically already exist. Then, finally, they also pointed to the role of universities playing a directly entrepreneurial role through creating new spin-off business ventures, and in allowing their employees to combine working for these new start-ups with their teaching and research duties.

The section 'Finance, institutions and the innovative milieu' dealt with the intractable issue of providing stable finance for a process as inherently uncertain as the innovation process. Without suitable finance for innovation, a technopole will not continue to thrive, with the risk that technological development becomes internalised within large companies able to bear the costs of that risk, reinforcing tendencies towards incremental rather than path-breaking innovation processes. Castells and Hall were two of the first authors to point to the importance of business venturing funds to the emergence of the clusters around Boston and Silicon Valley, as well as the importance of stable keiretsu financing to leading Japanese technology firms. Likewise, in their Chapter 10 they pointed to the problems that short-term approaches to finance can create, in leading to an emphasis on creating profit through financial re-engineering rather than creating new innovative products, thereby acting as a brake on innovation processes.

14.2.3 Technopoles as processes as well as places

The final set of conclusions highlighted that building an effective technopole is not just about creating a place, but ensuring that a range of different processes can function effectively together. The art of creating a technopole is therefore finding ways to create mutual benefits between these different processes. The first set of processes identified in the book are social knowledge exchange processes, as argued in 'The social organisation of technopoles'. The authors argued that one of the most important mechanisms by which technopoles created their competitive advantage was in anchoring particular social networks that exchanged knowledge and supported dynamic labour market evolution. Although those networks would spontaneously emerge as a consequence of the presence of innovative firms, these networks could also be actively mobilised and sustained with public support, and indeed that public support was a critical factor for technopole success. Support was also necessary to help create innovative milieux that supported the growth and expansion of technopoles' innovative activities.

In the section 'Some implications for regional development', the authors tied the micro-scale of technopole development much more closely into questions of long-term spatial rebalancing associated with technological development. They noted that there were clear geographical shifts in places' respective fortunes associated with long-term technology development cycles, which they framed in terms of long-term Kondratieff cycles. They noted that in the emerging spatial divisions of labour within the knowledge economy there were consequences for making technopoles successful in regions not at the forefront of technological development. But at the same time, they noted that serious long-term attempts to create technopoles in less successful regions could have positive results. In Chapter 10, they argued that the results might not meet policy-makers' expectations in creating new Silicon Valleys, but they could nevertheless be successful in creating new industrialisation complexes.

The final set of processes with which the volume was concerned was the underlying governance processes. The last two sections, 'The importance of time' and 'A winning formula?' were relatively brief, and both underscored a similar point, namely that a technopole process will rarely lead to the expected destination, but persistence will pay off in creating some kinds of benefits. The authors argued that technopoles take a long time to materialise, and they therefore need some kind of insulation from short-term pressures. They identified that where expectations are too high, and in particular where there will be immediate and fundamental change, when that change is not forthcoming technopoles can be left to their own devices. All too often, technopoles will then revert into speculative property developments with no considerations for the underlying technological milieu. The key issue from a policy perspective is continually adapting, interacting and nuancing the approach to build the kinds of synergies between actors that increase capacity to exploit emerging opportunities that draw new investment into those urban developments.

14.3 Key contemporary lessons from technopoles

Clearly, some of the lessons advanced by Castells and Halls retain a contemporary salience. A number of the chapters in our volume have returned to the importance of synergies for the success of technopoles, of ways of resolving different interests between actors, and coupling a variety of processes around a single physical space. There are likewise other findings that can be relatively simply updated to reflect evolving technological possibilities, such as more qualitative shifts in knowledge production, changing the role played by proximity in the innovation process and hence shifting – but not entirely eliminating – the importance of physical places promoting innovation. But at the same time there are also changes that were not foreseen by the authors, such as the rise of 'open innovation', and the increasing tendency for large companies to outsource their R&D, making innovation success increasingly dependent upon co-ordinating processes within global technological innovation networks. These have quite profound implications for technopole concepts, which cannot be simply ported across into the idea of open innovation campuses, because of the additional pressures and private interests that these global networks can bring.

To therefore provide a more systematic updating of the ideas presented in *Technopoles of the World*, we draw on the framework presented in Chapter 1 that has structured this volume, to draw together some of the main messages and findings that have emerged in these chapters, as the basis for developing a future technopoles research agenda.

In 14.3.1, we see that the issue of building coherence and synergy now has to take place in the context of extremely dynamic and loosely coupled ecosystems, involving agents with at best only an extremely limited local orientation. Effective technopole building therefore requires finding ways to bind them into this ecosystem but also to deal with the fact that regional coalitions more than ever before have a shifting character, with participants' interest changing quickly over time in response to these outside pressures.

In 14.3.2, we foreground the issue of governance challenges that arise in the context of these dynamic, shifting and potentially unstable coalitions, and the needs of territorial policy-makers to have clarity and certainty about stake-holder interest for regional innovation policy-making processes. Far more than Castells and Hall were able to do in 1994, we illustrate a number of the tensions that governance can create, and some of the potential solutions deployed by regional partners in seeking to operate in this complex environment.

In 14.3.3, we turn to the issue of how to meaningfully evaluate technopoles given the dynamism and uncertainties that seem to be an intrinsic part of their functioning and that have interests that are not readily reducible to a 'regional' level, as they function as key nodes in much wider innovation and knowledge networks. Reprising the themes of their long-term nature and the unintended benefits technopole policies can bring, any kind of evaluation from a regional-studies perspective needs to seek to explore the different kinds of processes taking place around technopoles, their inter-relation and their evolution over time.

14.3.1 Synergy management in dynamic, loosely coupled ecosystems

One clear area where academic debate has evolved is in a shift in idea of how regional innovation milieux operate, getting beyond rather rigid innovation systems approaches, emphasising structures, and instead to think in terms of dynamic – evolving and unstable – ecosystems. In the wake of the publication of *Technopoles of the World*, there was a 'systems turn' in innovation studies. These centred around conceptualising innovation environments in terms of the existence of sub-systems for knowledge production, knowledge exploitation, knowledge intermediates and policy-makers, with policy interventions focused around improving interconnections between these subsystems. But there was a parallel disquiet about the effects that this had on obscuring the importance of the people within these systems (e.g., Sotarauta, 2006), and in particular the institutional entrepreneurs able to reshape their own organisations to improve external connections and create regionally shared innovation assets (Sotarauta, 2011; Beer and Clower, 2014). There is an increasing demand, for example articulated in Volume 60 of this book series, *Leadership and Change in Sustainable Regional Development*, to better understand collective leadership processes. It is clear that synergy management in contemporary technopoles demands a better understanding of how processes of collective leadership function around these innovation ecosystems (Sotarauta, Horlings and Liddle, 2012).

A number of the chapters in this volume explicitly address the emergence of innovation ecosystems and begin to engage with ideas of collective leadership. In Chapter 3, Benneworth *et al.* note that the long-term commitment (since the 1970s) of the University of Twente (UT) to exerting a regional leadership role has seen the Kennispark technopole centred around the UT emerge as a dense innovation ecosystem; the Kennispark governance system was deliberately created in 2008 as a loosely-coupled system allowing partners to participate flexibly on their own terms for as long as they retained an interest in the project. The management of the physical space as well as the governance space has likewise been constructed with low barriers to entry, to try to encourage as many innovative firms as possible to be able to find a location on the site, and hence to maximise the knowledge overspills, synergies and benefits flowing back to Kennispark participants.

Chapter 4 specifically focuses on the issue of how projects create innovative ecosystems characterised by high levels of synergies of actors. Van Winden and Carvalho argue that there should be a reframing of the way technopole and science park management practices are understood and implemented to reflect this wider change (this volume). They argue in particular that the traditional four intervention areas in science park management, namely design for interaction, managed tenant mix, shared facilities and network promotion, need reconceptualising, reflecting recent shifts in the spatial organisation of innovation. They argue that while these four processes remain important, they are best achieved by managing four underlying processes: (a) helping their tenants to access knowledge held by others in the innovation environment; (b) helping tenants to participate in networks both within the science park but also externally; (c) providing specialised services and infrastructure that reduce the overall cost to tenants; and (d) ensuring the park has credibility and reputation as a serious knowledge location.

A second issue, mentioned at the start of this section, is the unexpected shift in the way that corporate innovation is organised. A the time *Technopoles of the World* was written (cf. Nelson, 1993) it was clear that there were national differences in the ways in which corporate innovation was driven, with the UK a particular anomaly in terms of the relative short-sightedness of corporate governance leading to an underinvestment in R&D and a tendency to buy in external technology sources. But what could not have been predicted was the fact that this tendency was a foretaste of a subtle re-organisation of innovation process. In particular, the pace of rapid technological development saw large incumbent firms withdrawing from technology development and seeking to buy promising high-technology start-ups as means of sustaining their competitive advantage. This was accompanied in many cases by corporate break-ups (such as that of the ICI R&D cluster at the Wilton Complex on Teesside), to allow large firms to focus on creating core shareholder value and near-to-market development and innovation activities. These trends have had clear consequences for the functioning of technopoles, in particular with the difficulties of finding large anchor tenants at the heart of these newly created innovation ecosystems.

One consequence of this has been the increased importance of the university as an anchor activity for technopole activities, not only as a source of new knowledge, highly-skilled staff, know-how and spin-off companies, but also as a means of providing continuity to these highly dynamic ecosystems. So in Chapter 2, for example, Etzkowitz argues that the characteristics of the contemporary university are precisely those necessary for creating, supporting and evolving within complex network innovation ecosystems. He proposes four characteristics, namely interactivity, independence, hybridisation and reciprocality as absolutely central to allowing universities to usefully fulfil this new role as ecosystem animateurs. It is not just policy actors who have to be sensitive to the needs of a wider coalition, but also universities, who use hybridisation and reciprocality of creating shared activities from which a range of partners can draw innovation benefits. Of course, it is always dangerous to promote a new 'model' of a university (Benneworth, 2014) but it is clear that these four characteristics are important more generally in understanding how actors engage within technopoles.

14.3.2 Governance challenges and integrating diverse stakeholder coalitions

What the chapters we have assembled show perhaps most clearly is that in the twenty years since *Technopoles* was published, the issue of governance has come to the fore (see Section 14.1). This is partly a reflection of the fact that in spatial sciences there has been a realisation that 'governance matters', that is that the processes by which decisions are arrived at affects their chances of success (Rhodes, 1997). This in turn reflects the reality that in the context of increasingly complex technological environments, no single expert policy-maker can have perfect knowledge about the situation, and therefore in order to have any chance of succeeding, policy needs to incorporate knowledge from a diffuse range of actors. As a consequence decisions are no longer made and implemented in a top-down way, but within networks. Within these networks, those with knowledge relevant to the situation have the opportunity to shape decisions in ways that benefit them privately. This changes the role of policy-maker from deciding on how to implement an outcome, to steering these networks to achieve the best public outcomes.

This change has clearly had some purchase on the creation of technopoles, where their success increasingly depends on producing valuable knowledge environments that can stimulate the creation and development of new, innovative and high-potential businesses. Thus, the traditional recipe of a top-down approach is no longer appropriate for creating these supportive, nurturing environments, particularly where there are already innovation actors present. What we have seen in a number of cases are examples of local authorities seeking to mobilise collective knowledge spaces to allow wider groups of actors to have a say in the construction of those technopoles. In turn, these coalitions and platforms are able to identify and form the unique competencies that can become the place-based assets. And in a number of the chapters we see these bottom-up networks becoming synonymous with the 'brands' these places are able to mobilise and with which they are able to attract new investments and improve their overall innovation environments.

But at the same time, we are highly sensitive that we are not advocating a simplistic model of the co-operative state, where actors mobilise their resources and assets in partnership with other actors. We concur with Lagendijk and Oïnas (2005) that it is absolutely vital to avoid uncritical reproduction of happy-family stories of collective innovation that grant the agency for improving a region's economic position to a particular set of institutional arrangements in a place based around partnership. In this book we see a variety of conflicts and tensions within these new governance arrangements; perhaps the most notable being those that arise when different logics and rationales simultan-eously underpin technopole creations, as in Taiwan and Barcelona (Chapters 7 and 9 respectively). These tensions are not just between creating optimal technological environments and respecting local needs (i.e., between different levels of governance arrangements) as in Taiwan, but also between different competing local rationales, such as between creating jobs and attracting investment in the built environment, as seen in Barcelona.

But this raises the question of whether there is an ideal-type governance arrangement for the contemporary technopole, and we would certainly shy away from crude generalisations. What is most important is developing a governance structure that allows long-term science-based development to emerge, thereby creating a regional innovative impulse. Different modes of competitive advantage through innovation require quite different and place-sensitive arrangements. Although both located in the Netherlands, the very different foci of Eindhoven's Strijp-S and Enschede's Kennispark demanded very different governance arrangements to stimulate creative urban sectors and high-technology systems and materials sectors respectively (see Chapters 3 and 4). Likewise, if the focus of the effort is substantive infrastructure investment and integration of the innovative environment into the urban fabric, then a quite different arrangement is demanded than where small efforts are needed to create synergies and connectivity between existing actors through curating particular knowledge spaces to that end. A key issue here is the relative power balance between actors involved in processes, and the fact that technopoles inevitably come to some degree to embody those power relationships. The focus on optimising technopoles' governance arrangements need be as sensitive to the underlying relative informal power structures as to the formal institutional arrangements.

14.3.3 Evaluating complex constructions of heterogeneous actors

The other key element of the shifting nature of governance in the contemporary society is the changing nature of accountability and autonomy. New organisational forms are being given increasing autonomy to implement strategies developed within stakeholder networks and advance policy-maker goals. But the obverse of this has been an increasing demand for these new governance arrangements to be held accountable, particularly where substantial sums of public money may be invested in their creation. In some cases, these accountability requirements may be no more arduous than responsible audit and transparency processes of outputs, to demonstrate where funds have been allocated, something particularly important, for example, for projects and locations supported by European Commission structural and cohesion funds (as in Barcelona, Madrid and Lisbon, see Chapters 8 and 9). However, there is also an interest in the more sophisticated evaluation of outcomes and impacts, to understand the extent to which technopoles are also able to meet their longer-term potential to drive structural territorial economic change.

This has placed pressures on evaluators to advance their methodologies, and in particular to get beyond simple balance-sheet calculations and cost-benefit analyses towards these outcomes and impacts. Technopoles should be understood as contributing to a wider process of change, and need integrating into the city-region space to maximise their benefits. Technopoles located in regions with strong existing economies will perform *primus inter pares* much better than those that are created in a technological wilderness as a kind of oasis in the hope of creating something radically different to what already exists. Likewise, the relative performance of technopoles depends to some extent on what kind of anchor tenants they are able to attract, as seen very clearly in the analyses from technopoles in China and Malaysia (Chapters 11 and 12 respectively). This raises the thorny question as to whether there is public value in investing in technopoles in places where there are not already conducive framework conditions, and hence what roles technopoles can play in stimulating re-industrialisation and economic development path switching in less-favoured regions.

The other context to technopole success, which needs inclusion effectively in evaluation, is the wider national context and the extent this creates propitious conditions for technopole success. Etzkowitz makes clear in Chapter 2 that the role of national policy decisions profoundly influenced the rise of Silicon

Valley's positive techno-entrepreneurial environment. Likewise, Perry and May are also able to show how the attempts to create science cities in England outside the traditionally favoured Golden Triangle was affected by dominant discourses of excellence that implicitly disadvantaged those places. Eindhoven clearly benefited from very high levels of direct support and indirect encouragement provided to the leading Dutch technology firm Philips, to ensure it sustained its R&D efforts over the decades out of pure national self-interest. Universities are themselves traditionally managed within national accreditation systems and therefore always have at least one eye on these national-level pressures in making their strategic decisions. Evaluating technopoles therefore needs to also find a way of incorporating these factors in the overall evaluation, as well as to reflect on the extent of whether particular kinds of national policy frameworks might be incompatible with local technopole stimulation policies.

The key issue in understanding the added value of technopoles given these ecosystem effects is in developing methodologies able to capture the synergy effects that technopoles bring (see 14.3.1). Evaluation needs to begin from the position of what are precisely the synergy improvements desired from a particular technopole intervention, and then gauge how the investments and interventions advance progression towards that overall goal. There is of course an issue, particularly for partners active in global technological innovation systems and production networks, that these will evolve in ways that local partners can have very little influence over. There remains this degree of exogenity in governing what leads to technopoles' effects, but at least being explicit about that in evaluation terms – and critically not over-claiming serendipitous successes – is vital to create a new mode of evaluating technopoles that does capture their roles in improving the situation of innovative firms in these global innovation and production networks.

14.4 The defining characteristics of the contemporary technopole

On the basis of our various contributions, it is possible to sketch out the contemporary defining characteristics of a technopole. It has always been our intention to be additive to rather than substitutive of the original concept, reflecting changes in the last two decades. But at the same time, there have been such wide-ranging changes, from the ubiquity of new kinds of information and communications technologies, to the rise of new advanced economies in China, India, Brazil and Russia, that inevitably this means that the technopole concept has changed substantively in this period. In particular we want to highlight what we see as being four vital elements of this evolution and shift. First, there has been a shift in the nature of the roles played in technopoles by universities, reflecting their increasing internationalisation in parallel with a stewardship of place. Second, there has been a shift in their location, with technopoles becoming increasingly integrated into urban fabrics, representing a Central Knowledge District for city-regions akin to the Central

Business Districts in traditional urban morphologies. Third, the nature of proximity provided by technopoles is changing, not merely offering physical co-location but helping to create shared identities, understandings and meanings that facilitate place-based technology transfer. Fourth, technopoles are embedded into longer processes of technological change, with the development of new platform technologies that are themselves producing shifts in regime, giving them considerable potential to serve as change agents.

14.4.1 The changing role of universities

The first dimension of change has been in the way universities engage with technopoles, and in particular the role played by entrepreneurial universities in technopoles. This is not to say that universities are *less important to technopoles*, but clearly there is a substantial difference in the way they contribute – they are *differently important to technopoles*. Understanding that difference is absolutely vital for ensuring that universities contribute effectively to place-based development. In particular we tie this changing role to the rise of the notion of the world-class university (Salmi, 2009), which although criticised as a confused concept within academic literature has become a highly alluring goal for policy-makers and university administrators alike. What characterises world-class universities is that they have the best teaching grounded on world-leading research, they attract elite students in a global market, offering the best facilities for students and faculty alike. In part through the ubiquity of university rankings (such as the *Jiao Tong Academic Ranking of World Universities* and the *Times Higher Education Top 100 Universities*), universities have come to see excellence in research, measured in terms of publications and prizes, as being absolutely critical to their long-term survival. This has changed the nature of universities' willingness to contribute to localised territorial developments and also their capacities and capability to contribute.

There are of course negative aspects to this development, with the rise of the world-class university idea creating a sense that local relevance is incompatible with global excellence. Many national research systems certainly create very strong disincentives for researchers to undertake the applied consultancy work for firms often at the heart of technopoles, and instead to focus upon globally excellent research. This runs the risk that universities only become involved in technopole projects as a means for them to access the kinds of resources to invest in strengthening their basic excellent research. With universities often being substantial or dominant partners within technopole projects, there is the risk that this driver leads to them being driven away from creating integrated synergistic spaces between firms and industries, and instead to becoming nodes in the global knowledge network with little local economic spillover. This can reduce the potential of universities as they have to manage themselves and their employees and permit them the freedom to engage with local partners, except when it can be demonstrated to contribute directly to creating world-class research.

At the same time, the changing nature of universities as agents active in multinational networks also has positive aspects for technopoles. It is not just that universities are able to gather knowledge and information globally, and embed it in their local environments, what Bathelt, Malmberg and Maskell (2004) identified as the 'global pipelines, local buzz' role played by universities. They also have relationships with partners globally, and those partners may choose to come to the university location to be able to engage better, co-create with and benefit from university knowledge communities (Benneworth and Ratinho, 2014). The presence of these partners at the site, even temporarily, can also contribute to local knowledge spillover processes, and hence strengthen the knowledge community, making it more of a 'place-to-be' within these global knowledge chains (Gertler, 1995). Internationalisation of universities therefore has the potential to increase the quality of the knowledge communities associated with technopoles and hence ultimately to strengthen their overall economic benefit, and the policy challenge lies in optimising this global–local tension.

14.4.2 The technopole as an urban institution

The second dimension of change has been the evolving location of technopoles. When one looks three decades ago to Hall and Markusen's (1985) *Silicon Landscapes*, Silicon Valley is portrayed as a rural idyll where budding entrepreneurs can experience both tranquillity and fulfilment in rural California. By the time of *Technopoles of the World*, there was a realisation that these nodes were evolving into whole-city districts, regarding the phenomenon as being primarily a suburban rather than rural phenomenon. Clearly, there has been a further evolution in the intervening period, with a realisation that technopoles have great potential as an urban phenomenon, to contribute to processes of urban regeneration as well as building new industries. This clearly has to be tied to the idea that this is no longer about building new technology sectors in separate out-of-town estates, but contributing to building collective knowledge pools upon which a range of different industries can draw to support their innovation processes and ultimately competitiveness.

It is now common in 'Third Wave' technopole policies for this urban dimension to be explicitly stressed and adopted as a policy motivation for technopoles. Chapter 3 has a number of examples where technopoles have been created to try to plug an emerging hole in the urban fabric, in Eindhoven or Helsinki, for example. Scientific entrepreneurs therefore fulfil the same role that creative entrepreneurs have played in artist-led regeneration projects in other places, and the creativity helps to build a district with a coherent brand that becomes part of its competitive rationale. Likewise, in Barcelona, there was a clear desire with the 22@ district to use the potential of knowledge-based development to drive a particularly tricky transition process from traditional to modern industries, and revitalise an inner-city quarter of Barcelona, thereby strengthening its overall global brand. There is a parallel evolution between the creation and re-creation of an urban fabric and the attraction-construction of a knowledge community that stimulates innovative competitiveness.

But at the same time we see that although these two logics may in some places be brought together effectively, they are not identical, and there may also be tensions between them that affect particular technopoles. In Chapter 6, Perry and May highlight the tensions that existed between two visions of science cities, around driving urban development as against rebalancing England's space economy. They came together in different places in different ways that ultimately shaped quite profoundly what these projects were able to achieve, and the balance between the private individual and collective territorial benefits they created. There is a strong tension between the investor and science/entrepreneur interests around urban science. Investor interests in substantial regeneration projects often revolve around issues such as investments in land reclamation, property development and infrastructure connections. Conversely, scientist-innovator interests are in bringing together teams of people who form coherent entrepreneurial knowledge communities able to undertake research, innovation and create new businesses. There are clear tensions in these urban science projects in ensuring that the physical and community developments evolve in parallel, and are central to successful projects in addressing the tensions that inevitably ensue.

14.4.3 Proximity in the social knowledge economy

The third dimension of change has been in the nature and importance of geographical proximity. Twenty years ago there was a clear materiality to physical proximity between actors – in translating R&D into production processes, there was a need for pilot plants and prototypes where upstream and downstream actors worked closely to use their knowledge collectively to solve problems as technologies progressed into the market. But surging developments in ICTs has meant that such physical co-location is no longer as important for exchanging knowledge in innovation processes. Knowledge pools are no longer exclusively embedded into physical communities, but can exist around other kinds of virtual communities creating 'knowing-in-action' (Amin and Roberts, 2008). This has had profound consequences for the ways in which technopoles create competitive innovation advantage if it cannot be assumed that all the necessary knowledge for innovation is held in a community physically anchored around a technopole.

It is therefore critically important to understand the wider dynamics and social structures of these knowledge pools, in particular the ways in which they interact with and become embedded in particular kinds of places (such as technopoles). Clearly, place matters to knowledge-producing communities, but in a different way to hitherto, because of the changing community dynamics. These knowledge-producing communities have tended to become far more organisationally flexible, operating as loose coalitions into which partners come and go depending on their relative interest in the innovation activities. Temporary organisational and gathering forms – projects, conferences, joint ventures – have become useful ways of managing this organisational flexibility. This in turn raises the question of what can be the relationship of technopoles to these new organisational forms. Perhaps a very trite answer is that they can engage with these temporary networks and ensure that they attract elements of the activity to those locations. In our eyes that is a very superficial answer, and no one would think it reasonable to assume a technopole is successful merely because it can occasionally attract and host an important conference in an emerging technological field. Rather we would see that the location of these conferences is a lagging indicator that the location is an important node in this wider global knowledge network.

Therefore, there is a need to better understand and rethink the nature of proximity and territoriality in technopoles. Although it has become fashionable recently to argue that there are different kinds of proximity (such as Boschma's (2005) distinction of organisational, cognitive, geographical, cultural and social), this seems to miss the question of how these kinds of proximity are coupled to particular places and physical forms – such as technopoles. Likewise, there is a following question as to what technopoles can do as active service managers to promote those different kinds of proximity, both to improve the success of their technopole as a whole as well as its constituent residents. Some of this is intuitively understood in the ways that some technopoles try to stimulate common culture-building activities between residents, and engage them in collective organisational structures, to improve their non-geographical forms of proximity, as well as selecting potential residents to ensure that there is a good 'click' between them (cf. Caniëls, Kronenberg and Werker, 2014). But this intuitiveness seems to suggest that more systematic understandings of the role of proximity in technopoles are needed in order to maximise their overall effectiveness.

14.4.4 Technopoles and technological regimes

The final defining characteristic of technopoles is their close link to their underpinning technological regimes, the way that particular societies choose to order and regulate the uncertain task of technological progress (cf. Nelson and Winter, 1982). With hindsight it is possible to distinguish how the archetypal technopoles of Castells and Hall were bound into national technological projects, both successful (e.g., Hsinchu and Silicon Valley) and unsuccessful (Academgorodok). Technopoles therefore need to be understood in the context of these evolving technological regimes and the ways in which national systems are seeking to organise themselves to achieve particular kinds of technological advance. This also provides a means for understanding part of the way that, as urban phenomena, they can provide particular kinds of proximity, as they can become central places in the co-ordination of the new epistemic communities that form the basis of the emergence of new technological fields and sectors.

Perhaps this understanding shows most clearly in emerging nations. China has a clearly articulated central mission of developing a technological regime that on the one hand ensures current prosperity and growth, but at the same time also drives towards technological upgrading and improving China's place within a wider global division of labour (a story for which echoes are also perceptible in the case of Malaysia). Technopoles can therefore be understood as providing a focus point for those desires and national technological projects, as a central point for the accumulations of investments in fixed and human capital that can drive further accumulation and transformation. At the same time we see in some developed countries that have been hit by austerity that this ambition for technological transformation has also been hit, and therefore the interest in technopoles has waned as a means of completing modernisation and transformation of these economies.

At the same time, elsewhere we can see efforts to revitalise technological regimes around responses to the 'Grand challenges of the 21st century' – those problems, limits and tensions emerging in late capitalism that must be addressed in this century if humanity is to survive into the next. These challenges are broad based and multi-disciplinary, and include issues such as resource scarcity, global warming, urban inclusion/sustainability, access to energy and civic security. There has been an emerging policy interest in the use of 'Living Labs' as experimental forms to create new knowledges to solve these problems, and technopoles may have a new lease of life in extending this notion of the micro-scale Living Lab to the level of the urban fabric, making them central nodes addressing these Grand Challenges. Clearly, in the case studies offered here we can see that cities are themselves wrestling with these problems and finding innovative solutions, and this is something that could be incorporated more systematically in our understandings of and policies for technopoles.

14.5 'Pointers to Policy' in exploiting technopoles' territorial benefits

As with the original volume, we conclude with a set of aphorisms to inform policy-makers.

Technopoles need policy-makers

Their embedding within technological regimes means that their evolution is framed by a wide range of policy decisions. Policy-makers therefore need to actively engage with technopoles and understand these needs if technopoles are to be able to develop and thrive coherently.

Technopoles are city districts

As technopoles have become an increasingly urban phenomenon, there is a reducing opportunity for them to be left to their own devices, as cathedrals in the desert. They function as central knowledge districts within broader city regions and require the special, sensitive treatment reserved for other urban 'crown jewels' locations. They need to be dense without being congested, and accessible without being overcrowded, and their needs require balancing with the wider urban interest in strategic city-regional management processes.

Technopoles are global nodes

The knowledge activities to which technopoles now contribute are distributed geographically across global innovation systems and production networks. But at the same time, there is still a role for particular places in representing attractions of activity. Ensuring that technopoles retain their wider external community connections remains critical, both in terms of the technological specialisations of public research organisations and the presence of key firms and business services related to these knowledge chains. Policy-makers need to consider how to attract, embed and retain these globally connected players for the benefit of the technopole as a whole.

Technopoles are local communities

The footloose nature of global knowledge production means that its local embeddedness is critical in determining its wider economic benefit. A critical need for policy-makers has to be to encourage local actors to plug more actively into elements of global knowledge networks present within technopoles. This goes beyond synergy management to provide reasons for coalitions of actors to work and interact to create place-specific knowledges that may be attractive to the wider global knowledge community, and thereby strengthening the place of these local communities – and the technopole in global knowledge-production networks.

Technopoles are physical infrastructures

Technopoles form part of an urban fabric and are thereby integrated into territorial infrastructure networks. This infrastructure requires considerable investment, and if technopoles are successful, investment needs to be secured and planned in a co-ordinated way to shape these high-technology spaces. Technopoles seek to change the regions within which they are located, therefore these physical investments must always be developed with an eye to the intended future situation.

Technopoles are community meeting points

Technopoles provide interactivity and communication, but these features are only relevant because they host communities of innovators who interact and co-operate to create globally-useful knowledge. People are at the heart of any technopole project and unless those people are interacting, innovating, being entrepreneurial and both creating and exploiting new knowledge, then the technopole will ossify. It is as important to ensure that there is ongoing policy support for encouraging interaction and growth as it is for ensuring capital investment and accumulation.

Technopoles are knowledge contexts

What gives technopoles their unique advantage is that people are working together on shared problems, giving them collective knowledge about how to solve those problems and apply those solutions to create economic value. What is important is the way that a local knowledge community comes together to work collaboratively, and also to create private benefits and improve firm competitiveness and growth. Technopoles therefore need to find ways to manage these collaborative and competitive tensions.

Technopoles are 'places to be'

What gives technopoles their competitive advantage is that they are 'places to be' to access particular kinds of knowledge. Although there has been a policy fad to develop smart specialisation strategies, what this reflects is the need for every place to create a niche for itself for those seeking to access particular kinds of knowledge. Although it is important that there is a wider demand for those knowledges, perhaps as articulated in terms of particular 'Grand Challenges', local uniqueness is arguably more important. Therefore, policy-makers need to understand what kinds of unique knowledge are emerging in their knowledge contexts, related to the specific interactions and activities they host.

Technopoles evolve over time

Just as at the time of the first volume, technopoles cannot be created in a hurry. Infrastructure takes time to develop but, more importantly, knowledge communities take time to come together and develop unique, shared knowledge that forms the basis of wider competitive advantage. Policy-makers need to recognise this long-term time horizon and have a realistic understanding of the likely steps on that journey to ensure they are able to appreciate what it is they are building up.

Technopoles provide long-term stability

Technopoles are a way of providing fixity and stability in increasingly flexible and dynamic global knowledge production networks. Anchor participants are absolutely critical, and universities are becoming increasingly valued for the roles they can play in anchoring urban science. But at the same time universities are private businesses and their interests must not dominate developments if they are also to retain the flexibility to attract and host other private residents in ways that create wider territorial benefits.

Technopoles embody diverse interests

Technopoles succeed when they become a way for a wide range of actors to meet their own needs. It is not just that they have a particular set of knowledge competencies that are attractive to many firms, although that is important. Many kinds of actors are vital to make technopoles work and each have their own interests and motivations for participating. Good technopoles ensure that these interests are made explicit, and that technopole development is sequenced in ways that ensure different participants are able to gain the necessary benefits.

Technopoles develop coherent strengths

Technopoles bring together very different kinds of actors, public and private research organisations, policy-makers, real estate and venture-capital investors, business services and advisors, as well as highly-skilled professional workers. They succeed because they are able to resolve these different actors' needs, but at the same time because they are able to cohere and become attractive to others outside the regional location. Arguably the most important task for policy-makers is to guide and steer these local partners to collectively identify, exploit and extend these strengths.

Bibliography

Amin, A. and Roberts, J. (2008) 'Knowing in action: Beyond communities of practice'. *Research Policy*, *37*(2): 353–69.

Asheim, B.T., Boschma, R. and Cooke, P. (2011) 'Constructing regional advantage: Platform policies based on related variety and differentiated knowledge bases'. *Regional Studies*, *45*(7): 893–904.

Bathelt, H., Malmberg, A. and Maskell, P. (2004) 'Clusters and knowledge: Local buzz, global pipelines and the process of knowledge creation'. *Progress in Human Geography*, *28*: 31–56.

Beer, A. and Clower, T. (2014) 'Mobilizing leadership in cities and regions'. *Regional Studies, Regional Science*, *1*(1): 5–20.

Benneworth, P. (2014) 'Decoding university ideals by reading campuses', in P. Temple (ed.) *The physical university*. London: Routledge.

Benneworth, P.S. and Ratinho, T. (2014) 'Back to the future of high technology fantasies? Reframing the role of knowledge parks and science cities in innovation-based economic development'. *Environment and Planning C*, *32*(5): 784–808.

Boschma, R.A. (2005) 'Proximity and innovation: A critical assessment'. *Regional Studies*, *39*(1): 61–74.

Caniëls, M.C.J., Kronenberg, K. and Werker, C. (2014) 'Conceptualizing proximity in research collaborations', in R. Rutten., P. Benneworth, D. Irawati and F. Boekema (eds) *The social dynamics of innovation networks*. London: Routledge (pp. 221–39).

Castells, M. and Hall, P. (1994) *Technopoles of the world: The making of 21st century industrial complexes*. London: Routledge.

Charles, D.R. and Howells, J. (1992) *Technology transfer in Europe: Public and private networks*. London: Belhaven.

Chesbrough, H. (2003) *Open innovation, the new imperative for creating and profiting from technology*. Boston, MA: Harvard Business School Press.

Gertler, M. (1995) '"Being there": Proximity, organisation and culture in the development and adoption of advanced manufacturing technologies'. *Economic Geography*, *71*(1): 1–26.

Hall, P. and Markusen, A. (1985) *Silicon landscapes*. Boston, MA: Allen & Unwin.

Henderson, V. (1997) 'Externalities and industrial development'. *Journal of Urban Economics*, *42*(3): 449–70.

Lagendijk, A. and Oïnas, P. (2005) 'Proximity, external relationships and local economic development', in A. Lagendijk and P. Oïnas (eds) *Proximity, distance and diversity, issues on economic interaction and local development*. London: Ashgate.

McCann, P. and Ortega-Argilés, R. (2013) 'Smart specialization, regional growth and applications to European Union cohesion policy'. *Regional Studies*, 1–12. doi: 10.1080/00343404.2013.799769.

Nelson, R.R. (1993) *National innovation systems: A comparative analysis*. Oxford: Oxford University Press.

Nelson, R.R. and Winter, S.G. (1982) *An evolutionary theory of economic change*. Cambridge, MA: Harvard University Press.

Paci, R. and Usai, S. (1999) 'Externalities, knowledge spillovers and the spatial distribution of innovation'. *GeoJournal*, *49*(4): 381–90.

Rhodes, R.A.W. (1997) *Understanding governance. Policy networks, governance, reflexivity and accountability*. Buckingham: Open University Press.

Salmi, J. (2009) *The challenge of establishing world-class universities*. Washington, DC: World Bank.

Sotarauta, M. (2006) 'Where have all the people gone? Leadership in the fields of regional development'. Sente Working paper 09/2006, Tampere, SF: Sente.

Sotarauta, M. (2011) 'Institutional entrepreneurship for knowledge regions: In search for a fresh set of questions for regional and innovation studies'. *Environment and Planning C*, *29*(1): 96–112.

Sotarauta, M. (2014) 'Reflections on "Mobilizing leadership in cities and regions"'. *Regional Studies, Regional Science*, *1*(1): 28–31.

Sotarauta, M., Horlings, I. and Liddle, J. (eds) (2012) *Leadership and change in sustainable regional development*. London: Routledge.

Index

For Product Safety Concerns and Information please contact our EU
representative GPSR@taylorandfrancis.com
Taylor & Francis Verlag GmbH, Kaufingerstraße 24, 80331 München, Germany

www.ingramcontent.com/pod-product-compliance
Ingram Content Group UK Ltd.
Pitfield, Milton Keynes, MK11 3LW, UK
UKHW021850240425
457818UK00020B/801